PRINCETON THEOLOGICAL MONOGRAPH

Series

Dikran Y. Hadidian

General Editor

1

REFLECTIONS OF RENAISSANCE ENGLAND

Life, Thought, and Religion
Mirrored in Illustrated Pamphlets
1535-1640

REFLECTIONS

OF RENAISSANCE ENGLAND

**Life, Thought and Religion
Mirrored in Illustrated Pamphlets
1535-1640**

By Marie-Hélène Davies

PICKWICK PUBLICATIONS
Allison Park, Pennsylvania

Library of Congress Cataloging-in-Publication Data

Davies, Marie-Hélène.
   Reflections of Renaissance England.

   (Princeton theological monograph series ; 1)
   Translation of: La gravure dans les brochures Illustrées de la
Renaissance anglaise, 1535-1640.
   1. England—Civilization—16th century—Sources.   2.
England—Civilization—17th century—Sources.   3.
Renaissance—England—Sources.   4. Popular literature.   4.
Popular literature—England—History and criticism.
5. Pamphlets—Illustrations.   6. Book industries and
trade—England—History.   7. Prints, English.   I. Title.   II. Series.
DA320.D29513   1986   942.05'5   85-32028
ISBN 0-915138-68-9

Printed and Bound by Publishers Choice Book Mfg. Co.
Mars, Pennsylvania 16046

For Horton

"For me, fair friend, you never can be old",
And "here's the joy; my friend and I are one."

CONTENTS

FOREWORD

There is no point in making this book longer than it is by an extensive foreword. It is an abbreviated translation of my original: **Les brochures illustrées de la Renaissance anglaise, 1535-1640,** which was originally published by the Presses Universitaires de Lille in 1979, but never had a commercial edition. Some imagery may have been lost in the curtailing, but none of the essential research.

In addition to all those whom I thank in the original French edition, I with to add my editor, Dikran Y. Hadidian, for offering to publish the work, and my good companion in work and play, husband and friend, Dr. Horton Davies for helping me in the translation.

Marie-Hélène Davies
Princeton, New Jersey

ABBREVIATIONS

B.L. & B.M.	British Library
B.N.	Bibliothèque Nationale, Paris
Bod.	Bodleian Library, Oxford University
Folger	The Folger Shakespeare Library, Washington D.C.
Hunt.	The Henry E. Huntington Library, San Marino, CA
S.T.C.	Pollard and Redgrave, **Short-Title Catalogue of English Books, 1475–1640**
T.P.	Title page

Chapter I

A HISTORY OF THE PAMPHLET
AND OF PAMPHLET ILLUSTRATION

Taylor the water-poet compared his debtors to eels, which slid away between his hands, never to be grasped. Such a comparison would apply to the pamphlet. From 1535-1640, the most varied pieces of literature were named pamphlets, from dialogues and prose work to poetry or works where poetry and prose are intermingled. Plays and controversial works or even learned treatises are also to be found in this category. Roger Ascham's **The Schoolmaster** is referred to as a pamphlet by Stony-hurst in his edition of Virgil's **Aeneid** of 1582. [1] Other authors sneer at the term "pamphlet", for them too common, and call their works "treatises" or "disputes" or by any other lofty term that might disguise the commercial nature of the writing.

To attempt to put some kind of order in this rather confused state of affairs, we shall retain three criteria, all necessary but not sufficient, whose combination is likely to present us with the true definition of a pamphlet. Those are: the subject matter, the absence of hard binding and the price.

The pamphlets, or brochures, were essentially ephemeral, [2] news before the periodical. They were generally written for a precise reason or occasion, for instance, the death of a sovereign, the marriage of a princess, the arrest of a thief. Some works were written on command, ordered by a powerful character for leisure or politics. Others were spontaneous controversial outbursts, discussing established values. Most of the time, a pamphlet was not written for art's sake, but shaped to the current fashion exacted by its clientele. However literary works could be included, if the sales warranted a popular publication. Short-lived like our paperbacks and newspapers, they were read and then doomed. They wrapped up tobacco or lit up the fires in the new-fashioned fire-place. Born to die in a day, a week or a year, pamphlets cheered up hearts or awakened passions, and then disappeared in smoke.

1

The term "pamphlet" derived from the French palme-feuillet. It meant literally what could be held in a hand, that is, a small, thin book. [3] Because of its insignificance, it was never bound, but only stitched by a thread or a thin leather lace. [4]

Pamphlets were the cheapest goods that could be obtained from a bookstall at the market place or in the shops and stalls of St. Paul's Churchyard. Plays used to cost sixpence; small pamphlets sold from tuppence to fourpence and works of greater consequence could reach a shilling. Price also varied according to demand and according to the illustrations it contained. In 1598, the Stationers' Company froze all prices and no pamphlet in regular print could sell for more than a penny, unless it was illustrated. [5]

A combination of these three criteria allows us to discriminate between pamphlets and books. Yet this is not altogether satisfying. Some pamphlets were very long indeed, although they treated modern subjects in a discursive way and other works considered as small books were very short. Consequently the definition must be fairly elastic, even when the triple criteria are adopted.

Censorship developed almost at the same time as the appearance of pamphlets. Immediately the Crown realized that these handy little tracts could be used for as well as against it, for better or for worse. In the laws and proclamations of the Realm, pamphlets and ballads appear side by side. They were the plague of authority, since they sometimes escaped its fine screening. Both tended to be written for the same public and used the same topics. If the narrative of the death of pirates was popular in prose, couldn't it sell in verse? Or alternately, if the song of robbing the Spanish Fleet brought music to the Elizabethan ears, others more historically oriented, might enjoy a true depiction of the feat. [6]

Censorship laws were of two kinds: some were directed at foreign imports, whereas others regulated the home market.

The English book market had a fluctuating relationship with the foreign markets. The Crown which had first welcomed the immigration of French, Dutch and German printers and the international exchange of woodboards, characters and printed sheets, became protectionist for reasons of state and religion, as well as of economy, around 1534. [7] However policy was not uniform from 1534 to 1640. Under Edward VI, England welcomed Protestant printers, who had fled repression, from France and elsewhere. They in turn had to retrace their steps under Catholic Mary, by an Act of Parliament of 1554. Another Act of 1555 forbade the use of all foreign labor, except for certain employment of which printing was not a part. [8] These Acts and laws were not socially inspired, but chiefly political and religious.

The same restrictions applied to the printers' and booksellers' attendance at the Frankfort Book Fair, [9] as some, like Prynne, tried to pass seditious pamphlets as paper, sometimes encouraged by corruptible customs officers. [10]

The last serious attempt at a blockade of foreign writings was undertaken in 1632. It affected Butter and Bourne, the publishers of foreign news called corantos, the ancestor of newspapers. It was not until 1638 that Butter and Bourne had their license to print these corantos renewed. [11]

In actual fact the censorship of books printed abroad was rather ineffective. Pamphlets found their way into England among blank sheets, in cargoes of cloth and even in wine barrels. And a false imprint from abroad often served to hide the provenance of certain pamphlets from secret presses in England. But the desperate desire to suppress such seditious literature on the part of authorities showed, as Dekker tells in **The Dead-Tearme,** the power of the pen. [12]

Sovereigns were alarmed and dealt with the English press in two ways: they chided and chastised through acts, ordinances and injunctions, while they flattered and cherished by the concession of privileges.

Laws, ordinances, and so forth, were numerous between 1540 and 1640: those of 1557, 1559, 1562, 1570, 1586, 1599, 1623, 1624 and finally 1637 were of the greatest importance. Only those directly related to pamphlets will engage our attention. The surest way of establishing an effective censorship was the granting of a royal charter to the "Stationers' Company" in 1557. [13] With regal contempt for publishers and printers, the Queen encouraged petty jealousies among them, and by a system of informers, succeeded in suppressing the majority of secret presses. Laws and decrees succeeded one another, frustrating the press, by limiting the number of printers and apprentices, the number of presses and the places where printing was permitted. The Crown thus hoped to reduce the area of search for its "inspectors." It certainly succeeded in killing the provincial press. [14]

The number of infractions perpetrated during the course of the years shows that the printers lacked neither imagination nor resources in evading censorship. Penalty ranged from small to heavy fines, sometimes involving the destruction of the press on which seditious books or libels were published and the imprisonment of the rebel printer. Around 1588 the fine for printing an unauthorized ballad was fourpence, but Day was fined five shillings for printing a pamphlet on the theories of Nostradamus. In 1627, Henry Burton was merely censured by the Privy Council for an anti-Catholic tract. [15] On the contrary, in 1595, Abel

Jeffes who had printed a translation from a French broadsheet saw his plant completely smashed. W. Phillips died in prison. John Allde was also incarcerated. William Prynne, a Puritan, was put in the pillory, lost two ears and had to pay a fine of 10,000 pounds for the printing of **Historio-Mastix.** Even so, it appears that censorship in England never reached the severity of its French counterpart, which caused the execution of many for seditious writings. [16] Later the Star Chamber was the main aversion of printers and booksellers. At its suppression in 1641, the market was flooded with a torrent of pamphlets.

However irritating to printers, home censorship was on the whole effective. It reduced the number of controversial pamphlets. In 1572 it succeeded in destroying the Puritan Press which had printed Cartwright's **Remonstrance to Parliament.** Only two important presses resisted the careful search in the reign of Elizabeth I: one was Jesuit, the other Puritan, responsible for the **Marprelate Tracts.** Finally censorship ran the latter to the ground. [17] Its effectiveness declined under James I, when Thomas Scott's **Vox Populi** which appeared in four editions in 1640, was re-edited and enlarged in 1622-24, and was even illustrated with a fine engraving.

The chief economic result of ordinances relating to the press in England was the stagnation of printing, a fact which produced another set of ordinances, threatening to take away the licenses from printers unless the quality of their work improved. But without exchanges from the continent, isolated England could only vegetate for lack of emulation. [18]

The Crown also tried to control the press by the granting of privileges and a royal printer was appointed. These privileges were to compensate for the financial loss incurred by certain printers for printing public notices and lampoons, pamphlets and tracts of monarchical propaganda. Then the Crown soon perceived in them a means of political control and a source of revenue. [19] The number of privileges increased with the successive reigns: R. Tottell printed law books; R. Watkins and J. Roberts were granted a 21 year monopoly for almanacs and predictions; Seres was to print Primers and Prayer-Books; Copland, the classics; Nicolas Bourne, news from abroad . . . Specialization made malcontents. In 1621, there was a dispute concerning the printing of ballads. Against W. Jaggard and later Boislore, Wood and Symcock, a protest was sent to the House of Commons arguing that a monopoly on ballads would cripple small businesses. [20]

This is one example among many which shows that the Crown was always limited in its desire for political control by the threat of social discontent and by economic considerations. Laws against the liberty of printing would cause famished printers to rebel against monopolies, as in 1577 when 177 persons were threatened with unemployment. Another revolt of the printers took place with William Carter, a Catholic, Hugh Singleton, a Puritan, and John Wolfe, as its leaders. For a while Wolfe was the hero of poor printers and booksellers, until in 1587, he defected to the other side, after having received privileges from the Company.

Monopoly then failed to control the printing of ephemera. In fact it encouraged literary theft, thus creating further disorder, a habit that even copyright could not control. Confronted with the poverty of printers, the Crown authorized anyone whose press was out of work to print the ABC and the small catechism.

Other measures showed that fighting against unemployment was a real concern. The number of copies for each impression of books and pamphlets was regulated, to allow for other editions as the market required. Finally many edicts and proclamations concerning the prices of such, attempted to deal with the economic health of the book trade. [21]

Wherever there is stern regulation fraud emerges. Apprentices and journeymen bettered their salaries by the black market. According to the tradition, workers were given one free copy of the works they printed. But often they printed more in order to sell them to poor booksellers. They also sold defective copies. Consequently the Company changed the ancient right, replacing it by a bonus of threepence a week. [22]

For the printer, the advantage of the black market was that he had no author's royalty to pay. [23] In this case the printing and the copy-editing were lax. [24] To disguise that a pamphlet was stolen, the title-page was often altered: thus Harman's **Caveat for common cursetors**, 1566, is republished under the title **The groundworke of conny-catching** in 1592. Authors sometimes had their own back by plagiarizing themselves, for instance, G. Markham whose books on horses were at the least repetitive, until the market could take no more.

Plays were particularly easy to steal. Authors lost their copyright to the company that played them, and therefore had no right to publication. However some tried it. Thomas Heywood, accused of such procedure violently denied the fact. Was he in earnest? If so, his play was purloined. [25]

Pamphlets were often what enabled a business to survive. In inventories made at the death of booksellers, one often finds that more than half the stock was composed of pamphlets, broadsheets and ballads, for fine books were financially hazardous. [26] An apprentice who had finished his training and sought to be established would start by buying ephemeral literature. If the sales were good, he would exchange some of his stock for books. This tells the economic importance of pamphlets in the book trade. [27] Reynes's advice to his workmen for instance, was to be as eclectic as possible. [28] Sometimes the dying master would give instructions for his best employees' fortunes.

Pamphlets, one must conclude were much in demand. But who read them? The old prejudice according to which three-quarters of Elizabethan England was illiterate has now disappeared. Merchants and artisans had to read and write in order to keep their accounts. Public schools, grammar schools and colleges would have little influence on the market, except for text-books. Lawyers were the chief purchasers of beautiful books. Teachers and clergy, traditionally poor, could only buy modestly priced books. As for the rural nobility, the gentry, either they were ruined or they despised the printed book and preferred manuscripts. Inevitably, printed literature was aimed chiefly at the middle-class, and the printed pamphlet was born the minute the English Press saw the light. Wynkyn de Worde observed that "Most of them [printed books] were small pamphlets." [29] Already newsletters had appeared and Faques in 1513 had printed **The Trewe Encountre** of the Battle of Flodden Field. Publishers were already eager for good relationships with the public. In the periodicals of 1620 they addressed them directly and allowed them to reply. [30] Authors were equally concerned with public taste and response and many of them put up with commercialism in order to survive, [31] while others like Parrot or John Earle poured their contempt on them. [32]

The general public as a whole and the lower middle-class in particular, first in love with stories, soon craved for learning and novelties. Taste hardly changes at all between the middle of the sixteenth and of the seventeenth centuries, although with the rise of Puritanism there appeared a greater demand for the didactic. Authors and publishers had to comply. [33]

Patriotism is rediscovered in the historical narratives of Robin Hood, Adam Bell, William de Cloudesley, King Arthur and of romantic heroes such as St. George, Bevis of Hampton, Guy of Warwick, Richard Coeur de Lion and Henry V. It was elated in the news of marriages, births and deaths of sovereigns. Publishers rushed to the registry to obtain the copyright of these news. Other stories inflamed national sentiment and pride, while others pitied the miseries of other nations. Finally, accounts of war and naval combats where England had the upper hand delighted the populace.

Religious sentiment is encountered everywhere. One read of teratology as a sign of God's punishment, or vices correlating with financial disappointments, or murders, [34] monsters and calamities borne by religious dissenters. Morality is tied to religion. Sermons were devoured and kept at the bedside, and religious controversy about Roman Catholicism, Anabaptists and the Family of Love, found avid readers.

Pamphlets could also express social concerns and demands. From Henry VIII's time versifiers wrote about taxes, monopolies or the problem of enclosures. Ballads and tracts provided publicity for the Virginia Company as in **News from Virginia,** 1610, in which Lord Delaware encouraged the Merchant Adventurers to assist the Virginia Company and thus minimize its disappointments.

Sentimentalism abound in the stories of young girls abandoned by their lovers or in romances of chivalric love. Books of jests and charades breathe the spirit of "penny dreadfuls." Servants and peasants love this sob stuff or more sensational stories. Mopsa in Shakespeare's **A Winter's Tale** wants someone to give her a ballad because she is sure to find a true story in it, [35] that is, a story in keeping with the drama of life. Most of the period pieces feature such characters as the stupid lover who borrows his valet's book of charades in order to impress his sweetheart.

Handbooks also became fashionable: treatises on astronomy, on agriculture, on the grooming of horses, on learning how to swim, as well as almanacs providing agricultural and medical advice with prognostications. These were in keeping with the new experimental scientific spirit. The public was also particularly addicted to stories of monsters which were interpreted in terms of the natural and the supernatural.

Women, too, were not only the object of tracts and ballads, but part of the clientele to be borne in mind. Bianca in **The Taming of the Shrew** was taught Greek, Latin and Mathematics, as well as the art of raising children, of how to please, how to dance and how to play music. (II, 1). Batista, a rich gentlewoman of Padua, thought she could give her daughters a good education (I, 1). Sir Thomas Overbury states that even the chambermaid loved to read, especially Greene's works and **The Mirror of Knighthood.** [36] Women were authors; for instance, the Countess of Lincoln published practical advice for her own sex in **The Countess of Lincoln's Nursery,** Oxford, 1622. The fair sex also held its own in controversies, and the opponents of Swetnam often show more wit than he. [37 & 38]

L. B. Wright is correct in declaring that tastes changed from day to day; yet there was only a certain span in their variety and the map did not fundamentally change during more than a century. Commercial authors swam with the current of actuality.

Pamphlets inspired by a phenomenological rather than a transcendental spirit, had to unite the useful with the agreeable. They had to attract the buyer by their lively titles and their layout, as well as by illustrations whenever possible.

The lover of pamphlets need only walk the district of St. Paul's, in St. Paul's Churchyard, Fleet Street and Paternoster Row, to find the production of his choice. Two kinds of shops were to be found: some were huge and spacious and served the double function of workshop and stockroom, while the other kind was transient, a sort of kiosk. Wealthy booksellers had both kinds. London Bridge in the second half of the century gained the same reputation as St. Paul's. Other areas also carried pamphlets: Bethlehem, Duck Lane, Little Britain, Holborn, Gray's Inn Gate and Chancery Lane. Most of the important publishers had a house of their own. [39] Some houses had a long history of printing; the Eliot Court house for instance printed for John Norton, Bonham Norton, John Bill, John Wolfe and F. Coldock. It reached its peak under Griffin and Haviland. [40]

Some bookshops were to be found outside London, but according to the law of 1583, most of them concentrated in the City, in Oxford and Cambridge. In the country books appeared on market stalls or in the sacks of colporteurs, who, like Autolycus in **The Winter's Tale**, went from city to city and from door to door. Forbidden books were apparently distributed to sympathisers. Chester, York and Coventry were the bastions of Catholicism around 1603, while Essex, Northampton and London were partial to Puritanism. All the same, Catholic books were found in the cellar of a wine merchant in London, which was large enough to shelter all kinds of religious confessions. [41]

Despite reactions against monopolies, one can observe a certain specialization among the publishers of ephemeral literature in the seventeenth century. Oxford and Cambridge concentrated on religious controversy: the first sided with Laud and the second with Puritanism. In London, W. Pickering sold interludes in the main, along with ballads, almanacs and thin brochures. W. Barley preferred minor works, beginning with illustrative plates as well as musical books. Allde, Harrison and Islip were interested in gardening. Butter and Bourne in Corantos. [42] The printers and publishers of Shakespeare's quartos were all minor businessmen. John Danter chiefly printed news from abroad and other cheap works, including the pamphlets of Nashe. Ballads were issued by some seventy-one different printers and publishers, who seem to have chosen them by subject matter. The editors of ephemera were mainly Ed. White, Th. Millington, John Bushby, Andrew Wise, W. Aspley, Charlwood, Roberts, Pavier and Butter, all of whom will be encountered again when specific illustrated pamphlets are under consideration.

Popular literature was by no means appreciated by all. It was usually disliked by the lettered who had no wish to mix with the mob. (Plate 1) They sneered at those who lived off their pen and made literature a trade rather than an art. They accused commercial writers of plagiarism and of popularizing and impoverishing the language of lofty books. [43] They called them sophists misleading the crowd into political-religious factions to destroy the peace and unity of the kingdom. The moralists joined in with outcries, accusing pamphlets and ballads of corrupting souls, perverting understanding, inciting to licentiousness, suppressing virtues and promoting vice. [44]

The popular press did, however, find a defender in Barnaby Rich. In **Allarm to England** he states that writing is not a matter of producing fine phrases, but of promoting a didactic purpose. Borrowing from authors, he argues, is common practice, but their sayings are none the worse for wear. [45] In his dedication to Prince Henry of **A Souldiers Wishe to Britons Welfare** with its revealing subtitle, **a dialogue between Captain Pill and Skill,** he writes that lofty literateurs need artificial discourses to hide packs of lies and dishonest actions beneath pleasant words, whereas he prefers those who will enforce the truth in a ruder language. [46]

Quarrels between fashionable writers became in turn another popular theme. The disputes between Harvey and Nashe and between Harvey and Greene were avidly read, until they were censured. Dekker in his epistle to the reader in **The Wonderfull Years,** 1603, rails against these scribblers who are worse than Goths. Whether Dekker's satire was intended seriously or not, it did not prevent literary quarrels from becoming as pleasant a sport as cockfighting for many. Did not Greene feel the need to come to late repentance, begging the readers' pardon for his lewd pamphlets? [47] Pamphlets also became the subject of wisecracks, whose wit was not always subtle as in Robert Chamberlain's **Conceits, Clinches, Flashes and Whimzies newly studied.** [48]

Pamphlets were the very image of Monster Opinion. When one head was cut off, seven others replaced it. They spread news, sometimes scattered discord, which the Crown found hard to stop. At best authorities could only build a containing trench to limit the progress of the flames. Literature, the very livelihood of booksellers, was a bill of fare, with enticing names for the various courses which often deceived when being eaten. Saint Paul's Churchyard resembled Place du Tertre in Parisian Montmartre, where tourists crowd over commercial painters, or a similar street in Quebec, the most French of Canadian cities. The publisher aimed at sales, happy when some decent work improved the mediocrity of the bulk of his production.

Commercial art is designed to bring beauty at the level of the mass. Why and how pamphlets were illustrated as well as the degree of refinement of the illustration will occupy the second part of this chapter.

The presence or absence of images in the pamphlets of the period can be partly explained by the attitude of the Elizabethans as regards the visual arts. No doubt some of them took Deuteronomy 5:8-9 seriously and banished images as idolatry. Illustrations probably reflect the struggle between the so-called medieval outlook, the spirit of the Reformation and the increasing intellectual curiosity which characterized humanism from the sixteenth to the seventeenth centuries. They reveal the divergent conceptions between the reality perceived by the senses and the apprehension of the suprasensible world: or better whether our world is only a false and artificial image of the world of ideas, or a means, however imperfect, yet useful, for apprehending it. [49]

The three main attitudes of the Renaissance with reference to images are evoked in **The Blindness of the Unhappy Jews.** The author reiterates the arguments of the Homilies on images in churches, rejects the total suppression of images advocated by the Turks, and declares himself in favor of profane images. [50]

The third Homily against idolatry did not condemn profane art; but the iconography of religious books suffered from religious taboos. Even though Primers and Bibles were provided with allegorical images or historical illustrations of certain Biblical events, or with representations of the Sacraments, the religious brochures remained for the most part unillustrated, or decorated with purely ornamental motifs. There are, however, some seventeenth century exceptions, chiefly those of Puritan provenance: in the writings of Preston, S. Ward of Ipswich and Th. Williamson, the print complements the text. Is this general lack of illustration to be attributed only to iconoclasm? It is hard to decide. [51] Understandably, the only representations of God are either symbolic or allegorical.

The second main reason for the poverty of the graphic arts--the ignorance of a large part of the nobility--allows the epoch to be divided into two parts: the reign of the Tudors, occupied by economic, social and politico-religious problems, and the reign of the Stuarts whose two queens, Anne of Denmark and Henrietta-Maria of France were enthusiastic patrons of the arts. A renewal took place. Treatises on art became more frequent and patrons less rare.

The Reformation had one positive influence on the nobility. It encouraged learning. After 1530, intellectualism became as fashionable as travelling abroad. However, art, formerly despised as handiwork, became part of the nobleman's curriculum only at the beginning of the seventeenth century. [52] It so happened that Bacon, John Dee, and later Peacham encouraged gentlemen to draw. Perkins exploded among the Puritan gentry the idea that it was culpable to be attached to secular art. Drawing was useful, they all said. Were there more experts at it, there would be less mediocre art around. [53] The art of illustration did improve.

It would be erroneous to conclude, however, that in the middle of the seventeenth century, most pamphlets were illustrated. Pamphlet illustration met with violent controversy, for instance in medical circles, where it was feared that they would replace first-hand experimentation. "Scientific" images eventually were found in sensational news of monsters, in almanacs and in navigators' tales.

This reluctance to illustrate is all the more surprising since the Elizabethans had a structured visual imagination. The concept of beauty remained at the center of many preoccupations since the neo-platonic philosophy deriving from Plato's **Banquet** and handed on by the **Enneads** of Plotinus, continued to teach that the Beautiful, the Good and the True are linked as the basic entelechies that form the One. Consequently the world of the senses, however distorted, was created by God and bore the imprint of supra-sensible reality.

They referred to Nature and the Bible as the books of God; to Christians with St. Paul, as "living epistles" and to Christ as "the image of the invisible God" (Colossians 1:15). God the supreme architect was also referred to as painter and writer. The appearance of a human being was the sign of his moral beauty or ugliness, and birth defects were considered the product of parents' wrong doing. [54] Dress and hairdo indicated one's position in society and one's station in life. [55]

They loved pageantry. [56] Plays, masks, mumming and other court amusements appealed to the eye as much as to the mind and disguise and visual tricks were often used. The importance of ceremonial and the plethora of costumes in historical plays, the love of exotic garb in foreigners, all is part of the Renaissance fascination for the visual.

Propagandists were aware of it, and Thomas Cromwell used dramatists like Bayle and Wylley to ridicule the Pope and Catholicism on the stage. Royal propaganda in the royal entries and progresses displayed the grandeur of the monarchy, while the liveried companies of London attracted attention to themselves by parading in their variegated colors.

Consequently one cannot infer that publishers were unaware of the importance of the visual message. Some claimed that illustration was a teaching device for the ignorant, a concept already in favor in the medieval times, since sermons in stone appeared in most Romanesque churches. [57]

Still one has to wait for the seventeenth century for life to flow again in the visual arts. In the Anglican liturgy a renewal of the theatrical element had taken place. Holy Communion, or the verbum visibile among the Laudian party was in greater honor than preaching, verbum audibile, which had been given the greatest importance by the Puritans. Ceremonial, ecclesiastical vestments, and stained glass windows are eloquent testimonies to the importance of allegorical and tropological iconography. The very titles of theological works appeal to the visual sense. They refer to gardens of hope, to the gangrene that is rotting England in the form of heresy, as well as to a beautiful bush to protect us from the sudden showers of sin. Most of these works, however, are not illustrated, because the theologians, with their imaginations impregnated with Biblical imagery had no need for further stimulation. [58] For the Puritan, the real illustration of the New Testament was "the doctrine and preaching of the Gospel." Preaching was an image in which the merits of Christ were mirrored [59] and Calvin frequently used the word "image" in the rhetorical meaning of the term.

Rhetoric was central to the artistic thought of the period. Artistic creation followed the rhetorical process: thought, invention and execution. This becomes clear in reading the words of Alberti in the **Ten Books on Architecture:**

> Him I call an Architect, who by sure and wonderful Art and Method, both with Thought and Invention, to devise, and with Execution, to complete all those Works, which by means of the Movement of great Weights, and the Conjunction and Amassment of Bodies, can, with the greatest Beauty, be adapted to the Uses of Mankind . . . " [60]

On the other hand, the aims of the visual arts correspond to the categories of rhetoric: delectare, docere, movere; to delight, to instruct, and to move the public. Rosamond Tuve in **Elizabethan and Metaphysical Imagery,** 1948, has amply proved that the rhetorical image strove to unite these three criteria. We claim that this is true of her poor sister. If rhetoric uses certain artifices of painting, inversely the iconology of the Renaissance employs rhetorical structures. Woodcuts could be simple pictograms like the illustration of Beaumont and Fletcher's **The Maides Tragedie,** 1630, showing the scene where Amintor wounds Aspatia, or like the composed picture illustrating William Sampson's **The Vow**

Breaker which narrates the entire story in the four corners of the woodcut. (Plate 2).

A simple image, however, could be read at different levels as, for example, in **A Nunnes Prophesie, or the Fall of Friers**, 1615. A unicorn upsets with his horn the tiara of the Pope who is sitting on his throne; his tail overthrows the cross and the keys fall to the ground. Clouds float over the entire scene. The allegorical interpretation reads: England will dethrone the Pope with divine approval. The image when read at both levels bears an anti-papal and pro-reformation message which reinforces the Protestant propaganda of the text. [61] Finally the picture can be both allegorical and composed of multiple elements, as for instance, the frontispiece of Keckermann's **A manducation to Theologie.** The sinner repents in the light of preaching, on the left, so that David and his lyre represent the love and devotion of the Church for God whose hand can be seen, on the right, emerging from clouds of glory. Woodcuts, etchings and engravings can then be interpreted, like the rhetorical image, at several levels, according to the degree of the reader's culture. They have an external meaning whose interior logic is intelligible only to the initiated.

The rebus, a minor form of art, if Camden is to be believed, was used by the master of rhetoric, Cicero, who punned upon his name, describing it as chick-pea. Printers and booksellers loved to play this game, which appealed to the ear as well as to the eye, using homophony to draw the attention of the readers. Thus Day's device represents an old man awakening a young boy: Arise for it is day! Grafton's sign is a small barrel (a tun) from which a graft emerges. Norton also uses a barrel and the letters Nor, while Seton has a barrel sailing on the sea. Woodcock's device shows a cock on a pile of wood, Martin's, a kingfisher, E. Wolf's, the fox and the wolf, Pavier's, a man engaged in paving. Henry Bell made a rebus with three components: a chicken (hen), an ear of barley (rye), and a bell. Rye was also used by Harrison whose mark represented a hare and an ear of rye shining in the sun. Islip loved them so much that he used four different ones for his name. All this was thought to be great fun. [62]

Emblems, that is, a picture containing a device, illustrated or not by a poem, were highly praised from the middle of the sixteenth century. Books of emblems became so popular from the 1580's, that Whitney arranged for the publication of **A choice of Emblemes and other Devises** in 1586. The fashion reached its peak with the collections of emblems of Peacham, Wither and Quarles. In emblems, the arrangement of objects, as well as the objects themselves, became symbolical. Whitney's definition of an emblem applies to any image, engraved or inlaid with a decorative purpose, which has some "witty device", obscure to begin with, which lures us toward the revelation of something we had not properly understood and forces us to undertake a disciplined moral life. [63] For Quarles, "an emblem is no more than a dumb word." [64] It is an almost magical image, a dynamic image whose signs appeal to cultural knowledge and are subordinated to a didactic design. Emblems appeal to different faculties in a human being: perception, reasoning and the memorization of the intuitions of ideas and intelligible essences. It is neo-platonic art at its best, uniting painting and poetry in the service of the IDEA. [65]

Printers and booksellers used emblems as devices. John Day for instance shows an old man pointing out a skeleton from which a tree emerges to a young man with the device: et si mors, in dies accelerat. Field uses the anchor of hope, Jugge, the pelican nourishing its young, a medieval symbol of charity and of the sacrifice of the Mass. Wolfe and Islip are fond of serpents and toads (calumny and envy) surrounding the roots of a palm tree with the motto: Il vostro malignare non giove nulla. Islip also borrows the emblems of Sambucus, including a mark comprising a column with the crowned head of a bird, a pair of scales, a cat, a snake, and a cornucopia. [66] Such emblems often appeared on the title pages of books or pamphlets as printer's advertisement, whether relevant to the contents or not.

Most of the time it is difficult to decide who is responsible for the illustration of pamphlets. In scientific texts, works on mathematics, physics, or astronomy, the author was often the instigator, as for instance in Harington's **An Anatomie of the Metamorphosed Ajax** which describes a modern privy in great detail. Sometimes there are clear allusions in the text. For example, in **The Murmerer**, N. Breton refers his reader to the illustration. In most cases, one wonders whether the image is any more than a commercial device.

In any case, all the engravings that genuinely illustrate the texts are there for mixed motives. They arouse the curiosity of the passers-by, they decorate, instruct or move. Contrived images are rarely objective but are destined to influence the reader; as dynamic images, they retain a little of the magic power of those of primitive societies.

Whatever the purpose of the prints which decorate or illustrate pamphlets, their first impact is esthetic. The quality of the paper, the darkness of the ink, the neatness of the line, the variety of the techniques--woodcut or intaglio--first come to our attention. The next question arises: how representative are the prints of the evolution in the technique of art in Renaissance England? These questions will occupy us briefly.

The maker of images, like the printer, lacked good ink,

good paper and good emulation. Some of the causes of the poverty of pictorial and graphic art are analyzed by Haydock in the preface to his translation of Lomazzo. Buyers underpaid; workmen no longer worked for the love of the trade, but for money only. Drawers and engravers were too poor to do good work and copper, canvas and oil, were costly. Further, there were few patrons and little interest. Cutters and engravers, then produced cheap commercial art in order to survive and lost the sense of values and decorum. [67]

Good paper was rare in England. Since for a long time parchment had been preferred, paper had often been imported from the Continent and England lacked skilled paper-makers. Good quality material to make the paste was rare, especially in times of plague, when clothes were burnt rather than transformed from rags into paper. [68]

Pamphlet paper, then was often yellow and porous, in both centuries, irrespective of the quality of the woodcut printed. For instance, the frontispiece of Copland's **Jyl of Breyntford,** 1560, reappears on the verso while the three characters printed on the verso come to mar the recto. The heraldic device of the verso of **The Man in the Moon,** 1609, blurs the representation of the monk with the hook appearing on the title page. [69] Even good prints came through, as for instance the title page of Taylor's **Jack a Lent,** 1620. Etchings generally appear on better paper: the process required quality paper, graphic art was improving and they illustrated mostly works of greater seriousness. [70]

Ink also lacked refinement. Good ink was made out of linseed oil to which was added a little rosin. In England it was made with fish oil to which was added a greater quantity of rosin. Since, moreover, it was insufficiently boiled or burnt, it dried slowly and badly. Besides, as blacking was expensive, it was used niggardly. Consequently one finds many pale prints like those on the title pages of the 1618 edition of **Thomas Coriat** or of **Adam Bell,** 1632, or of **News from the East Indies,** 1638. [71] Etchings, of course, had to use better ink, since all depended on the clarity of the print. [72]

The design was hardly better than the paper and ink: neither color nor tint-drawing is found. Most of the illustrations are woodcuts and the intaglio is almost exclusively represented by etchings which have sometimes been improved by drypoint.

Yet not all methods and styles are identical. Illustrated pamphlets reflect the evolution in the technique of woodcarving and etching. There is no need to remind the reader of the technique of woodcarving. [73] The line appears usually black on white. However, sometimes lines come out white on black, although the old relief method is still used: a black dress shows white folds like Hunger's on the title page of **Jack a Lent** (Plate 26), or on Mrs. Turner's garb in **The bloody downfall....** One could also be tricked into thinking of intaglio by J. Sylvester's **Lachrimae Lachrimarum** or Ch. Brooke's **Two elegies**, 1613, if in the latter the inscription <u>Interdum Lachrimae pondera vocis habent</u> did not come to prove that this is relief. [74]

Greater quantity of black areas is used in seventeenth century prints. The style of the woodcuts has changed. One's eye is immediately caught if one compares the ephemeral literature of the sixteenth century with the ballads at the begining of the Civil War. At the time of this study, we can give as examples: **The man in the Moon**, 1609, the devils of **Strange News from Antwerp**, the sorcery pamphlet on Dr. Fian [75] and J. Taylor's **A swarme of sectaries and schismatiques**, 1641.

The dotted manner consisted in dotting the background of a carving performed in the white manner. The few doubtful examples we have serve as ornamental letters and title frames. One border seems to ally the dotted manner and the black ink line method in J. Hooper's **A homelye to be read in the tyme of pestylence**, 1553. (Plate 3).

On the whole, the woodcuts we find illustrating pamphlets are fairly rough. One should not conclude that all woodcuts are rough and all engravings refined. The cuts of Dürer, of Hans Holbein and of Rembrandt would give the lie to this hasty assertion. But the woodcutters of ephemerals usually did speedy work.

Copper-plate engraving, the intaglio method, had the advantage of refinement and durability. Ephemeral literature rarely warranted such luxury, and yet a few etchings appear. Whereas, as far as we know, there is no work of the time available on woodcarving in England, John Bate in **The mysteries of Nature and Art** describes the pros and cons of engraving and etching. The problem with metal, he argues, is that the slightest error can be seen. Etching is an easier process than dry point, but it produces inferior results. [76]

Etchings mostly appear on or in front of the title page or on loose leaves attached to the body of the text. Their topics are varied: portraits as in R. Markham's **The Description of that ever to be famed Knight Sir John Burgh**. [77] A scene of Indian savagery illustrates **News from the West Indies**, 1638. A third example is found on a folded page in the middle of **Antiduello**. [78]

Some title pages are entirely engraved, including both letters and illustrations. Such frontispieces decorate for instance Gomersall's **The Levites Revenge**, or E. Benlowes's **A buckler**

against the fear of death, 1640. (Plate 4) These frontispieces appear more frequently after 1620, and for works of a certain intellectual or moral content, as for instance, in edifying treatises.

A fairly rare technique is that of double impression, which is used when a copper plate and letters appear on the same page, the techniques of which are mutually exclusive. We have found only four examples. The first and most interesting appears in 1607 in a tract against the equivocation of Jesuits; the mark left by the plate on the wet paper is clearly evident as are the imprints of the nails attaching it to the press. [79] In **Sir Francis Drake revived,** the plate is printed slightly askew and the careless compositor drew a line that interrupts the illustration. In addition, the plate was superimposed on "London"--the place of publication. [80] The process was costly, and therefore rarely used for ephemeral literature.

Mistakes in the composition of the title pages are, unfortunately, frequent. Often a picture is either slanted or cut unduly. In the **Anatomie of the English Nunnery at Lisbon,** [81] the frontispiece is printed askew. A boat happens to be cropped [82] or a horse's tail only appears, the rest of the body being trimmed away. [83] Sometimes even part of the title is cut. [84] Often errors are due to the haste of a negligent compositor, but at other times, woods were borrowed from another work.

Another defect in the quality of the printing is due to the wearing out of the board or the plate. As etchings fade away, woodcuts get coarser. [85] Both plates and boards can be grooved again. For instance the woodcut illustrating **Natures cruell step-dame,** 1637 is reused for the ballad **The downfall of William Grimmond,** 1650; [86] the latter print is thicker and the rough has chipped away. Another interesting transformation occurs in the woodcut adorning **Londons dove** which reappears facing the title page of **The dignity of preaching.** [87] Of the bird, only the claws and the tail remain printed on the black cloth covering the coffin.

Since woodcuts were not always made for the work they illustrated, the difficulty is to determine what proportion of these are original, that is conceived and realized for the pamphlet. [88] Publishers chose previously used illustrations, taken from the **Nuremberg Bible,** from the **Ship of Fools,** the **Roman de Renard, The Canterbury Tales** or any other popular work. Alternately the publisher would take out of his stock any decorative item: allegories, foliage, and architectual decorations. A borrowed woodcut could be a fragment or the reduction of a larger cut. Thus Foxe's **Actes and Monuments** provided scenes of torture; Topsell's **The historie of four-footid beastes** was a source for animal prodigies. The works of Ambroise Pare served for surgery.

Cawood the Rooke, 1640, modelled itself on **Renard the Foxe.**
Other cuts reappeared from pamphlet to pamphlet, as for instance
that of **Wofull News from the west-parts of England** (STC 10025)
in **A relation of the most lamentable burning of the cittie of
Cork,** 1622 (STC 5766). Death dancing on the coffins appears
both on Dekker's **A rod for run-awayes** and on Taylor's **The Fearful
Summer.** . . .

Some pictures were obvious adaptations of foreign woodcuts. The unicorn of Asia and the rhinoceros in **Webbe's Travailes**
are directly inspired from Dürer, so is the owl surrounded by
birds in Drayton's **The owle.** Brueghel's **Lean Kitchen** influences
the artist illustrating Taylor's **Jack a Lent.** The representation
of the Earl of Essex in the **Proclamations** is largely dictated by
the engravings of the French Boissard; it may even be borrowed
from him. [89] These are a few examples to show that continental
woodcutting and etching directly influenced their English counterparts.

Other illustrations are copied from paintings, like some
of the portraits of Queen Elizabeth. The portrait of Henry VIII,
in Rowley's **When you see me, you know me,** has been recognized
as a copy of the fresco painted by Hans Holbein on a wall in
the palace of Whitehall and subsequently burnt. [90]

Who indeed carved or designed the woods is most of
the time guesswork. Some rare illustrations were designed by
the authors themselves. Other authors, we know, like L. Digges
or G. Markham, closely supervised the printing of their works.
There are good reasons for believing that if they did not design
their own illustrations, at least they had to meet their approval.

Reliable and recent hypotheses have traced some woodcuts
back to embroiderers or purse makers. [91] Some illustrations
fit the pattern perfectly. [92] In a pamphlet on landslides, the
periphery seems to be made of chain-stitch allied to button-hole
stitch: the holes in the ground and the cracks seem to be filled
with lock-stitches. The trees are stylized as in needle-point and
the leaves have only three or five folioles. Five woodcuts are
particularly inspired by embroidery. In each the same striped
skies with coil-shaped clouds can be discerned; the trees are the
same and so are the hills and, **The baiting of the Popes bull** excepted, so are the character figures. [93] (Plate 15)

In **Hollands Leaguer,** 1632, the background motif is
inspired from weaving and finds a parallel in the rectangular
shapes of a fairly formal garde. The nails in the door could be
made in knot-stitches. Since drapers imported paper, it is extremely
likely that they would provide some designs. (Plate 5)

Other woodcuts, for instance interlude characters, can be traced back to the influence of card-makers: young men are often depicted as knaves, for instance "youth" in **The Interlude of Youth,** 1557, or "jealousy" in **Here begynneth a dialogue between the comen Secretary and Jelowsy.** We find him also in **The Churle and the Byrde,** 1550, as in various ballads. The original came from the French printer, Antoine Vérard, who worked in Paris around 1500. [94] Authentic examples can be found illustrating the pamphlets of S. Rowlands. His knaves of clubs, diamonds, hearts and spades symbolize the knaves of society, the rabble: diamonds work at sea, spades on land, and the knave of hearts helps the knave of clubs in catching gulls. [95] (Plate 6)

Some reproductions of cards can also be found in the pamphlets of R. Greene, but this is a slightly different matter as the characters themselves are not card-figures, but hold on to cards.

No one will be surprised if we stress the influence of bookbinders on the designing of the title pages and borders. [96] They probably provided the printer with a number of metal cuts which would print like woodcuts. Other craftsmen, such as makers of coats of arms and blasons must have played a significant role in print designing. Carpenters were also probably employed for the carving of the wood once the design was traced on the board. [97]

Most of these workers are anonymous. Copper-engravers, however, are often known to us, as frequently their plates are signed. Princes and personages, in the seventeenth century, according to the law of decorum, tended to receive the better treatment of the copper plate. Gustavus Adolphus appears on an unsigned plate of 1594 and in a plate engraved by Ge. Mountain for the **Swedish Intelligencer,** 1632. Royal portraits are fairly well-known. Even when they are signed, one can attribute the portraits of Elizabeth to well-known engravers. [98] The triumphs of James I, in 1604, delayed because of the plague of 1603, are illustrated by W. Kip and St. Harrison. Glover designs the plate of the Moroccan Ambassador in 1637. R. Vaughan and John Payne are both portrait engravers of the thirties. Thomas Cecil illustrates two works by Gomersall, and Marshall (the great Marshall) illustrates works as varied as the theological works of Sibbes and of Sym, **The Legend of Captain Jones,** a pamphlet of Henry Lord on the sect of the Banians, **The Assizes of Bread,** 1638, and **The Lover,** picturing Charles and the Infanta.

The illustration of pamphlets depended on authors' or publishers' tastes; yet it was not always consistent. Heywood's **If you know not me, You know nobody** is illustrated in three different ways, whereas Marlowe's **Dr. Faustus** always bears the same woodcut. What is the reason for this? It is hard to tell. [99] Changing the title of a work while keeping the same woodcut, changing the picture while keeping the same title, or changing the whole title page, seem to have been part of the salesman's tricks. These were used for successful works that appeared in several editions. The same work in a different garb looks like new. Stunning titles, woodcuts or etchings, all attracted the attention of the stroller in St. Paul's and were ingenious advertising devices.

From an artistic perspective, although some cuts reappear from one pamphlet to the next, still it is possible to follow the evolution of the visual arts in England through pamphlet illustration. Borders which were first imitations of manuscript illuminations as in **A devout treatyse called the tree and xii frutes of the holy goost [100]** (STC 13608), or in **Christmas carolles,** 1550 or in Hooper's **Homily,** 1553, [101] (Plate 3) gradually exhibit the impact of sculpture and architecture. [102]

Later, influenced by mannerism, imported from Florence through the French School of Fontainebleau, borders stress the primacy of ornament and are a blending of various techniques and styles. Interlacing on wooden columns or portals are added. [103] Gradually architectural and geometrical columns become more human. Busts either rest on pedestals in the years 1570-1580 or blend into columns that sustain that portal-shaped border. Most of these are Christian allegories. Later statues replace columns and the trompe l'oeil appears. Virtues, prophets and Pagan gods stand in their niches or bear cornucopiae or flaming urns.

Around 1580 the Byzantine style seems to prevail. A Hellenistic form of art can be found side by side with the Syrian type in interesting groupings. For instance, in **Riche his farewell,** 1581, David in oriental costume holds his lyre on one side, while on the other side Moses displays the Tables of the Law. Underneath demigods surround a medallion topped by an angel with unfolded wings.

Another example can be found in the evangelists' symbols of the tetramorph next to Athena representing Fides and Humilitas, in oriental costume, holding a sheep.

From about 1615, the new designing of the border seems to follow two very different tendencies, one purely architectural, the other "pictorial." [104] The former, inspired by Vitruvius, does not last very long. [105] Arches, influenced by neo-classicism, exhibit the style which will make Christopher Wren famous. The former fascination for the distortions of the organic and vitalistic have been replaced by a taste for the mathematical and the rational.

Next to this stream-line tendency, an architecturo-sculptural style can be found, also influenced by the <u>trompe l'oeil</u> technique of painting, as in the frontispiece of **The Sanctuarie of a troubled soul**, engraved by William Hole. It comprises five women, in various garb. Hope and Faith hold a chained heart pierced by love and kept burning by some oil or eased by some ointment; Fear pierces one side, while Pain caresses it with thorns. Underneath lie two nebulous bas-reliefs. On the left a figure flies away from the devil; on the right a lay equivalent of St. Martin of Tours gives away his cloak to a poor man. In between a medallion probably represents the author. The interest of this tormented picture is two fold. First, it is an admirable example of the excess baroque art runs into. Secondly, it shows the development of the sixteen-twenties toward the pictorial. [106] Sculptural borders also evolve toward the pictorial; this is evident if one compares for instance **A buckler against the fear of death**, 1640, with sixteenth century title pages. (Plate 4)

In engraved frontispieces, common under Charles I, a further move toward the pictorial takes place: the line gradually disappears as it yields to shadows intended to create illusion. A good example is provided by the etched frontispiece of Gomersall's tragedy, **Sforza**, 1628, which describes the destructive work of worldly wolves, using a town and some hills as background. Though some lines still remain, it is interesting to note the blending technique between the grass and the sheep, achieved by the mere difference of intensity. In the same way, the differentiation between the arm of the chair and that of the animal only comes from shadowing, a recent technique. (Plate 7)

How pamphlet illustration reflects the discoveries of modern art in England is the subject of the end of this chapter. How can we see in new cuts and etchings progress in the use of perspective, the advent of the chiaroscuro technique and of realism?

Early pictures dealing with essence, rather than existence lacked perspective. [107] So do most often miraculous events, even as late as 1613 or 1628. [108] Sometimes the stern of a ship is directed against the wind. [109] And whenever the new perspective according to the roundness of the eye is used, as in **A new spring shadowed in sundry pithie poems**, 1619, the general perspective is bad: the background wall has the same length as the foreground wall. (Plate 8) Archaism is often due to the negligence of cutters.

There is little opening onto the outside world or unifica-tion of subject matter. Antecedence tends to be expressed by the location of the composed picture, as one reads from left to right or from top to bottom, as in medieval polyptychs. [110]

Shadowing, however, can be found almost everywhere, except, until the seventeenth century, on the faces which remain flat. But shading appears often at random on clothes and landscapes. In Lydgate's **On the smyth that forged a new dame** (STC 17036), it gives neither fullness of shape to the characters nor depth to the landscape. In **The Churle and the Byrde**, 1561, the technique has improved; the artist shapes the robe of the peasant with its multiple folds. Curiously, however, the trees on which the bird perches and the peasant himself are given contradictory lighting. Why? Because two woodcuts are used to make one. [111] A series of hotchpotch shadowing can be found in **The story of the death of Peter Stubbe, a sorcerer**, 1590. The woodcutter, however, shows some basic knowledge of human anatomy.

Thus, one of the functions of shadowing is to enhance realism, as was increasingly fashionable at the end of the sixteenth century. The tabor of **Tarlton's jests**, 1638, is actually round. The tunic and the breeches in **Swetnam, the woman-hater** have a certain feel about them and one can make out the knees beneath the dress of Atalanta, who seems to have replaced James I as judge in the trial. [112] (Plate 9)

Shading also unified the scene while enhancing the main topic. The most striking example of such chiaroscuro occurs on the title page of R. Speed's **The counter-scuffle**, 1628, which describes a Gargantuan feast, probably borrowed from the Netherlands. Unfortunately, illustrations of this quality are rare. Sometimes, however, they will be found among the ornamental pictures that accompany pamphlets of intellectual or moral import. [113]

The most notable progress concerning most illustrations is the shift from intellectual sketching to verisimilitude. Allegorical images, that of **The murmurer** for instance, still achieve intellectual significance through the realistic painting of the anatomy of the body. The concern for realism can be traced in the evolution of the drawings of the heart: at first it is just delineated; then shadowing gives it relief; later the main artery is shown; finally it becomes the gory palpitating organ that we know. [114]

Only the best woodcuts or engravings can be compared to English painting. At best, at the beginning of the seventeenth century, they attempted to learn from the techniques of the portrait and of the miniature.

The taste for individual portraits arose from the growth of anthropocentrism and individualism. Sovereigns, courtiers, writers, preachers, travelers, all enjoyed posing for a portion of immortality. Portraits either remain allegorical or have a streak of realism in pamphlets. Woodcutting is first used, then etching. Satirical as opposed to formal portraits also appear, such as the illustrations of **A Game of Chaess,** made at Leiden, or of **Galateo Espagnol,** 1640. Only the formal portrait will be considered in this section.

A pharaonic portrait is the representation of a contemporary, in whom the artist has chosen a number of features expressing personality. It varies according to the perception of the artist and the <u>persona</u> of the model. Queen Elizabeth, for instance, forbade the diffusion of some unworthy portraits of herself and disliked shading which would mar the virgin-like quality of her youthful features. [115] On the other hand, she loved emblematic paintings which reminded her beloved subjects of the loyalty and affection they owed her.

There is little allegorical refinement in the woodcuts representing the Queen. Her nose is slightly arched and her upper lip strong. She usually appears in three-quarters face, after the Italian fashion, but keeps her eyes riveted on her subjects. Her coiffure is elaborate, her costume heavy with lace and gems, a symbol of her rank and of the pomp befitting the monarch. She bears the sceptre and the mace, representative of her power. Most often, in pamphlets, she appears on her ornate throne. The heavy embroidery on the seat, on the tapestry and on the royal garb, as well as the design of the border, get blurred. From all these trimmings, the face of Elizabeth emerges, striking in its simplicity, purity and clarity.

Other portraits of the Queen can be found. In a dedication from Churchyard to Sir Walter Raleigh, the letter "E" shows Elizabeth on her throne, clad in ample cloak. [116] Other portraits are medallions: the clothes of the Queen are still ornate, but she stands out on a white background, on which ELIZABETH D. G. REGINA can sometimes be read to remind her people of the divine right of kings. [117] The medallion can also be formed by intertwining rose stems, the emblem of the Tudor dynasty. They surround the Queen, square-shaped, with a rose at each corner. (Plate 10)

Portraits of the Queen do not stop at her death. In Heywood's **If you know not me, you know nobody,** 1633, Elizabeth wears a heavily embroidered dress. The edition of 1639 presents the Queen with a sharp face and narrow mouth, where delayed virginity has left its mark. (Plate 11a)

Marlin's etching facing **England's Elizabeth,** gives us a very different picture of the sovereign. Her face is shaded. The Psalms rest on a table near her. In court dress, the Queen wears a fashionable wing-shaped veiling which gives her an angelic look. The voice of God, supporting her, comes down from the clouds of glory: "Many daughters have done well, but thou surpassest them all." In the background, one can see the palace of Woodstock.

No sovereign holds the front of the pamphlet literature like Elizabeth. We know of only one portrait of her father, front face, a copy of Hans Holbein's mural for Whitehall. The portraits we find in the proclamations of the sixteenth century are all three-quarters face. Later figures, half-length or full-length, frontal or three-quarters view, stand out against a grey or white background. In Boissard-like pictures, the horseman holds the center of the page, while the background displays a seascape or a town.

In the seventeenth century, medallions become more and more fashionable. [118] Although some white backgrounds remain, most are grooved to give a darker effect. Some portraits stand against a plain tapestry. The eyes either stare at the onlooker or at a fixed point in the distance. In dress the stress is on embroidery rather than jewelry. The face is shadowed and wrinkled, for the real personality to appear.

Three portraits stand out. One woodcut is inspired by the three intaglio portraits of Prince Henry by Simon Van Passe, William Hole and William Marshall. [119] Prince Henry is about to throw the javelin; he is running, with hair pushed back by the wind and his taut arm is going to spring back and hurl the weapon. This is the only woodcut portrait, seemingly, that gives the impulse of movement.

A contrasting figure is that of John Donne in his shroud. The etching serves as a reminder accompanying the sermon that was delivered in the cathedral by this admirable preacher and metaphysical poet whose sense of theatricality moved the crowds. The portrait is both realistic and symbolical. [120]

The third portrait shows the ambassador from Morocco, Alkaid Jaurer Ben Abdella. The art of this etching consists in the contrast between the geometrical cross-scratched background and the blending, curving lines making the dark face of the Moor. Yet some of the shading in the face and the garb of the ambassador reminds us of the cross lines of the background. The picture is thus unified. The arched eyebrow is strongly shadowed as well as part of the eyes. The edge of the eyelid is lit up. What is stressed is the keen look and the determined chin. No doubt Ben Abdella was intelligent, but he was also hard to deal with. [121] (Plate 12)

Pamphlet readers also loved to see those of whom they heard most. Famous voyagers, like Sir Walter Raleigh or Sir Francis Drake and preachers like John Sym appear in many pamphlets. The image of John Sym, particularly is either enlarged or reduced according to the format of the pamphlet it illustrates.

A different sort of portrait can be found in epitaphs and funeral elegies. Although some medallions appear, most often the dead are represented full-length and recumbent on their death-beds, their coffins or their tombs, as medieval gisants. [122] In **Elegies consecrated to the never dying memory of Henry Prince of Wales**, 1613, the beloved prince is recumbent on a tomb. Its edifice reminds us of that adorning the title page of the **Triumphs of James I.** This fine woodcut appears on a folded folio sheet. Henry clad in princely robes, holds his javelin. [123]

The last funeral portrait of considerable interest concerns Henry Welby, who died at the venerable age of eighty-four. Facing the title page, Mr. Welby is sitting at his desk; left of him, a shelf full of books. Through the window, the print opens up with the view of a village nestled around its church, bordering a lake. The skill of W. Marshall, the engraver, appears in the delicacy and subtlety of the hair and beard as well as in the landscape. [124]

Portraits found in pamphlets are far from revealing the extent of the art of the portrait existing in England and certain-ly even less of the evolution of art. [125] Still they sometimes borrowed the miniaturists' techniques. About fifty illustrations belong to this group. Technically they illustrate the concepts of Nicholas Hilliard, who was also an engraver and fond of metal-work and embroidery. Considering perspective to be an optical illusion, he advocated the shortening of distances and opposed natural proportions to geometrical and visual proportions. He was also sparse on the shading which he thought was there to enhance the line only, never to replace it. [126]

To his school, we owe some of the finest clear woodcuts found between 1590 and 1640. **News out of Cheshire** (STC 24904) shows a miraculous fountain where the sick come in the hope of healing. The title page cut represents twelve characters in various attitudes. Everything down to the last detail is satisfying to the eye. In a corner a hut is made of stones that are clearly detached from each other as those of the wall that retains the fountain. The latter has two water holes shaped like an apothecary's bottles. A similar one could be found in Robert Record's **The urinall of Physick.** The woodcut gives an impression of neatness and precision. (Plate 13)

A whole series of woodcuts seems to belong to the same shop and school. In Dekker's **Belman of London,** 1608, the rounded paving stones of the street contrast with the rectangular stones of the wall. Similar to the wall of the fountain is the technical approach of **Laquei Ridiculosi** or of J. Vicars's **Mischeefes Mysterie.**

Other similar pictures could be inspired by Isaac Oliver, another miniaturist, who was more lavish on shading. In this category, we would be tempted to include the title page of W. Fennor's **Pluto his Travailles.** Others by their love or embroidery, remind us of George Gower. Such are, for instance, S. Rowlands's **The melancholie Knight** (Plate 14), or **A nunnes prophesie**, or other portraits of Queen Elizabeth. (Plates 11a and b)

One could discern other groups of woodcuts: those probably carved by various guilds come first to mind. But there are also others related by topic or technique; for instance those dealing with meteorological catastrophes. Because of the shape of their roofs, as of the frequency and shape of the wind mills, we would be tempted to say that they are imitated or come from the Netherlands. This is, however, only a hypothesis that remains to be proven.

Around 1640 the best pamphlet illustrations seem to be divided into two groups, which vary according to their techniques. Woodcutting seems to be influenced by the old crafts: card-making, embroidery, metalwork. Etching and engraving, on the other hand, encouraged by the recent discoveries of modern painting, endeavor to vie with their two formidable sisters in the Netherlands and in Italy. It can be concluded that, in any case, in the middle of the seventeenth century pamphlet illustration often aims at quality. Through them one begins to feel that English art is on the way. A century later it was to produce the marvellous etchings of Hogarth.

Chapter II

IMAGES WITH AN ESSENTIALLY DECORATIVE FUNCTION

This chapter deals with the decorative function of the illustrated pamphlets while acknowledging that motives other than aesthetic may also be involved. For example, a printer's colophon is an ornament but also a mercantile identification. If the royal coat of arms is found on the title-page of a work, the purposes for its inclusion are multiple. They may include: official propaganda, flattery, or a simple symbol. If the image of a fleet of ships is used, it may have little to do with the title of a pamphlet yet it may be a memorable ornament for an island nation or a memento of a distinguished admiral and patriot who is a peer of the realm. Hence this category must be employed prudently. Three principal types of decorative images will be under consideration: decorative letters, coats of arms, and ships. The aim will be to describe their evolution in the different roles they play in this period. Afterwards the ornaments of almanacs, sermons, and poems will be analyzed for their functions.

Ornamental letters are an irrefutable survival from medieval times: inspired by illuminated manuscripts, they offer many variations. There are letters decorated with motifs of leaves in a scroll, letters containing an animal or a person, [1] or a pure letter richly ornamented. [2] Some are separated from their woodcut, as happened in the middle ages: in this case the scene is independent of the letter but close to it, as in **A mournfull Dittie on the death of certain Judges and Justices of the peace,** 1590. Other letters, however, are inserted into the scenes. Clearly the contents of these scenes are different from those of the middle ages: the artistic quality of the illustration differs considerably from its hand-painted ancestor. The biblical or classical subjects are the main sources of inspiration, with the exception of portraits of sovereigns. For example, a servant carries an infant on a platter to a Thyestes dressed like Henry VIII. [3] Proclamations abound in classical subjects: [4] Europa and the Bull (296), Neptune on his chariot, brandishing the trident (308), and Hercules armed with his club opposing a peasant who holds a bull by the tail! (320)

The sphinx, of oriental inspiration, is another motif of illustrated letters. The saints form equally popular images. In the course of the seventeenth century the ornamental letter tends to evolve from the botanical or mythological motif towards depicting a reality closer in contact with daily life. One finds, for example, motifs of the egg-and-dart type characteristic of Jacobean furniture. Then, little by little, they die out. The most elegant letters tend to be found on broadsheets, because they are large enough for a scene to be printed clearly. In most brochures in quarto or octavo, the ornamental letter is reduced in size to fit the format of the page. Most ornamental letters are therefore of the convoluted or floral type, and very rarely representational. In contrast, a letter on a broadsheet is large enough even to accommodate a theatrical scene.

Decorated letters like the colophon, tend gradually to die out by the mid-seventeenth century. They appear either in the dedicatory epistle, or in the epistle to the reader, and most rarely at the beginning of the text itself. Increasingly they were reserved for elevated subjects like theology, law, or politics, and for elite works, and left the domain of common usage. Their demise merely shows that with the increasing availability of printed information they became superfluous; itself a common historical phenomenon.

The decay of decorative letters follows a half-century or century after that of the framing or bordering of the pages in the interior of pamphlets, towards the end of the sixteenth century. Rare exceptions survive, such as **The Assizes of Bread** where the frame shows the different activities of a baker. Some poems, such as **The passionate sparke of a relenting minde,** by Simion Grahame, a poem in praise of the king, justify typographical embellishment by the elevation of the theme. The encomium of James I and of Britain warrants the decorative border similar to that of a book of hours. Since the king is head of the Church of England, it would be wrong to think of this as sacrilege. The poem was approved by the authorities and justly so, for one could never find anything more nauseating in its platitudinous flattery. Samuel Rowlands, in the seventeenth century, also occasionally uses the frame on a printed page. Most frequently the bordering survives on the title-pages of abstract works, as will be seen in the case of sermons. Otherwise, it tends to disappear to be replaced by concrete illustrations. [5]

The same phenomenon appears on the tops of pages. Some woodcuts are still to be found with emblems of the king surrounded by the lion of England ornamented with a rose bearing the banner of St. George, or of the unicorn with the thistle of Scotland and the cross of St. Andrew above, **The Arithmetical Jewel** of William Pratt, for example, or the sermon in honor of the king, **Britannia Vota or God save the King.** But these works were printed by royal privilege. Apart from certain exceptions, the decorations at the heads of title-pages are often foliage and those too tend to disappear in the seventeenth century.

Coats of arms, on the contrary, survive better than letters or borders, though they are few in number. They are usually related to the author of the brochure--a rare case; to the person to whom the work was dedicated; or to the illustrious person who is written about.

The author's coat of arms appears only when he is himself a person of distinction. With Churchyard, for example, it is almost a habit, as in **A light bondell of livly discourses called Churchyardes charge,** etc . . . 1580. (Plate 16). He prints his arms on the back of the title-page of **A sparke of friendship** (1588): it is a griffin surmounted by three stars; from a helmet above emerges a broken staff encircled by a crown on a base of leaves or torn fabric from which two acorns fall. The device beneath the coat of arms is: EN DIEU ET MON ROY.

It is more common to find the coat of arms of the person to whom the book is dedicated. Such is the case with **The poor Orphan's Court,** 1636, whose initials, M.S., doubtless stand for Michael Sparke. The title-page bears the coat of arms of the king. The tract appeals to the crown on behalf of children and poor old people who die of hunger in the streets, due to social and official neglect.

Some printers use the coat of arms of the corporation or guild of London to which they are dedicated, as in the case of a broadsheet: **The armes of the tobachonists,** 1630. The coat of arms can also be found on the back of **Tabaco** by Anthony Chute, 1595, which boasts of the merits of smoking tobacco, just as he praised the smoke coming from the chimney in the middle of houses in olden times. The coat of arms also honors the person to whom the work is dedicated, as in the examples of the Earl of Essex and the Admiral of the Fleet. [6] It is, of course, to royalty that the greatest homage should be rendered because it is from sovereigns that the greatest favors can be obtained. Therefore the city of Edinburgh reminds Charles I of the munificence of the reception that the city gave him. On the title-page the arms of the city are to be found. (Plate 17)

In a society in which medieval survivals are still strong, the coat of arms often serves as identification, as in the case of the horsemen competing in the tourneys of long ago. Thus in a number of proclamations the coats of arms accompany the engravings made in honor or princes. Among others, those of Prince Henry and Mary, Queen of Scots, whose memory the engravings keep evergreen, as also of the Duke of Norfolk and the Earls of Essex and Northampton. The portrait and the coat of arms together advertise the importance of the elite members of the established order. [7]

Sir Francis Drake who had so often fought for England against the Spaniards with his device: SIC. PARVIS. MAGNA. appears with both portrait and coat of arms which equally catch the eye in **The world encompassed by Sir Francis Drake**, 1628. Both celebrate the person concerned; the portrait because it represents the person under the best circumstances, the coat of arms because, whether inherited or newly acquired, it is a mark of honor. **Prince Henrie Revived** provides an example of the role of a coat of arms as royal publicity. This Prince Henry is the first born son of the daughter of James I, Elizabeth and of Frederick the Count Palatine. The medallion of the infant is framed within four coats of arms. The English one is in the form of a lozenge, and the three others in the shape of a shield. The orb, the symbol of a Christian prince, also appears. The birth of Prince Henry was a cause of rejoicing because it compensated the English public for the loss of the greatly lamented Prince of Wales.

Of all those who died, Prince Henry, the elder son of James I, was the one most mourned. In all the leaflets concerning him, his heraldic sign can be found: a crown surmounted by the three feathers of the Prince of Wales. Here, in **Londons love to the royal Prince Henrie,** [8] his heraldic sign appears in the center of a sun with flaming rays. Perhaps this symbol is reminiscent of a catholic monstrance with the implicit deification of the Prince. In any case, the solar crown seems to indicate in both examples the coruscation of the souls of the two men and the promise of eternity. **Fames memoriall,** recording the life, the death, and the obsequies of the Earl of Devonshire, bears his shield on the title-page, roughly drawn. On the back, surrounded by Honi soit qui mal y pense an eye in tears, a symbol of mourning approved by the Order of the Garter, rests in the middle of a shining sun, a sign of eternity. Another example is that which ornaments the funerary sermon of Elizabeth Stanley. The coronet of her rank surmounts the arms of the Huntingtons.

Finally, the pamphlets sometimes bear both the royal arms and those of a London guild. This is the case in Buckminster's almanac which features on the top of the page the arms of the king and on the bottom those of the Stationers' Company. [9]

The paucity of coats of arms in pamphlets requires some explanation. There seem to be two main causes. First there is the ignorance of the great middle class public during the Renaissance era of the subtleties of the science of medieval heraldry. The rarity of tourneys and the changing of the armor of the combatant meant that it was no longer necessary to put up a sign which would transform an articulated mass of steel into a man defending his house. The public recognized only the most renowned shields, those of the great men of the kingdom. Furthermore, it is commonly accepted that the Renaissance saw an awakening of individualism. The portrait displays the features of the hero. The family badge fades out to give greater place to the individual portrait. This is why the Puritan Sibbes decorates most of his works with his own portrait.

The ships that ornament the pamphlets of the sixteenth and seventeenth centuries often combine the decorative with an illustrative purpose. The title-page decoration of **The Sculler [10]** is directly related to the title of the brief work. Other vessels often illustrate the accounts of naval battles. The reason for their inclusion in this chapter is that the types of ships represented are of very limited variety and that some others serve to ornament every other thing except tracts or narratives of navigation. These are types rather than concrete representations.

Curiously, the same symbol may be used for radically different purposes. For example, the same vignette decorates a decree on the fast on Fridays [11] and a religious tract condemning the cross at Cheapside: [12] in each case a fish approaches two ships of the merchant navy armed with cannons that shoot from their prows.

The same ship ornaments an order of Charles Howard, authorizing a search for J. Salisbury, [13] a ballad on Captain Ward, a famous pirate, and a wedding sermon entitled **The Merchant Royall**, 1607. (Plate 18) It reappeared in 1615 on **The Seaman's Kalendar, [14]** inside Rowlands's **The knave of Diamonds** in 1613 and in a news story describing a murder in 1618. [15] It is a three-masted ship, resembling a galleon because of its two rows of cannons, but it seems to be of much greater tonnage.

Publishers clearly used the same illustrations for different purposes and the ships were decorative and at the same time pointers to the merchant marine of England. For instance, a fishing boat figures on the statute in favor of the observance of fasting on Fridays; **A true and wonderfull Relation of a Whale, [16]** and **A true report and exact description of a mighty sea-monster, or Whale, [17]** show us the first English whalers. In this case the boats are illustrative rather than decorative. They occupy only part of the frontispiece. Larger fishing boats appeared in Dekker's **Penny-wise pound-foolish**, 1631, and John Taylor's **The Praise of Hemp-seed**.

Only two signs of the admiralty decorate pamphlets. That of Howard ornaments Digges's **Prognostication Everlasting,**

1576: it is a man-of-war flying the pennant of St. George, with the mainmast carrying the banner royal, as it should, consisting of lions and roses, and the mizzen-mast the arms of the Howard family and the emblem of the Order of the Garter which was part of that of the Admiral of the Fleet. (Plate 19) The illustration opposite the title-page of **A true Description of his Majesties royall and most stately Ship called the SOVERAIGN OF THE SEA** . . . 1638 [**18**] is an engraving on copper with an etcher's needle as remarkable for its technical perfection as for the precision of its depiction. It is a powerful man-of-war with four decks that has three entire rows of artillery on the three lower decks, and some supplementary armament on the upper deck. The impressive poop has three levels. The engraver did his best to show the arms and munitions in the interior of the ship, including the striking mouths of the cannons. Barrels of gunpowder and roundshot can be made out on one side, and swords, lances, and axes to repel the enemy in case of being boarded, on the other side. The prow is richly decorated with classical figures, notably those of Mars and Neptune. Even the trumpets that sound the signal for assault appear on this engraving that is so informative in its details.

The impressive bunting identifies the admiral's ship. The mid-mast bears the banner royal of Charles I: the lions of England and the lilies of France fill the first and fourth quarters, the harp of Ireland the second quarter, and the erect lion of Scotland the third quarter. The foresail mast carries the flag of St. George, and the mizzenmast the union jack, symbol of the unity of the three countries. Contrary to the previous example, the coat of arms of The Admiral of the Fleet, the Duke of Buckingham, does not appear. (Plate 20)

Up to the present only isolated ships, or pairs of ships have been considered. However, there are equally to be found prints representing a fleet. These can be divided into two groups: a decorative basis or a narrative exposition of the methods of attack of the British navy or of a foreign fleet. Already we find the mixture of types to be studied during the remainder of this part of the book. The ships certainly embellish the text, but also the celebrated actions of the fleets of which the author boasts.

The fleet commanded by Robert Devereux, Earl of Essex, is approaching the coast of Ireland, a reminder that the Queen's favorite was also lieutenant-general of Ireland. [**19**] Only two kinds of vessels can be made out: a pinnace starting to burn--that is a flat boat which can be easily handled and which is manoeuvred by oars. [**20**] The other vessels seem to be galleons, ships which by their length recall a galley, and by the height of the prow and the poop look like cockerels. [**21**]

The same type of illustration eulogizes Charles Howard,

Earl of Nottingham. In this case there are two fleets of different kinds. The one which fills the left side of the print commemorates the defeat of Philip of Spain in 1588: it is the Armada. With the exception of the three men-of-war in the front row, the rest of the fleet seems indistinctly composed of merchant ships, high and narrow and sufficiently raised up from the sea level, which were generally called carracks. Two vessels face each other; the one on the right seems lighter and speedier, and is doubtless a caravelle. The fleet on the right commemorates the sack of Cadiz which Charles Howard and the Earl of Essex commanded. The only distinctive characteristic of the English ships, is the bunting on the admiral's ship. The Spanish defence is composed only of galleys with their oars showing.

Even dominantly decorative illustrations serve a historical purpose for they disclose the various types of ships of the times and their functions. The ships with square sails are opposed to the galley with a triangular sail. Instead of a boat that was low in the water and slender, rapid but incapable of meeting a stormy sea, the seventeenth century preferred these floating fortresses with their cliff-like prows which rode up and down the waves without endangering the ship. The illustrations of our pamphlets show that in England the era of the galley was over. [22]

While predictive pamphlets have pedagogical value in explaining the mechanism of an eclipse, the illustrations of almanacs and calendars using vignettes and images of astrological man which are often repeated, serve no educative but only a decorative purpose. They transmit certain beliefs inherited from the middle ages: that is, the influence of the zodiac on the human body. This was so old hat as probably to bore the reader.

The form of the almanac did not change at all from 1540 to 1640. The almanac and the calendar, separated from the beginning of the sixteenth century, were no larger than a booklet and did not prophesy. It was the predictions that generally occupied themselves with such matters. From 1540 the almanac and the prediction found themselves under the same covering, but in the seventeenth century, they were often found separated: the prediction had its own title-page. From 1640 the prediction contained political prophecies destined to influence public opinion. [23]

The almanac did not always contain the calendar although the two are often found tied together. But in the middle of the sixteenth century if it contained a calendar, it was the legal calendar and not at all the astrological calendar which began with the winter equinox, on the 11th of March, and with days starting at midday, the day before the official calendar day.

In the sixteenth century three sorts of almanacs can

be found: the large type of which few examples survive and which disappeared almost completely at the beginning of the seventeenth century; the annual pocket almanac, the most common; and the almanac for several years. The two latter kinds are found between 1540 and 1640. [24]

Only a few examples of the great almanac are extant. Destined to contain only the most practical advice, in general they were not intellectual works. Astrological man, when he can be found, is small; the months and seasons or the signs of the zodiac often appear as woodcut vignettes. Almanac arrangement varies with their authors, but the two most frequent are: the upper part of the second half of the almanac is occupied from January to June, while July to December take up the lower part; the odd months from January to November use the upper part, and February to December, the even months, use the lower part. In 1546 and 1558 one can observe a slightly different order. The months are disposed in three rows and not on two and are to be read vertically: January, February and March are at the head of each. In H. Low's almanac of 1558 the signs of the zodiac are represented. In that of Askham, printed by Th. Marshe in 1555-56 the prints are divided in two; on one side the labors of the months, on the other the signs of the zodiac. The vignettes are imprinted in black on white, with the exception of some of the almanacs including the almanac of Thomas Hill of Oxford which are in red on white. The majority come from France and pass from printer to printer. It seems that John Turke and Marshe received the same because theirs are printed in French.

The themes of the illustrations reflect those of the illuminated manuscripts of the middle ages. The activities of man are entirely agricultural. In January, February, or March, laborers rest; April, May, and June depict pastoral life: sheep-shearing and the weaving of wool, sweet music and love. In July, August, and September, the earth yields its fruits: reaping the harvest and the ingathering of grapes are the usual occupations, while October, November, and December prepare for the winter and the following spring: tillage, woodcutting and the killing of the pig. [25]

The middle and the end of the sixteenth century witness the soaring success of the pocket almanac. Rarely found in quarto, it most commonly appears in octavo and even occasionally in sextodecimo. Four kinds of decoration can be found in almanacs: the title-page, astrological man, the months and the seasons. Two large sections were concerned with agriculture and medicine, but there are also tables of interest, the dates of fairs, and practical advice, in addition to the traditional calendar, as well as blank sheets for the readers' comments.

The title-page is generally ornamented with a border, with the exception of the almanac of Digges which presents astrological man on its title-page. Buckminster's almanac has a border of lace, others are in the mode of the mannerists. [26] In the seventeenth century the majority of borders, amid floral or scroll motifs, depict an object or a scientific allegory. The terrestrial globe is the most common as well as the most simple, and the astrological globe ornaments a good number of predictions, including that of Watson, in 1598. The quadrant or the compass, then the square, all navigational instruments, are rediscovered in others. Pond sees that his almanacs are decorated with such instruments and with the allegories of the liberal arts according to the neoplatonic categories of knowledge.

About 1589 the fashion is to have a border representing the allegory of the planets. Above, from left to right, we recognize Mars, Jupiter in the center, then Saturn; Mercury below, parallel to the Sun, and finally Venus and Luna.

Once again we see that if the decorative image does not adapt itself totally to its subject, it nonetheless creates atmosphere. The same image is used for different purposes, but is vaguely related to the text.

The success of the pocket almanac is followed by the decline of the vignette representing the seasons, the months and the signs of the zodiac. While still relatively common in the third quarter of the sixteenth century, it disappears almost completely after 1570 when the sketches or illustrations explaining the eclipses became more numerous. [27] An intriguing example can be found in Dauncy's almanac which ties the seasons to the age of man. (Plate 21) This phenomenon is probably explicable in terms of the general evolution of the spirit of the Elizabethans, from contemplation to reflection, from the decorative to the utilitarian. [28] As professor Morey has indicated, [29] there is a direct relationship between the degree of the instruction of a people and its need of decorative elements. It is not surprising to see one of the vestiges of the middle ages disappear precisely because education had penetrated to the middle layers of society.

Then why did astrological man survive so well? In general, in middle-sized or small format, he can be found in almost all the almanacs, whatever their size. In pocket almanacs he takes up almost all the page. Occasionally there is found below the illustration an inscription in Latin or an English verse. Its place depends as much on the author as the editor. In at least three editions of **A prognostication everlasting** of Digges, it appeared on the title-page; [30] for Nostradamus, it came immediately after the calendar, 1559, on the verso of A viii; Lewis Vaughan in the same year placed it immediately following the tables. For

Henry Rocheforth, 1560, the eclipses preceded the man of the zodiac on sig. B iiii verso. John Securis, a doctor, showed the anatomic man after the eclipses and before a long disquisition on medicine on the verso of A ii. Cunningham's almanac, 1564, is particularly ornamented. On the verso of A ii we find the man of the zodiac, then the eclipse, and, finally, each month is decorated with a vignette.

The place of astrological man in the almanacs appears to be stabilized in the seventeenth century. By royal privilege the publication of almanacs which had been confined under Elizabeth to Watson and Roberts, passed in 1603 to the Stationers' Company. This privilege in 1623 was extended to the two universities. The form of the almanac was then fixed. The great majority of zodiacal men were placed on A ii, or if there was no pagination, on the back of the second leaf, which comes to the same.

The form of astrological man shows no variation from the middle of the sixteenth to the middle of the seventeenth century. The old woodcuts, after being frequently recut, were practically used up so that eventually they were of poor quality. [31] Up to 1625 astrological man is almost always represented standing, facing the reader, astride. (Plate 22) After 1534 some examples can be found showing the viscera. [32] The figure in three-quarters of the cases is slightly inclined towards the left shoulder, but the head can also be in profile. [33]

The figurines of the zodiac often surround the body, sometimes separated by a crown of clouds, [34] sometimes accompanied by their graphic symbol, as in the almanac of Digges. Even rarer is the drawing of the planets on the right of the image, to the left of the person, with the signs of the zodiac printed on the other side. [35]

Although all these illustrations can be rediscovered in the middle of the seventeenth century, it is worth observing interesting additions. Astrological man appears from the back, or sitting on the world. His arms are still to the side. In place of the signs of the zodiac are found, either their graphic signs, or their names and the parts of the body they are concerned with. In the woodcut of the seated man, the names and signs are cut, but only the sign is used again in relation to the parts of the body. The underlying beliefs remain unchanged: Aries, the ram for the head and face; Taurus, the bull for neck and throat; Cancer, the crab for the chest and the stomach; Virgo, the virgin rules over the intestines and the belly; Scorpio, the scorpion over the private parts; Capricorn, the goat over the knees; Gemini, the twins over the arms and shoulders; Leo, the lion over the heart and back; Libra, the balance over the loins and their organs. The thighs depend on Sagitarius, the bowman; the legs on Aquarius, the water-carrier; and, finally the feet on Pisces, the fish.

Although after 1550 the pocket almanac was most frequently printed in black and red, astrological man and the borders remained in most cases in black and white to the very end of the century. In fact, the attempts to print in black and in color were catastrophic enough. The final result was unsatisfactory because the two imprints produced a confused effect and the colors ran into one another. The technique improved slightly in the seventeenth century, when the printer chose occasionally only to underline a part of the body, or even more, on the rarest occasion, when the entire man was in red ink. [36]

The astrological man in the almanac of Rudston, the mathematician, for the year 1607, warrants a special description. Although the brochure is only a simple calendar, yet the author shows the chief veins of the body and the best places for bloodletting. The man, hairy and Michelangelesque, takes up the entire page and the signs of the zodiac do not appear. The print is destined for surgeons and the inscriptions slanting towards the body explain the chief uses of the veins that are disclosed. This illustration is one step closer to a more scientific conception of the human body and is not exclusively decorative. (Plate 23)

The borders of the prophecies present almost the same characteristics as the almanacs. That of Erra Pater, printed by T. Snodham in 1562, is an exception to the rule. The author, himself appears below the title inside a lace border.

Finally, in the prophecies we find eclipses with repetitive or explanatory images. We have chosen to classify them in the second category for they generally spring from a pedagogical intention, although the same image can be found again in 1589 in Dade, Buckminster, Harvey and Gray, for example. Predictive illustrations will therefore be studied in the next chapter.

The study of almanacs leads us to the following conclusions. They were a vigorous survival of the medieval tradition. No variation in the simple representation of astrological man can be found until the second quarter of the seventeenth century. While trying to find enticing decorative borders for the title-page, which they changed from year to year, editors had to rest in the tradition. For economic reasons borders reappeared cyclically. On the other hand, not all the title-pages of the almanacs of a given year are similar. Was this because the woodcut was worn out? Hardly, since it continued to be employed even when it was split. Were the newest woodcuts then kept for the most famous almanac-makers? There is no evidence for such a conclusion. In any case, almanacs, furnished those who held their copyright considerable financial resources. If their price was modest--only two pence in 1611--the quantity of the sales more than recovered the publisher's initial outlay. As an official calendar, a reminder of important events in the year, adviser in agricultural and medical matters, the almanac was as indispensable to the Elizabethan family as our present-day diary. However, out of the thousands published, only a tiny fraction is extant. As witnesses to the beliefs and occupations of an epoch, almanacs and predictions offer us a vivid testimony. The tradition is so well anchored in the heart that Dekker, satirist of almanacs in **the Ravens Almanack**, 1609, does not change the order of the signs. All use the common reference.

Nothing needs to be added to what was said in the previous chapter concerning the illustrations of sermons and prayers. [37] Reference may be made to McKerrow and Ferguson's, **Title-Page Borders used in England and Scotland, 1485-1640.** The sacred and the profane are mixed together and, the survival of the ancient gods is incorporated in Judeo-Christian iconography. Prudence, Fortitude, Humility and Temperance take the form of ancient goddesses. Or, again, David and his harp face Moses holding the tables of the law. Sometimes the symbols of the four evangelists are found in the midst of scrolls and flowers. (Plate 24) At yet other times the title-page is composed entirely of grotesques. The seventeenth century tended to abandon the decorative title-page and to put nothing in its place. Certain authors like Sibbes or Sym ornament it with their portrait, most often in a medallion. Among Puritan preachers there is a renewal of the title-page illustrations of sermons in favor of pedagogy. The sermons of Ward will be considered later. [38] In conclusion the decoration of sermons follows much the same path as that of all other pamphlets: art for art's sake gradually wanes with the advent of art engagé.

The illustration of poems shows the same tendencies but the problem has different aspects to it. Prints are ambiguous; advertisements, ornaments, vague reminders of the text, and signs of a special brand of literature. Ballads, however, do not seem to evolve at the same rhythm as pamphlets. Intended for the humbler folk, and the most conservative part of the nation, they kept traditional illustrations even though almost all other illustrations evolved. [39]

Lace borders are found in several brochures, as in the almanacs and sermons. In the same way caryatids and scrolls also appear. More important are the images of characters in some pamphlets, but they are ideograms and human types rather than individual portraits. They add nothing new.

A large number of the prints on popular poems between

1540 and 1570 are entirely decorative. Vignettes mainly represent one or more protagonists. As indicated earlier, [40] the drawings are inspired by playing-card figures. Thus the same old man represents the secretary in the dialogue of David Garrick [41] and the peasant of Lydgate's poem on the boor and the bird, [42] while Jealousy in the first is the same woodcut as the young man in the second. The bird perched on a tree in the same edition of Lydgate's poems is found again in the later edition of Copland with another figure for the peasant. It reappears in a poem on the rivalry of the seasons [43] and on the condition of man. The young man reappears also later in an interlude of 1565, [44] (Plate 25) Obviously the printers of poetry and interludes took these vignettes from their stock trying to match them with the text. [45] If one accepts the theory that they derived from playing cards, then the young man is a knave, the married woman is the queen, while the juggler or the acrobat is the joker. This seems to us to be entirely possible. Many ballads were illustrated along the same line until the middle of the seventeenth century. [46]

One of the favorite characters of the old brochures is the knight. Two principal types seemed to be in favor: one where the horse is bedecked and its master caparisoned, and the other where the horse is completely covered while its master is bare-headed. Both master and mount, in the second case, are decked with feathers rising in the wind. Helmeted knights hold a banner, while bare-faced ones brandish a rapier or a sword. All wear spurs with rowels. [47] All, except **Syr Eglamoure d'Artois,** progress from left to right; he alone mounts his rearing horse brandishing a sword, with a town as background. [48]

There are also prints of St. George, the patron saint of England, crushing the dragon, although they are not as frequent as might be expected. Indeed his depiction offered the opportunity to express the patriotism of both author and publisher without servile flattery.

Historical love stories often have, in the sixteenth century, illustrations of a young man and a young woman facing each other. The girl, with untied hair, holding a rose in her hand, pricks herself on a thorn. [49] The married woman, with covered head, holds a cradle or a birdcoop in her hand; [50] and a flighty woman carries feathers, a symbol of vanity. These images continue until the seventeenth century.

Scenes decorating poems are more complex to interpret. Some have no clear relation to the text, like **A Description of the King and Queene of Fayries** by R. S., 1635. The title-page is a partial exception insofar as it represents a king and a queen followed by a nobleman. This, though not an illustration of the text, is near to being one. But the illustrations within do not seem to follow any pattern of thought. The subject-matter deals with fairies, and their clothes, customs, and activities. They wear cloaks made of gossamer bejeweled with the morning dew shining with the first rays of the sun, a description akin to that of **A Midsummer Night's Dream.** Yet without any apparent reason, the image of a devil pursuing an armed man is found on the verso of A vi. The poem goes on to praise the good fairies whose daily actions are favorable to humans: **The Fairies Fegaries.** Opposite this new title we find a woodcut taken from some historical narrative or illustrated Bible: from his monastery a monk observes birds dropping thistles on a tomb, chest, or altar. [51] Only two farfetched references are to be found in the text: the word "chanting" is used, alluding to Gregorian chant, and therefore to monastic life; but if the fairies sing divinely, does that make them monks? The second possible link to the text might be the suggestion of supernatural intervention, but this is mere eisegesis.

The third very short poem is the complaint of the lover who suffers yet loves his suffering. Opposite the title, Adam and Eve are leaving Paradise, while on the verso is the image of a prisoner whom a magistrate expels. Is this an image of the human condition? Is there a double meaning here? It seems unlikely because the succession of woodcuts does not form a true sequence. The inevitable conclusion is that this is a brochure which was typically illustrated at random. The short text might sell more easily if inflated with illustrations. [52]

More frequently we find some approximations between the illustrations and the text, as in the case of **Here begynneth a litell treatise of the Knight of Curtesy and the Lady of Faguell.** [53] A chaste lady falls in platonic love with a knight. On seeing each other both fall down in a swoon, but they swear to remain chaste. The lady's husband learns of this and makes the knight go far off hoping that he will die in combat and that his wife will love none but himself. In fact, the cavalier knight falls beneath the blow of the enemy and sends his heart to her whom he cherished. Deeply moved, she succumbs in her turn. The title-page depicts the interior of a stately house with diamond window-panes and a black and white tiled floor: a richly garbed man is conferring with a lady accompanied by her page. This could allude to the meeting of the unfortunate lovers, but nothing proves that the print was prepared for this poem in particular. It could serve for any meeting between two persons of the opposite sex.

The same approximation can be found in a broad story **Jyl of Braintfords testament.** [54] Its taste though often doubtful pleased a public with rather crude sentiments. The title-page represents her, a basket in her hand, taking leave of a clerk after having exchanged several loose pleasantries in front of his house. The subject of the poem, the testament of Jyl, takes place, in fact, inside the house where she makes her will. In the course of a carousal, Jyl, with her neighbors as witnesses, mentions in her will all the fools of society to whom she bequeathes a fart; the total comes to twenty-six and a half farts. The second illustration is more symbolic; it is composed of those ideograms referred to on the preceeding page. On the left we find Fantasy which gives the tone to the work, then Jyl the heroine, and finally another woman who seems to be there to fill out the picture. At the end of the poem the illustration of the title-page reappears.

One of the most interesting works for the approximation of its ornamentation to the story is that of M. Charme Her, **The wife happed on Morel's Skypp**, or, **The Taming of the shrew.** [55] The work may have inspired the play of Shakespeare. Its story is similar: two daughters, one kindly, the other a shrew to be married to a penniless and ambitious young man in search of a fortune. There follows a description of the marriage and the festivities. The corresponding illustration represents a line of four persons one of whom carries a carafe or a vase. Two possible interpretations would tie it to the context: perhaps those invited to the banquet are helping themselves to a drink, or perhaps they are bringing wedding gifts. The same image reappears at the end of the story when the young man, having tamed his rebellious wife, invites his parents to see how much gentler she has become.

Returning to the story, we find that the young wife begins her married life auspiciously. When the husband is away on distant business, however, she recovers her former humor, undernourishes his servants and treats them harshly. He returns, tries to improve her by kindness at first, but finding an obstinate resistance, calms himself by visiting his estates. At this point in the narrative, we find a woodcut displaying a man on a winged horse who leaps over a river; a great fish watches the horseman and his mount with an amazed air. What is Pegasus doing here? Is the man mounting the charger of resolution? The same illustration will also be found on sig. E ii, when the young man returns to his home to find out whether his wife has changed. Clearly, such an illustration is only remotely relevant.

Since the young wife persists in her cantankerousness, he decides to punish her. Here, without any clear reason for it, can be found an image of a traveler who is waiting for a boat and who is either telling a story to or asking the way from another figure. Is this a reminder of the title which is also a symbol of narration? Is there the suggestion of a trial? It is impossible to decide. After beating the shrew, he puts her in horsehide which he has previously salted, and leaves her there until she begs for forgiveness. Then when she is subdued, she finds the arms of her husband again, who is sad to have had to inflict this necessary punishment on her. The woodcut represents both the outside and inside of the house. A man with a bow in his hand, looks severely at a woman who seems to be reading. Outside a woman holds a serpent. [56] Here the illustration admirably concurs with the spirit of the text: the domination of woman by man; she submissively learns her lesson and the outside character would represent, either justice--the natural order of things dictated at that time that man should be the master of the house--or the wisdom of a man who has learned with firmness and love to tame his rebellious wife, or again, the symbol of the triumph of good over evil. The last engraving suggests the banquet to which the parents of the young woman were invited, for them to see how gentle she has become. The mother is mad, but dare not express her annoyance out of fear for her husband, while the father secretly rejoices - The complicity of men! On the back of the last page, finally, a woodcut of a different make represents a couple in a walled garden. Trees on the outside hide the lovers from the curious. Each wears a mantle richly ornamented with fur, and the lady has a ring in her hand; the spaces left for their words are empty. Does this image serve as a conclusion on conjugal love? [57] In any case it was not cut for the pamphlet. In the majority of cases of this particular pamphlet the prints included were more decorative than explanatory, didactic, or emotional in character. Still they were suggestive of the atmosphere of the whole. Since the woodcuts were thoroughly worn they probably were issued from the stock of the printer who chose the most appropriate with care.

In the final category, the illustration of poems, it is difficult to know whether the image is ornamental or explanatory. For many reasons they appear to us to be ornamental, but motivations are often mixed.

They seem ornamental if they neither add anything to the title nor explain it. For example, **Tarltons Jests,** [58] represents Tarlton standing on the pavement, blowing into a flute and provided with a drum. On his belt is a purse. The illustration is not explanatory. Everyone knows who Tarlton is and the image is no different except in technique from the portraits or medallions already spoken of [59] and similarly, in the animal series, **The beggars Ape** [60] has a monkey for illustration, while **The Mastive** [61] of Parrot and **A dog of war** of Taylor [62] and **Machiavells Dogge,** represent a dog, and **The country mouse and the city mouse** [63] two mice, the one facing the title-page, the other at the end of the story, which is a mixture of prose and verse. **Caltha Poetarum or the Bumble Bee** of Cutwoode represents a bumble-bee. [64] These illustrations, as the dates indicate, are products of the seventeenth century and have improved.

Certain sketches illustrating the title are equally valuable as ornaments. Among the most ancient the title-page of **A merry**

Jest of the Frier and the Boy: shows a young boy who plays a shepherd's pipe while watching his sheep not far from a town; a friar emerges from a bush and makes a sign to the child. Another seems to be Lindsay's in **The Testament . . . of our Soverane Lordis Papyngo,** a satire on the ways of the court by a bird who having become a courtier can no longer adapt itself, and dies overcome by its enemies. The woodcut of the title-page depicts simply a bird about to tell a story to a younger one. Of the same kind, but this time indisputably decorative, is the illustration of the title-page of **Jack a Lent** of Taylor, imitated from the Battle between the Carnival and Lent by Peter Breughel the Elder; it depicts hunger and Mardi Gras. (Plates 6 a and b)

The decoration of the poems in the pamphlets, contrary to that of the almanacs, demonstrates a clear evolution. Most of the <u>typically decorative</u> illustrations belong to the sixteenth century. At the beginning of the seventeenth century, we observe the effort of the printers to find illustrations more directly adapted to the subject of the pamphlets and more striking for the reader, whether symbolic, emblematic, or explanatory of the contents. [65] It can already be affirmed confidently that the tendency towards realism attributed to the seventeenth century is not a myth, but that the popular and middle-class public is aware of the new forms and prefers illustration to ornament.

Nevertheless one should use caution in determining categories. If the lacy type of borders raise no questions, the caryatids are problematical since they represent the virtues. Are they ornamental or symbolical? [66] As this chapter developed, the distinction became more and more fluid, the motivations more blurred, so much so that one shaded into another.

Chapter III

THE IMAGE AS A SOURCE OF INFORMATION

It is necessary to consider the evolution of the educational ideas at the end of the sixteenth and the beginning of the seventeenth centuries in order to understand the development in the spirit of the illustrations of the same period.

Educators of the time criticized the time spent in mere memory work and in the senseless repetition of texts the form of which the pupils remembered, but not the contents. That is to say, in Ciceronian terms, that the child or adolescent considered to be incapable of discovering arguments (inventio) and of judging wisely (judicium) first learnt the art of expression (elocutio), rhetoric. Education at school from the earliest years consisted in knowing how to defend the opinions given by the masters of antiquity in Latin, with the aid of writing and diagrams which were learned by heart. If this reasoning is pushed to absurd lengths, the conclusion would be that this education trained perfect sophists capable of defending any opinion thanks to the dialectical technique of Quintilian and the images of Cicero, without even reflecting on the logic argumentation. There was nothing new under the sun; it was all in Aristotle, Cicero, and Quintilian. [1]

This attitude to knowledge resulted in that provided with W. Baldwin's **A Treatise on Morall Philosophie**, 1547, for example, or the aphorisms of Meres, [2] almost anyone could sustain a diatribe. In the seventeenth century moralized images, which were called emblems, like those of Daniel, Whitney, Wither and Quarles, corresponded to the figures of speech.

In the domain of preaching, the logical consequence was that after reading the biblical text and deducing the lesson, the preacher had to prove that what was said was indeed right. [3] That took the form of attacks against himself made by himself and with a great reinforcement of citations taken as much from the Bible as from the ancients. The Art of preaching therefore consisted largely in rhetoric or the disposition of arguments which constituted the defense of the original position. The old school, particularly strong under Queen Mary, the Catholic, recommended a tropological and analogical interpretation of the Bible according to the teaching of Holy Mother Church: all was foreseen and preaching consisted in persuading the listeners to accept it.

Knowledge came to stagnation. Since Aristotle had already discovered everything, in literary as well as scientific matters, and Galen cured all ills, and Ptolemy was the master of all cosmography, and all were valued as authorities, all that was left was to defend their arguments with subtlety.

The result of this attitude is expressed in Bacon's **The Advancement of Learning,** where he declares that the masters have become tyrants or prisons instead of being advisers. [4] The moderns could in no way emulate the ancients since they only reflected their opinions as merely pale shadows. [5] Criticism and logic intervened in the organization of the arguments that projected the initial idea. Finally, in this servile state of the spirit, Elizabethans came to have poor self-opinion which led to discouragement.

The influence of these conceptions of education can be clearly discerned iconographically in the popular works. Concepts rather than individual persons or events are represented. Young is opposed to old, summer to winter. Similarly, an old man and winter give the same idea of decrepitude and sterility. Types of women are founded on the principal of differentiation: untied hair for the young girl, the head covered for the married woman, and feathers for the light woman. If these symbols were familiar, then a rapid glance at the illustration conveyed the general idea. The purely decorative image resembled the tropes and schemes of rhetorical discourse.

The so-called Ramist school opposed this static conception of education. [6] Irritated by the weakness of his own education, Peter Ramus proposed an alternative educational system founded on the predominance of logic over rhetoric. This meant that instead of applying logic only to the arrangement of the arguments, Ramus suggested that logic was concerned with the argument itself. It was an enormous revolution in thought that challenged authority. The argumentation became not a matter of form but of substance, which was to assert most sacrilegiously, that modern man prided himself on being the equal of the ancients. As a result rhetoric became no longer essential; it was otiose because the truth must be rediscovered and expressed in the simplest and most direct way possible. Bacon insisted, however, that to reject all that the ancients had said would be foolish, but judgment should be suspended until further proof.

The panic into which the partisans of the old school were thrown is easily imagined, for habit is the creator of security. If one of the principles taught by the ancients was erroneous, then the entire system ran the risk of collapsing. Consider the problems for two generations: the old school must have experienced the same disarray as the parents of our century; the former must have cried, "knowledge is dead," as the latter sighed, "all morality has gone."

Preachers felt the shock. The further one moves into the sixteenth century the more one observes a tendency to strip rhetoric. If the Anglican preachers often retained tropes and figures, at least they are linked with genuine argumentation. The use of tropology is moderated and figurative language among the Puritans tends to be translated into simple and direct terms. [7] However, at the end of the sixteenth century, the form of Anglican sermons remains divided into subtle parts difficult for congregations of average intelligence to remember: Lancelot Andrewes and John Donne will be adepts at this in the seventeenth century. The Puritans, however, adopted Ramism. Perkins, in **The Art of Prophesying** [8] divides preaching into three distinct parts: after the reading of the text, the preacher gives the sense of it in referring to other related passages of Scripture, then he finds some <u>useful</u> point of doctrine, and then finally, an innovation, he applies this doctrine to the lives of the congregation. That is to say that the sermon does not describe a circle on itself but is conceived in a dynamic and developing didactic perspective. The citations of the Puritans came almost exclusively from the Bible in order to concentrate the intellectual effort of the congregation on the essential. [9]

From the standpoint of the sciences, the empiricism of Bacon was opposed to the conceptualist system. If one admits that not all truths have been discovered then the deductive method founded on experience will supplant the inductive method. In this way, W. Gilbert speaks of natural philosophy as a novelty and does not refer to the ancients; W. Harvey, although an Aristotelian, finds it good to assert that his conclusions on the circulation of the blood are not derived from books but from experience he has had of dissections. [10] With reference to an apprenticeship to the sciences, Elyot affirmed as early as 1531 that a good sketch or a diagram will teach a child as much as talking for six months. [11]

The direct impact on iconography is evident. For the adepts of the new school, illustrations approximate reality instead of recalling prototypes. The relation between the subject of the pamphlet and the image on the title-page becomes more direct and close. Illustrations of narratives for instance demand the selection of the most significant passage in the text so that its quintessence may be taken from the pamphlet. Finally, in practical tracts, illustrations enabled the reader to visualize what could not be imagined or would take too long to explain.

Both schools, from the perspective of the illustration of pamphlets, were to be found in the seventeenth century. The break was not sudden. However, the introduction of the works of Peter Ramus about 1580 surfaced in the vitriolic disputes in Cambridge between 1580 and 1590 where the Aristotelian E. Digby confronted the Ramist W. Temple, and Thomas Nashe opposed Gabriel Harvey. The public at large were brought up to date with the new educational principles. [12] The middle class became interested in the new system because it was both practical and conformed more closely with the demands of modern society. [13] The upper middle class as well as the open-minded nobility read Gilbert's **Queen Elizabeth's Academy,** which sought to make the young man of a good family a defender of his country through practical activities. He learned how to draw maps of sea and land, how to operate a boat, how to administer first aid, and how to recognize plants in a botanical garden.

Because the middle classes were the chief buyers of pamphlets, printers and publishers quickly caught up with the new Ramist current of thought and illustrated their popular works in consequence. It is these works in particular that will be the concern of this chapter, while taking care to distinguish the illustration from the text. However, an image expressing the modern outlook will not necessarily correspond with a text of Ramist inspiration. It has already been established that the editor or publisher is the one who generally decides on the form of the pamphlet.

The modern form of iconography also attempted to make a more direct impact on the sensibility of the readers. To instruct was often to move and categories, once more, are not clear-cut. The illustration of the death of Henry IV of France, for instance, shows the king at the very moment when he was assassinated: it both conveys information by providing a visual description of the circumstances of the assassination; and also plays on the emotions of the readers. This is not the intellectualized conception of murder but the very image of a murder taking place. Although there is no single melodramatic gesture, this informative image plays upon our sensibility, whereas the print of the tortures of Ravaillac, on the contrary, appeals primarily to our emotions. [14]

For these reasons this chapter will be divided into two parts: the first will follow the evolution of the archetype in popular imagery towards an increasingly realistic interpretation of life concentrating on a limited number of popular authors.

Thereafter, it will be interesting to note the different works, theological, ethical, historical or practical· which use illustrations for didactic purposes.

In the previous chapter on decoration it was seen that many poems, ballads and sermons were illustrated with bowers, vignettes and archetypes. These images were conceptual, that is to say, they were independent of all verisimilitude. [15] Emblems, as suggested, also represented an ideational truth. But they had a dynamic concern to teach. Little by little one can observe an evolution in the emblem which changes from the moralizing image representing eternal truths to the representation of truths immediately applicable to the individual to whom it is addressed. This progression will be our immediate concern.

One of the first moralizing images to be found in the brochures appears on the verso of the title-page of a sermon of Luther's.

On A v the righteous receive the tongues of fire while on the left a sinner is struck by a key which represents the discipline of the community of the righteous, the Church. On the right, the hardened sinner is handed over to a Satan with bestial figure and forked wings. The second illustration on A iii verso represents Christ handing over the Gospel to the servants of God. In strict accuracy one should not here speak of an emblem; the image teaches the right path, but lacks the subtleties of suggestion in a true emblem. [16] The image remains medieval, like the west fronts of cathedrals.

Of a different type, is the emblematic woodcut of death that ornaments the back of the title-page of **The worldes vanitie** by Henry Raymonde. The illustration depicts death armed with its weapons, bearing a bier to the graveyard. The woodcut is old but the subject of the image and that of the verse coincide.

Two other woodcuts which interest us as examples are true emblems. Both are moralizing works. In **A feast for wormes** by Francis Quarles, a fervent Aristotelian and emblematist, a man stands in the desert clothed in a simple loincloth with bones at his feet; two angels support a dais above his head; above the dais is a crown obscured by clouds of glory. Reading from above to beneath one can see the legend: ad hoc, ad hoc, per hoc. The explanation of the emblem comes from above: the man who hopes for the crown of the kingdom of God must pass through early life and through death. [17] It is a message that is eternally true.

Fletcher's **The Historie of the Perfect Cursed-Blessed Man**, 1629, also explores the didactic possibilities of the emblem, but by an entirely different route. Two images are to be found. One of them is of **Christian Militans,** death on his left and the temptress who makes a gift of the riches of this world. The Christian soldier himself wears the helmet of salvation, according to St. Paul's Epistle to the Ephesians, 6:12. The other print shows Christ on the cross, the result of original sin. Eve above on the left, gives Adam the forbidden apple which the serpent has given her. God presides, represented by the tetragrammaton, while above on the right Christ ascends into heaven, a presage of salvation for forgiven man. Four other illustrations represent successively the miseries of man, the holy city, man blessed by God, and Redemption through the cross. Finally, man is seen as triumphant, with a palm in his hand and his head crowned with the aureole which God restored to him. [18] (Plate 27 a and b)

The emblem is not always the refined reappearance of the ancient medieval image. Samuel Ward, the preacher, uses it for didactic purposes, Taylor, the poet, for satirical ends. In "Wither's motto" Taylor contrasts his condition as a poet with that of Wither's, the author of devices. Wither, the very image of a successful poet, is seated on a rock with his eyes fixed on the clouds of glory that hide God. Below on the plain his enemies try to wound him in vain; on the other side of the rock lie worldly possessions: a country house, a horse and ship, and Wither thrusts aside a terrestrial globe at his feet. The second is Taylor's contrasting emblem: Taylor stands on a rock surrounded by a raging sea; between his straddling feet an open book lies on the world. He owns an oar, a boat and a book and gazes intently at the rays of the sun. His device contrary to that of Wither (Nec habeo, nec Careo, Nec Curo) is Et habeo, Et Careo, et Curo. What Taylor lacks is money and he never hides the fact. Taylor's emblem proceeds by allusion to Wither and not by a frontal attack. Taylor has an empty purse but he trusts James I King by divine right; the sun recalls for him the Son of God, the sun of righteousness. [19] The contrast is implicit. Wither poses as a cynic, while poor Taylor struggles against the difficulties of life as best he can. Poor Taylor, like Marot, is begging.

Emblems also function as personal advertisement. [20] On the frontispiece of Chapman's **Andromeda Liberata,** 1614, a hand emerging from the clouds of glory plunges a rod into a duckpond. The inscription MINI CONSCIA RECTI and the Latin citation above, Nihil a veritate nec virtute remotius quam vulgaris opinio (nothing is further from truth and virtue than the opinion of the masses) reinforces the elitist meaning of the emblem: whereas the duck and the reader, both ignorant, see the rod as broken, the wise man knows that it is an optical illusion. That is as much as to say "the vulgar must not approach my work." Such elitism will again be found in Milton. [21]

The title-pages of **Cornu-copiae** and **Pasquils Nightcap** of Nicholas Breton, 1612, and of Daniel's **Delia**, 1592, are comparable to emblematic images. They contain a message for the learned. Born of the image moralisée and flourishing when "characters" were in vogue, emblems were the product of both the unity of image and word and of neo-platonic thought. As neo-platonic thought weakened at the end of the seventeenth century, emblems became weaker and degenerated into the perverted reflection of an image depleted of supra-sensible inspiration. From a rich and vigorous life the metaphor becomes moribund, supplanted by the representation of sensible reality apprehended by human experience.

Ramist thought influenced even the illustrations of popular stories, an evolution announced by Sir Thomas Elyot who, though remaining Ciceronian, was nevertheless progressive. [22] However, hasty generalizations are inappropriate. A work could be illustrated for itself, yet also contain certain borrowed illustrations. Two examples can be given here.

The first is taken from several editions of **Bevis of Hampton.** It seems that this work was so popular that it justified being illustrated by custom woodcuts. [23] These represent an episode chosen from the text. They add nothing to its comprehension but allow the main events to be imagined, and for the difference, for example, between a Christian and a Saracen to be recognized. These are prototypical images which depict an action which they serve to recall. In this they are closer to Ciceronian rhetoric then to Ramism. Some of the woodcuts appear to have come from a foreign source: the combat against the dragon, as we have said about **The Pastime of Pleasure** [24] was probably taken from a book of natural philosophy. The body of a seated monster is carapaced and bristling with spikes, while its tail ends in a flamboyant head. This is of certain provenance but the marriage woodcuts are probably borrowed as well. The edition of 1582 has in addition illustrations taken from Catholic Bibles, while that of 1630 uses only woodcuts of Protestant marriages. A final probability: the edition of 1565 represents a town on E iv, but this town has no distinguishing characteristics from which one might deduce its origin. Here, then, is an example of a work whose iconography is well suited to its subject, and yet it is a mixture of indigenous and borrowed illustrations.

The title-page of **The Famous History of George Lord Fauconbridge** belongs to the same type. In contrast, one might take the more recent **Tom Thumb**, 1630, for the major part of the illustrations add a realistic touch to the narrative. The title-page which reappears on B shows Tom Thumb armed to the teeth with a cape for a joust in front of the king and queen. On A 4 one illustration gives several pieces of information on the life of Tom: his mother milks a cow which reveals his peasant origin; Tom is sitting on the edge of a basin in which black pudding is being made--in which he falls later--and a raven lifts him out, the subject of the ensuing episode. Another woodcut depicts Tom on the left hand of the queen where he has to dance a galliard. Finally, on the verso of B 2 the king calls in a doctor to save the dying Tom. All the illustrations are related to the work itself, and both subject matter and technique indicate that they are modern. Besides these, however, we find others the provenance of which is doubtful. On the back of the title-page and below the ending of the text there is a woodcut which is probably Jacobean and has served as a satire against the Catholic church. It deals with a funeral but one can only see the cortege on the back of the title-page and the lifting up of the body at the end of the story; all prelates have animal heads and chatter when they should keep a respectful silence. Cut thus into two, the first illustration seems to announce a fable and the last to show the interment of Tom Thumb. What attracts the attention, however, is first, the difference of style in these illustrations and then the fact that Tom on the bier has normal proportions, not those of a dwarf, which is contrary to the other illustrations and the tenor of the story. It is difficult to make out the subject of the vignette on A 5, but its style is clearly different. On the verso of A 6 the image of the courtier speaking to a servant is only an approximation to the text: Tom mounts a horse with the king and holds on tight to him. If the print had been made for the book, Tom's face would have appeared. Finally, two illustrations come after the end of the book, one depicting the father, the other the mother of Tom; we cannot be sure about the first, but the second is certainly derivative or borrowed. The lady has the air of a shrew, quite contrary to the context, and her coiffure is entirely different from that of her representation on A 4.

The illustrations of **Bevis of Hampton** and **Tom Thumb** are inspired at once by modern didactic needs and also by ancient theories. We are inclined to think that the economic needs of the illustrator in this case, rather than educational concerns, have influenced his choice of illustration. It is not less true that the evolution of the spirit of the clientele, which avidly breathes the fresh air of novelty, also directs him in his choice.

In considering the impact of the new educational theories on illustration it may be useful to choose a single author as exemplar. John Taylor, the poet, is admirably suited for this role because the majority of his work was printed at his own expense. There is, therefore, good reason to think that he is responsible for both content and illustration, and profit was always on his mind. Taylor therefore would reflect his own taste and that of the general public of his time. He is, without question, the most illustrated author of the period. Of the ninety-three works of his listed in the **Short Title Catalogue** we have found forty-four illustrated, which means almost a half. [25]

They seem typical of the evolution from ancient to modern illustration, since they include some purely ornamental images found in the printer's stock, some archetypal images, and both emblems and realistic images. [26] In general, repetitions occur only in successive editions of the same work. If the first edition is illustrated, the subsequent editions are also. The inverse proposition is not always true. For example, **An Arrant Thief** was illustrated only in its third edition, 1635, and similarly for **A common whore . . .** Most of these pamphlets were published by Henry Gosson, one of the publishers of ephemeral works. Otherwise one observes the names of E. Allde, E. Purslow, J. and N. Okes, and Griffith father of J. Beale, all printers of ephemeral publications. Finally, we find that E. Wright and N. Butter undertook the sale of certain works, since both, especially the latter, were specialists in "news", and "corantoes."

What may be said about these illustrations? [27] Altogether they appear original, placed on the title-page or on its back. [28] From our standpoint their principal function was to sell the pamphlet, for Taylor himself is aware of the lack of profundity in what he writes: he aims to amuse and not to be a man of letters. Wit is his to sell and this is exactly what he does. Illustrated from beginning to end are only the two pseudo-historical works, **A briefe remembrance of all the English Monarchs** and **A memoriall of all English Monarchs from Brute to King James.** The first contains high-quality etchings of monarchs from William the Conqueror onwards; the second, vignettes for every monarch, counting one hundred and sixteen before beginning the list from William to James I. The exceptional title-page of the work is a border made of fourteen of these vignettes. Its function is as much to help the memory as to create publicity. On the back of Taylor's pamphlets there is sometimes a list of his previous works, a delicate way of suggesting to the reader that, if he likes what he reads, he might find another brochure to his liking. [29]

There are two types of illustrations in the works of John Taylor: etching and woodcuts. Only two of his works are illustrated by etchings: **A briefe remembrance of all the English Monarchs** and **Taylor his motto.** In **A Juniper Lecture** a woman protects herself from the blows of her husband who is rising drunk from his bed. Among the rest there are two which are certainly borrowed: the one decorating **The life and death of the Virgin Mary,** [30] a Flemish work transposed into verses, showing a Flemish virgin with a large baby Jesus in her arms in front of a table on which rests a basket of fruit; the other is borrowed from Dekker's **Seven Deadlie Sinnes**. [31] **Jack a Lent**, as already noted, is a reworking of **The Poore Kitchen** of Peter Breughel the Elder. [32]

The prints illustrating the poems of Taylor contrast with those of the stories and jests of the sixteenth century. The new woodcuts of the middle of the seventeenth century emphasize black coloring all over. Thus most hats are black. [33] The illustrations also are more realistic representations of experiences and objects. For example, while **A common whore** remains illustrated by a woman with a feather, **A bawd** recreates the appropriate atmosphere of a brothel; with dishevelled hair and fists on hips, she is speaking to a man who claims a bottle of wine. In **An Arrant Thiefe**; the thief, rapier at his side and spurs on his boots, plunges his hand into the pocket of a man placed on his left. When Taylor speaks about the war in Bohemia, he shows an army on the march; gun on the shoulder, rallied by the drum and fife, the color-bearer advances from behind followed by halberdiers. [34] The old man in **The old, old, very old Man** is true to life, deep in his armchair, with a cushion at his back. A wife beats her husband [35] or is afraid of being thrashed in turn: [36] in both cases she treats him like a drunkard, a theme used as well as abused in the sixteenth and seventeenth centuries. (Plate 28)

Even when the image is fixed and it serves as an emblem or as a moral lesson, realism breaks through for the allusions are contemporary. On the title-page of **The Water-cormorant** there is a circle and at its center is a mariner's card. In the upper half of the circle the names of various cormorants are inscribed while on the left of the title-page their iconographic representation is to be found. In the lower part of the circle a cormorant eating a fish represents the author, who considers himself superior to other web-footed birds. The Jesuit wears a canon's hat and carries a revolver, an allusion to the Gunpowder Plot, then comes the separatist. A con-man breaks a ruler in two, while a drunkard drinks out of a pitcher, a gallant throws money away, and a pawnbroker points out his street. A judge fills his pockets and carries a basket, and a cutpurse holds a purse in his beak from which, with the aid of a knife, he has relieved the owner. A policeman marches with baton in hand, a jailer keeps his keys in his mouth; a vicar or his curate holds the key of the church in his hand; with his beak, the innkeeper pushes the plough, while the astrologer searches the skies and the lawyer and the undersheriff hold the hanging cord. The satire bears on all these pseudo-cormorants while the true cormorant remains in his element, water. [37]

Taylor's **Pastorall**, a satire of the Spenserian type, provokes a similar reaction of amusement by its illustration.

Each eclogue of Spenser's **Shepherd's Calendar** has its illustration, and the comic element in this case is provided by the way the persons are dressed. Both wear their best finery: court cloak, knotted garters, and carry the shepherd's crook while guarding the sheep. The sun shines on the mountain. The image not only illustrates the atmosphere of the poem, but emphasizes the ridicule of the pastoral idyll. Two other images are both satirical and emblematic at the same time; they are not against an idea or a social type but opposed to definite persons. One, as we have seen, [38] proceeds by allusion against Wither; the other transforms John Taylor's debtors into eels that are difficult to catch, for, as subscribers to **The travel of Twelve pence,** [39] they have not paid him. (Plate 29)

Taylor represents his times well in the remainder of his satirical and social illustrations. **The world run on wheels** shows the quarrel between a coach and a cart, but the image has diabolical resonances. In their totality, Taylor's works on social satire offer no original illustrations. Greene, Dekker, and the other precursors of journalism in England are illustrated in much the same way. [40]

In conclusion, the images of illustrating poems change from being an expression of concepts into the representation of living reality. [41] If, at the beginning of the sixteenth century, images were chiefly an aid to the memory, the new illustrations illuminate the text, either with the vividness of experience or with didactic wit.

The more didactic illustrators are considered next. Since the emblematic image aimed to delight as well as to instruct it appropriately appeared on the few sermons which were illustrated as a function of the text. [42] The sermon, essentially oral in character, is badly suited to visual illustration. Yet the Puritans whose sermons express the new Ramistic content [43] also publish illustrated sermons, as do Separatists. [44]

A sermon on marriage comes from Middleburg, where the Puritans had taken refuge after persecution. Two persons join their hands on which is placed a burning heart pierced by an arrow: the man and woman see themselves joined in hand and heart under the symbol of God, the tetragrammaton. The Eternal irradiates them. The entire scene is framed by two surrounding trees, joining at the top of the image. A similar illustration decorates **The lover** by Robert Crofts: the idea of hands and hearts reunited under the protection of God is the same, except that pagan symbols are added to the Christian vision of marriage: a man and a woman wear love-knots and two pigeons gaze at one another with a citation from Virgil: <u>omnia</u> <u>vincit</u> <u>amor,</u> <u>nos</u> <u>cedamus</u> <u>amori,</u> while the macrocosm represented by the sun and the moon pierced by the arrows of Cupid are on the left and the right of God. The same author's **The Terrestrial Paradise or Happiness on Earth** makes use of an emblematic image to preach that a chaste hedonism accords with innocence.

A Puritan sermon, **The White Wolfe**, 1627, includes two illustrations to comply with the author's desire. He wants the faithful to understand how to recognize the wolf even when disguised as a lamb. [45] Two images represent the subject. On sig. A 4 verso, the wolf is disguised as a lamb, on F 2 verso the wolf appears without disguise: here the wolf represents the Arminian tendency in the Anglican Church expressed by Lancelot Andrewes and Laud in contradiction to the Calvinist principles of the Thirty-Nine Articles. The Puritans feared to see the reinstallation of the Church of Rome, and the chief aim of the pamphlet is to alert them to the danger.

John Preston's sermon of 1630, **A sermon of spiritual life and death** represents four virtues: justice, fortitude, prudence, and mercy. [46] It includes a scene which has preaching as its theme. In a temple denuded of all images, a congregation is seated, and all listen attentively except two persons at the bottom. With his arms stretched out towards the congregation the preacher harangues them from the height of the pulpit. A great hour-glass-- of the type that has to be turned every hour--indicates the time that is passing. Finally, an important symbol can be discerned at the top of the illustration; it is the crown of England, in order to remind the king that John Preston, the Puritan leader, was formerly chaplain to the king, which made it easier to publish the sermon.

Another Puritan preacher's illustrations also warrant consideration. Three sermons particularly come to mind, but it also is intriguing to note that the vignette of the printer coincides with the subject of the sermon. **A Coal from the altar** represents a burning heart surrounded by a garland; the Greek inscription means "for God and for you." [47] A **Peace-offering** consists of a bowl from which escapes the fumes of incense or of sacrifice. The sermon entitled **All in All** is even more fascinating. The emblematic image comprises all the subtleties of the sermon and demonstrates admirably how the desire to return to the text and to the application of Scripture to daily life does not imply, even amongst the Puritans, any abandon of the older rhetoric. (Plate 30) On the top of the image can be found the sacred monogram of Christ [48] which signifies simultaneously the resurrection, the beginning and ending of days, the center and supreme judge. Then in the center Christ is found surrounded by the seven circles of heaven with their typological correlates: the branch of the tree, symbol of life, prefigures the brazen serpent, and the resurrection; Noah's ark signifies the Church, the cradle of the faithful; the tabernacle, the divine presence in Christ. . . . Here also metaphors of Christ can be found: for example, Christ is the sun or the morning star, he is the true vine from whom one gathers the wine of eternal life, or the bread of life, or the paschal lamb. Without Christ nothing exists and as a sign of mourning "Nothing" [49] is imprinted in white on black. With Christ one has access to the true world: on the top of the image on the left an astrological globe can be found, and at the right a globe of the world.

A woodcut on the title-page of **Woe for Drunkards** shows us the direct application of Christian ethics to daily life: here it is concerned with the traditional and satirical opposition between the good old times and the wicked present generation. Opposed vertically are the leg of an armed man, foot in the stirrup and his wheel spur, and that of a courtier, with a buckle on his shoe and his garter tied with a frilly knot. The dice and the playing cards of the present are contrasted with the Bible of ancient times. The soldier holds a halberd for the defence of his country, while the courtier carries a smoking pipe and a goblet with a serpentine knop, suggesting that the drink within is poisoned: o tempora, o mores is found translated on the last image: o manners, o tymes is symbolically written on the reverse. [50] (Plate 61)

Samuel Ward used logic and rhetoric to illustrate his sermons. The images appealed either to the experience of the biblical reading, or to the direct apprehension of sensible reality and to the values of popular morality. He uses both types of illustration in **All in All** and in **Woe to Drunkards**. In each case the message arises from a pedagogical concern and forms a sermon by itself. [51]

Pedagogy, in the purest sense of the term, lies at the origin of illustrated works, whether the science is pure or applied: arithmetic, astronomy, medicine, or what directly relates to human activities such as the construction of modern water-closets, hunting, fishing, etc. In general, the truly scientific works are published as books rather than pamphlets; though some simple treatises exist in pamphlet form.

Beginning with the most abstract, we find only one illustrated pamphlet on arithmetic, which has its image on the title-page. This is Robert Recorde's **The groud of artes.** This book intended for everyone represents on its title-page the interior of a house where four men are counting around a table; it is impossible to tell whether they are using the old system, from left to right, or the new from right to left; one of them explains the function of a table that he has prepared.

We know of no illustrated pamphlet on geometry. But manuals of instruction comprise some treatises of practical application for artisans. Because construction was an essential activity many small works on the subject were widely diffused.

W. Gedde wrote **A booke of Sundray draughters,** 1615, in order to inform glaziers of the aesthetic possibilities of their calling. (Plate 31) Carpenters also found practical advice from two main authors whose illustrations clarified the text. R. More's **The carpenters rule to measure ordinary timber,** 1602, and W. Bedell's **Mesolabium Architectonicum,** 1631, helped the carpenters to measure wood more accurately. The second work included a slide-rule with other diagrams.

Astronomy is widely represented with varying illustrations. The most interesting come from fragments and smack more of imagination than of scientific representation. Thus close to a letter of James I to Tyco Brahe, the astronomer, one finds an image of a woman talking to the scholar, representing the comet of 1572. The date of the print is 1632, seven years after the death of King James I. The representation of the comet of 1618 appears in **An astronomical description of the late comet** [52] or in **Cassiopiae Stellarum,** a prolix work. [53]

Many different types of scientific illustrations can be found in treatises and almanacs. The most illustrated subjects are the following: diagrams of the solar system or the earth, eclipses of the sun or the moon (far the most numerous), an explanation of comets, and diagrams of different instruments of navigation.

Diagrams of the astronomical world illustrate admirably the opposition of the two systems in vigor in the seventeenth century. To take only one example, White's Ptolemaic geocentricism [54] shows the earth at the center of the universe and the skies around it. Bishop Wilkins's Copernican heliocentricism, [55] whose diagram of the universe is both clear and complicated, displays the sun at the center of his diagram, the earth turns around it, while the moon gravitates around the earth.

Other planets turn round the sun. At the top of the illustration are the stars, the fixed celestial bodies. God, as Sun, enjoins all to love the whole world: <u>ame omnes</u>. The image is excellent and shows the planets illuminated from the side of the sun and the signs of the zodiac.

The second diagram also explains rationally the prodigy that filled the Elizabethans with fear: eclipses. Numerous almanacs of the seventeenth century did so. The eclipses of the moon were the most common. Their causes were explained by Bomenius,

Securis, Buckminster, Harvey, Hopton, and others. (Plate 32a) Monslowe was content to draw a moon entirely in black in 1581, while Buckminster in 1584 represented the more familiar face of the partial eclipse of the moon. Harvey's diagram is one of the most simple and is repeated in a number of almanacs, but it is not very clear at first sight. The best illustrations are unquestionably those of the seventeenth century. [56] Best of all is Hopton's prediction for 1607. It shows the revolution of the moon around the earth beneath the rays of the sun and how in a particular position--from the earth--it is impossible to see the moon because its face is hidden by the shadow of the earth. (Plate 32b) White's is even simpler and shows how the eclipse works.

It is also to White that we owe the best diagram of the solar eclipse. [57] It clearly shows the incidence of the diameter of the moon with the diameter of the sun perceived from the earth. It also demonstrates lucidly how this only appears from a single place on the earth, while the inhabitants of other latitudes at this precise moment see only a partial eclipse or no eclipse at all. These are all scientific images which differ completely from the emotive explanation of the sensational brochures. Allestree also explained the eclipse of the sun in 1633, but the illustration similar to Harvey's eclipse of the moon does not appeal to the imagination.

The comet was another object of foreboding. Three large treatises show it on the title-page, two in English and one in Latin. [58] A treatise of Blazing Starres represents a star making for the south-east. It may be observed that the cardinal points are oddly placed: the south above and the north below the image. John Bainbridge's brochure, the work of a physician, An astronomical description of the late Comet, 1619, is not a purely scientific diagram. The geocentric illustration displays a shooting star in the skies above the earth; the tetragrammaton of Jehovah surrounded by the clouds of glory is enthroned on high. In the lower part of the circle there is a legend: "lift up your eyes on hie, and behold who hath created these things" (Isaiah 40:26). The lesson of the inscription can serve as a transition to other representations of comets which, just as the eclipses, serve to frighten the people and to encourage them to repent and put themselves into the hands of divine providence. [59]

Two astronomical illustrations serve for practical application, both appearing in 1591. The one represents the seasons and encourages the reader to use meteorology, on the frontispiece of a work translated from Italian, Perpetuall and naturall prognostications of the change of weather. The other allows the reader to know on any day in the year when the sun will rise. It is R. Burton's, A briefe Treatise, printed by Charlewood, on astrology as much as on astronomy. (Plate 33)

Finally we discover some useful instructions on navigation. The most striking work in terms of its diagrams is that of Delamain on the horizontal sundial. [60] But the almanacs also contain valuable illustrations: Bourne's almanac, for instance, includes a mariner's card and a compass, [61] while Ford's for 1612 depicts a ruler and a theodolite. The fragments of the **Bagford collection** of London contain an almanac with a representation of a compass; at the end of each point of the compass there is the name of a port or a cape of England and the symbols which stand for them. [62] Similarly, **The Flye,** 1569, shows an anemometer and a table of the tides. The outer circle gives the names of certain capes and seamarks as well as the shallows on the south of England and the west of Brittany. The next circle towards the center translates visually the information given in the first intended for the ignorant illiterate. The next five circles provide, amongst other information, the tide tables and in the middle is the anemometer and the compass. [63]

Maps equally form a part of scientific images, as, for example, the work of Th. Hood, **The use of the celestial globe in plans,** 1590. They often are also means of propaganda. This is the case with the map representing the Armada in **The Birth, Purpose and mortall Wound of the Romish holie League,** 1589, which will be considered later. [64] To generalize, the majority of the maps in our brochures are sprinkled with letters which refer to the text intended to explain the map. Some are historical, such as **The troubles of Geneva With the warres which the Duke of Savoy hath made against it,** 1591, a brochure translated from the French and which depicts Geneva and Thonon in their natural environment, the Alps and Lake Leman, so that the reader may understand the setting of the action. Others are semi-historical and semi-geographic. Thus, **The Four Hollanders,** 1598, describes a skirmish off Java: the map facing page 17 shows the ships and the combat off the isle and the location of various markets: the pepper market, the Dutch market, and the markets for pomegranates, clothes, porcelain, fish and pork, as well as the principal buildings of the town. **The Relation of a wonderfull Voiage** is intended for mariners. The map opposite the title-page shows the route to follow through the straits of Magellan in rounding the Terra del Fuego to reach the South Sea. [65] The letter of I. B. printed by Bynneman (?1591) includes a map of Northern Ireland. However, the most instructive map and most remarkable for its technique is that included in **Gods Power and Providence** by Edward Pellham published in 1631 (Plate 34). It is a map of Greenland engraved on copper. On every side small vignettes describe the way to hunt a whale, a walrus, and a bear, and how to prepare them for eating. The map itself gives a remarkable description of Greenland, the dates when its various capes were discovered, the maritime commerce that flourishes there both English and Dutch, and of its fauna on land and in the sea. This map is at once a historical, geographic, maritime and zoological description depicted for the curious. It bears no signature, but it may come from Holland since the author in the course of his account refers to Dutch ships which were seen stuck in the ice in the same fashion in 1596 when making for Nova Zembla and similarly the sailors had to feed themselves on bears and whales. Is this a true narrative or a direct copy of the news from Holland? In any case, the author claims that the English have proved themselves to be braver than the Dutch.

Finally in this category of illustration, the first number of **An abstract of some special Forreigne Occurrences** printed by N. Bourne, ancestor of our present day journalists, displays a volcanic isle in eruption. We have not drawn attention to double hemispherical maps of Mercator: the terrestrial globe is the sign of Roberts and Watkins, printers of almanacs, but our brochures show no representations of the new maps of the world. All the same, the maps which we have considered: historical, geographic zoological, and maps of navigation appear to have represented reasonably well the knowledge of the seventeenth century and the public interest in new horizons. To these might be added the representation of Indian towns in **News from the East Indies,** but it is difficult to determine whether this offers a true map or merely an imaginative reconstruction. [66]

The intense interest of the Elizabethans in history will be sufficiently shown in our chapter on propaganda. In the seventeenth century all were passionately interested in the Thirty Years War. This is how the first modern journal of Butter and Bourne, **The Swedish Intelligencer,** was born. Contrary to most of the pre-journalists, Butter and Bourne tried to follow step by step the vicissitudes of the war and to give the most faithful summary of its developments. The first number showed Gustavus Adolphus. In 1632 there was an inset plate that explained the siege of Magdeburg and a map of Droeshout showing the relative positions of Tilly and the Count of Mansfelt. Letters give clues to the monuments in the town, the principal bastions and the fortifications. In addition, before page 115, there is a view of Magdeburg razed to the ground by the Protestant troops with the cathedral alone spared. The second, third, and fourth issues have similar maps. (Plate 35) The illustration serves truly for instruction, to describe the developments which a merely verbal description might misrepresent. [67]

Since death was a commonplace event, anatomical and physiological illustrations abound in pamphlets. Galen, the pioneer physician, appears on the verso of the title-page of a book of 1550, Moulton's **The Regiment of Health.** So far as we know he does not reappear. Renal apparatus illustrates **The Urinall of Physick** of Robert Recorde, so frequently reprinted that it must have become a bedside book. It includes a measuring apparatus for urine analysis and an image of the physician who holds the test-tube to the light. The heart appears on a broadsheet, which relates the presence of a worm in the left ventricle of John Pennant; one of the illustrations shows the worm spread out, the other the worm in the heart. The image is only semi-scientific because the auricles are not visible, the artery and coronary vein are shown in section, but the draughtsman tries to represent the exterior fatty tissue of the heart by great white surfaces. The author refutes Hippocrates who affirmed that the heart was free from all illnesses. The astrological man in Rudston's almanac, previously referred to, [68] is the only pamphlet illustration of veins which frequently appeared in books. Also, another illustration with a practical application is that of Ambrose Paré, which shows the different kinds of wounds a man can receive: a temple hit by a stone, a bludgeon from a club, a hammer blow, a wound dealt by a rapier or a sword, or by an arrow or a lance, or a burn caused by boiling tar. [69] The man in his birthday suit receives no less than seventeen wounds.

Animal ills are also illustrated. Thomas Spackman, the physician, provides the remedy for bites from a mad dog. **A Declaration of such greivous accidents as commonly follow the biting of mad Dogges**, 1613, represents a dog entirely in black and white, a sign of sickness. The foam issues from his throat, his eye has an evil look and, with a raised foot, he seems ready to bound. Apart from the treatises and works of Markham which are almost always illustrated, [70] we have found only two treatises on the sicknesses of horses. Nicholas Malby in **A plaine and easie waye to remedie a Horse that is foundered in his feete**, 1594, inserts two images: the one on the left shows how to bleed a horse. The animal is standing, with tubs in front of both back and front feet. Lines mark the way the blood should flow. The image on the right displays the horse some days after the bloodletting now cured and spirited. (Plate 36)

L. W. C. praises the same kind of remedy in **A Very perfect Discourse**, 1624. The author teaches the reader how to know the age of a horse and includes a diagram of the veins of the animal. However, no illustration of the sicknesses of a cow or a sheep can be found, two animals the economic importance of which, however, have made them the object of treatises. The horse is doubtless more fragile and once the anatomy of the horse is familiar, the cow would seem to correspond fairly closely to the same physiological system. [71]

Small agricultural treatises show the reader how to get best results. It is clearly much easier to draw an illustration than to proceed merely by a verbal description. **The silkworms and their Flies**, a work in verse by T. Moffet, is one of those brochures which contains everything and nothing. It is the history of clothing since Adam and Eve, a eulogy of worms since antiquity, but it oddly also contains allusions to lovers. The illustration of the title-page represents the metamorphosis of the worm, into a chrysalis and then into a butterfly. A treatise on the culture of the silkworm is, however, much more scientific: **Instructions for the increase and planting of Mulberie Trees,** 1609. It contains many plates. The silkworm is first installed on plates covered with mulberry leaves, then the mulberry plants grow in the greenhouse on different levels on which the worms are attached, and, lastly, there is a detailed plate showing the transition within the chrysalis of the worm into a butterfly. Once they become butterflies, says the author, the male and the female mate; after laying her eggs the female quickly dies; the breeder must take up the eggs, put them on silk, and shut them in a wall-cupboard until the next season. (Plate 37)

We have also found two illustrated treatises on gardening: the one, **[72]** of 1618, **A new Orchard and Garden,** of William Lawson is intended for women as well as men. The man plants the orchard while the woman looks after the herb garden. There is also a treatment of bees. The title-page represents an enclosure where three men are busy. One grafts, another uproots a tree, while a third prunes. The lesson is that work bears its fruits. On page 11, another image depicts how to establish a garden surrounded with trees and hedges; steps will break its monotony. The other treatise of 1640, **The expert Gardner** deals only with the grafting of trees and the establishment of a formal garden. More pedagogical than the first treatise, it is addressed to the ignorant. **[73]** The compiler indicates the best season for planting trees, as well as the tools the apprentice gardener needs. An inserted plate, more than the numerous illustrations of the work, shows the shapes of useful tools for looking after trees.

Another practical pamphlet is the fascinating **An anatomie of the Metamorphosis of Ajax,** 1596. A voluminous work, it explains the construction of modern water-closets or privies. Thinking that the place frequented daily for necessary activities ought to be decorated, the author explains to us the construction of this place which will require an aquarium for goldfish. The ingenious system uses the principle of Archimedes. Two illustrations peppered with letters referring to explanations in the margin, provide all the information necessary and the way to operate everything from the bolt to the pit. In another illustration the scholar, Ajax, in the great robe and headgear of a doctor, sitting on his throne, makes the sign for Satan to depart. The flushing chamber placed on the horizontal part of the seat indicates that this is a new system as well as a fish tank. But no diagram indicates how the water will rise to the fish.

Finally, the same instructional concern is evident in two treatises on games: **The famous game of Chesse-play,** 1614, and **Hocus-Pocus** junior, 1638, intended for a wide public. The one teaches how to play chess and depicts a table with chessmen, the other performs conjuring tricks with the help of many sketches.

The dates of the illustrated pamphlets considered in the latter part of this chapter prove that the desire for instruction was well established by the end of the sixteenth century. The desire to understand and to analyse prevailed. The image evolved therefore from a conceptual to a perceptual representation of reality. [74] At the same time a purification of the image occurs since its primary motivation is functional. As McLuhan has said in **The Gutenberg Galaxy,** [75] the neutral world of the visual succeeded to the magical world of the ear, where only facts speak.

Nevertheless, if in this chapter we were principally concerned with the neutral reality of information, we ought not to conclude that all factual images are necessarily neutral. If indeed truth is stranger than fiction, it will be the art of the illustrator or the journalist to present this facet of reality which will elicit an emotional response from the reader of pamphlets. Consequently, if the purely informative image is born of the concern to combine the useful with what pleases the eye, the image as the source of emotion, will be even more complex since it adds to the desire to move the reader, both information and decoration.

Just as the formal Elizabethan garden starts with the planting of trees in alternate rows and develops, as a result of pruning and purifying, into a complex system where the spectator forgets the initial scheme, the same is true with our illustrations whose creation responds to motivations whose intertwinings escape our perspicacity.

Chapter IV

THE IMAGE AND EMOTION

People want facts, but they also need thrills. This accounts for the popularity of our sensational newspapers, the imaginary relation of apparently true experiences, the so-called "news" of foreign affairs, especially the macabre and the thrilling. The minute by minute accounts of the Judicial Committee of Congress in the United States which decided the fate of President Nixon, and whose members each in turn left to weep, exemplify this. [1] The public demands the human touch that a factual narration would bore to tears.

Naturally, there are continuities between the reporting of news between the Renaissance and the present day. First, there is the desire to escape the dull diurnal and confining routine by the enjoyment of drama. The Englishman of the sixteenth and seventeenth centuries was far more emotional than the reserved Englishman of today.

The Renaissance man of good breeding was not afraid of emotions but from an early age was trained to express his convictions adequately. The art of the orator and that of the actor are constantly paralleled. Vehemence was a part of the exercises in rhetoric practiced by schoolchildren; for example, it should be observed that Chapter 10 of Mulcaster's **Positions** is headed, "Of loud speaking. How necessarie, and how proper an exercise for a scholler." Kempe and Brinsley in their treatises on the education of children insist on the role of elocution. [2] **Vociferatio** was not only recommended to the rhetor, but as a necessity for good health, since the child thus expelled the humours that affected the chest and head. So, in discourse, the whole body was in movement, and to speak motionless was to be dull. Renaissance man mistrusted the introvert, who was thought to be either a hypocrite or a nervous depressive. Clearly, this is why Orsino in **Twelfth Night** howls his love for Olivia, and why Malcolm advises Macduff in **Macbeth** to express his agony for fear of seeing his spirit explode with suffering. [3] Macbeth himself, by contrast, has an absorbed air which promises no good, and Lady Macbeth, so strong in the moment of action, becomes mad for lack of a confidant. All Shakespeare's villains are introverts. Extroverts like Sir Toby of **Twelfth Night**, however crazily sensuous, are never completely evil, for their folly finds an outlet which prevents the venom coming to a head. If Toby is mad, he only hurts himself.

The sane therefore express thoughts incarnately. Quintilian, whose book was the basis of the education of young people, had already said this in his **De Oratore**. He showed the orator at the end of his plea breathless, hair dishevelled, toga half-undone, exhausted as much by physical as by intellectual effort. [4] Thomas Wright in **The Passions of the mind**, 1601, expresses the subtleties of speech. The orator must know how to excite or calm the passions of his audience by the intonations of his voice and the gestures of his body. [5] His feet alone must remain immobile.

Although the new Ramist rhetoric had an impact on the place of rhetoric and logic in discourse, it never doubted the importance of vociferatio. The Ramists, quite as much as the Ciceronians, were anxious to see the message of the word reaching the auditory they addressed. Elocution in its bodily expression where soul unites with senses in the expression of conviction, replaced verbal rhetoric. The Puritans, for the most part adept Ramists, were well-known for the vehemence of their sermons which were meant to touch the minds and hearts of their hearers. So much was this the case that Anglicans of the center or of the right wing ridiculed their many gestures in preaching, thinking that metaphors, analogies, and schemas were much more fitting. [6]

Thus the seventeenth century man, far from the modern Englishman whose hands stay in his pockets during a sermon or a university conference, was closer to the Welshman of our days, with his sense of the dramatic and his tendency to emphasis. Attitudes and gestures were codified in Ghisi, **Wits Labyrinth**, published in England in 1610, a counterpart of moral emblems. In 1571 Thomas Hill, in his treatise **The contemplation of mankinde**, republished in 1613 and known under the title of **Art of Physiognomy**, explained human attitudes as a function of moral behavior with the aid of appropriate illustrations. For example, the prostitute holds a bouquet of feathers in her hand. Later still, in 1644, John Bulwer also illustrates suitable gestures by images in his **Chirologia** and **Chironomia**.

Undoubtedly one could relate this taste for expressing emotions to the entire philosophy of the period we are studying, since physical appearance reflected moral reality, the ugly moral turpitude, and the beautiful serenity and integrity. The witch bore the mark of Satan on her neck or on the secret and carnal parts of her person. The deformed child was thought to be the fruit of its parents' vices; signs in the heavens and inclement weather the indications of divine displeasure. It is therefore logical that behavior, too, should have obeyed this rule. Crossed arms signified introversion and melancholy. [7] A furrowed brow marked displeasure. The closed hand indicated stinginess. All these signs of behavior abounded in plays and the verses reflected the stage business. They were also expressed in the popular pamphlets, a vivid reflection of the human presence.

Decorum was the ideal expression of the individual, of his qualities and defects, as also his place in society. Sir Toby in **Twelfth Night** arranges for Sir Andrew to sin against decorum by improperly jumping and dancing. Why so? Was he not expressing himself? Emotional though the Elizabethans might be they distinguished between justifiable emotions, such as indignation at the murder of a king, or the anger of a father faced by a recalcitrant son, the misery of seeing one's family ill, and irrational emotions provoked, for example, by greed, jealousy, disorderly conduct, or lasciviousness. Decorum does not exclude passions; but passions have to be justified by a certain moral and social code, the expression of humanity at the level of the individual. It is the middle way between the excess of individualism and tyranny. The stoic countenance is only a late development in the seventeenth century. [8] In our period nothing is more despised than the mask, connected with hypocrisy and only perspicacity can discern the wolf in sheep's clothing from the real sheep. [9]

Pamphlet-publishers, like orators, are acutely aware of the emotional impact of images, as objects of attraction or repulsion, as moral movers of humanity, and as the satisfaction of a need of the imagination or of novelty. On the whole, taste at the times of the Tudors and the early Stuarts was for the strong rather than the refined. Setting aside the two emblematic images representing marriage, of which we have already spoken, the entire collection of pamphlets illustrates catastrophes, murders, or executions. Few joyful events can be found in the illustrations of brochures, but for the baptism of a prince, a marriage, or royal progresses.

Theatre and pamphlet illustrations often follow the same path. Theatre audiences, and readers of illustrated pamphlets, were infatuated with the same topics. Scenes where gulls were swindled by sharpers, as in the pamphlets of Greene, provoked the hilarity of the spectators, [10] so strongly that it was impossible to stop the peels of laughter. [11] Stephen Gosson objected that while present at a comedy or a tragedy, people were so governed by their passions that they lost all sense of moderation. The one made people laugh beyond what was reasonable, while the other caused an excess of suffering; [12] both addressed themselves to the small fry, as did our pamphlets. Under the pressure of emotion they would run amok in the theatre, losing control and thrashing anyone in their way. [13]

The themes of the drama of the time reappeared in the illustration of pamphlets: the cuckolded husband, murders and middle-class drama. The terror of an eclipse reverberates in tragedy and shines lugubriously on the front of divinatory pamphlets. The deformity of Richard III finds a parallel in the teratology of the times. To sum up, one might suppose that the public which read sensational illustrated brochures was also present at public hangings, noisily grabbing the heart of the victim, watching spirits being conjured up, participating existentially in the action of the theatre, rushing to the nearest bawdy-house or throwing themselves on their wives at the end of a seamy play, haunting the taverns, drinking and dancing the night through like Sir Toby in **Twelfth Night**, Falstaff, or Gargantua, all great drinkers and trenchermen, [14] a people hungry for strong sensations to match their appetites.

Some pamphlets are entertaining. The four principal writers of accounts intended to distract the public by the narration of tricks accomplished by sympathetic cutpurses are Th. Harman, Greene, Dekker and Rowlands. All four, write under the cover of morality, warning young inexperienced people how not to fall into the traps laid by tricksters. Greene is the most brilliant of the four, having had experience in his own life of the trickery of which he writes. All are largely illustrated. The illustrations of Harman's **A caveat for Common Cursetors** are not specially comical. Most show the punishments undergone by those condemned by the common law: the pillory, the tied bundle of rods intended to thrash the offender, the whip whose knots pierce the flesh, and the gallows. This seems sinister enough to us, but it was part of the daily distractions of the life of other times. [15]

Next came the series of conies or scoundrels, with the illustrations of Harman and Greene. Almost all of Greene's illustrations come from **The Groundworke of Conny-catching,** a new title for the previous work of Harman, **A Caveat . . .** One can see there, looking from below to above and from left to right: a dispute between a male and a female rogue, the justification of trickery, the coney breaking into a house by forcing the lock, a lady tricked by a fool who passes a card to her, a coney who after abstracting the cards shows them to the public. The first vignette blown up and edited, like all the others to which we shall refer, decorates **A disputation betweene a hee conny-catcher, and a shee conny-catcher,** the second, **The Defence of Conny-catching,** the third, **The second and Last part of Conny-catching,** the fourth, **The third and last part of conny-catching,** and finally the fifth, **A Notable Discovery of Cosenage.** [16] All of these pamphlets, including that of Harman, appeared in 1592, which implies collaboration between the two authors and between their printers, J. Danter for Harman, Thomas Scarlet and John Wolfe for R. Greene, and between their publishers. [17] To finish the description of Harman's frontispiece, on the top of the illustration are the punishments for the offenders which do not appear on any of the brochures of Greene: the gallows, the tree from which often the hanged man was suspended, the birch and the seated judge with the book of laws under his arm. (Plate 38).

Of the same type, half-amusing, half-indignant, were the pamphlets on swindling by S. Rowlands. The illustration gives most of the attention to the playing cards, since one or more knaves of the four suits, clubs, diamonds, hearts, and spades are found again and again. [18] A parallel to the series of cards is that of the watchman of London, or bellman, of Rowlands and of Dekker. **Diogenes Lanthorne** of Rowlands appeared in 1607, with the image of the barrel which served Diogenes as a house. The watchman of London is one of Dekker's favorite persons. He appears with or without his dog on the frontispiece of a number of his satirical pamphlets on the customs of London. Also it can be found with two rogues, man and woman, on the posthumously published work of Greene, **Theeves falling out,** in 1615.

Among the joyful pamphlets the jokes of Tarlton or the adventures of Robin Goodfellow are to be found. [19] The latter's continuation, **The second Part of Robin Goodfellow,** displays in an image what would not be ordinarily encountered except by reference to a theatre, the smutty side of the men of the sixteenth and seventeenth centuries. Robin, horned, with the half-body of a billy goat, displays his private parts. He occupies the center of the image, with a broom on his shoulder and a candle in his hand, the hunting horn in a bandolier, while in the background people with hats on dance to the sound of his flute. A pitcher of wine, near to Robin Goodfellow, suggests the atmosphere of joyful inebriation.

All these narratives are short stories or poems. The only joyful news pamphlet, except for the narratives on the Court-progresses or triumphs of sovereigns, marriages or births in broad-sheet or small format--is the account of the journey of Kemp. William Kemp, a comic actor and popular dancer, who never refuses a jig accompanied by an air of a naughty song, swears to dance all the way from London to Norwich. He leaves on the morning of February 10th, accompanied by his drummer, Thomas Sly, and a witness, George Sprat; great crowds gather on his route, encouraging him and inviting him to drink. On March 5th he reaches Norwich after being slowed down by the snows of winter. Altogether Kemp would have spent nine days in dancing from London to Norwich, although these were not consecutive days. The title-page of the pamphlet shows Kemp dancing, accompanied by his drum. [20]

The rarity of illustrated brochures of this type should be noted: for Kemp, it would seem that the Elizabethans felt an exhilaration comparable to that of the fanatics of the Tour de France at the arrival of the maillot jaune, or the inhabitants of Pampeluna at the moment when the bulls are let loose in the streets. If the majority of illustrations of news carry information, most often they also appeal to the sentiments of fright and terror, in describing a very sinister event. [21] At the dawn of the journalistic era, these were tragic events aimed at reaching the crowd with a sense of the misery of mankind. Almost all of these pamphlets affect to be minatory, priding themselves on ridding man of evil and exhorting to repentance.

Among the narration of murders, this may well have been the case in **Heavens speedie Hue and Cry** written by Goodcole, pastor and chaplain of the prison of Newgate. [22] He truly writes out of compassion, to help the ignorant and to convey the horror of crime. The two culprits, Thomas Sherwood and Elizabeth Evans, known as Countrey-Tom and Countrey-Bess, have lost their humanity, since they have departed from the image of God. They are monstrous beings, creatures of Satan and yet worthy of compassion. Both came from good families, but foolish love caused their ruin. The young girl, disavowed by her family turned to evil. Goodcole does not challenge the decision of the family. He deplores her actions and yet expresses Christian piety for Bess. The large illustration does not represent the murder on the title-page, as in other news pamphlets, but the weapon of the crime, the club that killed the victim, Mr. Claxton.

Preachers and pastors were the authors of a good number of these murder accounts. John Hilliard, published **Fire from Heaven** in 1613, and Thomas Cooper wrote **The Cry and Revenge of Blood** in 1620. Cooper was the friend of judge Montaigu, then became the preacher to the Fleet, and author of booklets against Papists and tracts against witchcraft. Finally, Goodcole dealt with popular subjects for homiletical dissuasives, such as adultery, witchcraft, and murder. We have an incomplete list of illustrated pamphlets, but the preachers are the quickest to mount the emotional ladder of violence and to use horror in a minatory manner. [23]

The news pamphlets relating a murder can be categorized in different ways. First, they are chiefly works of the seventeenth century. The previous century was less daring in depicting reality in all its crudity. There the vivid evocation of the concept, such as theft or murder, could not have the same emotive impact as the representation of the very scene. Is it not true that it is possible to read accounts which if represented on the stage would be insupportable? The seventeenth century which understood the impact of the image as related to real experience as opposed to the apprehension of truths by learning, applied this to daily life. However, certain categories are to be discerned: the relation of the event for itself or as a function of certain political or religious truths.

To start with the most simple, the telling of middle-class dramas, we find the murder of two friends who quarrel over a question of money after having overheated their senses in a tavern. Then after some time, overcome with remorse, the culprit kills himself in seeing the distress he has caused the wife of his victim. The brochure entitled **The Bloody booke** [24] presents on the title-page the final scene in red and black. The wife is kneeling in front of the body of her husband, while the aggressor pierces himself with a sword. (Plate 39) Another image of a suicide after a murder is that of John Batterham in **A true Relation of a most desperate Murder**, 1617; the man shot a magistrate, then hung himself in prison. [25] There is also the somber account of the murder of an avaricious miller, killed by his servants, when his wife went to her mother-in-law to have her baby so as to spare her husband the cost of the confinement. The illustration represents the mill which the third servant is leaving whom the two others do not look for until he has done his dastardly work. The miller is sitting in an armchair opposite a fire in the kitchen hearth. The two servants, harangued by Satan, take him from the back; one of them holds a pickax which he brandishes above the head of the victim, ready to strike him. [26] The image, which is divided, provides all the information, the circumstances, the weapon of the crime and the place of the murder. The psychological reason is not expressed, for the victim does not have his fists closed, a sign of miserliness, but his hands are open. The title of the pamphlet says that he sleeps, but his eyes in the illustration seem wide open.

Readers were also intrigued by murders perpetrated in the family, as in **Two most unnaturall and bloodie Murthers**, 1605. The first, which the title-page illustrates, is the murder of a wife, and children by Master Calverley whose wife's sickness had driven him to madness. The image represents the devil who urges the young man to kill the wife and children with a cudgel, while a dog is terrified by the scene. This is the explanatory story: a young orphan, promised in marriage to the daughter of his tutor, is going to marry a young Londoner. The young woman, learning that he had been affianced before marrying her, became so worried that she developed tuberculosis. The young man, feeling responsible for the sadness of his fiancée and for the sickness of his wife, gets bitter. He becomes melancholy and needy after squandering his goods. His wife sells her dowry for him. But one day, overwhelmed by excess of melancholy, he kills his wife and two children. The image depicts him dishevelled and beside himself. The motive seems to be madness.

Two horrible and inhumane Murders done in Lincolnshire, 1607, presents another example of a husband who finds the sickness of his wife unbearable. The two murders are shown on the title-page and the illustration seems to be of Dutch manufacture. This is not unusual since news and illustrations passed from country to country. On the left, Thomas Cash strangles his sick wife while pretending to succor her, and on the right John Dilworth burns the murdered body of his wife in the hearth.

Infanticides also appear. Even more horrible than the murder of his children by a father is that committed by a mother. Goodcole in **Natures Cruell Step-Dames** relates the murder committed by Elizabeth Barnes and Anne Willis against their own children. The cut shows the mother in a wood decapitating the child. The same brochure shows a father violating his own child. (Plate 40)

Finally, there is an accidental infanticide in **Newes from Perin in Cornwall,** 1618. A prodigal had left for the Indies because of a falling out with his family. His parents received no news of him for many years and assumed that he was dead. After his mother has died of sorrow, the father remarried. Meanwhile the son, grown in wisdom and riches, wishes to return to the paternal home. A tempest overwhelms his ship in the open sea off Cornwall. Arriving on dry land, he seeks shelter from his father who does not recognize him, after having requested his sister and the friends whom he has confided in, to join him in the morning in order to effect a reconciliation. As a sign of good faith, he has brought money to pay off the debts of his father. The father and stepmother are unaware of all this, and the young man seeing that the woman is troubled at the thought of lodging a stranger, gives her his purse as a token of good faith until the next day. The stepmother, made greedy out of poverty, urges her husband to kill him in order to rob him. The sister arrives next morning and asks to see her brother. The old man, horrified by his crime, climbs to the bedchamber and kills himself on the body of his son. His wife, in turn, climbs up, finds the two men dead, and kills herself in despair, since the drama has taken place at her instigation. Finally, the distracted sister arrives; she contemplates the scene, but her stepmother prevents her from killing herself in recounting the story to her.

Four illustrations decorate this event in different ways. A boat in <u>sig</u>. B. depicts the voyage of the son; later we find the motive of the crime and then the crime itself. Here the motive looms larger than in the narrative: The young man hands the purse to his family which the stepmother hastens to hold, while the father is flabbergasted at seeing so much money. The youth is dressed simply but tastefully, with a rapier in his scabbard, holds his hand on his heart as a sign of good faith. Money is the motive for the crime; the wife holds her right fist closed, a sign of cupidity. The last illustration, which appears both on the title-page and on <u>sig</u>. C2, depicts the father's despair; with a knife close to his throat, he kills himself; drops of blood issue from his wound and from that of his son whom he clasps. The stepmother, dressed in black corresponding to her black designs, is on the verge of death, bent in pain, maintaining herself on her arms and legs as she tells the story, while the sister, twists her hair in sorrow. A slight inconsistency can be seen in the two illustrations representing the scene; for although on the title-page and on C2 the young man lies on a pallet on the floorboards, yet on B2 the victim is depicted on a bed with four legs. The illustrations, however, were well-related to the narrative.

Other illustrated pamphlets are more propagandist than factual. Three antipapal pamphlets attribute murders to the murderer's conversion to Roman Catholicism. **Three Bloodie Murders,** 1613, recounts, among other murders, that of the preacher, Mr. Storre, by one named Cartwright. This is an unusual murder since the culprit proves his sadism by cutting up the victim before killing him. The illustration represents the crime: a man on the right seems to raise his arms as a sign of execration. [27]

A woman from a well-to-do family and of a religious disposition kills her children after twelve years of a happy marriage. Why? Because the poor woman converted to Papism; after having attempted in vain to convert her husband she kills her children out of despair at seeing them born and nurtured in heresy. Overwhelmed by hysteria, she thinks that her children have become saints. The illustration represents a well-dressed mother in a rich interior; the devil helps her to kill her two and five year old children. The devil holds the weapon of the crime. The unhappy woman, using her garter, kills a child peacefully sleeping on a bolster.

The last conclusive example is, **The Cry and Revenge of Blood,** 1620, by Cooper, preacher and member of Christ Church, Oxford, who obtained his information from his friend Montaigu. Norron, a rich Papist with limitless cupidity tries to appropriate the vineyard of his neighbor, a poor widow. He has her elder son, who defended her interests, put in prison, where he dies. The second son comes to reclaim his inheritance; two men in the pay of Norron drag him to an inn and knock him senseless as he leaves it and throw him into Norron's pond. The third son returns with his sister. Both are clubbed to death and join their brother in Norron's pond. The murderer, later haunted by the memory of his successive murders, decides to drain his pond. Thus his heinous crime is discovered. In sig. I2, one sees the man hanging, justice having prevailed. The illustration on the title-page depicts the story in its totality: above on the left the elder son in prison, below the second son struck on the head by a club by a man who is encouraged by Satan, and below the third son and his sister lie dead. The right side of the image depicts the scouring of the pond; bottom right, a body is found, while a man brandishes an accusatory rod. Meanwhile another man in the center of the pond holds up a bone belonging to the two other victims who start appearing. The woodcut is beautiful and careful in its details.

A factual pamphlet can also serve as anti-separatist propaganda. **A true Relation of a barbarous and most creuell Murther,** 1633, recounts several murders. All the murderers are Separatists, nonconformists, innovators in matters of religion, members of the Family of Love or other dissident sects. The image on the title-page represents one of these crimes, that of Enoch who decapitates his mother and his brothers with a hatchet; he is seen carrying two heads out of the house. The right part of the illustration depicts his punishment: the gibbet.

All these murders were ordinary murders. All were related as the expression of the disapproval of God and all served to exhort man to sudden repentance. On the whole, the murder and the punishment of the criminal by justice were rarely represented in the same pamphlet. However, there are three suicides and two hangings. The inverse is also true. Usually the representation of the punishment excluded the image of the crime itself. Why was there this separation? Publishers were probably concerned with economy, but they also believed that crime often brings its own punishment. Sometimes society applied the punishment, sometimes the criminal's own conscience.

An unusual subject for illustration is the murder of the King of France, Henry IV, by Ravaillac in 1610. The woodcut which deals with a lofty subject is finely produced. The king and his companion are in a coach, which, by anticipation looks like a royal catafalque. It is entirely black; only the royal feathers are white as well as the horses. [28] The king behaves with decorum. He dies with dignity, giving no sign to betray surprise or emotion. His companion tries to turn the weapon aside, but is too late. Ravaillac, with inflamed eyes, directs the dagger right to the king's heart. The illustration is entirely different from all those previously considered: it is striking by its dignity and lack of sensationalism. [29] It might be expected that the image would be censored as indecent since it showed a king submitted to a vulgar assassination,--a touchy topic, since the sovereign could be alarmed that his subjects should be witnesses of how easily God's representative could be stricken without divine interference to save him. Or it might also be thought that the illustration would show the skies in tears or in anger, with the French writhing in their misery while Henry IV would remain dignified before death facing God with a clear and pure conscience. But only the facts were displayed. The factual character of the death of the king contrasts with the horror of the punishment of Ravaillac. A unique crime received an extraordinary punishment. Like Chastel in 1594, Ravaillac after being tortured on the rack, is quartered by horses. [30] The illustration of **The terrible and deserved death of Francis Ravilliack**, 1610, shows Ravaillac's execution while the judicial authorities and the hangman watch him. [31] (Plate 41)

In England the death of conspirators against the person of the king was never shown on brochures. But the deaths of conspirators against the kingdom and their tortures were depicted in pamphlets. The phantom of H. Percy the traitor returns in red on the title-page of a pamphlet bearing his name. There is an example of a purely political crime in **The overthrow of an Irish rebel**, 1608, which recounts the death of the rebel O'-Dogherty. O'Dogherty was originally a friend of England, well received in London and at Court as long as one of his friends, Doewra, aware of the problems of Ireland, was governor of the County of Derry. Unhappily, he was succeeded by George Paulet in 1606, a brutal and undiplomatic man, who one evening insulted and cuffed O'Dogherty. This put the fire to the gunpowder and O'Dogherty vowed revenge. He attacked Derry and killed Sir George Paulet. But on the 5th of July, 1608, he was taken in turn by Chichester on the rock of Doon near to Kilmacrenan and shot in the head. His head was sent to Dublin and transfixed on a gate of the city. The illustration represents two heads, not one. The cross and the barrels of powder remind the reader of the famous conspiracy of the Gunpowder Plot which still haunted the memory of the public. The brochure taught a shocking lesson-- the price of treachery.

A religious offence was of the same nature as a political crime. One recalls Hacket, Arthington and Coppinger who went through the streets of London, proclaiming that Queen Elizabeth should be dethroned, and that Hacket, this wild man who bit the nose of his schoolmaster without restoring it, [32] should reign in her stead. Catholics were represented as wishing the destruction of the kingdom. Puritans and Separatists also threatened the equilibrium of the nation.

Th. Heywood's **A true discourse of the two infamous upstart Prophets, Richard Farnham . . . and John Bull,** both weavers, does not display, but only implies, the hanging of the two individuals. The frontispiece shows the two at work, the person on the left with the Bible open in front of him; in the background two threads from the loom appear in the form of a hanging cord. The reader is reminded that this is a new version of the same heresy as Hacket's. [33] John Bull and R. Farnham went through London's streets proclaiming that they were possessed by the Spirit of God, that they had been molested like Christ in Jerusalem, and like Him they would resurrect and reign in the heavens. The crowd that was so keen to follow them was equally keen to witness their hanging.

The life, apprehension, arraignement and execution of Charles Courtney in 1612 shows us an escape from prison. From the top of the watchtower a person holds a rope by which the other person can slip down to the ground. Unhappily for them, the two men are recaptured and both are hung at the gate of the prison. A curious head appears at the window of a house close by. The image is clear and beautiful; it reminds the public of the fate of rebels. All the punishments to which we have referred have their minatory value as examples; in filling the multitude with horror they discourage sedition.

A crime against the common law was generally punished by hanging. [34] In the case, however, of grave crimes, the hanging was followed by the taking down and dismemberment of the body. It depended on the crowd and the authorities whether the condemned man should be dismembered living or dead, or at least insensible. After Hacket's execution, his body was immediately brought down and his heart was thrown to the crowd. That also happened in the case of O'Rourke in 1591, guilty of treason, or of the Catholic priests executed in the same year and who, at the moment of being dismembered, called on St. Gregory to the great surprise of the executioner. [35] There is no example of an illustration of a body brought down after execution except in Harman, nor any of the cutting up of the cadaver. [36] Possibly the visual representation of such horrors in the press would create qualms of conscience among some of the witnesses to such events. To participate in collective hysteria is one thing, but to see its effects in cold blood is entirely different. The crowd, sometimes impressed by the dignity of the condemned, was moved by compassion. On such occasions they did not ask for his heart and begged the executioner to wait until he was completely dead before dismembering him. [37]

Extraordinary torture was kept for a murderer and informer, Griffin Flood. The title-page shows him attached to stakes and crushed by weights. Two persons bring the weights with which to load the tortured man until death. Opposite the title-page is the representation of one of his crimes, the murder of a vine-grower: three persons are present; one loses blood from an open wound and the second is being stabbed with a dagger by a third person. Apparently the plate was printed on the wrong side. (Plate 42)

These illustrations were intended to dissuade the public from imitating troublemakers, on pain of receiving the same punishment. However, the punishment of those condemned by the common law is not always the subject of the illustrations of the brochures relating to their misdeeds. Such is the case in two different deeds that are reported. **The Arraignment of John Selman,** 1613, depicts a cutpurse, executed for the act of felony committed in the chapel royal of Whitehall in the presence of the king and the nobility. He can be seen, purse in one hand, holding his cape in the other. The second example reports the death of Sir Thomas Overbury, assassinated by the intermediacy of Weston and Mrs. Turner, in the pay of Lady Essex, daughter of the Howards. The paid killers appear on the title-page on their knees with a repentant air. The text denounces the Court: it condemns Lady Essex, while denigrating Overbury. Such ambitious courtiers, he insists, get what they deserve.

The intrigue was complex. Overbury, a courtier and a man of letters, in the service of the favorite of James I, helped Rochester to gain the favors of Lady Essex, a fast woman. But when they wished to get married, Overbury opposed it strongly, as much from a concern for the happiness of his friends as in order to control the political support of the viscount. James I, in order to expel him from the court, offered him a post abroad; he refused and was imprisoned for lack of respect to the crown. Lady Essex vowed his death. She placed at the head of the Tower of London a man in her confidence, Helwys, who engaged his henchman, Weston. Weston, to whom Mrs. Turner, the keeper of a house of assignation, had given poison, mixed it with the food of Sir Thomas Overbury so that he would die by inches. One day the countess, tired of waiting for him to die, sent him poisoned confectionary. The doctors, knowing that Overbury had been ill for some time, thought he died from natural causes. It was only the confession of the murderer that brought the plot to light.

Hitherto the majority of brochures illustrated capital punishment or torture. [38] The taste for these bloody images was rediscovered at the end of the nineteenth century, if Sir

Walter Scott is to be believed. We have found only one example of minor punishment: the placing of John and Alice West in the pillory, whom two little devils and the crowd watched. The text refers more to Alice than to John. Benefitting from the credulity of the people, Alice pretended to be the friend of the king and queen of fairies and asked for money in order to implore the good fairies on their behalf. She made a young girl sit down in her garden for several hours with an empty pot, in the hope that it would be filled with money. Imagine the fury of the young lady when after a prolonged wait she found she had lost her money and her time! Alice was the brains of a group of tricksters. Their case was not referred to the Assizes, as in the case of murder, but to the Old Bailey where minor offenses were tried.

We can conclude from the dates of these brochures on murders and their punishments, that they represent a definite trend in the taste of the seventeenth century. Theatrical imagination is transformed into diurnal reality. Images remind the readers of the hangings and tortures that fascinated them then as now corridas or films of violence. [39] While they canalized the destructive forces of humanity, they equally served as dissuasives from violence in depicting the consequences of wrong-doing. [40]

The frequency of sensational reports relating murders and executions is unrivalled except by that of catastrophes and monstrosities. Animals and fabulous beings found in the narratives of travellers, like those of Thomas Coriat and Webbe, must be distinguished from the monsters which, like murders, calamities, or inclemencies of weather, are signs of the displeasure of God. Catastrophes awaken the curiosity of the reader, while monstrosities have a prophetic value. A large number of them appear on broadsheets, as well as on quarto or octavo. Only one of them, published in Amsterdam, **A monster late found out and discovered,** 1628, by Rawlidge is really diverting. It is not concerned with a real monster, but with the distortion of the spirit and the senses by alcohol, and the tricks played by the keepers of taverns and bars. The illustration represents two young sons of Bacchus who follow a lady keeper with a curvaceous figure. The one is led by the nose by the pitcher of beer he holds on his hand and to which he is attached by a bar of iron. On his left foot he wears a small cask in the guise of hose. His companion, tied to him by another bar of iron leading him by the nose, is also covered with vine leaves, grapes like horns, and both sport a pipe. The woodcut is symbolic and humorous.

The same humor, however, is never found in the pamphlets published in London. Other woodcuts are more serious. The pamphlets of the 16th and the 17th centuries only differ in the format and making of illustrations. Up to about 1590 monsters tended to appear on broadsheets, while they decorated quartos or octavos after this date. Moral conclusions remained the same. [41] **Strange Newes** of 1613, for example, is eloquent on the origin and nature of monsters. The author, William Leigh, was one of the most popular preachers under James I and preceptor to Prince Henry. First he evoked the fall of man, the cause of the events of his time; meteorites, meteors, monsters, for Nature, so he said, "having suffered violence through the fault sees its order perverted." Humans are solely responsible for this state of things and are the only beings to degenerate. But one might ask: what about the animals? Why are there monsters among them? The author replies: the animals suffer through our fault; then follows a long enumeration of monsters, including their place of birth and the reason for their existence. For Leigh most were bastards or the children of bastards. Other authors find it more difficult to account for monsters. For instance, **The true reporte of the forme and shape of a monstrous child,** 1562, is careful to note that the child is perfectly legitimate, that the parents had other children that were normal in previous marriages, but that this child, the first of their marriage, is deformed. No blame rests on the parents for the author does not infer that they were divorced or adulterous.

Again and again the question of the imperfection of a divine creature was raised. In **Gods Handy-worke in wonders** of 1615, the author attempts to justify God. God, so he says, gives us his signs in his mercy. Lest anyone should think that these monsters are a defect of the creation, it should be recognized that they too sing the glory and omnipotence of God. [42] The misshapen child is born through either the fault of the parents or from the need to remind men that they should be humble, for the downdrag of original sin weighs heavily on everyone. It is like a wart on the nose. The author then gives the example of a poor woman whose two children were hermaphrodites. The fault devolved upon the father who, when she became pregnant, ceased to have any respect for her. Occasionally an illustration is to be found which combines several monsters, as in **A true relation . . .** (Plate 43)

For most, a monster is therefore not a divine mistake, but a divine punishment or warning. Factual rather than theologically explained accounts are rare; the descriptions of the catch of marvellous fish on 11 October 1568 [43] and 16 June 1569 are of this kind.

The representation of the monster at the top of the pamphlets and broadsheets is sometimes factual, sometimes symbolic. The description of the fish taken off the coast of Holland in 1566 is purely symbolic: it is a devil-fish and its scales are like beggars' bowls, its eyes like an owl's, its mouth like a parrot's beak, and its tail like a priest's cape. It is a satire against Mother Church. [44]

Another attack against Catholicism is **A true and Wonderfull Relation of a Whale.** Out of a black whale there escapes a Catholic priest bearing from Rome an indulgence for English and Irish Papists whose names the parchment reveals. In the distance there is a whaler and small fish gravitate to the whale. The blackness of the whale elicits in the reader a sense of the physical and moral horror of Papism. [45] (Plate 44)

The pig, as distinct from the fish, is almost always a symbolic representation of the times and manners of England: the pig with a dolphin's head born near to Charing Cross in 1562, the pig with long ears and a misshapen body of 1572, the pig clothed in lambskin but with tiny ears, its sexuality exaggerated although disguised, with long trotters and hard nails. All these representations allude to the laziness of the English from the fact that if they have ears they do not listen, and even if they hear, they do nothing as a result. The pig is therefore The Englishman; fat, greedy, dirty, and slothful.

Two prodigies can be linked with monsters. **True and Wonderful,** 1614, recounts the appearance of a dragon in Sussex which destroyed everything, both man and beast in its track. [46] This fabulous creature is seen erect above four of its victims whom it has laid low. Its forked tongue hisses, while fire issues from its throat. Its body is covered with scales and its belly is red. It has a white scaly collar. Two embryonic wings, about the size of a football, jut out from its back. What does it stand for? Is it the growth of the High Church position in the Church of England through Lancelot Andrewes, or the threat of Catholicism since Cardinal Bellarmine had directly attacked King James I, a controversial subject about 1610? These are merely conjectures which receive no proof from the text itself, but are suggested only by the description of the serpent or dragon.

The second prodigy is the apparition of a headless bear to a delirious woman. [47] The scene represents the miracle. The very pious husband prays that God will cure his wife, but at midnight when she calls him and the candle is extinguished he too sees the headless bear. He summons the household so that they can witness the vision. [48] The bear is the devil who possesses the wife; but suddenly a little child brings in a light and the wife improves. All fall on their knees and give thanks to God. The illustration depicts the development of the scene in detail. The story is authenticated by six witnesses. [49]

Other pamphlets illustrate human monsters. The mystery of Siamese twins, whether brothers or sisters, haunted the Renaissance. To our knowledge there are three examples, in 1554, 1566 and 1613, of which two are illustrated and printed on broadsheets. [50] The two first examples are joined at the belly, the last at the back. All three mothers agree in thinking that they signify an exhortation from God to repentance. [51] The children are, respectively, two girls, a girl and a boy, and two girls.

Even more frightening are the malformations of children. Some appear authentic, others seem imaginary. Between 1560 and 1570 broadsheets representing human monsters flourish. Most do not bear the name of the author. [52] A child was born in Sussex, at Chichester, with a misshapen head, distended belly and puny arms and legs. The umbilical cord, extraordinarily long had been cut near the mother and not at the child's navel. In 1562 a child was born near to Colchester with stumps of limbs. In the Isle of Wight in 1564 a child was born with pubic hair surrounding its navel and its thigh bone projecting. The woodcut shows the child and a detail of the deformed part. In 1566 in the parish of Mitcham in Surrey, a girl was born with a perfect body except for excrescences of flesh on the neck and loins. The young child is pictured from the front and the back in two woodcuts. Contrary to the previous examples this child will survive. Finally, in 1568 in Maidstone in Kent, there was born of an unmarried mother, a boy with a mouth twisted on the right side, with a left arm attached to his side, a left leg growing up instead of down and the right leg twisted towards the left; besides, a picture of the child's back shows an excrescence in the shape of a rose. The tale of horrors could continue indefinitely.

As time passes by these monstrosities become more and more extravagant. A child speaks in the belly of its mother in 1599. [53] **An example of Gods Judgement** includes two illustrations: the one on the title-page shows a black child, armed with a sword at the time of birth, with his left hand shaped like a tail. His brother appears in the course of the text, with two heads, one black, one white. In Kent, in 1609, a monster was born whose body was disproportionate in relation to his shortened arms and legs; the child lacks a neck.

Two other brochures deserve attention. **Gods Handy-worke in Wonders**, 1615, tells of a certain number of misshapen births. Those of the title-page, from our standpoint, seem to be too incredible to be real, even supposing these were cases of bestiality, which none of the booklets we have read ever mention. [54] One of the children has neither head nor left arm; its mouth is located on the chest under the male member; it has embryonic breasts and its private parts are confused: testicles or an attempt at representing a vagina? We would incline to the second interpretation since the text speaks of a hermaphrodite. The second child looks like a bird, except that its body is human and it has a fox's tail covered with feathers. **A wonder worth the reading,** 1617, depicts a horned being without a neck, legs and arms immeasurably swollen; its arms jut out from behind the head.

The fad for monsters appears to have weakened after 1620. How is this to be interpreted? Was it because the publishers had enough material with which to astonish the public? Or was it because the respect for human nature had grown so great in an increasingly anthropocentric universe, that it forbade the exposure of its weaknesses? Or again is the cause to be found in the progress of the sciences which attributed these phenomena to the accidents of nature rather than a punishment from God? Or did it seem more prudent, given the rise of agnosticism and rationalism to keep silence on what seemed to many an error of the creation? We would not presume to decide which of these interpretations is the more likely. Yet it is a fact that public sensitivity gradually lost interest in teratology, to concentrate its attention on the phenomena of everyday reality: changes in the weather, or twists in the psychology and the manners of mankind.

Just as in primitive societies the death of the sun each evening is followed by the anguish of the coming night and the fear of never seeing the kind luminary reappear, so for the Elizabethans and the first Stuarts natural disasters presaged the death of the world and the judgment to come. From the most natural to the most strange we find: the cold, floods, the plague, fires, earthquakes, storms and comets, the battles of birds and miraculous visions.

The cold Yeare, 1614, is a dialogue between a citizen and a man from the North telling each other of the misfortunes of winter. The man from the North clearly symbolizes man on the verge of old age. Winter also is as symbolical as realistic. [55] Taylor describes the winter as a plague that is fatal to dwellers of the countryside. Sig. B2^V and B3 recount the misfortunes caused by cold, the subject matter of the title-page cut. Below, on the left, a peasant attempts to free his animals trapped by the snow: a cow, a sheep, a pig; two birds, one white, the other black, have perished. On the right, contrasting the rustic life with the one of the town, are two courtiers throwing snowballs, the single joyful note. In the background, on the left, three horsemen have difficulty in advancing, so thick is the snow. One of them almost falls, for his horse has plunged into a hole which the snow has hidden. On the right a man helps a poor woman who carries her frozen child. This pitiful scene is shadowed by a leaden sky from which threatening flurries of snow fall. The woodcut is finely detailed, and like the other weather woodcuts evokes the reader's compassion. It is a reminder of the misery and fragility of human life, which a single drop of water is enough to crush and whose only hope is in God. (Plate 45).

Flooding is another inclemency of weather, capable of destroying man and his habitat. Two dates appear to have been particularly fatal: 1607 and 1613. Both produced illustrated pamphlets. The same illustration is used for the title-page of **A true report of certaine wonderfull overflowings of Waters**, and for the verso of the title-page of **More strange Newes**, both of 1607. The title-page of the latter represents a traveller arriving in a town; he sees a fire on a hill, a sign of the presence of God. The flood itself is depicted with all the pathos of its realism: men climb trees; men and women, flocks and herds, houses and churches, are all caught in the accident and can hardly keep their heads above water. A baby is seen floating perilously in its wooden cradle. A man is seated on the roof of his house trying to escape from the rising waters. All the domestic animals are depicted there: cows, oxen, asses, pigs, goats and sheep, rams, rabbits, and finally near the church the horse, the most noble of them all. Only the dog is missing but since the cut is not absolutely clear, perhaps he can be made out with difficulty on the left. The anger of God is as pitiless as the obstinacy of man in sinning. [56]

The illustrations of the two pamphlets of 1613 are equally frightening in the horror of the calamities they depict. **The wonders of this windie winter** displays a black sky from which the rain falls in buckets, while the heads of two messengers of God in the upper corners of the woodcut emit wind and rain. Below the spectacle of desolation, men and boats in distress, houses in ruin, trees uprooted, the sail of a windmill torn off, the spire of a church shattered can be seen. **The last terrible tempestious windes and weather** displays an image of the same technique, probably from the same illustrator, but much more dramatic. The theological interpretation is emphasized by the presence of the devil on the spire of the church. The scope is more vast than in the last image and more urbanized. In this case it deals with the destruction found after the tempest. In the previous images it was difficult to decide whether it was the overflow of a river; here the scene clearly takes place on the seashore. The low tide exposes men and women lying drowned on the sand, as found by their families. On the beach among the pebbles and shells one can make out a clam and a scallop shell.

These catastrophes could be local as well as national. Indeed the latter pamphlet mentions boats which sank with their goods: wines, oils and pewter. Gravesend and Windsor were cut off for the watermen were unable to reach them, except at the risk of their lives. The loss of houses and cattle impoverished the peasants in depriving them of their savings or even of their livelihood.

Still the calamities of the weather were nothing compared with those caused by the "black sickness," the plague. There are many kinds of plagues, of which the worst, the most murderous and the one which spread most quickly, was the bubonic plague of bacterial origin. [57]

This scourge raged through England so many times that the memory of it must have been intolerable for the survivors, if one is to judge by the rarity of its illustrations. It appears most often as a cause of dissension between the town and country. [58] Dekker and Taylor use the same woodcut to depict the two bubonic plagues of 1625 and 1636: in the distance the city of London appears; on the right peasants rise in revolt against the Londoners, who flee at the risk of infecting the rest of the country. Near the haystacks a man, a woman, and a child are dying, while in the distance one can make out the feet of a man already dead. Death allegorized, with an arrow in each hand, strikes everywhere, dancing on the coffins. Six of them can be seen, of which four are arranged in the center to suggest a St. Andrew's cross which was inscribed in chalk as warning on the contaminated houses. [59] In the sky, the hand of God emerges from a cloud, brandishing the whip of chastisement.

Another scourge of the century was fire. The houses of this time, made of straw, wattle and of wood--stone was kept for rich houses and monuments--burned at the least provocation: a coal from the hearth, an uncontrollable flame, a sudden wind when leaves are being burnt, and an entire district or most of a village was consumed while the powerless inhabitants watched.

D. Sterrie narrated the destruction of Beckles, where one of the major fairs of Suffolk was held: the catastrophe of 1586 cost twenty thousand pounds. [60] The woodcut shows the flames that have reached the entire town and the curious onlookers and some unhappy citizens who lift buckets of water in the vain hope of putting out the fire. Misfortune and the wrath of God have ruined the town. The same is true of the monastery of St. Michael of Antwerp in 1612. [61] God, it is argued, has chosen to destroy this place where the princes and dignitaries of the entire world were visitors, because of its idolatrous images. A ball of gilded copper decorated the top of the spire. In the cloister, plays were occasionally performed; one day Satan came to sit on the cross of the spire, threw a vengeful stone against the chapel and set it on fire. The fire destroyed among others, a painting of Rubens. God let the monastery burn to punish the monks for their idolatry. The author introduces religious propaganda into the news item. [62] The woodcut shows the monastery near the river and far from the town seen in the distance at the very time when Satan from the air is about to throw the stone. As it destroyed the roof, a draft came into the chapel and was responsible for the fire.

The cold, inundations, the plague and fires, unfortunately, were not rare events in the lives of the men of the sixteenth and seventeenth centuries. But these were known as natural events. Earthquakes seemed more unnatural, as well as astronomical happenings. **A shorte and pithie discourse** by T. Twyne, contrasts in spirit with **A true relation of a very dreadfull Earth-quake,** 1612. Though the former does not deny the part played by divine providence in the origin of earthquakes, still it attempts at a rational explanation. The title-page woodcut is ornamental rather than illustrative: it could bear the title, "The reflections of a scientist on the world". A man is sitting, pen in hand, and writes down his observations in a copybook. On the other side of the river God watches a town from his clouds of glory.

The second pamphlet on earthquakes advertises its contents from the very first: "Read and tremble". In fact, the cut does not show an earthquake but a comet, equally feared at the time. Five scared characters are awed by the event. One kneeling on the top of the hill prays God to spare him; he is parallel in composition to two other characters on the right: the first is also kneeling whereas the other, too old to bend his reluctant knees, is leaning on a staff. Two other persons, from the inside of the town have left the walls of the city to watch the phenomenon. The star shoots through a sky that is both starry and cloudy. The text is even more terrifying than the picture: in Westphalia people who had fled an earthquake to go and pray on a hill, died, struck by lightening. Comets, clouds of fire and of blood are vividly described; the reader is spared nothing since the aim of this pamphlet is not scientific accuracy, but a moral exhortation to repentance.

The final topic deals with miraculous apparitions. We have already seen those of the dragon and of the headless bear. [63] In Cologne, dead men come to life again, the subject matter of **Miraculous news,** 1616, first printed in the original city, then at Antwerp, and last in England. This is a good example of news circulating within Europe, passed on from one country to the next. The title-page shows a woodcut of three skeletons leaving their coffins; from right to left, the first beats his chest, the second burns and the third tears out his hair in despair.

Preceded by thunder and lightning, then the three men rose from the tomb to predict the judgment to come. **Looke up and see wonders,** 1628 represents a fight in the sky, a prophecy of the imminent end of the world. Yet the pamphlet wishes to

86

be reassuring and begs the reader not to be afraid but to bless God that the tempest is raging far away. Here, the woodcut is less reassuring than the text. Two laborers work in the fields; one of them falls, struck by what he sees in the skies. His companion with his back to the vision, continues to work unawares but the crowd on the left, watches in amazement, lifts its hands in despair and impotence before the marvel. Angels at the corners of the heavens, blow wind; thunder rolls on White Horse Hill, near Oxford. [64] First the roar of one cannon is heard, then many join in; balls emerge from the mouths of the two huge pieces of artillery, while lower down the horsemen of the sky confront each other. Three suns appear, then a drum is beaten sounding the retreat of the armies.

All these scourges, blazing stars, the appearance of three suns and the transformation of water into blood, the reddening of the wheat, birds in battle, [65] visions of an army in the skies, a spire being struck by lightning, the birth of monstrous children, and the struggles of animals that have turned wild, appeared in a voluminous pamphlet: **The Prodigies of Germany**, 1638. A woman rises in mourning garments and shouts around, "Woe to you!"

"Let those who have ears, hear", for all these pamphlets demand an emotional response from the public, founded on horror, astonishment and terror, deriving their information or their interpretation from the Apocalypse of St. John, one of the popular books of the time. [66] It does not seem that the arrival of the apocalyptic year 1600, removed the fear the common man had of seeing the world come to an end. The preachers from the height of their pulpits cried: "Be ready" and the people continued to live in terror.

If rationalism was the prerogative of intellectuals in the seventeenth century, the pamphlets which we have just described seem to prove that, among the majority, it was still in an embryonic state. Although the thinker might turn away from God towards man, the people remained theocentric in heart. The book of nature was for them supremely the mystical book and the apocalyptic imagination supplied what was missing. Their main contact with the intellectual world was through the Sunday sermon and the country preachers were not always as learned as they might have been. Rationalism might have undermined some of the reliable convictions of the past, without uprooting superstition anchored at the bottom of humanity. On the contrary, a wave of credulity arose born of the insecurity which reigned in their hearts and was changed into reliance on apocalyptic predictions and on witchcraft. [67]

Once more a mixture of the genres is revealed. Many of the authors of sensational news pamphlets, seemed to have been concerned with social order or preoccupied with theology. They knew that nothing convinces with more intensity than an appeal to the emotional reactions of human beings. All used the importuning of the heart to convey their moral message: respect for the social and divine orders.

Chapter V

PROPAGANDA

Our world is so submerged beneath economic and political propaganda, that we believe that it is a recent phenomenon. This is a great mistake. When the Greek Creo buries Antigone alive because she flouted his authority and covered her brother's body with dust, he publicly shows the world that he is not to be disobeyed. This is governmental propaganda of the dissuasive kind. When the Romans paraded in the streets of the cities they had conquered, that was another act of political propaganda. The humiliating display of defeated chiefs attached to their chariots is also used as a dissuasive, since it proclaims the might of the Empire and the folly of rebellion. In both cases propaganda is direct and vigorous. A more devious and subtle form of propaganda, and one often used by tyrants, is to embellish their territory with monumental architecture and statuary and to restore historic cities, as well as to improve the highways. The result is that popular pride is swollen and patriotism is inflated.

For the general public propaganda means the partisan praise or deprecation of an idea or a person by means of the press. Defamation is part of it. Pisistrates, for instance, used to expose the defects of the public enemy. [1] In Greece this appears to be a standard procedure of political life. To extend the proverb: all is fair in love and war <u>and politics</u>. In **Julius Caesar**, Shakespeare surely expresses his aristocratic scorn for the mob. It is ruled by the last one who has spoken. If Bolingbroke in **Richard II** wins popular opinion it is because, contrary to his inflexible cousin Richard II, he multiplies favors and smiles.

Until the end of the fifteenth century, propaganda, in England as well as in Europe, is a sporadic and unorganized phenomenon. After the Reformation in the sixteenth century, it becomes an essential governmental organ. England, especially is faced with the problem of transforming a Catholic majority, (who even as they are disappointed by the Roman Catholic Church, still obey its spiritual chief, the Pope), into a Protestant majority, whose temporal and spiritual head is to be the King. The English entrust him not only with their material welfare but also with their spiritual well being.

Thomas Cromwell, a great propagandist in the reign of Henry VIII, uses various propagandist methods. Defamatory stories are circulated within the country about priests and their misdoings. Later propaganda becomes organized. The pulpit, the theatre and the press are all used separately or simultaneously. Writers are hired to publicize the official creed. Three main types of publications appear: those that defend the revolution that took place, those that praise the new order of things, and those that defend the interests of the citizens. The latter insist that it is better to obey the orders of the prince than to rebel and fall under the axe. [2]

Thomas Starkey and Richard Morison are the two main pamphleteers under Richard Cromwell, but their pamphlets are not illustrated. Not that Cromwell underestimated the power that images had on the soul of the common people. Indeed, he encouraged the attendance at plays representing the Pope as the devil's chief supporter. These plays tended to replace the popular interludes like Robin Hood, whose seditious contents displeased the authorities. [3] The lack of illustrated pamphlets is largely due to the lack of development of the printing press.

Political and religious indoctrination penetrates the eyes by means of plays and pamphlets and the ears through the Sunday sermon. During the sixteenth and the seventeenth centuries, the scope of written propaganda widens as it uses drawings either to praise or to ridicule, like the weekly satirical magazines of the present. While originally political and religious in character, the propaganda disseminated by illustrated pamphlets is more diversified under Elizabeth and extends to the field of economics. As the role of the press is asserted, the government adumbrates its uses and fears the power it may have on public opinion. Because of the close scrutiny exercised on the printing presses, forbidden literature, printed hurriedly, sometimes in the dark of the night, will not benefit from the propagandist advantage of illustrations. Indeed, Catholic pamphlets will bear none. [4]

Governmental or semi-governmental propaganda--that is, works written by unpaid friends of the government--is not of equal importance under the Tudors and under the Stuarts. Although illustrated propaganda pamphlets are not produced until the reign of Elizabeth I, the earliest Tudors are interested in the image that circulates among the crowd. Even "Bloody" Mary endeavors to justify her unpopular marriage to Philip II of Spain. Christopherson writes a treatise for her, which shows by devious ways and with genealogical trees in folio, that Philip is in fact a descendant of John of Gaunt. [5]

We have seen that propaganda was reaching the rabble under Henry VIII's Cromwell. Elizabeth returns to her father's policy but adapts it to her temperament and to the modern means. She wants to appear as the virgin queen, dear to the heart of her people. Not that her policy is notably more tender than that of any other sovereign of the Renaissance. She is prepared to sacrifice a few heads for reasons of state. But to her people she always justifies the unfortunate executions that she has ordered. So much so, that in the House of Commons she declares that the main glory of her reign is to have gained the love of her people and to have governed in harmony with their will. [6] Whether her deeds went according to her words or not, the queen cared about her image.

Contrary to the Tudors, the first Stuarts intend to govern as absolute monarchs and consider that the people should have no knowledge of or influence on the affairs of the state. This may be a realistic view, but it proved fatal to the royal policy. The Stuarts openly hold the view that their predecessors carefully hid, namely that the people cannot be sufficiently informed of the twists and turns of diplomacy to be capable of expressing a sound and solid opinion. Unfortunately the crowd does not like to be told that it is ignorant. It was used to discussing political affairs under Elizabeth. As a child becomes furious when his privileges are revoked, so the populace resented the political secretiveness of the Stuarts.

The result of this regressive policy is totally negative. The Londoners do not become apathetic about English politics. On the contrary, they flare up at the time of the Thirty Years War. And since the king does not explain why he does not rush to the rescue of his daughter and of his son-in-law, he is accused of passivity and grows unpopular. [7] This desire on the part of the Stuarts to keep the affairs of the state secret, their disinclination to become demagogues, and supremely their superbia, are factors partly responsible for the death of Charles I. Some sovereigns in Europe could afford to reign as absolute kings, but this the democratic tradition in England refused to tolerate. Hence the numerous contentions between the early Stuarts and the Parliament and their growing unpopularity.

Although royal policy leaves little room for propaganda, nevertheless there are many illustrated propagandist pamphlets in the seventeenth century. Not all the king's men agree with the royal silence and some publish governmental pamphlets. Englishmen become increasingly intrigued by the events of the European war where Catholics and Protestants fight for hegemony in Germany. Propaganda, which emanates less and less from the Crown, passes into the hands of popular and controversial writers. It rises in the pamphlets first, then it blooms in the first periodical, which, directly or indirectly, will comment upon royal policy. There is the beginning of a freer press, whose role will increase as it reflects more and more uncensored public opinion.

* * * * * * *

Political and religious propaganda are therefore typical of the reign of the Tudors. Positively, it will encourage the people to trust the Crown. Negatively, it will deter the subjects of her Majesty from following the enemies of the realm.

Though some have little patience for the sitting itself, all sovereigns, whether Tudor or Stuart, enjoy having their portraits made. All wish to be seen by their subjects with their most flattering features emphasized and in garments that suit both their figures and their social standing. Not only is the concept of kingship apparent and to be revered, but the personality behind such an office is to be admired. The portrait is there to show how perfectly suited the personage is to the title.

Never has any sovereign sensed more acutely the need to appear this way in the eyes of the public than Queen Elizabeth. [8] If one is to believe Roy Strong, the particular interest of all of the portraits of Elizabeth is that none of them seem to show her features accurately, at least so far as may be determined from the various documents that we possess. Yet the Queen must have been recognizable to her contemporaries. In the pamphlets as well as in the literary portraits of the time, like Lyly's, the Queen is either Arastea the beautiful, or Judith, the formidable, and though living, she is represented as a legendary character, for she is truer than fictitious characters. The myth of the virginity of the Queen harmonizes with the image of stability that emerges from her portraits. This type of representation of the goddess queen survives after her death as the naming of the pamphlet, **The Maiden Queene Entituled The Britaine shepheardes teares for the death of Astrabomica**, 1607, indicates.

We are left with two portraits of her cousin and enemy Mary Stuart. Both appear in the Proclamations under her son' reign, James Stuart. The first is a simple intaglio medallion. The Queen of Scotland wears a wide low-neck collar. The date of this broadsheet is unknown. As it was printed by John Norton it is reasonable to assume that it appeared between the accession of the King and the death of the printer in 1612. [9] In the other portrait we have of her, she is in the company of her consort

Henry, Lord Darnley, the father of James. Reynold Elstrack, the famous engraver, designed her with all the pomp and veneration due to the mother of the King of England. The queen occŭpies one quarter more space than her husband as a sign of her importance.

The portraits of James the First are not numerous in the pamphlets. He probably thought that aloofness would be more proper to his degree than the vulgarization of his image, which would be in keeping with the rest of his policy. Also he positively loathed sitting, which explains why the portraits of his majesty are so scarce, so inaccurate, and so imperfect. [10] He mainly appears on political works written in Latin or on pamphlets issued by the Virginia Company. In John Vicars's **Mischeefes mysterie,** 1617, the idea of the sovereign appears more than the likeness of the living king himself.

Although Charles did not share James's repulsion for sitting in order to have his portrait made, his idea of the mystery that should surround kingship is similar. The title-page of Duval's tract on the Anglo-Spanish marriage is the only likeness we know of until 1641. Prince Charles, hand in hand with the Infanta Mary of Spain, receives the blessing of Christ. This is a tract in Latin of 1641. Though beyond our period, it is worth mentioning. As the whole of London rejoices to see Charles back, having escaped from the ferocious Scotsmen, great revelling ensues and a pamphlet appears showing the king triumphantly entering his capital. Royal propaganda is also achieved through the displaying of the rich entertainments of the court and of the royal triumphs and progresses. Elizabethan illustrated triumphs and progresses, generally appear on broadsheets. Very few seem to have been published, contrary to expectation.

The honorable entertainment given to her Queen's majesty in progress at Elvetham, 1591 and **The royall passage of her Majesty from the Tower to Whitehall,** 1604, are, if we are able to believe Nichols, the only remaining traces of the passages and progresses of Queen Elizabeth. [11] **Arches of Triumph,** for the accession of King James, only appeared in 1604 as the plague raging in 1603 stopped the festivities which usually accompanied the coronation of a new monarch. The narrative of Stephen Harrison and the seven engravings of William Kip emphasize the decorum due to the monarch, head of State and Church. They exhibit a marvellous taste for a mixture of antiquity and orientalism: London, pygmies, Italians, the Dutch, New Arabia, the garden of cornucopia and the Temple of Janus are all represented. These engravings probably appeared as broadsheets and were posted on the walls of London, as they can be found in the Bodleian in Oxford, among the proclamations as well as in the book just quoted. It does not seem unreasonable to believe that the Londoners may have been able to buy them, with or without the text.

The return to London of the beloved Prince Henry is the occasion of an illustrated pamphlet in 1610: **London's Love to the royal Prince Henrie.** On the recto of the leaf preceding the title-page, a rare place for an illustration, one can see a ship all decked with flags. Facing the title-page is another smaller ship, also dressed. The two woodcuts are typical of the ambiguous functions. A ship is one of these decorations that can be found everywhere. In this particular instance it corresponds to part of the story, as the citizens of London launched some boats on the Thames to go and greet the Prince, coming back from Richmond. After the death of the beloved heir, an illustrated pamphlet appears affirming allegiance to the new Prince of Wales, Charles: **Civitatis amor,** 1616.

Royal festivities given on the occasion of the visit of a foreign prince find very little echo in the press, not even that of Anjou to Elizabeth. Yet at a time when curiosity for Africa and the East is at a peak there appears the picture of the ambassador of the Prince of Morocco in **The arrivall and intertainments of the embassador from the Emperor of Morocco,** 1637. (Plate 12)

With the reign of Charles I, it seems that royal entertainments develop refinement. Whereas earlier, they were both aristocratic and popular pleasures, they later become mainly the privilege of the court. The works of Inigo Jones speak mainly of an elite, aware of the artistic innovations that Italy inspired. Their minds are used to intellectual games. In his masques written by some famous collaborators like Ben Jonson, one feels the growing distance between the sophisticated king and his court, on the one hand, and the cruder mob of London, on the other. And yet the people remain devoted to their king since in 1641, they sweep away the differences that grew over the years to explode with joy at the return of their king from his perilous journey to Scotland. [13]

Apart from these narratives and that of the marriage of Lord Haye to the daughter of Lord Denny, [14] there is very little news about the rejoicings or the doings of the court. We may well ask why, as we are used to the tittle-tattle of gossipy newspapers scooping the courts of modern Europe. Is it because it would be impossible in a crude woodcut to recover the intensity of the royal pomp experienced by the Londoners themselves? Since they partook in the festivities, the illustrated narrative would appear as a come down. This would be an argument, but would it not be hard on the country folks to deprive them of the sense of exaltation recorded through such a picture?

Another hypothesis may be that the Crown felt that

the depiction of obvious luxuries was dangerous in itself. Let the people know that the court has entertainments, since this is in accordance with the decorum required of the prince. But to let them know how many and how grandiose they are may excite subversion among the poorer sort. Also the aristocrats, who could have financed the printing of a pamphlet on the visit of the queen to their mansion houses, often felt like Goneril or Regan at the visit of their father, King Lear and his royal train of debauchees. So they would be the last to want to recall such a visit, for fear a second one might come.

Political propaganda does not merely include the display of personal prestige. The justification of the policy of the time and indoctrination are also part of the political game. There men like Cranmer under Henry VIII, Bancroft and Cecil under Elizabeth, Seymour and Bacon under James I, have their part to play. The Stuarts, as we have seen, do not believe like the Tudors, in the importance of giving the "right" information to the people of England. But friends of the government take the initiative. In the amusing mood, we shall note a pamphlet by Colbe. Two heralds from England and from France are seen disputing which of their two countries is the more worthy. Each, with excessive patriotism, praises the merits of his own country. The Frenchman, being pre-sumptuous, says that no other country in the world is more beautiful than his sweet France. The Englishman not lacking humor answers that to the virtues of France, England adds modesty, and the debate continues.

In this category, the number of illustrations is still fairly scarce. Illustrated Elizabethan propaganda seems mainly economic in character. In 1590 there appears a tract by Jenings on the harm caused by feeding badly, that is, not eating enough fish. The title-page represents a boat from the merchant navy. It is printed by Roger Ward, living in Lambart Hill near the old Fish Street of London, an important detail since the pamphlet is set to impress by its image and by its place of impression as well as by its contents. [15]

Similar propaganda in favor of the merchant navy can be found in the proclamations. In 1596 an illustrated broadsheet shows a fisherman's boat in which the men are hauling in the net full of fishes. One also sees two light-weight ships towards which a fish is swimming. The seal of the Queen frames the whole. It is explained why the law has prescribed fish-days to the exclusion of any other meats. England being surrounded by seas, a strong naval force should be maintained in times of peace and of war. Mariners need to sell fish in order to survive. To abide by the law is not only healthy for your body and for the salvation of your soul. It is a civic duty. [16]

In 1616, there appears a brief of the orders given by the Crown to the Society of Arms of London. The title-page shows both a halberdier and a musketeer. The pamphlet was devised to encourage the people of London to keep up their soldiering. England is constantly on the qui vive due to the fragile balance of power in international affairs in the sixteenth and seventeenth centuries. [17]

To include Thomas Heywood as one of the propagandists of the Early Stuart period, does not seem altogether arbitrary. He was a member of the Lord Admiral's company and a staunch supporter of monarchy at a time of tension between the Crown and the Parliament. His allegiance and admiration for Elizabeth does not prevent him from writing in favor of James or of Charles. What conclusions can be drawn? That Heywood was totally devoted to the royalist cause regardless of who the monarch was? Or were some of his works ordered by the government? The elegies on the death of Prince Henry and on the death of James I, a play like **The royall king and the loyall subject,** and mainly the illustrated pamphlet on the royal boat being built at Woolwich, tackling the controversial problem of ship-money and dedicated to Charles the First, seem to be propagandist works. [18] In the latter work Heywood indeed stresses the fact that the building of such a beautiful boat should encourage the subjects of the king to give more ship-money. [19] The etching is remarkable in its execution; every detail of the ship can be seen. [20]

Where does governmental propaganda stop and where does private exposition of royalist convictions start, is one of the problems we meet. This is not so easy to determine when letters may have been lost or purposely destroyed so as to leave no evidence. The first conclusion we can reach is the scarcity of illustrated pamphlets in governmental propaganda. And again to answer "why?" is difficult. It may be a matter of decorum, since a work nursed in high circles could not bear the usual crudity of popular illustration. On the other hand the urgency with which the royal message had to reach popular opinion before it was set, might not have allowed the etching of plates worthy of the subject. But mainly the works of propaganda required an intellectual maturity which was alien to the lower classes. The argument could not be summed up in a picture and therefore rendered it superfluous.

Negative propaganda, however, could use satire. Its target was more simple and it could hit the mark by publicizing the theme with one single satirical picture. It affected the antagonistic feelings of the mob and the picture acted as one catalytic agent. This is why most of the illustrated propagandist material on the part of the government or its friends is turned towards foreign affairs. To unite the people against a common foreign enemy saved them from domestic dissensions. There censorship was vigilant. Yet under James I there appears the first open illustrated critique of the interior regime.

The first tract seems a simple, gossipy murder story: the assassination of Thomas Overbury. [21] Yet its implications are anti-royalist as the king is shown to back the villains of the piece. This is a very sleazy affair--one of these untangled murders that the Renaissance left us to unravel without success. The narrative deals with the dangerous liaison between Rochester and Lady Essex, which was blessed by the king. The victim was Thomas Overbury, a friend of Rochester, whom Lady Essex sacrificed to her passion.

The pamphlet is a disguised satire of the frivolity of the court of James I. Robert Carr, viscount of Rochester, is the first Scotsman to sit in the House of Lords, as he attracted the eye of James I. The favorite is also entrusted with the financial accounts of the realm. The scandal discredits the favorite and the wisdom of a prince who chooses an unreliable man for a responsible position. The implication of the pamphlet is therefore to show the folly of the king, who follows his passions rather than his wisdom. [22]

But anti-Jacobite propaganda reaches its peak with the pamphlets of Th. Scott, former chaplain to the king, dean of Norwich cathedral, and a convinced Protestant. The first tract he wrote about the Spanish marriage planned by James I for his son in the hope of reversing the balance of international affairs and of making the enemy into a friend, **Vox populi**, 1620, is not illustrated. It is important though to know it, to understand the others, which are [illustrated]. He attacks the Spanish ambassador, Count Gondomar, in charge of the negotiations between Charles and the Infanta of Spain. **Vox populi** imagines Gondomar, back in Spain, unravelling to Philip II, his king, his plans in order to fool England, and buy its courtiers into establishing Catholicism again. He describes the enthusiasm of crowds of Englishmen attending Mass in the Chapel Royal. This tract expresses the fears of Th. Scott and of the old Protestants seeing Catholicism admitted at the court and the rising of a new tendency toward pomp in Anglican liturgy. Scott did not have to wait long for a royal response; **Vox populi** was banned and Scott had to leave England for the Netherlands.

It did not stop him, however. **Vox Regis** published circa 1623, is an apology for the preceding tract. The frontispiece was engraved by Crispin Van Passe I and shows James I in the House of Lords. On the right the bishops are sitting, on his left, the peers. At his feet his son Charles, his daughter Elizabeth and his son Frederick, for a short time king and queen of Bohemia, are kneeling, probably imploring his aid. The royal canopy bears inscriptions from **Ecclesiastes** 9:10 and from **Proverbs** 21:1. Both remind the king of his divine right; he is God's deputy and should go about His divine business, prior to any other commitment. He should be strong and resolute. [23]

Scott's reminding the king of his duties hit strongly home since the people of England could not understand why James did not commit himself in the affair of the succession to the throne of Bohemia. Protestantism demanded his allegiance and blood pleaded for his love. Yet James does not dare to enter the war, nor does he send any troops before 1624. For he hopes to make a friend out of the old Elizabethan enemy. When the plans for the Spanish marriage fail in 1624, then James joins in with France and the Netherlands on the side of the Palatinate against the Hapsburg. Meanwhile Spain manages to neutralize England, as Elizabeth had done for France, when she led all to believe that she might marry the Duke of Anjou. The mottos written on the royal canopy are therefore an obvious criticism of James's policy. (Plate 46)

Above James another quotation from the Book of **Ecclesiastes**, 10:2, [24] encourages James to set his heart to his task. The bishops and the peers also prompt James to action. The motto above the bishops reminds him that God seconds any enterprise undertaken in His name. [25] The peers renew their allegiance. They are always ready for action. [26] On each side of the three kneeling figures two other biblical quotations appear. At the very bottom of the print, both the nobility and the people, enthusiastic for action, offer their hearts, their purse or lift a flask of wine to signify their joy at James's supposed decision to enter the Thirty Years War. Again two biblical inscriptions, one from **Judges**, 5:9, the other from 2 **Samuel**, 3:36, support the righteousness of the popular reaction. [27] The first reminds the king of the importance of popular opinion as the rulers of Israel are praised for their democratic sensitivity. This is tantamount to rebuking the king for his haughty authoritarianism. Never did the illustrated press dare thus to propagandize the King. One can guess how angry the King became.

Vox Dei [28] uses another technique: association of ideas through pictures. Christ from his niche holds out a triangle containing monarchs. The top of the niche bears the title of the pamphlet surrounded by clouds of glory. Christ, with his head coming out of the clouds of glory steps on the image of death and of hell. One reads, "O Death where is thy sting, O Hel where is thy victory" (The sting of Death is sinne: **I Cor.** 15). On the pillars surrounding the niche on the left, from the top downwards and from left to right the lion, the dragon, the unicorn and the lyre can all be seen. In the center of the triangle, James I is surrounded by the medallions of Frederick and Elizabeth, left and right. He is also surrounded by his grandchildren. Above him, at the top of the triangle, Charles is crushing the popish princes. In the corner left, the Duke of Buckingham defeats factions and venality, whereas in the corner, right, Sir John Ramsey, the Count of Holderness, wins over the traitors. The suggestion remains the same as in the previous pamphlets; let Protestants unite against the Catholics.

In fact these tracts voice even more a hatred against Spanish power than a criticism of the royal policy. We have not yet mentioned the second part of **Vox Populi,** both etchings of which are most representative of the anti-Spanish tradition in England, as we shall see below. Therefore it seems wise to retain them as prize-pieces for the following section: anti-Spanish propaganda.

* * * * * * *

Of the pamphlets dealing with foreign affairs the greatest part is concerned with the English resentment of Spain, growing in the sixteenth century. This feeling became inflated over the years to the point that anything that had to do with Spain was evil: historians call it the Black Legend. [29] It lurks within the people under the reign of Mary Tudor. Her persecutions of the Protestants are largely imputed to the evil influence of her Spanish husband, Philip II. Furtive at the beginning of the reign of Elizabeth, it suddenly flares up in the 1580's, and keeps on blazing until about the middle of the Thirty Years War. Anti-Spanish propaganda becomes anti-governmental propaganda under James I, as the new monarch endeavors to pacify the former enemy. It certainly occupies the front stage of our illustrated pamphlets.

It appears at various levels. Politics and economics are linked in the skirmishes between England and Spain in the West Indies. The political conflict bursts out in the naval fights preceding or following the Armada. But the whole affair is mingled with religious hostility, since Philip II is one of the sustaining pillars of Catholicism. The European politics of the sixteenth and of the seventeenth centuries are so complex, the motivations are so tangled, alliances are so quickly established and broken off, that strict categories are out of place here. One can only speak of outstanding features. Sometimes anti-Spanish propaganda insists on the religious aspect of the Black Legend, sometimes it dwells on the balance of political and armed forces in Europe. But the fact that politics and religion in Elizabethan times are so linked as in the Irish contentions of today, must never leave the scholar's mind.

Illustrated pamphlets represent only part of anti-Spanish propaganda and considering Elizabeth's prudence in political matters, it is not surprising to see the first illustrated pamphlet appear in 1585. In the first period of her reign she does not want any open hostility, and should anyone question her about her privateers, he always found her surprised at the news of a skirmish between English ships and Spanish ships.

The first anti-Spanish poem we know of, is a ballad of Ralf Norris on the fall of Antwerp. A small cut placed in the top corner left, shows the town, in fact any town. [30] The word "Spanish" is not uttered but the author alludes in disparaging terms to the cur that destroyed Antwerp (1st stanza). He thinks England should in no way trust an enemy who amiably flatters his prey, the better to pounce upon it, as it would be unguarded. [31] These are already the themes that we find in the later development of anti-Spanish propaganda: pro-Netherland tracts. The date is important since it marks the breaking off of the negotiations between England and Spain about the Low Countries. William the Silent, the great champion of Protestantism, is murdered in Delft in 1584. Hence there ensues the fall of Antwerp in August, 1585. In 1586 Sir Philip Sidney dies in Arnhem. His national funeral is followed by crowds and immortalized by Theodore de Bry in 30 etchings. In 1585 a colonial incident starts the battle. Spain orders that any English boat found in the Bay of Biscay should be seized. Drake returns the compliment by attacking St. Domingo and Carthagena. [32]

Nothing seems to appear, however, in illustrated pamphlets, before the revealing publication of the orders of the Duke of Medina for the invasion of England. A ship serves as an illustration and the contents of the booklet are rather disappointing. The propaganda comes in the foreword. It excites English patriotism in stressing with what sadistic care the Spanish navy was preparing for the invasion of England. As for the body of the booklet, one finds there only the usual recommendations that any admiral would give his fleet for any voyage whatsoever. The ships should not attack without due command. They should not get mixed up. They should not flee if they are attacked. The use of the pamphlet was to show the people of England that they should get ready and that the news of a Spanish attack was not a ghost, or the phantasm of a politician's brain. [33]

The year of the Armada, 1588, is, naturally, rich in anti-Spanish publications against Philip II, against the Spanish ambassador to France, Mendoza, and against Alexander Farnese, Duke of Parma and governor of the Low Countries. Ballads sing the unexpected victory of England, with the queen inspecting the troops at Tilbury. Deloney sharpens his pen against the Spanish foe. He crows over the defeat of the great galleass, commanded by

Don Pedro de Valdez and over the death of Captain de Moncaldo. He excites popular resentment by describing the barbed iron cat-o'nine-tails specially prepared, so he tells us, to lash and tear the flesh of Englishmen, pull out the sinews and nerves and pierce their veins. Deloney concludes ironically on the soft-heartedness and the Christian charity of these sanctimonious hypocrites, one of the favorite themes of the time. [34]

The most remarkable illustrated pamphlet on the Armada dates from 1589, **The Birth, Purpose, and mortall Wound of the Romish holie League.** [35] This tract tries to kill all Catholic birds with one stone and contains a satirical map, with letters, as were used at the time, referring us to the comments of the writer. (Plate 47)

Vignette A shows Satan near the Holy See surrounded by monks. Vignette M depicts the sickness of the Holy League. The Pope hopes that it will heal, but the devil, disguised as a doctor, says the truth: it must die. On a small table near the devil-doctor lies a collection of medical instruments commonly used in the sixteenth century: clysters, sucking-glasses, urinals. . .-- a passing blow at the medicine of the time.

The map itself has very little in common with geography. It is purely allegorical and endeavors to represent the misdemeanor of the Pope and his partisans. The Catholic party in France with the Duke of Guise, and the Spanish cruelty to the West Indians, are all described. Yet there is a sea and the crescent-shaped armada sails within two shores. But the delineation of these coasts bears little resemblance to England or to the Continent.

If we start from the right-hand land and go from top downwards, one sees the following: in F the Pope threatens to flog Philip II if he does not obey the bull excommunicating Elizabeth and help the league against her. In G, pressured by a monk, Cardinal Allen, through a cannon, fires two seditious tracts against the queen, urging the English Catholics to welcome Philip of Spain (on the map one can see only one tract). In D, Henry of Navarre, followed by his famous white steed, appears as a defender of the Bible, which is resting on a lectern. He seems to be deeply involved in the reading of the Holy Scripture. B depicts the mass murders organized by the chief of the Catholic party in France, the Duke of Guise. He himself is dislocating the joints of one of his victims and as a result various heads and limbs are already arranged for display on a trestle. An envoy from the Pope pours out a bag of gold at his feet. In I, a representative from the queen, probably Drake, sows the seeds of trouble among the Spanish. This refers to the raid on Cadiz where Drake took the Spanish ships unaware as they were preparing to attack England. Although he did not succeed in destroying the Spanish fleet and munitions, the expedition had to be postponed for a year, and this gave more time for the English forces to get ready.

On the other side of the sea, most probably the Channel, but perhaps the Atlantic or the Indian Ocean, two Spaniards are destroying Indian idols. The printing of the picture is not clear, but one reads "Spaniard tearing out painted saints from India's womb". This is an illusion to the Black Legend and to the cruelty of Spaniards towards the aborigines living in their colonies. Right at the bottom, in E, Elizabeth puts her trust in Christ. As firm as a rock she sits, crowned with the laurels of peace and holding out the English banner.

The sea extending between the two pieces of land, is strewn with galleys and sea-monsters. This gives an accurate picture of the Armada which was mainly composed of galleys, galleasses and gallions. In H, the famous fleet, supposedly invincible, unfolds, crescent-shaped. In K, the Spaniards become scared, as they see the Dutch fleet approaching. An important historical event is then recalled. When the Spanish ships having avoided Calais, then in English hands, anchored between Calais and Dunkirk, Howard sent his suicide-boats to set fire to the fleet. To avoid them the Spanish fled to the coast of Holland. But the Dutch came to the help of the English and fought their oppressors. The Duke of Parma, who was to join the Armada, did not dare to come out of the Scheldt, for fear of meeting the Dutch fleet. The intervention of the Dutch, had a double function: it weakened the Spanish fleet and prevented its reinforcement. This was priceless help for the English. [36]

The iconography of this tract, proves to be far the most interesting political one we have encountered. One map sums up clearly the Protestant point of view on the European wars of religion and the Elizabethan drama.

The relationship between England and Spain suffered for a long time from the blow of the Armada. Anti-Spanish feeling keeps growing and even when political stress becomes less, popular opinion remains belligerent. Any Spanish defeat is a subject for rejoicing. In 1589 there appears an account of one of Drake's voyages to the West Indies. The maps engraved by Baptista Boazio are the most interesting visual account of Drake's activities found in illustrated pamphlets. The booklet was written first in Latin, then in French, and printed by R. Field and R. Ward a year apart. The seven engravings show a bird's-eye view of the attacks of Drake against the Spanish possession of Santiago, Santo Domingo and Carthagena. They also show an iguana, an alligator and a flying fish. None of these maps is sewn within the pamphlet but all are contained in a small accompanying pouch. [37]

A tract from an official source justifies the seizing of ships at Lisbon, as they supplied wheat to the Spaniards. This piece of literature issues from the presses of the royal printer, Christopher Barker. It has a vignette on the title-page and bears the arms of England on the verso. It informs the royal subjects of the success of the Drake-Norris expedition to Lisbon. It also aims at justifying the action of the English captains to the Germanic Hanseatic League as sixty ships of theirs were also involved. This piece of propaganda is therefore conceived for national rejoicing and international justification. [38]

One of the most memorable incidents among the skirmishes against Spanish power is the taking of the Great Carrack, off the Azores, in 1592. Its narrative appears both in Hakluyt and in Purchas. The feat is also related in the **Sea-mans Triumph**, 1592. The title-page could illustrate any sea-fight. The contents of the pamphlet are fascinating, though the anti-Spanish sentiment and the feeling against the rival Portugal are somewhat confused. It tells us how Frobisher and Hawkins took the Madre de Dios, an enormous Portuguese ship, that contained, so the tract tells us, up to six or seven hundred passengers and was bringing back considerable riches from India. The pamphlet praised the English for their humanity to their foe. For whoever reads between the lines, this means, contrary to the attitude the Spanish or the Portuguese would have had towards the English in similar circumstances. After having overcome the crew of the ship and captured the remaining living, the humane English admiral sends over his personal surgeon to nurse the wounds of the survivors. [39]

The opposition of the kind-hearted Englishman to the Spanish blood-thirsty brute is part of the tradition transmitted by the Black Legend. The suggestion that the Spaniards are even worse than the Infidels is made clear in the relation of the travels of Richard Hasleton. Delivered from the Turks and made a prisoner by the Spanish, he has to bear all the tortures of the Inquisition. He admits, however, that those are only applied to him after he has made an attempt at evasion. But he spares none of the gruesome details. [40] Therefore, according to the Black Legend, England always appears as the poor innocent victim of Spanish foul play. Any attack that England initiates is but fair reprisal against past Spanish malevolence. The taking of the Madre de Dios is not an isolated incident but one of the most glorious.

Few pictorial narratives of sea-fights against Spain succeed this feat. Apart from an affray off the shores of America [41] most illustrated pamphlets concern events of the past. Drake is the great hero. Two pamphlets appear in Stuart times, possibly to remind the new dynasty of the old feud. One is written by his nephew, [42] the other by his chaplain. [43] Both illustrations are similar in spirit and design, but the second is superior in technique. A bust of Drake, in three quarters face, shows him with his left elbow leaning on a table covered with instruments of navigation. His right arm rests on a two hemisphere map of the world, similar to those made by Mercator. This map is dotted to indicate the course of the voyages of the great navigator. Top right, the hand of God emerges from the clouds of glory and with a celestial rope guides Drake's boat around the world. This replica of the larger map on a smaller scale rests on Drake's coat of arms. In the second illustration engraved by Crispin Van Passe, the face and the pointed beard of the voyager show greater sharpness and realism. **The world encompassed by Drake** also contains a planisphere engraved by Robert Vaughan. While the illustrations contain no satirical attack against the Spaniards, the contents stress the hostility of the two countries and praise the numerous defeats imposed by Drake on the enemy. [44] (Plate 30)

Another typical feature of the anti-Spanish literature of the time, is the stress on the inequality of the fight between gigantic Spain and puny England, echoing the Biblical encounter between small David and huge Goliath.

The natural conclusion is that God is on the side of Protestantism against Catholicism. [45] Needless to say, Spain always bears all the blame. [46] This was good propaganda, both partisan and prejudiced.

Toward the end of the sixteenth century, anti-Spanish propaganda returns to an earlier theme--the war in Flanders. The interest in sea-fights was waning. The action was now on land and the attention of the English reverted once again to continental Europe.

In order to understand the conflict in the Netherlands, we must revert to earlier history. Historians seem to consider that the long warfare in Holland is largely due to the imbalance of power, and the changes in European alliances. Charles V had counted on England, Spain, and the Netherlands remaining allies. After the death of Mary Tudor, Philip II, rebuffed by Elizabeth, is forced to marry a French Princess. The treatise of Cateau-Cambrésis strengthens the relationship with Italy and estranges him from Northern Europe. France and England, intimidated by the proximity of such a powerful country, encourage the revolt of the Netherlands. To crown it all, Philip II sends over to the Netherlands governors whose authoritarianism and lack of sensitivity to the needs of the natives are astonishing. Cardinal de Gravelle, and after him the Duke of Alba, who lacked diplomacy though he shone in the arts of war, both set the country ablaze. [47]

One way of sapping the power of Spain is to encourage the Netherlands to gain their independence from Spain. In the midst of the sixteenth century, England sends some thoughtful pamphlets to convince the Dutch of their right to freedom and of the staunch friendship of their sister across the North Sea. To return the compliment, Philip of Spain sends over tracts to incite the English Catholics to sedition. [48]

Illustrated propaganda written against the Spanish domination in the Netherlands becomes more frequent at the turn of the century. Then Elizabeth sends over Sir Francis Vere to take an active part in the fights in Brabant. [49] Hence, in brief, there appears a narrative of the battle of Tournai in 1597. The brother of Sir Philip Sidney, Sir Robert Sidney, fights there. [50] A vignette tries to represent the glorious victory over the Spanish troops. One also finds within the same pamphlet an account of the pacification in France and of the attempt to pacify the Netherlands. The latter illustration is far the more interesting. [51] William Barley published some news from the Netherlands and pitied the state of dereliction in which the war had left her. At the back of the title-page, a crude picture of a burgomaster has been printed. [52]

The woodcut illustrating **A true coppy**, 1598 warrants lengthier comments. It describes the events taking place in the Low Countries from 1594, written top left, to 1598. Two circles, like the rims of a pair of spectacles, in the upper part of the woodcut denounce Spain, the arch-deceiver. The lower part attacks those provinces that treated with the enemy. Top left, the Stadtholder of Holland is attached to the pillar of Inquisition. The links that bind him are tightened by a monk, while the Duke of Alba, sword in hand, tests the firmness of the knots by which the prisoners are tied. Around the circle is the inscription: "the mouse with his gnawing teeth doth free the lion", a reminder of the fable of Aesop. Top right, the prediction has materialized and the freed lion confronts Philip II. Deceitful Philip, obeying the orders of the Pope, keeps a collar of captivity hidden behind his back, whereas he openly holds out an olive-branch, the emblem of peace. The wise lion is not taken in, which is explained in the inscription: "The Lyon being at libertie will weare a Collar no more."

Immediately below, one sees two proofs of Spanish double-dealing: on the left a girl is buried alive in Brussels in 1597. On the right the Armada occurs precisely at a time when peace negotiations were in process. The woodcut is not realistic since Holland is represented on the left of England, but it is symbolical. Last, the lower center of the picture shows a nice Dutch father accompanied by his two children, meeting the Janus-faced representative from the subdued provinces. The latter holds out an olive branch, but hides a sword behind his back. From the clouds of glory, God points out an accusing finger at the treacherous provinces. (Plate 49) This woodcut sums up in all points the Black Legend: Spain and her friends are hypocritical and cruel tyrants, paid by the Pope.

When the attention of the English public turns towards the Thirty Years War, anti-Spanish propaganda becomes more sporadic. A new swirl of hatred occurs at the time of the negotiations for the Spanish marriage between Charles, Prince of Wales, and the Infanta of Spain. The failure of these negotiations, re-awakens the pamphleteers. We have seen, in the section on anti-governmental propaganda, that some of the tracts of Thomas Scott showed how diffident he was about the Anglo-Spanish attempt at rapprochement. [53] The part we now want to deal with appears as the second section of **Vox Populi.** It is a satire of the Spanish count which is addressed to Frederick and Elizabeth of Bohemia. On the title-page, the Spanish ambassador stands near his chair which has a hole in the seat, one of the common jokes about the count whose bladder was not as resistant as that of a Falstaff. We see him on top sitting in a sedan, pulled by animals, whose long ears are no doubt those of donkeys. He wears a wide head-dress, and an ample cloak lined with fur, and carries a staff. In the edition of 1624, two additional engravings are to be found. The first represents the Spanish Parliament in session. Two crowns rest on the table which are coveted by the devil with the hideous smile who stays in the background. The Parliament seems to be in a turmoil and the devil himself scratches his head as his plans have failed. Charles and Buckingham, full of anger, left Spain, shaking the dust off their feet.

In the second engraving, the council of Jesuits, monks and priests are sitting in England, wondering how they can help the cause of Catholicism. Although the devil is not present, the association of thought from the Parliament to the council can easily be made. [54]

Despite the vigilance of the Crown, the Globe opens its doors to one of Middleton's plays, **A Game at Chess,** on the sixth of August 1624. It holds the stage for nine days and then is suppressed by public authority and on the request of the Spanish ambassador. What is surprising is that it should have been played at all. Some really powerful person must have protected Middleton, since three illustrated editions of the play are now extant, all of which have intaglios as their title-page. The first and second editions bear the same title-page. The etching is divided in two sections: in the upper one, eight characters are sitting around a chess board. In the lower part the main protagonists in the game appear: the fat Bishop (alias Dominis), the Black Knight (Gondomar) and the White Knight (Charles).

The third edition purports to be printed in Leyden. In

the lower part of the picture only the fat Bishop and the Black Knight are left. Are they enlarged because of the composition of the print or are they allegorically fatter? We cannot tell. We shall not enter into the details of this exciting play. Let is suffice to say that the reading of it provides us with most of the components of the Black Legend. And yet each of the protagonists of the episode of the Spanish marriage appears exhibiting the main features of his character. [55]

The last etching worthy of analysis represents the convent of the English Nuns at Lisbon, famous in England for its debauchery and hypocrisy, which is not true of the College of Jesuits in Rome. The picture is divided and subdivided. In a, b, and c, a nun is going to confession. In d, the grill separating the sister from the father confessor is lifted and they go arm in arm towards the more intimate recesses of the monastery. In f, they kiss and fornicate whereas in g, a nice meal is being prepared to enable the lovers to regain strength. In i, one of the monks pours a barrel of gold coins into the cellar of the monastery. The contents of the pamphlet mock the so-called spirit of chastity and poverty as practiced by religious orders and especially by those in Spain (again we have a confusion between Spain and Portugal). Similar criticism will appear in the satires addressed to the whole Roman Catholic world, as will be seen later. [56]

If one is to compare the number of pamphlets dealing with anti-Spanish propaganda, those referring to the rest of Europe are hardly worth mentioning.

The ambiguous feelings between France and England leave us with very little illustrated documentation. Here Henry of Navarre holds the scene. During his reign, favorable to the Catholics, though not adverse to the Protestants, six illustrated English pamphlets are published. The first praises his victory against the leaguers and the Duke of Parma at St. Denis in 1590. The illustration of the siege of Paris undertaken by the King, Monsieur de Chatillon, and Turenne appears on a folding sheet sewn within the pamphlet. Two monks and a priest are executed for their treachery to the king. St. Denis is delivered to the mercy of the king who will afterwards establish his headquarters there. One sees the fortifications of Paris, military tents pitched around the capital, the threatening guns. In the distance the Ile de France displays its windmills and its small villages. At the bottom of the picture, the Seine, hardly bigger than the smallest of streams, passes calmly by. [57]

The next event illustrated in England is the war of Piedmont; there the Huguenots led by Henry of Navarre are opposed to the Duke of Nemours helped by Philip II of Spain. England is particularly eager to see France free from any Spanish domination.

Two pamphlets refer to this historical happening. **The troubles of Geneva,** 1591, the first and the more interesting of the two, contains a lettered map in <u>sig</u>. B.2. Since no comment about these letters can be found in the text, one can only assume that the map was printed either for a foreign press or for a book and was reused for the pamphlet. It marks fairly accurately the location of the disputed towns: Geneva on Lake Leman and the <u>bailliages</u> of Thonon, Ges and Ternier, which had been restored to the Duke of Savoy by the Lords of Berne in 1567. The pamphlet blames the Duke of Savoy and praises the citizens of Geneva for their courage in putting up a hard fight. The second tract, in 1601, extolls Henry IV for his victory at the fort of Mont-Millan. The title-page woodcut shows a street in what could be any town.

Three other pamphlets concern the reign of Henry IV, King of France. On the title-page of the news of his coronation, published in 1594, he appears in a medallion. [58] The two other pamphlets deal with his tragic end and with the tortures inflicted upon his murderer, Ravaillac. [59] The English take as much interest in this king as they did in the Stadtholder in Holland who was a champion of Protestantism. The convictions of the French king are somewhat different since he converts to Catholicism for reasons of state. Yet with all his might, he defends the oppressed Huguenots and grants them their liberty in worship. For the first time, England does not fear her rival on the other side of Calais. But the fact that within half a century, two chiefs of state were murdered, one Protestant and the other favorable to the new form of Christianity, shocked the minds of the Elizabethans who believed in the divine right of kings. [60]

As a sign of the alteration of the governmental policy towards Spain, the official press issued **A Congratulation to France upon the happy alliance with Spaine,** displaying a face of the new king of France in a medallion. Whether this piece of news would have been welcome to the people seems fairly doubtful and the picture of the new king was more likely to be spat upon than admired for his friendliness with Spain, the enemy. But the king thought otherwise.

The brochures give a fairly accurate idea of the relationship between England and the Low Countries. We have seen England as their staunch political supporter against Spanish domination. [61] This sympathy does not diminish in the early seventeenth century. **Strange Newes from Antwerp,** appears in 1612 [62] and **A vision or dreame contayning the whole State of the Netherland warres,** in 1615. It assumes that the new phase of war waged in the North is a consequence of the previous conflict between Spain and the Netherlands. This time the enemy could be considered to be the emperor, because although the king of Spain waged the war, the emperor gave his approval and encouragement to Philip

II. Underneath the title a monk, holding up an olive branch, keeps a whip hidden behind his back. He tries to catch the bridle of the horse, but the horse, having thrown off the rider, gambols in freedom and taunts him with the words: "Who wants to ride me?"

Political friendship between England and the Netherlands is also marked by common naval exploits. We have already seen how opportune the Dutch intervention was at the time of the Armada. Another joint effort occurred, for the attack on Saintes Maries was jointly undertaken by four English pinnaces and one ship from Amsterdam. Facing the title-page is a plan of the fortifications of the island, as they are attacked by the allied ships. [63] Therefore the political friendship between the two countries is distinguished by their common hatred of Spain.

Tracts also clearly exhibit economic and colonial rivalry. Had there not been the common danger of Spain, they might indeed have been enemies. [64] In 1598, **The four Hollanders** depict a skirmish at Bantam, in the East Indies, between an English ship and several Dutch ships. A map, facing p. 17, shows the geographical position of Bantam divided by a river with an extremely difficult bar to be overcome by visiting ships. One also notes its fortifications and the naval skirmish off its coasts. A map of St. Helena displays cuts of the east side and of the west side of the island. Coins are represented in another picture. This informative pamphlet has a propagandist value: it aims at persuading popular opinion of the danger of Dutch colonialism for English economy.

The peak of the colonial conflict occurs at Amboyna in 1624. The East India Company has a tract published four times about this unfortunate event. The last three editions include, facing the title-page, a cut borrowed from Ambroise Paré's works. It shows the various tortures that were alleged to have been inflicted on the English. The prisoner is attached to a plank supported by a trestle. One man pierces his liver with a dagger. Two children heat his feet with a torch and a candle, while two men do the same with his armpits. Another man is approaching and is about to pierce the other side with a spear. At the very bottom of the cut one distinguishes the railing of a jail from which other prisoners are forced to witness what happens to their companion. [65]

Propaganda, for England, sometimes consists in stressing the nation's own superiority. This is the subject of Edward Pellham's tract on fishing in Greenland. The English survive where the Dutch did not. The English resistance and bravery are subtly extolled in comparison with that of the Dutch, who had been caught by the ice in the same place, in 1596. Within the pamphlet there is an intaglio map which shows the coasts of Greenland as they were known at the time, and the potentialities for fishing and hunting. (Plate 34)

Five pictures on each side illustrate whaling and hunting the walrus. They can be read from left to right and from top to bottom, in order to give us the whole story. A comparative study of both animals shows us that a whale measures about sixty feet in length and a walrus is comparable in size to a steer. In order to catch and kill the whale with a harpoon, men leave the main ship and get into dinghies. They circle the mammal and the harpoon is thrown as strongly as possible. Then the dinghies haul the whale up to the vessel; there it is skinned and cut, as it still floats on the sea; fat is brought to the shore and melted into oil. Oil is then loaded in barrels on the trawler. Finally the fishermen work on the whale-bones. The last two pictures show the hunting of the walrus with a spear and a tent bubbling with activity. Right at the bottom of the map, bear shooting is presented. Side-arms are only used in a defensive way to enable the marksman to come sufficiently close to the bear, so as not to miss it. [66]

The interest shown by the English in the Thirty Years War was at least equal to their passionate concern at the time of the Armada. The rivalry between the Catholic Ferdinand of Styria and the Protestant Frederick, Count Palatine, for the throne of Bohemia degenerates into a war involving the whole of Germany, and later most of Europe. [67] England was expected to side with Frederick because he was a Protestant and because he had married the daughter of James I, Elizabeth.

The underground stream of the proto-Protestant spirit in England that ran from the Lollards onwards, combined with the spate of anti-Spanish hatred, made the people passionately interested in the development of the war. In 1620, John Taylor's **An English-mans love to Bohemia** expresses the national joy and impatience at preparing to help Frederick. The woodcuts on the title-page and on its verso probably come from one larger wood block cut in half, since the frame in both cases occupies only three quarters of the picture. They show a military march, with marksmen, musicians and halberdiers. Gustavus Adolphus's intervention on the side of the Protestants, fills the people with joy. He is a good warrior and his victory against the imperial army led by Tilly is celebrated by Butter and Bourne, two new-fashioned pamphleteers whose journalistic ideas were not always appreciated by the king and the censorship. After many problems with the authorities, they succeed in establishing the ancestor of the modern newspaper, a weekly called The Swedish Intelligencer, and their affairs prosper. The first issue is illustrated by a beautiful engraving of the king of the Swedes by G. Mountain. The king rides his rearing horse, while in the distance, a battle rages. [68] This beautiful etching has one weakness: it does not illustrate the new military techniques used by Gustavus Adolphus, particularly the thinning out of the army into a line only three or four soldiers deep. Other pamphlets are issued, giving news from Holland, [69] and England's heart echoes the cries and groans from Germany. The Protestant spirit is set aflame by means of the press and indignation against the Catholics scales the peak. The Catholic soldiers ravage the country like the ten biblical curses against Egypt in the time of the captivity of the Israelites. May they be cursed in turn! [70] (Plate 50)

* * * * * * *

Political propaganda consisted in praising the sovereign and the home regime, in eulogizing one's allies and painting one's enemies in somber hues. Anti-establishment propaganda uses more devious stratagems: it praises the king for what it puts him under pressure to do; it flatters popular opinion so far as it differs from the king's; or it attacks the courtiers to sap the diplomatic efforts of the Crown. It does not as yet openly rebel against the person of the king, nor attack the idea of the divine right of kings. Political propaganda, whether governmental or anti-governmental uses persuasion and dissuasion.

Though politics and religion are very much linked in the sixteenth and seventeenth centuries, the illustrated pamphlets that deal with specifically religious themes use mainly dissuasive propaganda. They appeal to the aggressive, vengeful spirit of the nation. Because of censorship, our view is warped into taking, most of the time, the point of view of the Church of England and, in particular, that of the high church tradition from Andrewes to Laud. Apologetical works, previously referred to will not be considered in this section. [71] Here we are mainly concerned with satire.

The bulk of religious propaganda, with its political undertones or overtones, can be divided into three unequal sections. Anti-Catholic propaganda has the lion's share. Towards the end of the century the satires are directed more specifically against the Jesuits, whereas previously the Pope, the priests and the religious orders were all hit with the same stone. Around this time, there are many Jesuit priests sent over by Cardinal Allen from the College of Jesuits in Rome to evangelize England, who die as martyrs of the faith. At the same time Elizabeth, weary of religious indiscipline passes an act against all dissenters, whether Catholic Recusants or Separatists.

Anti-Separatist and anti-Puritan satire, at least as far as its expression in the printed material is concerned, occupies a much smaller space. It began in the theatre, but at the end of the old century and the beginning of the new, the divisions among the Protestants of England are no longer hushed up.

Towards the middle of the seventeenth century attacks against the Roman trend of Anglicanism start being voiced. The Puritan party is gaining in the House of Commons and William Laud becomes more and more unpopular as he encourages the use of Roman ceremonial in the service. The fight between the last two tendencies will hold the stage in the illustrated popular literature of the middle of the century, from 1640 onwards.

We have seen that anti-Catholic propaganda flourished slyly in sensational literature [72] and in anti-Spanish tracts. [73] Therefore we shall dwell no further on these categories. In what follows we are concerned only with tracts directly attacking the Pope or the Jesuits.

A number of constant features can be discerned in anti-papal iconography over the hundred years that separate the Reformation in England from the rebellion fomenting in 1640. These follow almost to the letter the advice given by Cotton to Henry VIII in **A discourse touching the reformation of the lawes of England.** [74] The satire is not directed against an individual but against the office of the papacy and therefore ideograms more than realistic delineation of persons and circumstances will be used. Religious propaganda although first issued from the royal presses, gradually passes into the hands of private citizens. The Protestant spirit is so deeply ingrained in the popular mind that a reversion to Catholicism in royal circles meets with great unpopularity in the seventeenth century. England was indoctrinated beyond return. [75]

The Pope is therefore represented in the pamphlets according to the fourfold medieval interpretations of the Scriptures as expounded in Cassian's **Collationes.** If we are to apply these interpretations to the Protestant satirical spirit, our guess is the following. The historical Pope is the bishop of Rome; according to allegory he is the Pharaoh of Egypt; his anagogical representation would be Satan's minion and his tropological implications would be found in his encouraging the English to deceit and lese-majesté.

Like the Pharaoh of Egypt, the Pope forces the people of God to idolatry whereas they are constantly robbed by his gluttony. He is the tyrant filling his flesh-pots with the riches of the poor. It is therefore the duty of the people to be disenchanted from his spell and to see him for what he is. [76] In

Garter's **The third new yeeres gift and the second Protest**, 1576, a herald blows the trumpet that declares the shame of the tyrant. On the verso of the title-page the same woodcut is found, whereas on the page facing it, the pope is seen presiding on the scaffold, maintained by murder. All weapons serve his ambition: spear, musket, flail or fire. With his triple tiara firmly fixed on his head, he is sitting on a fat cushion, with bulging belly, while four monks obey his blood-thirsty orders. [77]

The beginning and the endynge of all popery, or popish kingdom, 1583, by W. Lynne anticipates the downfall of the Pope, as the tyrant of this world and a servant to Satan. On the title-page the plump Pope is struck by the light of God. His horse has been brought down and he cannot rise again. Behind him, the cowardly cardinals and monks are taking to their heels. Within the pamphlet many vignettes are to be found. The constant theme is the association of the Pope and the devil, through the bestiary. The story is told almost like a _fabliau_. The Pope gives money to the bears, symbols of the cruelty of the Evil Spirit. The Holy Spirit watches him. [78] The second vignette uses the lily flower of France to overthrow the crowned eagle (the head of the Holy Roman Empire). God judges him severely as His hand, emerging from a tree orders the Pope to be devoured by wolves. Later the pontiff is shown with one hand strangling the crowned eagle, while the other keeps the French rooster at a distance with a satanic fork. On _sig_. E the Pope meets with the devil under a tree. The latter gives him his orders written on a scroll. [79] The next image displays the Pope carrying the fasces. He blesses the _Agnus Dei_, carrying a sword in his mouth. From Satan he receives the keys to the kingdom of this world. (Plate 51)

Since his covenant with the devil, the Pope, holding the keys, keeps the serpent under his pontifical vestments. With the help of the snake and that of France symbolized by the rooster, he puts the lamb into bondage. The eighth woodcut shows the Pope, keys and razor in hand, standing on the imperial crown. A wolf keeps the sword with the cruciform hilt in front of his eyes. But the angel withdraws the keys of power from the Pope who holds the fasces. At the Pope's feet, a peacock spreading out its tail, represents the vanity of the Roman Catholic Church.

But the Pope will not relinquish his temporal power. He surrounds himself with bears--princes and men-at-arms--to defend his realm. He keeps the Bible closed next to him, and forbids its reading by anyone but himself. But the unicorn (England) interferes to knock over the tiara. And yet the Pope is still surrounded by a king and a queen and one of the oxen that he yoked is looking at him with admiring eyes. On G ii, the Pope is attacked by a she-bear, nursing her babies: the ox of the preceding images was metamorphosed and, tired of being exploited, turns against his oppressor. On <u>sig</u>. G iii, the wolf abandons the Pope and takes away the keys of the kingdom of the world. The fifteenth and last vignette shows his "holiness" sitting naked on his empty chest, as pardoning money obtained from indulgences no longer flows into it, while a commoner is mocking him.

A summary of the themes of the woodcuts illustrating this tract gives us most of the usual accusations against papacy in the sixteenth century. The Pope instead of being the spiritual leader of Jerusalem, prefers the flesh pots of Egypt. Ordained to serve the will of the Lord, he chooses to satisfy his own ends. Even so he turns against the Lamb to embrace the laws of the devil. He therefore is a traitor to Christ and a fiend. It is fair that having sold the cause of God in order to satisfy his own cupidity, he should not only be deprived of his spiritual leadership and unmasked, but also punished by what hurts most this man of the world: the deprivation of his earthly goods, that he usurped and kept, through avarice. [80] **A little treatise**, 1548, has a woodcut designed by Hans Holbein, expressing the anger of Christ against those who let their sheep be devoured by the wolves, while they are attending to their own carnal dissipations, so mercenary are their souls. [81]

Another important tract, by Th. Williamson, **The Sword and the Spirit**, 1613, shows at the back of the title-page, the author, writing in his library. On his table there lie the hour-glass and a skull, two emblems of the flight of time and <u>memento mori.</u> A shelf supports the books that guide his scholarship. Page 4 gives a view of the printing press and of the working typographer. Later, ten illustrations are devoted to papal satire. In the first, God, the judge, weighs the Bible on one side of the balance and the icons and trinkets produced by man on the other side. Garter had already listed those in **A new yeares gifte**, 1578: indulgences, crucifix, beads, bells, cherubs, sword, candelabra, tiara, monk, bishops' mitres, and cardinals' hats, keys, medals. . . . All these do not weigh anything as compared to the Scriptures.

The second picture shows the sacrifice of the Mass, much criticized by the Protestants, whether they spoke of consubstantiation like the Lutherans or of memorialism like the Zwinglians as opposed to the Catholic transubstantiation. The Pope is then seen in sumptuous garb and adored as if he were a god, thus encouraging idolatry. In the fourth emblem the Pope holds one of his bastards in his arms, the fruit of his coupling with the wife of the devil; indeed, chastity was hardly the forte of the Renaissance popes. The Pope should choose between the narrow path that leads to salvation and the broad highway of destruction that leads to the gates of hell, but he no longer does.

In opposition to popery is the Word delivered by the

preacher who holds the attention of the congregation which crowds in to hear him preach. Room has to be made around the pulpit for them to sit on the floor. On F 4 of this book with double pagination, the devil spurts out of the mouth of a man who had laughed at preaching. P. 79, James I, overthrows the Pope, and crushes him with his heels, as he would a serpent. The ninth picture, inspired from "The Book of Martyrs" of Foxe, shows an auto-da-fé. To this Catholic act of violence, the English Protestants reply by beheading a traitor and exposing his head on a pike on the ramparts of the town, as an intimidating measure. All these cuts, probably made out of fine wood are remarkable in their neatness of design and in the quality with which they are printed. The last picture sums up accurately the position of the state in matters of religion.

Pamphlets issued from Spain and from Italy as well as from the presses of Douai encourage Catholics to revolt. The government is acutely aware of the danger and the fear of rebellion sometimes becomes an <u>idée fixe</u>. Walsingham, for instance, cannot rest at peace while the Queen of Scots lives in the prison of England, as the residual political hope of some Catholics. With his numerous spies, he knows how to trap the impulsive Mary in his toils. Aware of the importance of popular opinion, he denounces the genuine or the contrived conspiracies in which the Catholic queen is supposed to have had a hand, and produces genuine and faked letters from Mary Stuart. Books have been written in which Mary appears either as the villain or the saint. She is likely to be neither, but pays the toll of circumstances and of her own impulsiveness. Anti-Catholic feeling is kept alive by the news of the conspiracies of Ridolphi [82] and of Babington. These and the Powder Plot under James I, keep the minds of the people in a state of uneasiness.

Catholics therefore, are the cankers in the English rose, as they are pictured on the back of the title-page of **Certain very proper . . . similies,** by Fletcher. Catholicism is a tree of vices which the angel of Truth is hacking down. Justice, a wise old man, endeavors to overthrow him who reigns on top, a monster, half-man, half-serpent. The seven deadly sins are inscribed on the trunk of the tree. On each branch caterpillars with the heads of men are creeping, each representing some vice. From the left to the right the following are to be seen: pawnbroking and usury, extortion, blasphemy and perjury, ambition, scorn and disobedience; self-love crowns the top, then infidelity, simony, false prophecy and ignorance, vain-glory, excess, false seeming and curiosity, and last idolatry, heresy, hypocrisy and dissimulation. The text in front of the tree refers to the Gospels of Matthew and Mark and the parable of the withered fig-tree.

In 1611 there appears a tract praising the generosity

and magnanimity of Elizabeth and James I towards the Catholics, as opposed to the cruelty of the Catholic queen, their predecessor. The contrast in the text is echoed by self-explanatory pictures. One woodcut is inspired from the "Book of Martyrs", showing the martyrs of the Church of England dying on the stake. Another illustration pictures the Pope riding on a hydra-lion with seven crowned heads, who orders his assistants to go and kill the prince. Out of all the mouths, frogs, diabolical animals, escape, for their words are those of the evil spirit. Both pictures are cleverly chosen, as both show that, if some cases of Catholic persecution can be found in England, it is more gentle than any of the penalties inflicted on the Protestants. Besides, this is a case of self-defense: Catholicism must be hindered from killing, or worse, damning, simple souls, and the sovereign must be protected. The Church of England showed that it could use as clever propaganda as the Inquisition of Spain. [83]

The animals representing the Pope are derived from the fabliaux tradition, from puns or from the mixture of western, Byzantine, Sassanid, and African traditions that form medieval iconography. **Renard,** the fox has a prize place in the first half of the sixteenth century. The Pope is a sly, and unfortunately, clever, blood-thirsty being like in **The rescuinge of the Romish fox, otherwise called the examination of the hunter,** 1543. [84]

After 1570 and the issuing of the bull of excommunication, the Pope is represented as a bull or a calf. The pun was a facile one. [85] Nor did it fade out quickly. The Pope is either an ass, a bull or a calf. In 1579 **Of two wonderful popish monsters witnessed by Melanchthon and Luther,** produces two German pictorial satires of some elaboration. [86] The ass version of the bishop of Rome, adds cupidity to the implied stupidity of the stubborn beast, since one of its hooves is changed into a griffin's clawed paw. His sexual organs, well in evidence, are turned towards the back, a sign of lechery and hypocrisy. A rooster projecting from the rounder face of the devil figures his lower parts and the symbolism hardly veils the physiological reality. The ass is standing in front of the Vatican, with its flag up. The other woodcut shows a monk as a calf, bursting out with fat and as monstrous as the ass, its spiritual leader.

Although most of the anti-Catholic caricatures of the seventeenth century aim at a higher level of satire, animals still appear. **A straunge Foot Post with a Packet full of strange Petitions,** 1613, refers to a 1592 papist plot in Scotland. On A i^v, a bird looking like an ostrich is carrying a key in its bill, its head turned towards a horsehead lying behind. [87]

As a whole the representations of the Pope in the seventeenth century tend to be less allegorical and more historical, anagogical and tropological. One of the interesting pictures we have found is the transformation of a printer's mark into an anti-Catholic satire on the title-page of **The Parricide Papist**, 1606. [**88**] The printer's mark has become the whore of Babylon, with a crown on her head, her hair badly groomed and falling at random, while her nakedness is covered by a single fig-leaf. [**89**]

Considering the frequency of anti-popish publications, four main events seem to have set the presses going: the excommunication bull in 1570, the Armada in 1588, the following reprisals from England, and the Powder Plot in 1605. [**90**] To those can be added the attempts at a Spanish marriage that delays the involvement of James the First in the Thirty Years War. Under the pressure of all the forces of papism gathered against her, England, with the help of God, boasts about being unchanged, immota, true to herself. In 1617, **Balme from Gilead to recover conscience**, by the Puritan Samuel Ward, shows the Pope, the Jesuits and the devil gathered in a circle to blow the wind of revolt on England, in the center. But the country remains insensitive to the infernal commotions and remains unchanged. This piece of work was so popular that it was published six times between 1616 and 1628. The same year, a similar picture appears in Vicars's **Mischeefes mysterie**. Who inspired whom? This question remains unanswered. (Plate 72)

A new outburst of anti-Catholic feeling is recorded through the printing press, as the Anglican worship reverts to the Roman Catholic pomp, under the Early Stuarts through the influence of Andrewes and Laud. [**91**] The building of the two royal Catholic chapels at Oatlands and at Somerset House is most unpopular among the people, who saw in them a betrayal of Protestantism. [**92**]

But the anger of the Puritans reaches its peak when Cosin issues the Anglican equivalent to a Catholic Book of Hours, **A collection of private devotions**, 1627. The Calvinists remaining in the Church of England protested violently against this around 1627-1628. Henry Burton's **The baiting of the Pope's Bull**, reminds the king of the anathema cast on his grand-mother's cousin, Elizabeth; it attacks the devotional practices of Henrietta Maria and yet is dedicated to Charles I and to Buckingham. The title-page shows how Charles, like the unicorn, overthrows the Pope's tiara, a picture reminiscent of Lynne's **The beginning and endynge of all popery**, 1583, with is reedited the same year. Below the protagonists, a bishop reads the bull to the minority of English Catholics, whereas the Protestant majority kneels at the feet of the king, signifying their allegiance, and sing his praise. [**93**] A prelate absolves the Catholics from their oath to the king, as the poem facing the title-page indicates. A supposed letter from Urban VIII who issued the anathema against Elizabeth in **In Coena Domini**, alludes to the division within the Church of England. The Pope rejoices in seeing Charles more tolerant towards the Catholics since his marriage to a French princess. But he fears the Puritan faction eager to see all Catholics imprisoned.

Another Puritan sermon, **The White Wolfe**, also appears in the same year. It attacks the Arminianism growing within the Church of England. Facing sig. b, a woodcut showing the wolf in sheep's clothing expresses the fear of seeing the church of the bishops become Roman in disguise. The other, facing F 3, shows the wolf as he really is. It is up to the people of England to use their common sense and discrimination. There are two sorts of wolves, he says: the papists and the Arminians. [94] Beware of the false sheep. [95]

Needless to say, the Puritan attacks on the Arminian heresy within the Church of England do not stop in 1629. Henry Burton and William Prynne, among the most renowned, keep fighting though they venture their lives. However, only a few of their works are illustrated; three in Burton's [96] case and two in Prynne's. [97] A. Leighton denounces the episcopacy in a tract printed secretly. [98] Between 1620 and 1640 there is hardly any respite in the attacks of the Puritans against Arminianism.

One could add to those works that have already been quoted, a sermon by Walter Sweeper, **Israels Redemption by Christ**, 1622. E. Goodman, in **Hollands Leaguer**, 1622, compares the Church of the bishops to a London whore, as the Roman Church had been compared to the whore of Babylon. Hollands Leaguer was one of those famous red light houses abounding in the suburbs of London. Though besieged by all, Dona Britannica remains mistress of her own house. This is an allusion to the Montaigu affair, which the Parliament had initiated. Manwaring, Montaigu, and Sibthorpe, finding strong support in Laud, finally win the case. The illustration shows the house.

The previously devious attack on Laud becomes direct in 1640, in **Fortunes Tennisball** which criticizes those who prefer their own glory to the cause of truth. The work closes with some satirical epitaphs against some of the dignitaries of the realm. Laud's reads thus:

> Paint Pope and divell, make this stranger laugh;
> Mix his own shame and ther's his epitaph.

In comparison, the attacks against Separatism and Puritanism seem relatively scarce and mild. In fact, illustrated pamphlets give us an extremely small portion of the subject that was so popular on the stage. We find only three pamphlets on the theme.

The first is addressed to the Anabaptists who had found a notorious refuge in Münster in Westphalia. The second is part of Taylor's social satire in **The water-cormorant**, in which the Separatist, the Anglican clergyman, or the judge are railed at, in turn. The third, more violent, foreshadows the pamphlets of the forties: **A whip for the back of a backsliding brownist.** There are also, of course, those indirect attacks by means of the "strange news" like **A true relation of a most barbarous and most creuell Murther,** 1633.

Why, then this relative silence of the press? It is probably due to the desire on the part of the Church, not to overstress the growing division within the reformed Church. What was printed could very well slip abroad and give evidence against it. It was, of course, a common opinion, but news went slowly and inaccurately, so that what was not in the press might be brushed aside as rumor or false or exaggerated report. To convince the English of the necessity of adhering to the Church of England and not to the new Calvinistic "fad", persuasive action is used. Cartwright and Wall are imprisoned, and the Separatists Barrow, Greenwood and John Penry are all hanged in 1593. When Cope and Morrice try to defend the Puritans in the House, they are put in jail. Later on under the Stuarts, Leighton, Prynne, Bastwick and Burton have their ears chopped off and the Puritan printer Lilburne is imprisoned. These were strong means of persuasion.

And yet the Puritans have many friends among the middle-class in London and the turn of the century and the seventeenth century see them growing in Parliament. To publicize too much the sternness of the Church of England might cut both ways and harm as much the persecutor as the dissidents. Hence Puritans might become martyrs dying for the faith, and the Church their oppressor. This surely is the feeling when in 1628, a ballad praises John Felton, the murderer of the Duke of Buckingham, instead of lamenting the victim, De Villiers. From 1624 to 1637 many edicts are issued against the freedom of the press, especially in religious matters. This, however, is to little avail, since 1641 will see the outburst of the quarrel between Arminianism and Puritanism, laid in front of the public's eyes.

Meanwhile only those of schismatic or Presbyterian tendencies or sympathies in the Church of England are vituperated in the press. In 1640 the ballad on the "backsliding Brownists" promises to thrash those Brownists that left England for Holland, which the woodcut humorously displays. **England's complaint against her adjoining neibours the Scots** is also illustrated though the cut is of no particular interest. The text protests against the belief of the Church of Scotland in the parity of ministers and in the priesthood of all believers and accuses the Scots of attempting a new Puritan "Powder Plot." This was bound to increase the tension between the two countries. [99]

The political and religious alliances of European countries occupy the foreground in most of the illustrated literature of the time; Catholicism, Arminianism, and Dissenting Protestantism are also one of the main concerns of the reading class. The pamphlets concerning the Turks, however, can be viewed as both religious and economic literature. Four of them illustrate the opposition of Christians and Infidels in the seventeenth century, the sixteenth century press being too involved in the dissensions within the Christian Church to consider the Moslems. Valesco's **News from Rome**, 1607, translated into English, shows on the title-page an army looking both ferocious and asinine; the woodcut is probably of Italian origin.

Jews and Turks, opponents who only share hatred against the Christians, are represented in the same way, with a turban, and present the same characteristics for the folklore of the time. They are both weird and sly. The Londoners could see them in the play acted by the company of the Queen, and read about them in **The travels of Three English Brothers.** Their ferocity in naval warfare appears in **A famous Victorie Atchieved in August last 1613.** The title-page woodcut illustrates a sea fight. The usual trend of military propaganda can be found: one reads that the Christians are all the more to be praised for their victory as they fought against the ferocious enemy, far superior in number to themselves.

Last but not least comes the relation of the tortures imposed on Christopher Angell by the Turks, which appears in 1617. Ch. Angell, a Christian Greek, prays God to protect him against the sadism of the infidels. The images in the pamphlet are extremely rough, designed as it seems by a clumsy child, technically some of the worst we have found. In sig. A 4, the victim is bound, hand and foot, to some frame-shaped stakes, as two Turks are preparing their sabres. At the end of the booklet, a small character shows a bigger man with the head crowned with thorns; probably a stylized depiction of Christ. The meaning is not clear, but it may refer to the common idea that being martyred is the supreme honor befalling a Christian, since this is the ultimate imitatio Christi. Within the text is a letter from Sultan Morat, swearing hatred to the King of Poland. It also gives a summary of the main encounters between the Turks and the Christians. A portrait of the Sultan is to be found, in intaglio, facing the title-page. It is the only good print in the pamphlet. According to common tradition, the Turks are even more perversely cruel than the Spanish Inquisitors. Indeed, though the latter belong to a cruel race and are the devil's advocates, yet as their religion has a common root with Protestantism in Christ, they cannot be quite as bad.

* * * * * * *

Compared to the two giants: political and religious types of propaganda, economic propaganda seems puny. Some tracts have already been considered among official propaganda. Insofar as eating fish is a means of keeping the navy busy and ready for any warfare, it partakes as much of political as of economic propaganda. [100] Others have already been described within foreign policy, especially those concerning Spain. [101] or with Holland. [102] Very little remains to be studied.

Another major worry of the Elizabethan times concerned the exportation of wheat. After a drought, or after the plague, the crop was generally meager. Yet profiteers still exported wheat from England, selling it to the highest bidder. Charles Fitz-Geffrey delivers and prints three sermons on the subject, stressing the importance of keeping a store of wheat in England and of burning the earth once the crop was in. **The curse of Corne-hoarders with the blessing of seasonable selling** shows a walled garden which four men had set aflame, thus destroying the vermin. [103]

Commerce and colonization inspire the illustrated literature from the last quarter of the sixteenth century on. In 1572, a letter and a map are published suggesting that Northern Ireland should be peopled with Englishmen who would till the ground. The map shows the shape of the country, its agricultural resources and its habitat. [104]

The acute awareness that England stifles within its own frontiers and the desperate need for expansion is at the origin of tracts in favor of colonialism. [105] Their illustration is usually fairly stilted: one or several ships serve as a vignette under the title. The text, however, varies from the sixteenth to the seventeenth century. The first texts tend to speculate, as they refer to the experience of other nations in colonialism, Spain leading the dance. The later texts draw conclusions from the English experience. [106] They appeal to the courage of the nobility, to the right of England to a colonial empire. This, so they affirm, is a good way of fighting the Spanish, of solving the problems of overpopulation in England, and of providing a market for its industry.

The sixteenth century tracts on the voyages of Hawkins, Drake and Gilbert in the West Indies mainly stress the anti-Spanish combat. [107] The Jacobean pamphlets insist on the necessity of finding new fishing-grounds in Newfoundland [108] and of founding an English colony where the motherland could export its manufactured products. Smith issued a pamphlet, published by mistake under the name of Watson, which draws its conclusions from the failure of the first English settlement in Virginia. [109] Curiously enough, the name Watson does not appear in the list of the colonists drawn in the works of Captain Smith, the initiator of the whole expedition, [110] unless this is an erroneous spelling of Th. Wotton, the surgeon. The failure of the English plantation is due more to their lack of organization than to the hostility of the aborigines. Indeed, the latter start by collaborating with them, rather than fighting them. But the Indians, fascinated by new tools, have an unfortunate tendency to hide them, thus causing disturbance for the new settlers. [111] Smith does not express any animosity against the Indians. The map accompanying the pamphlet was engraved by William Hole in 1606, though on top and left a vignette dated 1607 shows the king of Indians in council. Was the plate engraved at two different times? It seems so.

In 1618 the account of Raleigh's journey to Guyana is illustrated with his portrait. The narrative of the journey of this great promoter of English colonialism differs in tone from the previous pamphlet. The generation gap can be felt for Raleigh is once more looking for Eldorado. His techniques are those of the abhorred Spain: violence and pillage, whereas Smith aims at peace. Finally Raleigh, weakened by sickness, comes back to England, having failed. He entrusts the expedition to his Captain, Kemys. His arrival in England is greeted by the news that Spain, angry at the raid on San Thomas, has asked and obtained his head from James I. Meanwhile, Captain Kemys, ashamed at his lack of success had done away with himself. [112]

Colonial propaganda makes use of national pride and aggressiveness towards other European powers. Thus the relation of the journey of Cornelius Schouten is published to whet the English appetite for competition in naval matters. C. Schouten had reached the Pacific by sailing south of the Straits of Magellan as one can see on the small woodcut map illustrating the title-page. [113] Another devious way of prompting national initiative is to praise the success of the ancients or of the previous generations, as opposed to the passivity of the new generation. This "o tempora, o mores" method is used in the two tracts that commemorate the exploits of Drake against Spain and both bear the portrait of the national hero. [114] This is effective propaganda since the mind of the man of the Renaissance oscillated between two poles: the hope in progress, through science, and the feeling of inadequacy created by a longing for the past golden age.

Colonial propaganda is also diffused in the tracts of the Virginia Company bearing the seal of King James. (Plate 53)

Indeed, a charter is granted to them by His Majesty in 1606, revised in 1609 and later in 1612 when the king adds Bermuda to the possessions of the company. [115] Most of the pamphlets issued by the company are to inform their members on the state of the colony, to encourage the immigration of gentlemen and of scientists to Jamestown and to reassure the people on the welfare of their children.

The latter point deserves a brief explanation. The state, worried by the growing number of delinquent children who remained financially dependent upon their already poor parents, arranged to let the company take them over to the new settlement. In this way, the streets of London would be rid of possible evil-doers and the youngsters might get a new start in life. The company was to take them on the condition that when their apprenticeship was over they would each receive 15 or 25 acres of land. The company thus acquired cheap labor and to give land away was no problem since it was plentiful. Therefore, three lots of poor children were thus exported to Virginia, in 1619, 1620, and 1622. [116] **A Declaration of the State of the Colonie and Affaires in Virginia,** 1620, is published precisely at the time of this new experiment. It bears the seal of James I. If one believes statistics, many died on the way or when they reached the marshes of Virginia.

It seems that neither the Pilgrims that left for Massachusetts in 1620, nor the East India Company, made as many efforts to attract general attention and support as the Virginia Company did. The narratives proceeding from the East India Company appeal to the imagination and the epic sense of the readers of the time. They expect the readers' admiring contemplation of those travellers who dare face multiple obstacles; they hope for gratitude, but they do not ask for participation. The Virginia Company, on the other hand, wants people to be involved.

As to the settlement in Massachusetts, it is more due to the religious ardor of the Separatists than to the hope for a commercial enterprise. It proceeds from an elitist point of view. This land that they conquered would be the land of God's elect. Therefore the tracts proceeding from them are generally without illustration, and have religious contents, aimed at justifying their point of view. [117]

If we consider that many pamphlets were either omitted or mentioned briefly, because of the lack of interest of their illustration, there is no doubt that propaganda played a huge part in the popular literature of the time. If the sixteenth century gives us few illustrated tracts, the general state of the press is to be blamed. Whereas political and religious propaganda is well organized in the England of the sixteenth century, the seventeenth century sees the methodical arrangement of their economic and colonial counterparts. Thus the virtues of capitalism and of colonialism are hammered into the people's minds, a direct consequence of industrial development.

As to the quality of the illustration, it becomes more entertaining in the seventeenth century as the slight distortion of reality replaces the symbolic fable. Yet it also shows that tradition is dying out. The signs and symbols that made medieval manuscripts understandable are no longer grasped by most; and the allegorical world of faith is slowly dying out for the realistic world of scientific proof. The need to touch to believe is there as the new discoveries in the world of science and of geography tend to show that the old pictorial alphabet inherited from the forefathers is no longer adequate. So many things had changed within a century!

Political and religious propaganda first managed by the Crown, gradually shifts into private hands. When the Stuarts stopped the make-believe monologue from the Crown and its supporters to the people, personal initiative developed and limited freedom settled in. Thus the obduracy of the Stuarts deprived them of the support of the nation who, informed from other circles, were no longer systematically indoctrinated.

Thus gradually the press is freed and its role is enlarged. It becomes the publicizing organ of private individuals and mainly of colonialism and trade. As the faith in traditional sayings and images weakens and as new realities and enterprises come to change the policy of England, propaganda becomes more necessary in order to attune the mind of the people to the new music. The colonists are acutely aware of its role and use drawings and maps to dispel foreboding phantasms that would deter personal involvement in the expansion of the new world. Instead of the terrifying products of imagination, they know how to substitute slanted reality in which the worst features are carefully omitted. Its relative verisimilitude is likely to attract the curiosity of the most adventurous or the most radical.

Chapter VI

DAILY LIFE

Our concern is no longer with bishops and kings but with knights and pawns on the chessboard of daily life. This chapter will deal more with cabbages than kings, with gardens, houses and dress, and games like chess. Chapter VII will present the rainbow of society with its various vocations, while the last chapter will end in the clouds of heaven or amid the flames of hell, as it surveys the creeds and the credulity of the age.

In dealing with the everyday life of humanity the problems of its nature or its destiny are bracketed out in order to concentrate on life's daily worries, its occupations and its distractions. The woodcuts also show some permanent features such as the struggle against sickness and scourges, the friendship with domestic animals, and the fascination of public executions. They also reveal some changes proper to the evolution of any civilization in the areas of fashion, housing, furniture, transportation, the workmarket and the social ladder. Sociological changes are also mirrored in the pamphlets of our period.

Renaissance humanity is viewed from the traditional standpoint of seven ages. Dauncy's almanac for 1614 links the ages to the seven planets. Babies appear on several occasions; the idea is evoked by the cradle which the dame rocks in **The Maydens Crosse rewe**, 1540; the reality, as a picture of the grandson of James I reported in **News from the Palatinate** whom Peacham eulogizes in **Prince Henry revived.** Children often wear the fashionable lacy collars. They can also be found depicted in the news of monstrous and malformed births and murders of children. [1]

The lazy boy who has to be pulled by the ear to get him to go to school is shown beating a schoolmate or fighting over a ball as on the title-page of Nowell's **A catechisme.** Most frequently, he appears in the accounts of infanticide, as for example, in Yorkshire, when Master Calverley kills his wife and his two children. [2]

Lovers appear regularly in popular iconography. The Knight of Courtesy sighs for the Lady of Faguell without a trace of impropriety. He is a survival of the old school of courtly love. Some are more daring, hopping into ladies' beds or caught leaving their bedrooms. They do not linger in their mistresses' arms, because women, they think, are deceivers. [3] Obsessed and fickle, the lover romances all the fair ladies and wears the most extravagant clothes. He hails one of his numerous future conquests on the title-page of Thomas Brewer's **A knot of Fooles**, 1624. The serious lover, however, always aims at marriage; this is the subject of Robert Crofts's treatise, **The Lover**, 1638. On the contrary, Swetnam's advice to young and foolish men is never to meddle in marital matters and to give in only to irresistible carnal desire. [4] (Plate 74)

Soldiers answer the call to arms, and women value the combats that test the virility of their men. The **Geste de Guillaume** may be recalled: Guinevere would not open the gates to her husband fleeing from miscreants until he had sent them packing. **Frederyke of Jennen**, or horrific stories like **The martyrdom of Saint-George**, 1614, reveal the nostalgia of the public for derring-do. Sir Philip Sidney, poet and warrior, has the good manners to die on the battlefield. Webbe, the royal gunner, chases glory into the very mouth of the cannon. [5] Seventeenth century moralists and women both complain, that men are now cowards, thinking only of effeminate elegance instead of masculine war-games. [6] England under James I longs for peace, but not all Englishmen do so. Taylor, the water-poet, praises the merits of the soldier in the Thirty Years War in **An English-mans love to Bohemia**, like Dekker in **Warres, Warres, Warres**; detesting war, he yet honors the warrior. Thomas Heywood, in **The Iron Age**, recalls the heroic age when one woman, Helen, let loose the war between two peoples. [7]

The fifth stage of man's existence is more sedentary. He works in the city or in the fields, depending on his social status and educational training. With the exception of the apprentice, he will be considered in a later study of vocations. The sixth and the seventh ages are times of wisdom; conclusions drawn from both the mistakes and the successes of his life, man is gifted with prophesy, like John of Gaunt, who, on his death-bed, still advises Richard II. **Keepe within Compasse**, 1619, is the advice of a father to a son. [8] So is **The wise Vieillard**, 1621. Many other similar brochures flourish, showing wise old men sitting in their armchairs or at their studies. Such include John Taylor's **The Old, Old, Very Old Man**, 1635, the life of Thomas Par, who had reached the hoary age of 152 years, and **The phoenix of these late times, Or the life of H. Welby**, 1637. At a time when mortality was common, due to the general lack of hygiene, to wars and to epidemics, the sexagenarian was a rare phenomenon, while the centenarian was almost a miracle.

The deadliest enemy of our period was not the fire which burnt a village or a town like Cork in Ireland, nor the tempest that sank the ships, nor the floods in which men and beasts perished, nor the freezing cold, nor the comets, nor even the eclipses which spread fear. The terror of the Elizabethans and Jacobeans alike was the plague. As an ordinary plague, appearing sporadically, it affected a few; but as an epidemic, bubonic plague ravaged entire towns, where the density of population allowed it to propagate with the speed of a prairie fire. London, where both boats and rats disembarked, was decimated in this way. A number of proclamations on plagues witness to the panic of the inhabitants. [9] James I and Charles I renew the measures taken by Elizabeth: gathering funds to succor the affected city, appointing inspectors to count the dead and mark a blue or red cross on the doors of contaminated houses. Their statistics were verified by those of the pastors who had to bury the dead at night. Orders were strictly enforced, and anyone disobeying them would be imprisoned. [10]

The intent of the law was admirable, but its execution otherwise. Dekker devotes six pamphlets either in verse or in prose, or in a mixture of both, to this scourge; he observes the failures of magistrates, ministers and physicians, more concerned with their own than the general safety. [11] **A Rod for Run-awayes,** deals, in heroic style, with the battle of God against the people of London and warns deserters. (Plate 55) The title-page shows the country police trying to force people to return to London. Some runaways are on foot, while others are in carts or carriages. A 1630 broadsheet depicts rich people fleeing death in comfortable carriages, while the rest, in the background, leave on foot or on horseback. [12]

Many died on the way for the neighboring peasants resented the citizens carrying the contagion. Should the testimony of Dekker be insufficient, **A dialogue betwixt a Citizen and a poore Countrey man and his wife** is eloquent. On the title-page, the citizen approaches the cottage surrounded by a black fence. A white barrier blocks the entrance behind which the peasant woman invites him to enter. As for her husband, he pinches his nose to avoid the virus. [13]

The story runs as follows: a rich Londoner flees the plague and asks shelter of one of his tenants who cannot pay his rent. The tenant refuses to lodge the citizen because a neighbor lost his wife and two children who caught the plague from a rich old man he had lodged. A vigorous discussion ensues. The citizen insists that the plague kills animals but not good Christians. The peasant says he wants to keep his dog and suggests that only unbelievers want to flee London. Finally, the peasant agrees to feed him. At this point his wife appears, sees that he is rich, and for greed and charity prepares the straw bed for the citizen. The latter is happy to be lodged. The pamphlet concludes by encouraging the peasants to be charitable, but condemns the rich for deserting the towns and abandoning the poor to their tragic destiny. [14]

In **A Rod for Run-awayes**, Dekker proposes that the magistrates should fine the rich who abandon London to provide funds to help the poorer Londoners. Often, the poor living in the asylums and hospices had nothing to eat, because the staff had fled. The poorer shops remained open, while the apprentices and their masters died of hunger. [15] Henry Petowe, in **The Countrie Ague**, represents London as a woman ravished by sorrow, whose open arms welcome penitent deserters. The cut displays the walls and gates of London, St. Paul's Cathedral and the Thames.

In **The Wonderful yeare**, Dekker describes London in the time of plague with its streets strewn with aromatic herbs in the hope of avoiding the contagion, and its robbers of cadavers. **A Rod for Run-awayes** fails to reach the same heights of eloquence or depths of pathos. Restless bells toll for the dead, ceaseless like human sinning. [16] Not all suffer as a result of the plague. Apothecaries, physicians, butchers, cooks and gardeners thrive, for the doctors prescribe treatments with rosemary, juniper, absinthe, spices, emetics of ammonia, which display more their botanical than their medical knowledge. [17] The truth is acknowledged, at least in part, by Bradwell in saying that the plague of 1625 is incurable. However, he continues to give the old remedies.

There were many different kinds of plagues, although the word "plague" was applied to every epidemic, for example to the typhus of 1637-1638. The microbic plague was far less deadly than the viral plague. Dekker declares that more than 12,000 persons perished in London in less than six weeks and that more than 40,000 persons died in the epidemic of 1603. Preachers tried to console Londoners with the thought of joining God's elect in heaven. The law, however, forbade them to encourage their flocks to break the sanitary regulations or neglect medical remedies, under pain of imprisonment. [18] The desparate Londoners gathered in crowds, seeking comfort, at St. Paul's Cross, as can be seen on the title-page of Brewer's **The weeping lady**, 1625.

The obsession with death characterizing this period is due to its frequent recurrence in the plague. Death is more than an allegory; it is a too familiar daily companion. Still the allegory appears in all the pamphlets and broadsheets referring to the plague. It dances on the caskets, brandishing an arrow as on the frontispiece of Dekker's **A Rod for Run-awayes.** [19] It haunts the town, with its hourglass. [20] It walks on the tombs of the graveyards, carrying a coffin. [21] It warns the Christian, and exhorts him to repent. Armed with a spade and a pickaxe with which to dig the grave, it raises its trumpet on high on <u>sig.</u> C 2 of **A dialogue betwixt a Citizen, and a poore Country-man.** Death is at every turning, on the frontispiece of funeral pieces. [22] It fights time, armed with a scythe. [23] It spares no one, neither rich nor poor, nor the brave, nor the cowardly. Sometimes the dead return to warn the living and to exhort them to repentance: three men rise from their tomb and give news of hell. [24]

In **A terrible battell between time and death,** 1606, death complains of having become an obsession. People even design rings surrounded with the inscription: <u>memento mori,</u> in gold. But, it says, men do not really love death, otherwise they would not be so attached to their possessions. For example, it continues, while concentrating only on amassing more money, the usurer forgets death. The dialogue allows Rowlands to paint a satirical image of society.

Other maladies proliferated during the Renaissance. Unlike the plague, they did not appear in the illustrated pamphlets. Few medical works, almanacs excepted, bore illustrations. Moulton's **Regiment of Health,** 1550, could be considered as a popular treatise. On the back of the title-page, Galen speaks to one of his disciples. Thomas Spackman provides a remedy against rabies: the dog on the title-page is foaming at the mouth. [25] A translation of Ambroise Pare's **The method of Curing Wounds made by gunshot** shows a man pierced by all kinds of weapons.

The most amusing brochure, dealing with illness, though not a medical treatise, is **The praise of the Gout** by Bilibaldus Pirckheimerus, translated by William Est in 1617. It is a social satire: the poor suffer from cold and hunger while the rich stuff themselves, with their ill-gotten gains. Thank God, justice does exist; they suffer from the gout! If you do not wish to suffer from the gout, reflect and read. The title-page provides us with a picture of the seventeenth century doctor, wearing a pointed felt hat, and long robes, and feeling the foot of an old man, whose costume seems to suggest that he is a magistrate. He cries with pain and the doctor says "foh", in contempt.

The diet of the rich then was certainly not subject to the obsessions of our times. William Harrison, whose description of England is so flattering as to arouse suspicion, calls the table of England the most abundant in Europe. Red meats are found plentifully, while white meats, milk, butter and cheese are the food of the poor. [26] Such a well-garnished table can be seen in **The deceytes of women,** where the guests are eating and drinking to surfeit. [27]

The delights of the table and of love are depicted on the title-page of S. Marmion's **Cupid and Psyche,** 1638. The table is laid with plates, a knife and a spoon; in a metal bowl, varied fruits spell abundance. A servant brings in a rib roast of beef and wine flows from the pitcher to the cup, poured by one of Cupid's disciples. It would be wrong to conclude that the nobles ate daily to excess. Usually, the family only took their portion of the food and sent the rest back to the kitchen to the servants and to the poor who pressed at their doors. Occasionally during banquets the poor waited in the great hall and caught what fell from the rich man's table. As the great hall ceased to be used for more intimate rooms, the poor were relegated to the kitchen.

If one is to believe Robert Speed, the company of **The Counter-Scuffle** was not in the least intimidated by the laws and regulations concerning fasting in Lent. The captain, the jeweller, the priest and the lawyer make hogs of themselves. Their modest repast comprises eggs preserved in salt, butter, crabs and lobsters, fish of every kind, steaks of gammon, beef tongues seasoned with mustard, a shoulder and a leg of lamb, a roast side and a knuckle of veal, all to be seen on the title-page.

Such a meal called for drink to aid the digestion. The English popular drink was made of barley or of wheat boiled in water and then fermented with yeast. Every family could brew this light beer or ale. Darker beer was imported from Holland. In **A Dyetary of Health,** Andrew Borde thinks that it may suit the Dutch but that it is fatal for the English. All the same, by the end of the sixteenth century, most of the English had adopted this drink made of hops and their cultivation developed in the country. [28]

Beer could be drunk in tankards, like those that Eleanour Rummin held full in each hand on the frontispiece of the new impression of 1624 of John Skelton's poem. Similar ones were downed by the sons of Bacchus in **A monster Late found out and discovered,** 1628. According to Heywood in **Philocothonista,** beer mugs took many different shapes, some like the ones we know to-day; others had the form of dogs, cats, monkeys, horses, while others resembled a fish in appearance and sound.

Alcoholism among the poorer classes is hardly surprising when one reads that the children had a right to two pints for their breakfast and domestic servants could claim a gallon. The king might control the quantity drunk in inns and taverns, but he was powerless in dealing with domestic abuses. The acts of 1604, 1606, 1609 and 1623 demonstrate by their frequency the difficulty that James I, that sober Scot, had in limiting the ravages of alcoholism. [29]

Beer was not the only cause of drunkenness. Our pamphlets generally prefer to show us the evil effects of drinking wine, since wine was mainly imported. **Philocothonista**, 1635, surveys the list of current wines in England: French table wines, sweet wines of Spain and its islands, Rhine wines and, surprisingly, wines from Greece. To these are added home-grown decoctions such as blackberry wines, elderberry wine and liqueurs. **Pasquils Palinodia**, 1619, is a story of cuckoldry intended to serve as a drinking song. On the frontispiece, a man draws a pitcher from a cask of Spanish wine. A bacchante, goblet in hand, bears a musical instrument. The man warns the already tipsy woman: huc, huc, perides.

The drinking scene on the frontispiece of **Philocothonista** is hardly appetizing: each drinker has an animal's head. The clinking of the cannikins becomes more rapid and the innkeeper or his maid bring in two extra pitchers. One of the drinkers turns aside to vomit without having reached the chamber pot put on the ground for that very purpose. [30] The scene depicted in **The Counter-Scuffle** is hardly more tempting: drunken men fight with shoulders or legs of lamb. Plates, dishes, bottles and goblets are lying anyhow with the fish and some of them have rolled under the table.

Seventeenth century writers attempted to make the public more aware of the dangers of alcoholism. In beer, the poor forgot the sadness of their lot, the emptiness of their bellies, and the ugliness of their shacks. The rich had more refined pleasures: the delight of dressing up and the purchase of elegant furniture. While occasionally drunk, it was not their regular condition, for the more joyful their life was, the less likely they were to be the prey of Bacchus.

The delights of tobacco are generally linked with those of tippling as in **The Scourge of Drunkenness**, 1619: a man as hairy as a monkey, smokes a pipe while whipping himself. The illustration was taken, the pipe excluded, from Wither's **Abuses Stripped and Whipped**, 1617. Similarly, a toper smokes a pipe in Heywood's **Philocothonista**. (Plate 56) Harrison condemns the use of tobacco like most writers of our period. The exceptions were a few rare individuals like Buttes who recognized that smoking had certain therapeutic effects. [31] Tobacco, at first the privilege of the rich, later also reached the popular classes. **The Roaring Girl,** a comedy by Dekker and Middleton, shows Moll, the cutpurse, cheerfully drawing on her pipe. Tobacco burned money, but never as much as the extravagance of dress which sent several courtiers to the debtors' prison. [32]

Man, born naked as a worm, would be unable to endure the intemperate English climate--subject of so many conversations--without a covering for his body. The need for nourishment developed into refined culinary art and the need for clothing developed into the most extravagant fashions. Many proclamations were issued against those who dressed above their station in society. [33] Who could distinguish the servant from the mistress of the house, if the former gave up the serge, for velvet and silk? [34] Or who could tell the difference between a woman and a man if the woman wore masculine garb? James I shared the opinion of his predecessors about women's fashions. He loathed the yellow starched ruff, a fashion started by the sinister Mrs. Turner. Inculpated in the assassination of Sir Thomas Overbury, she was led to the gallows wearing yellow, so that the fashion might end like the head that planned it. [35]

The illustrated pamphlets offer a vast panorama of the fashion of the high middle-ages up to the most recent period of our interest. Old blocks account for the survival of so many fifteenth century dress designs, especially in the illustration of poems, old histories and jest-books.

The fashion of the early 1500's appears on the title-page of **Here is a necessarye Treatyse . . . The Maydens Crosse rewe**, 1540. [36] The young girl wears a kirtle with high neck-line, a surcote with hanging oversleeves and tight-fitting undersleeves. Now a woman, carrying her child's cradle, she wears a gown with open surcote and a V neck-line and a hennin with a gauze veil hanging. Women's fashion at the very beginning of the sixteenth century is characterized by its sobriety. In **The knight of Curtesy and the lady of Faguell** (n.d.) the lady's gown is becoming, with shaped waist, full at the bottom, and fastened to the hand to make walking easier. It has a round low neckline, a fashion immediately preceding the square neckline.

This new style appeared in the illustration of **Jyll of Breynforts testament**, 1560. (Plate 57) Like the lady of Faguell, Jyll wears a simple headdress; because she is a commoner, it is made of starched linen. The square neckline of her ample kirtle is covered by a stomacher in V-shaped black material. A gown with turned back cuffs covers the kirtle, shaped at the hips. Like every good wife, she wears an apron to avoid being soiled. [37]

On the back of the title-page another version of the styles of 1500-1530 is to be found. No stomacher hides the breasts, but a short necklace is worn instead. The neck of the gown is still square, but the waist is emphasized by a narrow sash knotted in front. The gown is held up by a link which ties it to the oversleeve. In fact, in 1530 the gown is held together by a girdle. The illustration is outdated. Her headgear is more elaborate: the face is framed within the open diamond which distinguishes the English hood from the French which follows the contours of the face. The English hood is shown again in **The deceytes of women,** and lasted until about 1540.

The early masculine style is considered next. **The Knight of Curtesy** wears the doublet with full skirt, the trunk-hose with prominent codpieces, the broad-shouldered gown lined with fur with slit hanging oversleeves, the craze under Henry VIII. He wears his hair long, under a large velvet crowned hat and on his feet are square-toed shoes, which were by a royal decree limited to six inches in width.

The style of Henry VIII's time cannot be described without analyzing the garb of the sovereign himself. It appears on the frontispiece of S. Rowley's **When you see me, You know me,** 1620. The king wears a slashed doublet with full skirt. The slashes make it a striking contrast of colors and material. The skirt is open in front to show the stuffed codpiece. The doublet sleeves have long vertical slits and fit closely to the wrists. The sleeves of the gown balloon to the elbow where they are close fitted, and to them are attached hanging sleeves. The lower part of the hose is also close-fitted. Two garters are tied on the outer side. The low cut shoes with inset strap are hardly any more than mere toecaps. The king wears a short cloak faced and lined with fur, which was the style of the day. His head is covered with a broad velvet hat with low crown, trimmed with a large ostrich feather, which goes all the way round and falls on the right side. The accessories are two narrow sashes, one of them bearing the rapier and two chains as emblems of his dignity. (Plate 58)

Thĕterlude of youth, 1557, gives several choices in the Henrician style. Charity wears a wide-skirted doublet with a square neck which reveals a shirt with a standing collar; his cape with wide slashed sleeves and his square-toed shoes and buttoned cap were popular between 1520 and 1550. Youth is also clothed in a wide-skirted doublet, but the waist is already stressed by the ornate girdle which supports the sword. The sleeves are wide to the elbow and close-fitting to the wrist. His bonnet has slashed brims and feathers. On his feet are instep-strap shoes. Fantasy in **Jyll of Breyntfords testament** also wears the doublet with square neck which was in favor between 1500 and 1536, [38] but he sports the Milan bonnet, in fashion between 1505 and 1540. [39]

A relic of the fourteenth century, the armor, can be found as recently as 1560, in an illustration from **Frederyke of Jennen.** The armor is articulated; the helmet resembles the head of a toad with low jutting forehead. The tunic is tight-fitting and padded. The foot is covered with articulated steel shoes, which replaced the rigid shoe at the end of the fourteenth century. The armor that St. George wears in combat with the dragon is much lighter: a metal doublet and a skirt of articulated steel.

The visor of the helmet is lifted. Shoulder straps appear. This costume marks a transition between medieval armor and lighter wear, which abandoned all metal by the end of the sixteenth century. [40] Nothing could appear more civilian than the dress of the musketeers on the title-page of Dekker's **The Artillery Garden** or on Taylor's **An Englishman's love to Bohemia**, as compared with the medieval breast-plates. The change, involving danger, was required by the increasing mobility of warfare. It may be recalled that Sir Philip Sidney died because he removed his leg-guard to become as vulnerable as his wounded friend. Such chivalry marked the end of an epoch, like Don Quixote's feats.

The fashion among the common folk follows at a distance that of the court. Its materials are duller and coarser, although the lines follow the new trend.

The masculine mode takes a decisive turn about the year 1545. The square-necked or crew-cut doublet with full skirt becomes considerably shorter and reveals the trunk-hose. [41] The title-page of Harman's **A Caveat for Common Cursetors**, demonstrates that the new style has reached the streets. The man holding the horse wears the typical working-man's high-necked, long skirted coat which is buttoned in front. His traced trunk-hose are bombasted; the codpiece has disappeared while the garters are undecorated. The man on the right, who holds the whip, has a very high-necked doublet with the beginnings of a ruff. All wear the hat with a round crown, generally of felt, while their hair is cut short. The woodcut of 1573 which illustrates chapter X shows another style. The high-necked doublet is still buttoned, but the bombasted trunk-hose emphasizes the codpiece. Trunk sleeves with close-buttoned wrist were in fashion from 1550 to 1570. [42] Even the ragged Jennings wears the wings in fashion from 1545 to 1640, to hide the joining of the sleeve to the body of the doublet.

As the new century progresses, doublets get shorter and the now visible trunk-hose get longer. The skirt of the doublet is reduced to a mere band hardly any wider than the belt, as can be seen in Garter's **The third newyeeres gift**, 1576, or in R. Greene's **A quip for an Upstart Courtier**, 1606. The standing collar gives way to the ruff around 1570. While of modest size for the masses, it is impressively large among the courtiers. **A quip for an Upstart Courtier**, 1592, contrasts the ancient with the modern doublet.

Trunk-hose take many varied forms. The onion-shaped "Spanish kettledrums" appear in Harman's work. In Harman's edition of 1573 Nicholas wears bell-shaped hose. Hose are often decorated with laces or with panels of variegated material, until about 1610. [43] Between 1570 and 1615 trunk-hose with cannons appear, which descend in a tight fit from hip to knee, or just below. Generally, the material of the cannons is no different from that of the top of the hose; they are lined to ensure a tighter fit. The codpiece tends to disappear; 1590 marks its death in high society, but it lingers on among the masses until 1600, as can be seen in N. Breton's **The court and country**, 1617. (Plate 59)

1570 sees the birth of venetians, a new type of hose. Garter's **The third newyeeres gift**, 1576, provides an example: pear-shaped and gathered at the waist, they fall naturally down to the knee which is gartered above and tied in front. Another variation is illustrated in **A quip for an Upstart Courtier**: these are close-fitted and maintain the line of the boot, like those in **The Blacke Dogge of Newgate**, 1596.

Stockings are not considered because they cannot be seen in woodcuts, but the garter, subject of much discussion and immortalized in **Twelfth Night**, on the legs of Malvolio, evolves with the century. The plain functional garter is a slim band of material, hardly noticeable; like that of the two figures in the 1573 edition of **A caveat for common cursetors**. The decorative garter is regularly tied on the outside of the leg, so as not to prevent walking, in the manner of Henry VIII. About 1560, however, crossed garters became fashionable. The garter is now placed in front or below the knee and is crossed behind the knee while being tied in a bow in front, as in **The third newyeeres gift**, or on the side.

Shoes had a round or blunt pointed toe. The two editions of **A caveat . . .** show both models. Boots are generally turned down to display the lining; buskins often protect the stocking which can be seen between the boot and the trunk-hose. It can also be tight-fitting as can be seen in the 1592 edition of **A quip for an upstart courtier**; the old model is on the right, the new on the left.

Hats vary, worn by all, all the time, except for the nobles who took them off at church, in the royal presence and in salutation. The buttoned cap is retained as also the flat cap. [44] The felt hat with the round crown is worn with or without a feather as in Greene's **A quip . . .** The court hat is also illustrated in the same pamphlet: with raised crown and small brim, it is often ornamented with osprey or plumes. The copotain, a felt hat with medium brim, has a sugarloaf crown. It was chiefly worn during court festivities until 1560 when it became a great favorite of the London populace. It could be worn slightly cocked as in the work of Luke Hutton and was decorated with gems. The hair beneath it was generally short and swept out behind the ears.

While there are many documents extant illustrating the masculine fashions of the second half of the sixteenth century, a few deal with the feminine styles. Fashion seemed to be above all the privilege of man in an anthropocentric society. However, Gosson's **Quippes for upstart newfangled gentlewomen,** an anti-feminist pamphlet, was complementary to Greene's work on men.

The ornate embroidered kirtle contrasts with the simple material of the open gown. The bodice of different material is separated from the bottom part of the kirtle, as in Heywood's **If you know not me, You know nobody,** 1633, and in Gosson's **Quippes . . .** The neckline is low and square as in the previous century, or high and fitted with a ruff of comparable size to men's. This fashion starts around 1570. Gosson's **Quippes** and Tedder's **Recantations,** 1588, both satirize the enlarged ruff, known as the cartwheel. The head, like that of decapitated John the Baptist, gives the impression of being served on a dish. [45]

Near the end of the century, the fashion inclines towards the rebato, a lacy fan-shaped ruff or band attached to the top of the bodice, like the regular ruff, but open in front. At the same time the wired headrail is attached to the shoulders, as in Heywood's **If you know not me . . . ,** in the 1633 edition and **Englands Elizabeth.** (Plate 11) The sleeves, with or without slits, are bombasted and are often called bishop's sleeves; they are tightened at the wrist, with or without handruffs. There also are trunk sleeves: those decorate most of the portraits of the queen and the title-page of **Quippes.** Cuffs were fashionable either as handruffs imitating the neckline, or as laced bands. The first is shown in Tedder's **Recantations** and the 1639 edition of Heywood's **If you know not me . . .** The second appears in the three other portraits of the queen referred to and in **Quippes.** (Plate 60)

The bodice with a long stiff stomacher is usually deep-pointed, **Englands Elizabeth** excepted, following the male fashion. The hips are enlarged to emphasize the thin line of the waist. The verdingale, or Spanish farthingale, gives impressive dimensions to the hips. The farthingale is first made of circular hoops sloping wider and wider towards the bottom of the kirtle as seen in the illustration of Mary Queen of Scots found in the proclamations. [46] The queen seems to prefer this type of farthingale, though she switches with the fashion to the padded roll of French farthingales which enabled the dress to fall freely. Heywood's play and E. N.'s **Caesar's dialogue,** display it in its most naked form, tilted at the back. In **Quippes,** however, the circumference is already reduced.

Two kinds of coiffure, looking much alike, were in fashion, often covered with a Mary Stuart Hood. The latter was made of light material and, curved with a dip in front, it made the face appear wider. The first style had the hair parted in the center and waved or curled on the temples as in the **Recantations.** The second was also center-parted, but the hair was gathered over crescent-shaped pads. [47] The court bonnet and the Mary Stuart Hood were often ornamented with an osprey or begemmed.

Among the accessories, gloves or laced handkerchiefs were the height of fashion. [48] A chain or a ribbon was suspended from the waist with other accessories. These included a mirror, a handkerchief, and a purse. Long metal chains were worn around the neck as in the **Recantations** or in **Quippes.** Queen Elizabeth loved gems and chains.

Hers was also the epoch of the fan made of ostrich feathers, which led Gosson to compare woman to a peacock for her legendary vanity. [49] The handles were chased in silver, as in **Quippes.**

The fashion of the common people was much the same, although more conservative. Some peasants still wear the skirted doublet or the tunic-like coat and "tights" with prominent codpiece, as late as the middle of the seventeenth century. The usurer retains the copotain, the ruff, and the fur-faced and lined coat of olden times. [50] The goodwife too retains the older, simpler fashion rejecting the farthingale. [51]

Children's clothing followed parental fashion, with cheaper material. The frontispiece of Nowell's **A Catechism or Institution of Christian Religion,** 1583, shows the teacher slightly out of fashion in his long fur-edged gown, teaching rowdy children wearing up-to-date clothes.

As previously noted, Stuart documents are more numerous than Tudor ones for fashion. Male attire changes from stiffness to suppleness. Bellypieces, stiffened with buckram, in fashion at the beginning of the reign of James I, and, the heavily-pleated venetians [52] were discarded in favor of doublets of silk or other supple material, which were unbuttoned to show the shirt frills, of open jerkins showing the doublet, and of long-legged breeches tied under the knee.

Stiffened doublets can still be found as late as 1660, but they went out of fashion in the thirties. In **Three Bloodie Murders,** 1613, the V-shaped waist becomes rounder and lower and the band-like skirt is made of narrow tabs, usually eight in number as in the work just referred to, or with wide tabs. The front tabs often dip to a sharp point as in Rowlands's **The Melancholie knight** or the person on the left in Taylor's **An arrant thiefe.** The doublet is buttoned in front or joined with laces or ribbons. The high standing collar is ornamented with a ruff, a laced band, which around 1620 becomes the laced rebato. [53] Doublets were often covered with a jerkin, a sort of waistcoat. The epaulettes in fashion under James I, gradually widen into wings as in **An arrant thiefe**, then diminish and disappear at the same time as the fashion for stiffening. Doublets were often paned and sham hanging sleeves sometimes start from the shoulders, instead of from the elbows as formerly. These can be seen on the title-page of **Taylors Pastorall**, 1624.

Trunk-hose are lengthened, lose their wadding and are sometimes prolonged by cannons as in Taylor's **The praise, antiquity and commodity, of Beggery, Beggers, and Begging:** the beggar on the right represents the courtier and wears a tight jerkin, which was beginning to replace the doublet. His trunk-hose with cannons are decorated with clocks, sewn on the side. Occasionally a garter with a rose terminates the breeches, sometimes a knotted ribbon. **Three bloodie murders** gives an example of the first and **Taylors Pastorall** of the second. The French velvet cloak trimmed with lace and thrown casually over the shoulder came to England and the beggar-courtier wears it turned up to show off the lining. He also wears soft leather bucket boots with boot-hose tops, called <u>lazzarines,</u> in the style of Louis XIII. On their heads were large cocked felt hats with hat bands, a feather or an osprey.

For the Puritan Samuel Ward, the new shoes, decorated with small or large roses, are a sign of the degeneration of the times. In **Woe to drunkards,** 1627, he contrasts the spurred boot on the muscular foot of olden times with the effeminate gartered and elegant contemporary leg; its foot rests on low heels for the first time for many centuries. The same symbolism is applied to the upturned sleeve: he contrasts the halberdier with his iron arm with the modern arm with padded shoulder and laced cuffs, holding a drunkard's cup and pipe. Modern fashion is the subject of street-talk and of popular pamphlets. Thomas Brewer, John Taylor, Samuel Ward and many others, all get into the act. (Plate 61)

Half length hair was then waved or close-curled. Later, long-flowing locks reached the shoulder in cork-screws. A little waxed moustache grown on the upper lip contrasts with the vertical straight beard in the Van Dyke style. [54] Hats vary from the sugarloaf shape inspired from the copotain used by the citizens, to a castor type with feather or osprey used by the elegant. [55]

Feminine fashion provoked much controversy. Two styles confronted each other. Up to 1625, the first resembled Elizabethan court fashion. The other modern style, modelled after the men, was more supple, elegant, and refined. [56] The illustrations in the three editions of Swetnam's pamphlet: **The arraignment of lewd, idle, froward and unconstant women,** namely those of 1615, 1619, and 1628: show the evolution of women's fashion. The first two follow the ancient style, the last, the new. [57]

The pointed bodice of the gown was no longer stiffened as in the past but emphasized the lissomeness of the figure. Occasionally the more elegant adopted the male doublet as in both the 1628 edition and the title-page of Westwood's **The fair maid of the west**. As in masculine fashion, the wings worn by women became larger and then diminished in the new fashion. The style of sham-hanging sleeves reappeared, as in both works just referred to.

None of these pamphlets, however, informs us about the new fashions in hair-dressing. Hair was still brushed up high over the roll. In Rowlands's **Well-met gossip**, 1619, the married woman and widow wear a tall cocked hat, while the young girl is fashionably hatless. [58] The new hair style appears in R. Crofts's **The lover:** the hair of the young girl is divided in three: the hair in front is cut to form a curled fringe; the hair on either side is curled in corkscrews while the rest is caught up in a bun. Occasionally both men and women cut their hair half-length. **Hic Mulier or the Man-Woman**, 1620, satirizes the unisex fashion, both in the text and by a woodcut. [59]

Accessories also imitate men's with the long embroidered or laced gauntlets and handkerchiefs. The fan of feathers or silk is still in fashion. The two first editions of Swetnam's tract show the former, the third, the latter. Jewels are still worn: pearl necklaces, often short, and chains. In the thirties luxury becomes discreet, elegant and tasteful.

Middle-class women in the 1634 edition of **The Arraignment** wear ruffs or bands with simple lace-trim. Their head-gear, however, remains occasionally old-fashioned in shape: copotains or bonnets, but they are decorated with contemporary lace. In **The pleasant and sweet history of patient Grissell**, the heroine, who is spinning wool, wears a doublet with a ruff and a simple gauze veil on the back of her head, while her hair surrounds her face. A knight on horseback passes by, with rebato collar and felted plumed hat, while a countryman rushes by, in short-skirted doublet with high collar and venetians. [60] Even the Puritan followed the style of the day, while criticizing its excesses.

With the refinement of manners and the awakening of the visual sense, fashion became more supple and subtle under James I. In the third decade it reached its apogee, under French and Italian influences.

The Tudor extravagance in dress was equalled only by the lavish expenditure on houses. Yet, in the pamphlets, there is little exterior or interior evidence of this. There are some illustrations of castles as on sig. B of **Newes from France** or on the title-page of **A true Relation of a very dreadfull Earthquake,**

1612. This form of construction, however, was only a vestige from the past, and from Henry VIII's time, the house changed from a military to a more civil aspect. From the beginning of the century, up to the Revolution, the mansion was constructed in the form of an H or an E, as can be seen on the frontispiece of Goodman's **Hollands Leaguer**, 1632. The house is entered by a great wooden portal with metal studs and the different levels give a sense of space and of many rooms. Since this particular house was a brothel, it may seem ironic to take it as an example of a radical change in architectural structure. In fact, however, at this time more intimate rooms were preferred to the great central hall. When the laws of Henry VIII forbade great gatherings for fear of reviving feudal revolts, [61] great halls then fell into disuse, except for the reception of the sovereigns and their retinues during a royal progress.

The mansion depicted on <u>sig</u>. C 2 of William Lawson's **A new Orchard and Garden** shows the total abandonment of the central chamber. The house is divided in two separate parts, according to the recent plans of Inigo Jones for the palace of Greenwich. A road, as in the medieval hospices of pilgrims, unites the two sections and allows carriages to leave their occupants at the door, without the inconvenience of rain. We now have a sense of horizontal amplitude. [62]

The mansion still had to receive sovereigns. Queen Elizabeth loved journeying and visiting her noble subjects. The great hall was replaced by a central gallery where one could pay homage to the sovereign who was retiring to the royal apartments. The seventeenth century saw the development of a balustraded terrace on the second storey from which the garden could be admired. In **Mischeefes mysterie,** a tract dealing with the Gunpowder Plot, James I is enthroned on the terrace of the palace. The curved columns of the balustrade are thicker at the base and thinner at the top; above each one rests a sphere. [63]

It is impossible to say precisely what these houses were built of. If the illustration is exact, we might think that the surface was white-washed. The four little garden rooms of **A New Orchard and Garden** seem to be made of brick, a material greatly in favor in the seventeenth century, because the oak used for construction or furniture-making was the fuel used for baking the clay in the brickyards. [64] The shortage of construction wood became so serious that a proclamation of James I forbade the use of timber for decorative addition on the façade. The king's command was respected in London, but not always in the provinces. [65] Walls get thinner as the building is used for domestic purposes rather than as a fortress. The thickness of the earlier walls appears clearly on the title-pages of **The Treatise of the knight of Curtesy and the lady of Faguell** and of **The smyth whych that forged hym**

a new dame: the setting of the window shows this. On the title-page of R. Wilson's **The pleasant and Stately Morall, of the three Lordes and three Ladies of London,** the stone building is characteristically modern and the windows are aligned with the walls.

Glass windows are also a novelty. Dating from the end of the fifteenth century they became popular in the sixteenth. They replaced the former oiled paper, parchment or linen. This was an expensive luxury since the taxation of property was founded in part on the number of windows. For practical reasons, Bacon recommends that they be few in order to avoid suffering from the heat of summer and the cold of winter. His essay No. XLV advocates the bow-window for the country which provides an excellent place for conversation or work. In the galleries of a house, he prefers colored glass that tames the light. **The bellman of London** shows latticed glass, as opposed to latticed parchment. Most of the time the difference cannot be noticed on the woodcuts. It is also difficult to distinguish between colored and transparent glass. It would be reasonable to suppose that black windows appearing on country houses are either parchment linen or colored glass. **[66]**

Formerly the room was organized in relation to the window. In the sixteenth and seventeenth centuries it came to be centered on the newly developing fire-place. This can be found in both the mansion and the cottage, as one can see on the title-page of **A Horrible Creuel and bloudy Murther,** 1614. The entire interior of the house is turned towards the hearth; the master's armchair and the decorative items above the mantel-piece.

The mansion is set off not only by its refinement and decoration, but also by the elaboration of its garden. Harrison notes the improvement of gardens during Tudor times. Their beauty is the product of their attractive structure and the variety of color brought by the flowers. **[67]** The garden imitating those of Italy or of France may be square in shape as in **Hollands Leaguer,** or rectangular, as in **A New Orchard and Garden.** Bacon wishes to see the land of the mansion triply divided into a lawn, a heath and a formal garden.

"The garden is best to be square", he writes, "encompassed on all the four sides with a stately arched hedge . . . The arches to be on pillars of carpenter's work or some ten foot high." **[68]** The formal garden is divided by paths which lead from one level to another by means of steps. **[69]** The fountain is in the middle of the garden, as seen in **A New Orchard and Garden.** The central part consists of an arrangement of boxwood, bricks or tiles which border the beds in a geometric design, as in C in our illustration. The garden in **Hollands Leaguer** is not as formal; its boxwood does not form a maze, a favorite device of the seventeenth century.

Nooks are provided for lovers. One can also see a bower in which lovers are embracing. [70] (Plate 5)

In addition, the utilitarian garden is arranged aesthetically. W. Lawson's **A New Orchard and Garden,** teaches how to mix the functional and the beautiful. The rectangular garden is divided into four equal squares. A stream borders it on the north and the south, while a central pathway affords easy access from one part to the other. The first two squares are planted with trees and flowerbeds. The two other squares comprise on the left the orchard and on the right, the formal garden, while the final two are a kitchen garden. Artificial hills are found on the four corners, relics of the middle ages. Sometimes, little paths ascended them. At other times the entire border of the garden was artificially raised, from which a little tour of the whole could be made. The author suggests that the labyrinth should be planted with fruit-bearing shrubs, to increase the pleasure of the senses. [71] (Plate 62)

While the mansion stands out by its luxury and novelty, the homes of farmers, tenants, laborers, and artificers, are strikingly conservative. As in clothing, the common people follow fashion at a distance. The mud hut has its place in **The wife happed on Morel's skypp** or **The taming of the shrew,** on sig. E 3. The wife, sitting in front of the hut is putting away her husband's hunting bow.

The other dwellings in our pamphlets seem to belong to the first type described by Sir John Summerson: [72] they have a large interior all-purpose room with an adjacent kitchen or larder. [73] The house almost resembles a barn and it was not unusual for humans and animals to live there together. [74] The secondary room is usually windowless. A house of this kind is often built without foundation or ceilings. [75]

In **The history of the noble Marques,** [76] the dwelling has a first story which must have been used as a bedroom, if one judges by the openings in the wall. The roof shows the presence of a chimney, rather than an old-fashioned open hearth. Harrison observed that towards the last quarter of the century, the English village numbered ten or twelve chimneys instead of the two or three earlier. [77] Robert Greene deplores the disappearance of the ancient hearth in **A quip for an Upstart Courtier,** as he argues that smoke was good for the health. In John Norden's **Surveyor's dialogue,** 1607, the conservative baillie opposes the surveyor who is in favor of the modern chimney. [78]

One of the reasons why the country house did not grow larger can be found in the Statutes of 1589 which prohibited more than one family living under the same roof. The materials of which the houses were constructed depended largely on the site. However, the poorer houses were made of wood, mud and straw or of wood and clay, white, red or blue, on which the mortar was placed. Sometimes the interior was covered with plaster of Paris. Tile-roofs were most common, as in **The wonders of this windie winter,** or in Gad's **The wandering Jew telling fortunes to English-men,** 1640, or thatched roofs as in **The history of the noble Marques.** [79] Both the barn and the windmill were generally made of wood. The latter was raised on a pole; this way it was possible to turn the body of the mill so that the wings catch the wind. Many mills are depicted in the pamphlets, among them **The wonders of this windie winter,** 1613, **A Horrible Creuell and Bloudy Murther,** 1614, or Markham's **The English Farrier.** Their disadvantage was their fragility in a storm, for the size of the body of the mill greatly exceeded that of its base, so that it tended to break under the pressure of wind. One such mishap is depicted in **The last terrible tempestious windes and weather,** 1613.

The construction of the urban dwelling was different from that of the country house. The wooden house at the beginning of the century yielded slowly to construction in brick or stone. This was directly related to the decrease of available timber. Wooden houses were set on foundations of masonry, strong enough to prevent the woodwork from deteriorating from the humidity of the soil. Two or three thicknesses of insulation were covered by a layer of wood which was to support the uprights of the house. At their upper end there was another floor on which were placed the transverse beams which projected over the lower floor. The procedure was repeated until the roof was reached. Between the oak uprights the walls were raised in wattle and daub. When viewed from the front or in the profile the house widened as it climbed. This is clearly shown on the title-page of **A true discourse of the occurrences in the warres of Savoy,** 1601. The house in the foreground has three stories and an attic which may have been used to board domestic servants. The one next to it has two stories and an attic. The openings are numerous and casement-windows suggest the presence of glass.

Harrison informs us that in rich houses the glass of Burgundy, Normandy, and Flanders was preferred to the cruder English product. Another kind of window is seen in R. Greene's **The Honorable historie of Frier Bacon,** in the edition of 1630. The glass is finely divided. Sash windows existed; **The life . . . of Charles Courtney** may provide one example, unless it is a window closed by a latch. [80] Brick and stone houses are illustrated in **Swetnam the woman-hater arraigned by women,** 1620, and in Th. Heywood's **The Iron Age,** among others.

London is the living image of the phenomenal boom in construction that took place at the turn of the century. In

1563 a number of French and Dutch refugees sought asylum in London to escape from the political and religious persecutions in their countries. This resulted in a greater demand for accommodation and a renewal of building construction. [81] Elizabeth and James I were unable to limit construction in London. Stow says that the regulations were so poorly obeyed that builders had to be summoned to the Star Chamber. [82] The West End of London, according to Stow, was the most active in construction.

Dekker's **A rod for run-aways** provides a panorama of the capital on its title-page, which is repeated on the title-page of Taylor's **The fearefull summer.** Seen from afar, London can be recognized by St. Paul's with its belfry struck by lightning on June 4, 1561. The base of the belfry, however, remained. St. Paul's Cross, the great center of próclamation and preaching, was renovated and a brick wall constructed round the pulpit in 1595, as shown on the title-page of **St. Paules-Church her bill for the Parliament.** Its congregation asked for a subsidy with which to repair a room which had been burnt. (Plate 63)

A gate of London appears on the title-page of **The life . . . of Charles Courtney.** Its principal modern function was hanging criminals. A curious head, excited by the spectacle, projects from one of the neighboring houses. Newgate, outside the city, was reserved for those guilty of minor civil offences and lodged insolvent debtors, among others. Its gate appears on the title-page of Mynshal's **Essayes and characters of a prison and prisoners.** The prison also lodged robbers, like Taylor's main character in **The Arrant Thiefe.** Men went to Newgate, while their female accomplices found themselves in Bridewell.

Beside Paris Garden, a bordello, **Hollands Leaguer,** [83] appears on the title-page of a pamphlet on the Church of England. The house is surrounded by a ditch, both for its protection, which explains the presence of the armed guard, and to prevent flooding, since it was situated in the marshes. Holland, the madam, rents the house and there keeps happy company. With the exception of the pamphlets on the plague and particularly Henry Petowe's **The countries ague,** which shows the different gates of London, no other London sights can be distinguished in the rest of the pamphlets.

Towns or villages were grouped around one or more churches. Most churches were built of stone in the gothic style, but the belfries were wooden, hence their vulnerability to tempests, as in **The last terrible tempestious windes,** 1613. The church is a monument to stability by its construction. It is not only the center of worship and theology in England, but also of social activities: it is there that the latest news of the village is passed on, as in the market. Its almsbox and notice-boards recording testamentary gifts gave hope to the poor.

The floors of the houses indicated the degree of poverty or wealth of the inhabitants. Erasmus wrote to the cardinal archbishop of York that the plague probably came from the dirt floors of the London houses. They were often strewn with rushes; but frequently new layers were superimposed without removing the older. Consequently spittle, together with human and animal excrements, were mixed with spilt food [**84**] and remained to breed pestilence, as in the hut of **The wife happed on Morel's skypp.**

Some improvement took place in the course of the sixteenth century. In **Well-met gossip,** 1619, the floor is made of wood. Many houses in the illustrations of the pamphlets have oak or tiled floors. Oak floors can be seen in **News from Perin,** 1618, **Vox Graculi,** 1623, and in the narratives of the murders of Enoch ap. Evan and of Arden of Feversham.

Tiled floors were not rare, especially in castles and mansions. Checkerboard tiles appear in **The knight of Curtesy and the lady of Faguell,** surrounding the forge in **The smith whych that forged hym a new dame,** n.d., and in the almanac-maker's house in Dekker's **The owles almanach,** 1618. Tiles could also be self-colored as in the houses of the miller of Putney, [**85**] of Dr. Faust, or of **Frier Bacon,** 1630.

In rich houses walls are covered with wood panelling, either simple as on the title-page of **The owles almanach,** or sculpted in low-relief. At the turn of the century, stone wall interiors reappeared, as in the olden days of fortified castles, but they were far thinner. Finally, some became unadorned brick. (Plate 9) The illustrations do not always indicate whether the walls are of stone or brick.

The poor climbed to an upper story by a ladder, whereas the rich went up a circular staircase in wood or stone. The steps formed triangles, as on <u>sig</u>. K ii of **The deceytes of women.** The straight staircase with landings is an Elizabethan innovation. Steps are rectangular and lead by a landing to a higher story. [**86**] Blaxton's **The English usurer,** 1634, shows the lower part of such a staircase, but it seems to lack a balustrade. Balustrades in carved wood were the pride of rich houses. (Plate 67)

Even when the actual construction was not always luxurious, the growing wealth and the improvement of the quality of life at the end of the sixteenth century can be traced in the furniture and tableware. Dire poverty did exist. John Taylor discovers Hastings, the weaver, one cold night in winter, without food or drink, without pallet to sleep on, or stool to sit on, or light. Yet this is not the picture given by the illustrated pamphlets. Their poor always possess a bed, a table, and a chair.

The bed is the most important single article of furniture, since birth, rest, sickness, recovery and death, are experienced there. The style of the bed changes in the houses of the rich. In the first half of the sixteenth century, the canopy over the bed is fixed to the wall; rich hangings exclude the light, as can be seen in **The deceytes of women.** It is unclear whether it has drawers or not, since its base is masked by white twill and the rich counterpane. The bolster and the pillows are filled with soft down; on a low beside table or stool, the chamber pot is placed. During the day, the curtains are drawn to provide additional seating.

The four-posted bed appeared towards the end of the sixteenth century and remained popular until the nineteenth century. The new style is found in John Taylor's **A bawd,** 1635, [87] and in W. Sampson's **The vow-breaker,** 1636. The bed has now its own ceiling and the pillars are more or less ornate. In **The vow-breaker,** they are architectural columns surmounted with balls. In **A bawd,** they are masked by the curtains. (Plate 2)

The bed of the poor is far less elegant. **News from Perin** demonstrates that they had no draperies to keep out the light and the cold. Within the pamphlet the headboard appears simple and straightforward resting on feet, while on the title-page only a miserable mattress is placed on the ground--a luxury, however, as compared with the simple straw pallet and log. Pillows of hemp, horsehair, or down, were kept for women and children.

The table was next in importance, as it often dictated the style of the seats used with it. The mobile table of the middle ages, resting on trestles gave place to a smaller, firmer, and lighter table that could be easily moved. From 1535 to 1640, there is little change in style. The massive and solid fashion of the Elizabethan age is extended to the Jacobean. In a 1590 ditty about judges, the table with column feet is fixed on a wooden platform. As a result the stools have to be very high. [88] The only difference between the tables of Gower's **The painfull adventures of Pericles,** 1608, and of **The English usurer,** 1634, is in the feet and the rails which unite them: the table is simple, straight, and uncarved.

The table in **The famous game of chesse-play,** 1614, by A. Saul, is more shapely. The feet are made of balusters resting on a ball and the stool harmonizes with the table. In **Well-met gossip,** 1609, the plain table rests on ball feet. The table of **Arden of Feversham,** 1633, has curved feet. The only table markedly different from the rest is that of **Vox graculi,** 1623; two large feet, each curved in an X-shape, are united by a strut.

While the stools and forms more or less follow the shape of the table, the chairs or armchairs keep their independence. The monumental seat was kept for the master of the house or for some guest of distinction. Almost unknown in the interior of the rural house at the beginning of the century, it became more common at the end of the Elizabethan era. The stolid armchair, as it was at the end of Henry VIII's reign, was adapted from ecclesiastical use. The back became lower as in **The famous game of chesse-play**, or remained high as in **The owles almanach.** The arms of the latter are curved, those of **A horrible creuel and bloudy murther**, are straight; occasionally the back is sculpted, as in **The praise of the gout**, 1617. In most of the illustrations, the finials of the chairbacks are ball-shaped. [89] Towards the end of our period the chair or armchair is often padded on the seat or on the back. It is covered or in tapestry, as in **Vox graculi.** The cushion that was separate from the stool in **The praise of the gout**, becomes attached in the mid-seventeenth century. Finally, an adaptation of the Roman chair which first appeared under Queen Mary, became fashionable in the seventeenth century. **The English usurer** shows one on its title-page. The furniture becomes more harmonious and more comfortable, the sign of a sedentary civilization.

Tapestries and other hangings, as well as carpets, decorate the mansions of the rich. The palace of Whitehall appears on the frontispiece of S. Rowley's **When you see me, you know me,** 1613. The folds of the curtains reveal the heavy silk embroidery, while the king places his feet on a delicate carpet. Carpets were still rare among the middle-classes, and straw still covered their floors in the seventeenth century only to be replaced gradually by matting. [90] Carpets were still kept as table or bed-covers, whether they ended with a fringe, as in **The painful adventures of Pericles** and in **Hocus pocus junior,** or by plain piping as in **The arraignment of lewd . . . women,** and in **The English usurer.** Sometimes the carpet ends with an embroidered edging as in **Arden of Feversham.**

Crockery, cutlery and other household implements also improved. While originally made of turned wood, plates, dishes and spoons of pewter became popular amongst the poorer sections of the nation. The court, however, ate out of gold or silver. As can be seen in a miller's house, these objects were no longer merely functional, but were used to decorate the chimney-piece. [91] Inns displayed fine collections; one can be glimpsed in **A bawd.** Glassware was even rarer. The single example ornaments the title-page of **Vox graculi:** two bottles, one with a bulging body, and the other squat and round, rest on a bookshelf.

Brass and pewter candlesticks illumine the night, but did not always reveal noble acts. One discloses the murder of

Arden of Feversham, and a sconce, fixed to the wall, the rascality of **Hocus-pocus.**

Though comfort improves in the seventeenth century, one could hardly call the epoch sanitary. The efforts of some to supply a hygienic lavatory system found little favor. One ingenious inventor was John Harington, who in **The metamorphosis of Ajax,** anticipated our modern water-closets. The chamber-pot and the pierced chair, were used by the majority.

If Erasmus had survived to the middle of the seventeenth century, he would have observed a considerable evolution in the houses and the equipment of the rich and middle-classes: inlaid wooden floors, mattresses, beds, pillows, and washable crockery. Did dire poverty benefit from these improvements as Harrison suggests? We wonder. Rather it seems to us that Taylor's description, going from London to Salisbury, is more realistic. [92] Our illustrated pamphlets show only relative, not desperate poverty, since they were written for a middle-class public, they did not wish to embarrass their readers by exhibiting the almost naked body of poverty.

Although the Englishman's home was his castle, it was not his ivory tower. He delighted as much in outdoor sports as in indoor pastimes. On Sundays, after morning prayer and sermon, adults and children needed relaxation. In winter, it was not unusual to see them snowballing, as in **The wonders of this windie winter,** 1613. In summer, of course, they were rarely prevented from practicing all the sports.

Sports were, in fact, subject to very strict regulations. Statutes forbade many sports to be practices on all working days. Besides all sports were not open to all people. In 1541, an act of Henry VIII was passed, which encouraged archery and forbade bowls, tennis, dicing, and cards. [93]

James I and Charles VII both tried to regulate pastimes. Both working and noblemen had to toughen in the military art. Both kings felt that unless games were open to their subjects, they would get drunk in the taverns. Consequently, provided they attended divine worship, the king would allow them to take part in archery, jumping, equitation and dancing, on Sundays. They also celebrated May Day, feasted at Pentecost, and practiced masked dancing. The baiting of bears, bulls, and dogs, however, was forbidden. [94] The proclamation added, somewhat illogically, since it advocated archery, that no one should bear offensive arms, in order to avoid rioting and disorder.

There are many representations of archery, [95] but

the best is the title-page of Matthew Walbancke's **Annalia Dubrensia**. This is a pot-pourri of poems in honor of Robert Dover, who, in James's time gave an almost olympic dimension to the Cotswold Games. [96] (Plate 64) First comes new-fangled fencing: each adversary is given both a sword and a dagger. Jumping and wrestling are followed by exercises requiring agility: an acrobat stands on his hands. Dogs pursue game in a maze. Two greyhounds chase a hare. Stakes and hammers are thrown, while on the left women dance to the sound of bagpipes. This is followed by another hunting scene and tents are prepared for a chess tournament. Other men play at bowls while drinking beer. Finally, there is a mounted hunting scene and the throwing of the javelin.

The illustration corresponds almost exactly to the description provided by the poet, William Denny. Trussell is happy on this occasion, because, he says, for some mysterious reason, all public celebrations require the approbation of the law. He alludes not only to the royal sanctions but also to objections raised by the Puritans and the Catholics, which Charles I strongly reproved in his re-issue of **The book of sports.** [97]

Nobles had little difficulty in finding a convenient sport. Generally they would have no truck with the sports and jousts of the common folk. However, in the provinces, the vicar and the squire often played together. The duel, a plague of the seventeenth century, which decimated the flower of the nobility, appears in **Antiduello** and on the title-page of **The maid's tragedy**, 1630.

The mounted hunt was the outstanding noble sport. Often nobles trained falcons to hunt small game. Books on falconry are frequent, from Latham to Markham, but most of them are too lengthy to be considered as pamphlets.

Aquatic sports were also popular. C. Middleton published **A short introduction for to learne to swimme.** Although the title-page has no illustration, the work comprises forty. They show the different positions of various styles of swimming: the crawl, the breast stroke, the back stroke and diving. Cows watch the naked swimmer in amazement.

Fresh-water fishing is praised in I. D.'s poem, **The secrets of angling**, 1613, as a sport much favored by the universities, [98] presumably because it was conducive to meditation. Fishing rods were usually made by fishermen, while the line was of horse-hair and silk, guaranteeing firmness and lightness. The emblematic illustration of **The secrets of angling** is most impressive. One of the fishermen, crushing a snake underfoot, catches a globe; the other man catches a fish, while another fish emerges from the river to see what is happening to his mate.

Cock-fighting is the subject of Wilson's **The commendation of cockes and cock-fighting.** The brochure is partly informative, through its anecdotes, and partly moralistic: it compares the courage of cocks and men. It begins with a doubtful reference to **Genesis;** God has given man the sovereignty over all things for his needs and his pleasures. This is as much as to say that God has given men cocks for the sadistic pleasure of seeing them murder each other. [99]

There are three kinds of cocks: the fighting cock, the half-breed cock, and the cowardly cock. The third is only good for roasting. After the eulogy of fighting cocks, anecdotes on cock-fighting in Norwich follow. One of these was called Tarleton, for it always went to combat with a noisy fluttering of wings which resembled Tarleton's drumming. [100] G. R. Scott states that Wilson's information is defective. In fact, there was only one kind of fighting cock; furthermore, he gives us no information on the preparation of the cock before the fight. [101] On the title-page of the treatise the poor cocks can be seen; one red, the other black. They fly at each other with their back feathers partly shaved.

There were, of course, more humane sports. Country dancing, called morris-dancing, was the delight of young people, as witnessed by the joy of the crowds watching Kemp dancing his way from London to Norwich. **Kemps nine daies wonder,** 1600, recorded the event. Tarleton played the drum so as to delight fair-goers like Jyll of Breintford. [102]

Polite society avoided popular fun and games. Stubbes says that more than one girl lost her virtue at the fair. They danced or dined at home to the sound of the viol or of the theorbo, like the boon-companions of Shakerley Marmion's **Cupid and Psyche.** In **Robin Goodfellow,** the lascivious Robin often presides over the May dances; on the title-page he leads the dance as a minstrel.

When weary with sports and out-of-doors celebrations, all went home to parlor games, as they were then defined. These were varied and numerous and could be divided into legal card-games and illegal dicing-games. [103] The division is made according to the degree of chance.

The game requiring most intelligence was undoubtedly chess. G. B. in **Ludus scachiae; Chesse-play,** 1597, praises the game which demands brains, wit, vivacity, discipline and memory. The game is an admirable exercise for the politician, for the player must prepare his attacks in advance and parry the counter-attacks. [104] This brochure is decorated only by a border of vine-leaves and grapes, but there are other brochures illustrating the game. A. Saul's treatise shows two players opposed; the game has not yet begun. **A Game at Chesse,** 1624, and its new edition of 1625 bear two engravings, both showing the game in progress. **[105]**

Backgammon, however, did not require as intense an effort. Most of the game is left to chance. Arden of Feversham is assassinated during the game. The illustration shows the folding tray with two compartments on which are painted twenty-four arrow-heads with alternating colors, each matched by its opposite arrow-head. The pieces all appear in white, doubtless for printing reasons. Normally they are black and white to indicate to which player they belong. **[106]**

There was very little change in the official attitude towards card games. All kinds of games are mentioned in the interlude **Hyckescorner.** Primero was the popular game at court, soon to be supplanted by quadrille and ombre. Sir William Forrest in **The poesye of princylye practise,** allows the prince to play chess, a permission which was granted to the people only once a year, at Christmas, to the great displeasure of Stubbes. His objection was that Christmas had become an occasion for giving oneself to pleasure rather than to prayer.

Dekker satirizes card-games and the busy courtier who starts to play in the theater, even before the curtain has been raised. **[107]** Tarot continued in favor and new games included Trente et un, the game of A, which is very like whist. Both Greene and Taylor, the one in prose, the other in verse, exhibit the diversity of games. **[108]** Greene specializes in what goes on under the card-table, in the tricks that are played in the London taverns. Several of those are revealed in **A notable discovery of cosenage, The art of conny-catching,** 1591. For instance, a countryman is picked among the crowd by a confidence man who pretends to recognize him. As a reparation for his assumed mistake, the former offers the latter a drink. While they are at the tavern, an accomplice arrives who offers the dupe a game of cards and they find a fourth partner. They play a game of chance and one of the tricksters keeps on winning. After several games, he asks the countryman if he would like to be his partner in winning, which offer is accepted. Then, during several hands the crooks let him win until he is sufficiently enticed to bet all that he has. It is then that the trap is sprung and the victim is caught.

Illustrations taken from card-games are numerous. It was observed previously that many of Greene's popular pamphlets on the sharpers of London were enlargements of those on the title-page of **The groundworks of conny-catching. [109]** The title-page of S. Ward's **Woe for drunkards** presents dice, a goblet, cards and lace-edged garments, all signs of degeneration. Rowlands uses card-figures to symbolize the abuses in society; **The knave**

of hearts, 1612, deals with games and betting. **Hocus-pocus junior,**
1638, is a complete treatise on conjuring, useful for private or
public entertaining. The entire art of prestidigitation depends
upon deflecting the attention of the spectator. The treatise deals
not only with dice but with the illusion of beheading, or of making
a child's head appear in a jug of water.

Puritans objected both to betting and to plays. Theatrical
illustrations are of two kinds; those which show one or more of
the characters and those which represent a crucial scene in the
drama. The majority belong to the first category: among them
are, **Hyckescorner,** Marlowe's **Tamburlaine,** Rowley's **When you
see me, you know me,** Beaumont and Fletcher's **A king and no
king, English-men for my money,** and Heywood's **The fair maid
of the West.** [110] Cooke's **Greene's Tu quoque** has the advantage
of showing the leading man at the same time as the main character.
R. Wilson's **The three lords and the three ladies of London,** 1590,
presents the characters as if they were made of wood.

In illustrations of the second category, we find that
the main action of the drama appears on the title-page. Arden
of Feversham is shown murdered while he is playing backgammon.
[111] Marlowe's Dr. Faust is seen in the midst of the astrological
signs which Satan has given him, causing his spiritual loss and
the despair which grasps him at the end of the play. In Greene's
Friar Bacon and Friar Bungay, the friar is asleep at the crucial
moment when the statue speaks, and the servant on the watch
is too stupid to understand the message it transmits. **A faire quarrell**
by Middleton and Rowley and **The maids tragedie** by Beaumont
and Fletcher enable us to witness the two duels essential to their
plays. (Plate 88a) Heywood's **A maidenhead well-lost** presents
a slight variation. The image is divided: on the right, one sees
the two interlaced lovers; on the left, on the table, five men
uncover a box which contains the girl. [112]

It is chiefly a portrait of the common man rather than
of the aristocracy that the illustrated pamphlets offer us of daily
life. We never penetrate the jealously guarded and highly decorated
castles. The elegance of English mansions is made easily available
in our modern books, as the furniture and the architecture are
brought to light by the historian. What is discovered is that life
in the sixteenth century has improved little by little until the
middle of the seventeenth century. In short, we see the slow progress of the masses towards a more refined civilization. These
are the problems and anxieties of everyone who is not protected
by privileges from experiencing the harsh reality of everyday
existence.

Chapter VII

A MIRROR OF SOCIETY

Everyday life in Renaissance times varies according to degree. Rich noblemen wear luxurious materials and follow the latest fashion in clothing and in housing. They eat off gold or silver plates; they are allowed to play cards; they dance to the sound of the pavane, the allemande or the galliard. Should one therefore conclude that the rich and noble men can do as they wish and that only the poor commoners are bound by the restrictions of proclamations and statutes?

Certainly not. It is true that the poorer classes, dressed in cloth or in felt, cannot gamble as they please, that Sunday is kept for sports under the strict supervision of the parish, to the exclusion of other days. Through necessity, they live in shanties and their dress is strictly practical. But the commoners also include those merchants whose wealth is coveted by the poor nobleman's daughter and the nobleman, having lost his revenues, must wear his clothes threadbare.

Nor is it true that noblemen are free to do whatever their fancy dictates. We have already seen that the nobleman is not allowed to join in the noisy dances around the maypole. He should not let himself be beaten by a man of inferior class. Eating in the kitchen is to fall from his rank and Sir Toby, who drinks and cultivates the friendship of maids, is only a degenerate. It is not healthy for man to shun his social responsibilities. [1]

Each man in this society that aims at more stability than actually exists, should fulfill his function in the environment and position that God assigned him. But the spirit of feudalism is on its way out as the power of plutocracy asserts itself through the mobile and rising class of merchants. Yet the belief still persists. The meaning of his life directly relates to the satisfaction of having carried his burden, as Christ did His cross, according to the divine plan. To lead a righteous life, true to God and his sovereign, mindful of his neighbor, kind to his friends, and just to his servants, is the aim of the man of the Renaissance. Sent

by God on the earth to tend it, man, like Atlas, bears the burden
and the responsibility of the way of the world.

Yet it is not good for man to be alone. God, in his
kindness, gave woman to man to help him on his long and arduous
path to the gates of heaven, serving God's kingdom on earth. [2]
Even so, some of the pamphlet writers toy with the question of
whether woman is in fact a help or a supplementary burden. As
to the women, some dare consider themselves equal to 'the lord
and master' of nature. Indeed, do not two ruling queens succeed
each other on the throne of England? There is no shortage of
treatises in favor of or against woman. In the illustrated pamphlets
the issue reaches its peak with the Swetnam controversy. His
pamphlet against marriage which insists on woman being the worst
evil for man, arms the fair sex with the pen of wit which will
turn often sharper than that of their accuser.

The quarrel was not new. But amour courteois had raised
woman to a rank between the saint and the pagan goddess, and
painted her with subtle hues. To win her heart, man submits to
many a test, braves numerous dangers. The medieval tradition
largely inspired from France changes at the Renaissance as the
eyes turn to Italy. The Petrarchan lady is as exacting as her medieval counterpart, but contrary to the latter, she never gives way.
Thus instead of inspiring man with moral strength, she destroys
his virtu, as man wears himself out in the hope of possessing
her. She is cold, insensitive and cruel, and nothing can deter her
from her pride, reach her and move her. Her influence on man
is finally negative, as frustration creates anger and a desire for
self-destruction. Her main role is to provoke the poet into writing
his complaint.

Though some of the bourgeoisie may be challenged by
the subtleties of medieval courting and of Petrach, most of them
tend to prefer the spicier reality of the wife of Bath. Most of
the illustrated pamphlets dealing with the role of woman as part
of a couple hardly aim much higher than the morals of the fabliaux,
and differ considerably from **Astrophel and Stella**. Gosynhill swears
against the fickleness of women, their tendency to gossip, and
their extravagance in **The Schole house of women**, 1550 and in
A dyalogue betwene the comen secretary a. jelowsy, 1560(?),
ornamented with stock-type characters; [3] jealousy wants to
get married and asks the secretary's advice. For instance, here
is the answer to whether it is possible to subdue a shrew:

> Yes wyth good handlelyng as I ayme
> Even by and by ye shall her reclayme
> And make her tame as ever was tyrtyll
> To suffre kyssynge and tyklynge under the kyrtyll.

There is no need for us to conclude what is the main attraction of woman for man; the text is self-explanatory. The rest of the dialogue is amusing in tone and is not to be taken more seriously than the stories of _ménage à trois_ in our Broadway comedies.

The quarrel gains in seriousness after the publication of Knox's **First Blast of the Trumpet . . .** A convinced Calvinist, Knox believes that letting a woman rule England is to go against the laws of nature. He quotes the Bible and argues that perfection in a woman consists in obeying man. Since Eve is responsible for the Original Sin and cursed in **Genesis,** she is henceforth, condemned to suffer to have children and obey the laws devised by her husband. It is therefore indecent to see a woman, and a spinster at that, ruling England and nothing right will come of it. [4]

The validity of the arguments of Knox for the Elizabethan mind is corroborated by the legislation of the time, which shows the expected role of woman in the community. It was codified on paper in **The Lawes Resolutions of Women's Rights,** 1632, and is worth mentioning. [5] Woman who takes no part in legislation is nevertheless ruled by the same. The reason why she has no voice in Parliament is that she is responsible for the expulsion of Adam from Paradise, and his disgrace. [6] A woman hardly exists, in any legal sense, apart from marriage. From the age of seven, her father can look for a husband for her. At the age of nine, she should be given a dowry. At twelve, she can, if she is obdurate and prepared to renounce her dowry, marry the boy she loves without the consent of her father. Around fourteen she is of age and at sixteen, she is already getting old maidish. Therefore it is not surprising to hear Lady Capulet tell Juliet that she should seriously be thinking of marriage and that many a friend of hers already has children. [7] An unmarried girl is often a heavy burden to her family.

In wedlock, the woman is totally obedient to her husband, and depends upon him, body and soul. She is "covert", that is, like the brook that joins the bigger river and is absorbed, losing thus its name and its identity. Her new personality should model itself on her companion, her lord and master. [8] As a counterpart, her husband owes her help and assistance. He is answerable to the law for any of her misdemeanors, a heavy responsibility. A letter from John Chamberlain shows that the seventeenth century will make no progress in this respect. The bishop of London tells his clergy to reprimand the women of their parish for their mischievous conduct. It is not decent for them to follow the masculine fashion, have their hair cut and give themselves emancipated airs. Indeed, the king proposes to punish the husbands if they do not put an end to the excesses of their wives. [9]

Through the legislation, therefore, woman's status is that of a minor in society. If she does not marry or bear children, she has hardly any more importance in this Christian civilization than she would have had in ancient Achean times. Copland describes the widow in **The seven sorrows of women**, 1568(?), illustrated by eight woodcuts. She is seen nursing her husband before he dies. Then she has to wear her mourning garments and bury him. Four men are carrying the body while the parson blesses the corpse. The husband is then put down into the ground and the unfortunate expectant woman is thus bereft of a father for her child. The grave-digger covers the coffin with earth while the woman is helped by a friend or by another woman belonging to the family. The fourth woodcut within the text shows her praying at church and thinking of her first night of deprivation in bed. Then, such is the irony of life, things gradually go back to normal. The neighbors come and go. She starts going out of her home again. Soon, the last picture shows her cursing her husband who forbade her to remarry.

The male point of view that woman is nothing without him finds a counterpart in the female point of view, related by a male in S. Rowlands's, **Well-met Gossip**, 1619. Three merry wives confide to each other the drawbacks of marriage, from the female point-of-view. A virgin, a married woman and a widow are sitting on the second floor of a tavern and drink some wine, as shown on the very fine title-page. This is a more refined version of **Elenour Rummin** by Skelton. The customers of Elenour Rummin drink downstairs in the common room, those of **Well-met Gossip** go upstairs. The former pay in goods whereas the latter pay in coins. Though both drink pots after pots of wine the difference in social class is made clear. The women of **Well-met Gossip** are from the city whereas the others belong to the suburbs or to the country.

The three women talk of their favorite subject: men and love. The young girl expresses her scepticism about marriage, but the widow and the married woman, though partly agreeing, still think that marriage is the best of all evils that can befall a woman. Without false coyness, unlike our Victorian ladies, they directly refer to the sexual advantages of wedlock. Virginity forces a woman to chastity, a very grim prospect. The rest of the pamphlet describes the life of the couple, its joys and its strains: what man allows woman to drink, and the way he reacts when she is slightly too "happy." The pamphlet expresses a male point of view but it is also sensitive to some of the female opinions.

In **The Bride**, Samuel Rowlands expresses the feminist quarrels through a more violent debate. The title-page is much less refined than that of the previous pamphlet: a woman holds two children, which, we would assume, might represent the contents of the brochure: motherhood. But in fact the inside dialogue is a conversation on the advantages and disadvantages of marriage without any reference to the role of the woman as mother. Unmarried girls claim that they are men's equals, and even that they sometimes are superior. Marriage is therefore the enslavement of woman who has to suffer the whims of her husband, his continual scolding on the way she manages the budget . . . And to add to it all, he makes a cuckold of her! He exploits her and flatters her when he wants his pound of flesh from her, or wishes to make her work harder. The girls decide that marriage is evil, and that they are having none of it.

The married woman is not original in her answers, but she presents them intelligently. Liberty is not good for woman who needs a guide for her life. Man is certainly wrong if he goes out with other women. But woman is not blameless either. She had an unfortunate tendency to tease him sexually, without any intention of fulfilling her promise. Those who think that they can keep chastely away from marriage are presuming on their own strength. There follow some salacious details worthy of Chaucer's "The Miller's tale." I know one girl, the bride says, who pretended she abhorred men; but one day her belly started to grow. The guilty party was, of course, Welsh, as the Welsh are renowned for their amorous inclinations. [10] The pamphlet continues with the praise of marriage and of the virtuous woman, a reflection of the thought of the time. [11] Her first duty is to keep an eye on the household and not to meddle with the outside occupations of her husband. She is queen over the house and reigns over the children. Her second task consists in keeping open house for the friends of her husband. But when she wants to have friends in, she should ask her husband's permission so that he will not be jealous. She must manage her budget parsimoniously, and not be extravagant in her expenditures on clothing. It is not suitable for her to spend her time gossiping, since she is not supposed to serve as the gazette to the town. The tavern and the theatre are not proper places for her to be found. Fifthly, a modest woman does not assume that her huband can err, or that he may sometimes act foolishly for, as a rule, men are wiser and more intelligent than women. In the shop, she should never be allowed to strike a bargain, for the woman who makes a decision in business will soon want to wear the breeches in the house. Her sixth task is to pacify her husband, when he is either bothered or angry. She must honor her husband and always speak of him with respect to other women. And last of all, she must perform these duties with love, for better or for worse.

If the fifth duty is excluded, the advice given by Rowlands is not so far from that given by a mother to a daughter, even today. Wilkinson in **The Merchant Royall**, 1607, had already summed up the duties of the middle-class woman, by comparing her to a merchant ship according to the biblical model, in **Proverbs** 31:14. The sermon is a good example of Aristotelian rhetoric, proceeding through similitude and dissimilitude. Address to a young aristocratic couple, it can be summed up in a few sentences. Woman, like a ship finds man as it is sailing, aimless on the sea. She takes him on board and he becomes her captain and she the rudder that he directs. She differs, however, from a ship in three respects: she belongs to one man only and not to a crew, she should not be bedecked like the ship, and her captain can take her right back home. And yet, she belongs to the merchant navy, because a sensible woman brings back so many riches to her companion. She definitely is not a warship, for she is not to be firing insults, nor is she to grumble. A woodcut ship, of no particular beauty, adorns the title-page of the sermon.

The sermon drags on, a little wearily, and one finds a curious allusion to divorce at the end, to refute the possibility of it, of course, but it seems rather untimely. The married couple will have to stay true "'til death do us part", a time when one of them will join the Lamb, because the Lamb allows neither divorce, nor separation. [12] The awkwardness of the suggestion is amusing though perfectly defensible on theological grounds.

The three pamphlets that we have just analyzed are favorable to woman. They reassert that it is not good for man to live alone and that a wise woman is his best asset, physically, mentally, and economically. They also ascertain progress in the condition of women, from the time of patient Grissell or Griselda, whose story is related by Th. Dekker. Griselda who is seen threading in a shack, bears everything from the lord, her husband. He has her daughter and then her son taken away from her; he repudiates her because of the baseness of her birth; she suffers all without a groan. He even asks her to greet the woman that she thinks he is going to take for a new wife, and she accepts. Whatever tyranny is imposed on her, she obeys in silence. But the husband, who was only testing his wife and finds her a model, praises her and cherishes her for ever and gives her back the rank of marquess.

Such passivity is not that of the wife of the end of the sixteenth century. Either, like Jyll of Braintford, she goes shopping to the market, or like the married woman of **Well-met Gossip**, she helps her husband in the shop. Her role in the mercantile society now developing in England, is more active. It cannot afford idleness. The mistress of the house has to give the right instructions to her servants and be on the lookout for leaks in any budget that she herself does not fully control. Whatever the reason the picture of woman is no longer, in the seventeenth century, that of passive endurance, but of active obedience.

Some men resent this new role assumed increasingly

by the English woman, though G. Matsys had painted the Flemish woman helping her husband in the famous painting of the Banker and his wife in which the mirror reflects the outside world. Whether anti-feminist pamphlets are the result of a literary fashion or express the resentment of a majority of males, is hard to tell, but they certainly abound.

Among the illustrated pamphlets, **The deceyte of women,** 1560, is more interesting by its numerous illustrations than by its text. The title-page is appealing. Woman, armed with a whip, muzzles her husband and spurs him forward. This beautiful woodcut seems of German make. All the other images of the text were carved by a different hand. They relate some of the numerous stories of feminine deceit from biblical or classical antiquity. The text itself consists in the alternation of these stories drawn from tradition and their modern equivalents. From Judith to Helen of Troy, all women are deceitful, a theme which recurs in **The arraignment . . .** by Swetnam.

Not all pamphlets are openly misogynous. Then, as today, there are men who think that every woman is fickle except for their mother, their sister, their wife, their daughter and some of the chaste friends whom they have met. What disturbs man is the "new" woman who wants to follow the latest fashion, in clothes as well as in civilization; she menaces his security, by disturbing the secure image he inherited about the subordinate role of woman in society. One of the symbols of this change is her clothes.

Many pamphlets illustrate feminine fashion and all are disparaging. We have seen that **The Merchant Royall** strongly recommends a man not to bedeck his wife. Gosson in **Quippes for Upstart Newfangled Gentlewomen,** 1595, formulates his principles: peacock vanities bring nothing to her soul; on the contrary, they spoil it for eternal life. The various issues of this pamphlet are illustrated according to the fashions of the times. **A Discourse against Painting. . . of Women,** 1616, by Tuke, with the same type of image on the title-page, ridicules the plastering, the star-shaped spots and other beauty aids used by the women of the time. Modesty is the woman's way to man's heart and to salvation.

The same type of woodcut again illustrates the frontispiece of **The arraignment of Lewd, idle, forward and unconstant women,** 1615, so that the misogynist, walking in the streets around St. Paul's may immediately pick up his favorite literature. This tract suddenly hit the mark as it gave the impulse for a new outburst of literature. The quarrel armed men and women and both sexes took up their pens for the fight. The author claims that he is only attacking fickle women, but within the body of the pamphlet he asserts that nothing good should ever be devised or achieved by women. It is dedicated to light-headed young men and advises them to stay single. He draws the list of the women who should be avoided: the good and the bad ones; the good-looking and the ugly, the rich and the poor. Should they be stubborn enough to want to marry, they should choose a young and supple woman and keep away from widows. By nature woman is vain, exacting and extravagant. She flatters man until all his fortune has disappeared in her dress or her pleasures and the poor husband works all day whereas she thinks of nothing but foul-play. She paints her face, curls her hair, she is superficial and her ideal is to be married to a courtier. [13] Swetnam's prejudice, not only against women, but also against the court, can easily be perceived. Yet his was often the typical belief of the middle-class.

In a third point, Swetnam, to give more strength to his argument, reviews the faults of men and those of women. Men, he confesses, sometimes get drunk. But this is their only shortcoming, whereas women have all the defects. Was Swetnam's pamphlet indeed the product of inebriety? Who knows? Anyway, it was taken seriously by a number of the ladies of the time, who, indignantly armed themselves not with the whalebones of their corsets, but with a sharp and often witty pen. Their answers far surpass Swetnam's tract in their light-heartedness and erudition. [14] Unfortunately they are not illustrated. Yet, to give a single instance, Ester Sowerman, in **Ester hath hang'd Haman,** accuses Swetnam of blasphemy when he asserts that God created woman with one of the bent ribs of Adam, which, according to him, accounts for the crookedness of women. [15]

One must confess that Swetnam's pamphlet is not particularly brilliant. Moreover, his arguments are often so lightweight that one feels he is providing opponents sticks to be beaten with. The play **Swetnam the woman-hater** exposes him at the bar surrounded by a group of middle-class women who threaten him with a knife. (Plate 9) Their pointed caps are a sign of their class. In the center, Atalanta, in lieu of James I, has the seat of the judge. In fact the misogynist only appears in a few scenes, whereas the main theme of the play deals with the crossed love of Aurelio and Isabel using the typical devices of the theatre of the time: a lost and found brother, disguise, masquerades, dances. . . . In Act I, Misogynos appears elated, because he has sown trouble in every family and he laughs at the credulity of people. [16] Meanwhile, his pupil Sanfardo undertakes to defend the fair sex. In Act V, women are taking their revenge on Swetnam and torture him, using the whale bones of their corsets. They tell him he is ignorant, his book is condemned and he is expelled from the stage. [17] Swetnam is pleasantly satirized. The tone of this bears a resemblance to Pope's poem of the eighteenth century, **The Rape of the Lock,** as women are already armed with the instruments that contribute to their beauty.

In 1620, another exchange of pamphlets, this time both illustrated, keeps the question alive. **Hic Mulier** criticizes the adoption of the masculine fashion by women. On the title-page, a woman who went to the hairdresser to have a hair-cut is looking at herself admiringly in the mirror. She is dressed in the elegant masculine fashion, starting around the middle of James's reign. She then tried on one of those felt hats with a long plume typical of the court fashion of the time.

Just as Copland had written two complaints, one on the disadvantages of marrying early and the other on the drawbacks of marrying late, immediately after **Hic Mulier, Haec Vir** appears. Both pamphlets were probably written at the same time and the woodcuts seem to come from the same shop. A man and a woman confront each other. The woman rests her hand on the pommel of her sword, while the man brandishes feathers and a mirror. She defends her right to liberty, and equality. Perenniality is not of this world, she says, and to prove it, all one needs to do is read the book of nature. So societies change and the role assumed by individuals. But man wants fixed rules for ever, which is not realistic. Times have changed and he should be prepared to acknowledge the new role of women. The conclusion, however, emphasizes the need for man and woman to amend and return to a more traditional way of life. [18] (Plate 66)

After 1620, as with all subjects, this one becomes less fashionable and is gradually dropped. Taylor's eulogies on a bawd and on the prostitute are amusing, but they do not bring any water to the mill. His pamphlets which combine erudition and saltiness, are mainly journalistic, but offer no conclusion on the crucial problem of the place of women in society. As typical phenomena of a mutable society, feminism and anti-feminism, then as today, express the discomfort accompanying the necessary acceptance of change, and the vanity of clinging to the banks of the river of civilization. Like adolescence, they manifest healthy signs of growth, however disconcerting to both parties concerned.

The conflict of generations between parents and children is not reflected in the press to the same extent as the differences between man and woman. Fathers do complain in plays about the lack of obedience of their children; and the advice of parents to children remains fairly traditional. [19] Yet, Kempe in his pamphlet, **The Education of Children**, 1588, deplores that with the rise of capitalism, parents are more concerned with the financial welfare of their children than with their education. His little book could be called "in praise of knowledge." He regrets that seamen, merchants and voyagers should be satisfied with their own ignorance whereas they could become judges, advocates, or even justices of the peace or preachers. He represents the point of view of the intellectual, prejudiced against the commercial world. Education should be the main parental concern, and within education, linguistics.

Keepe within Compasse and **Live within Compasse,** both show a pair of compasses on the title-page. The mother and the daughter in the second pamphlet hold a Bible where they will find the rules of their lives. The ideal is the <u>via media,</u> as expounded in antiquity by Seneca.

It is true, however, that the whole of society is changing thus bringing insecurity to the family. The balance between the nobility, the clergy and the working classes is gradually upset by the upward mobility of merchants. Some professions die, while others are created. Fear is borne in the hearts of the rich that they may be upset by the new social climbers who can become radical without detriment to themselves. The forces of conservatism ally against them. Harrison divides England into four social classes: the gentlemen, the citizens or the middle-class, the yeomen, the journeymen and the craftsmen. [20]

England's granary is entrusted to different hands. The lands of the Crown are enlarged by the dissolution of the monasteries under Henry VIII. Some are sold to men whose recent nobility is due to services rendered to the state, and the royal need for funds in the treasury of the Crown. The old nobility is the most respected since the domain has been inherited over generations. The new rule forces all noblemen to appear at court at least once a year. This was a serious drawback as some of them could not spare the money to buy the new clothes that this imposition required without endangering some of their patrimony. Also, it stopped them from looking after their land for some part of the year. Among them other noblemen chose the political career. The Earl of Essex and the Duke of Buckingham are among the most famous. Others, like the Howard family devote their lives to the defense of England, on land and on sea, and must leave the responsibility of their "pleasaunces" and farms to family and yeomen. Dukes and peers all possess landed property, a part of which is devoted to the pleasures of the family and the rest is given to farming. Inversely, there is a feeling that no one is truly noble, if he does not possess a piece of land.

Recent patents of nobility, generally acquired by soldiers, often result in the acquisition of land. Sir Francis Drake, Sir John Hawkins, and Sir Francis Vere, for instance, are examples of men who have been knighted for their services to the Crown. [21] There are some that complain that the titles are cheapened under the Stuarts. Sir John Oglander reveals that at the time of the expedition of La Rochelle, the Duke of Buckingham, being short of money, allowed the admirals of the fleet to create forty baronets. The letters patent of nobility were thus sold for a hundred and fifty or two hundred pounds compared with the usual thousand pounds. [22] One can easily imagine that the first move of these recently ennobled men was to acquire some land.

The more recent nobles as well as some rich merchants who have bought some land are not deeply concerned about the best way of tilling the ground. A. Standish in **The Commons Complaint**, 1611, raises this issue with others. [23] The new landowners are interested in both the prestige that their property confers upon them and its rentability. Their land is therefore a capitalist investment, like their ship, or the bulk of velvet and silk they acquire.

The gentlemen farmers of olden times who spent most of their time in the middle ages, fighting for the king or for his lord, now devote most of their time to their land. Thanks to almost constant supervision and the re-grouping of land due to the enclosure system, they no longer need as many hands. To these factors can be added the impoverishment of other squires. The journeymen, out of work, tend to wander over England, join in with people of disrepute and steal for a living. [24]

Standish complains as he sees good tilling ground converted into pasture either by the new landed gentry or by the old gentry who have become poor, because it requires less workers. The result is that food is expensive and that poor journeymen can no longer survive. He suggests that hedges should be planted with fruit trees [25] and that chicken houses should be built instead of the pigeon houses fashionable under James I. Between pages 20 and 21, he draws a model printed from a block. The grounds are surrounded by a ditch full of water, in order to defend the chickens from the blood-thirsty fox or weasel who eat the eggs or kill the chickens. The ditch is bordered with trees because England desperately needs construction wood. [26] In the water some ducks are swimming and another pond is built in the center of the land for the animals to have permanent drinking water. The hen house itself includes a door made out of horsehair, so that the hens can go in and out while the heat is kept within. Poultry does not cost a lot in feeding: some oats, a few fish that will multiply in the ditch, and the peasants will be all the richer for the selling of the eggs and meat. A good mix will comprise some roosters, hens, capons, ducks and mallards. The wood, once cut, will form poles on which hops or flax can be hung to dry, since most of those two products rot for lack of sufficient ventilation.

Another illustrated treatise, **The ordering of Bees**, 1634, by J. Levett, is designed to help the farmers with a better and more profitable management of their farms. The work is an acknowledged compilation of the two best books on the subject--those of Googe and of Southern--but it is simplified and explained for the common man. Facing the title-page, a beehive is set up on a low table and protected by woven straw. The work is concerned with protecting the bees from the cold and advises the breeder on the kind of flora that will best serve his purpose.

Peasants were not always poor. The yeoman was sometimes far richer than the gentleman farmer. In the seventeenth century he often tries to rise in society by buying manors. His son often goes to Oxford or Cambridge and his daughters are married to some nobleman and receive as a dowry enough for them to be able to live off their land. This change in the pattern of society is reflected in the pamphlets of Greene and Wilson: farmers' sons dress in velvet hose and abandon cloth breeches; they are to be called "gentlemen" and no longer "goodmen". The title-page woodcut of **A quip for an Upstart Courtier** shows precisely the quarrel between the recently rich who does not dare to confess his base birth and the peasant who is proud of his cloth breeches worn for the nursing and feeding of England. The envious peasant accuses the upstart of pride, mercantilism, and Machiavellism. [27] The bitter peasant then reviews all the classes of society, and finds only a score of fairly honest people. [28]

Below the yeoman in the social scale, rich enough to be able to lend money to the Crown, as Wilson states it, and an archer in the infantry, [29] there come the tenant-farmers. They belong to two categories. The free-holders are, as their name indicates, free men, who are answerable to the law of the realm and owe military service. On the other hand, the farmers who hold their tenancy from customary usage, are attached to the manor, either by soccage, or by a lease of one year, seven years or of an even longer period of time. [30] If they do not pay their rent, they are to be evicted. This last type of tenant appears in our pamphlets. He is seen on the title-page of **A dialogue betwixt a cittizen and a poore Countrey-man** by Brewer, bitter against the rich landlord who is insensitive to the fluctuation of the harvest. [31]

Last in the country world, there appear the workers, journeymen or seasonal employees. They offer their labor at the time of the fairs. Sometimes as they are unemployed, they put snares in the fields and the woods and have to appear in front of the justice of the peace. The plaintiff in **A dialogue between the plaintiff and the defendaunt**, 1535, is one of those culprits, who as a result of being caught has to spend some time in prison. The illustration gives no clue to his surreptitious activities. The blame is laid, as stated before, on the heads of those who have converted arable land into pasture. [32]

Traditionally, the shepherd does not share the acrimonious temperament of the tiller of the earth. He earns very little but is fed on the farm; he is given a crook and plays the pipe, as he sits watching his flock as in the vignette of **The merry jest of the frier and the boy.** The leisurely aspect of this country occupation appeals to some of the members of the court who play at shepherd and shepherdess on the title-page of **Taylor's Pastoral,** a theme dear to the French queen of the eighteenth century, Marie Antoinette. This occupation was also rich in biblical associations that raised it to one of the most venerable vocations, the ministry. Holbein has shown examples of bad pastors in **A little treatise,** 1548.

The shepherd was therefore a symbol of humility, poverty and concern. The calling was not restricted to men. The father of patient Grissell is a poor man who lives in a shack built by the man for whom he works. To supplement his income, his daughter tends the sheep and spins flax or wool. [33] An additional problem arises for poor men after the law of 1566. Until then it was possible to build a one-family house on an acre. After 1566 no one is allowed to build unless he has four acres. Thus the poorer sort were almost pushed into becoming nomads and sometimes ruffians.

Nor is living in the country free of taxes. All pay the tithe to the clergy [34] and the tax to the parish, in which case they will fear neither the constable nor the justice. [35] Those in turn protect them and their cattle against vagrants, Londoners fleeing from the plague, and from various other injustices. Some are honest, others can be bought; Greene's two characters, Velvet-breeches and Cloth-breeches agree on this point. Chicanery is the plague of countrymen. One brings an action against his neighbor whose hen has scratched the trees of his orchard. [36] The judge meanwhile puts them both on the same side by ruining them while the usurer who has advanced the money for the expense of the lawsuit is thriving. [37] (Plate 67) The heavy expenditures of the parish are divided between the richest of the yeomen or far-mers. They consider it an honor to be churchwarden or inspector of the inn. The duty of the sergeant of the guard does not tempt anybody, though, as no one makes friends through enforcing the law and, on the contrary, this is a way to create enemies for life.

The time table of the farmer's life is represented in the vignettes illustrating the almanacs, hanging on the wall of the kitchen in the farm. Some bear the traditional cuts on the occupations of each month, others bring further information on the recent discoveries in agriculture. In the almanacs of Buckminster for 1590, of Grey for 1591, and of Neve for 1616, for instance, the peasant will find when he should sow, plant, graft, castrate the animals, shear the sheep, prune the vine and cut his hair.

The farmer also uses the almanac for medical advice.

Buckness, in 1589, specializes in veterinary writing. Buckminster and Neve include a medical treatise. Greene's Cloth breeches trustingly follows the remedies he finds in his almanac and goes to the apothecary's only if his horse is sick. [38]

Almanacs also provided the countryman with a list of the fairs of the realm, either local, national or international. Bartholomew Fair at Smithfield or Sturbridge Fair in Cambridge are the most renowned of the third category. One could see there theatrical performances and autos-da-fé. [39] Unfortunately we have no visual representations of the fairs in the pamphlets, except a glimpse of Jyll of Braintford going to the market with her basket in her hand. The market often takes place once a week in London (two come immediately to mind--those of Smithfield and Leadenhead) or in the boroughs. Most of the London markets are organized according to specialization (meat in Smithfield and flowers in Covent Garden, as examples), whereas the small town market endeavors to bring all that is needed for a household to survive the rest of the week. [40] This is the place where the women exchange most of the gossip of the preceding week, the news that was not available the previous Sunday as they came out of church.

Although there is an element of stability inherent in country life which is not shared by city life, nevertheless a slight evolution can be observed during the first third of the new century. Not only do treatises show progress in the art of the orchard and garden, [41] but new plants are grown besides the traditional ones. Peas, beans and the usual cereals are cultivated, but hops and apricots (or "apricocks") have to be mentioned as new developments. [42]

The passion for silk clothes also influences agriculture. At the beginning of the seventeenth century, England imports thousands of mulberry trees in order to develop the silk industry. [43] Treatises follow, showing the countryman how to deal with the fragile insect. **The silkwormes and their flies,** 1599, by Moffet, proposes to boost the advantage of the raising of the silkworm in England. Only the title-page bears a woodcut and the treatise is more erudite than useful as it reviews the history of clothes from Adam to the present time. Of far more use to the farmer is Stallenge's pamphlet **Instructions for the increase and planting of Mulberry Trees,** 1609. It comprises detailed instructions and woodcuts that show precisely how to organize the breeding: the exposure necessary to the planks where the leaves and the worms will be placed, the way the worms reproduce themselves, with the various stages shown, and the spinning-wheel needed for the unravelling of the silk. (Plate 37)

Country folks have many enemies. Drinking and betting

are not the least. In **Eleanour Rummin,** they often pay for their drinks in kind: one is said to have brought a chicken, the other a cradle or a cot. [44] And yet, when sober, the wife objects to her husband coming back drunk. A picturesque cut in Taylor's **A Crab-Tree Lecture,** 1639 exposes one of these marriage scenes. Armed with a ladle, a wife prepares to greet her husband under the apple-tree. He tries to smile and look at her with sheepish eyes to calm her fury, but she is tired of seeing hard-earned money disappear in alcoholic fumes and she keeps on hitting him. [45] Robert Greene depicts another scene, in **The art of Conny-catching,** that of the countryman coming to London because of the fair; as he is unsophisticated, he soon becomes the easy prey of the coney-catchers hanging around the tavern.

Whoever speaks of England should mention the weather, which the pamphlets illustrate with particular vigor. Floods (Plate 68) and winds carry off the house and the barn of the countryman. This one sees on the nice woodcut of **The last terrible tempestious windes and weather,** 1613. The floods were followed by a harsh winter in 1614 and the farmer's cattle are killed for lack of proper covering and insulation. And yet the wretched man struggles to save them as on the title-page of **The cold Yeare,** 1614. (Plate 45)

The plague is also one of the crosses that the countryman has to bear, hence his lack of charity towards fleeing Londoners. But the plague often kills his servants and journeymen, his dog, his cat, his sheep, his cow and his horse. Thus he is left with no help to till the ground and no dairy foods. Years of famine ensue until he has earned enough to build up his farm anew. [46]

The best help the farmer has is his wife, when she is thrifty. Her role in the farm is very considerable. She prays in the morning before getting up, and she sweeps and tidies the house. Then she milks the cow, makes sure that the colts have suckled the mare, and skims the milk. After this she prepares the children's and her husband's breakfast and shares the meal with her children and the servants. She orders some flour from the miller's and fetches it herself, to be sure she will not be cheated on the weight. During the day, she makes butter and cheese, gathers the eggs in season, feeds the pigs and the fowls. She takes care of the herb garden and of the fields planted with hemp and flax which, once gathered, she will turn into thread, as shown on Taylor's pamphlet. [47] After having woven the flax into sheets, she cards the wool and knits it into warm clothing for the winter. Such is the life of a countrywoman. [48] Illustrated pamphlets show her milking the cow as in the pamphlet on Dr. Fian or in **Tom Thumb;** alternately she spins like the wife of Morell [49] or patient Grissell, sitting on the threshold of her cottage. [50]

The ballads also show her tossing the hay. No wonder Fitzherbert compares her jokingly to a horse. Like the horse she is cheerful in disposition, she must obey the slightest push from her master, her brow and her hips are wide, and she is fragile and difficult to keep. More jocularly still, he infers that she can easily be jumped upon and that she spends her time biting her bit. [51]

The horse is the subject of more than one treatise, the most famous and repetitious being by Markham. **The English Farrier**, 1636, is illustrated and has the advantage of summing up briefly what Markham often expounded garrulously. It tells how to keep a horse in good trim. The title-page cut shows the various uses of a horse: saddle-horse, draught-horse or pack-horse. The veterinarian and the farrier are in action. Inside the pamphlet another cut shows the anatomy of the horse.

After the horse, the cow and the ox are the best helps that the countryman can buy. The cow produces milk and cheese, the basic food of the peasant. Oxen are good for tilling the ground. Sheep produce wool and salted pork is a good food to have to prevent the family from starvation in winter. As black pudding, made immediately after the killing of the pig, out of its blood, cannot be kept fresh for a long time, the farmer gives some to his neighbors. The neighbor will return the compliment when he in his turn kills his pig. Thus, with a little forethought, pigs were killed at weekly intervals to prevent any spoiling of the rich food they produced. [52]

Let us therefore imagine the older English countryside, open, with scattered trees and mills, gradually closing up with color patches edged in by stem-stitches. [53] The contrast between one field and another is more noticeable, but the mill unifies the whole, and its ever-moving wings in a country where the wind hardly ever stops, gives cheerfulness to the landscape. The miller makes the flour, a fairly rich man since he can use several full-time servants and live in a house where pewter decorates the mantleshelf. But servants are sometimes jealous of their masters. We see them murdering E. Hall, a miller, at a time when he is anxious about his wife having a baby. [54] The miller does not, however, possess a spotless reputation. Like the butcher he is renowned for cheating on the weight of his merchandise and he is highly unpopular.

In town, that is to say, in London which is larger than any other town in the realm, men from all crafts, trades and professions swarm around the streets. Vagrants and pretenders appeal to the charity of the richer sort while liveried men stroll like so many components of the rainbow. The Elizabethan onlooker can see a variegated parade of bright serge, soft velvets and delicate silks according to the rank in society. A little tract bearing a rough woodcut of the coat of arms of the Lord Mayor's order, gives the numerous occasions when the people of London may see the Lord Mayor and his councillors in their traditional costumes: [55] for the municipal elections, St. Bartholomew's fair, for the taking office of a municipal official, the coronation of the monarch and for a number of events from the religious or juridical calendar of the realm.

In the streets of London, one can also hear the bustle of the conversations of those who study at the Chancery or at the Inns of Court. The latter accommodate those sons of noblemen, gentlemen or yeomen who did not go to Oxford or Cambridge. [56] There one does not only study law, to become a lawyer or a judge, but one also acquires the basic economic and financial knowledge to become a usurer or a merchant. That Bar is not a smooth profession. Generally unpopular, judges and lawyers are often the objects of popular railing. Not only Greene and the popular writers take a pound of their flesh, [57] but Johnson, who is recruiting for the Virginia company, welcomes almost anyone, except for magistrates, whom he expressly recommends not to apply. Though he does not give in detail the grudges he bears them, yet he indicates that they are as vile as papists and that the company neither needs their money nor their presence. [58]

The unlearned multitude shares this feeling of disgust. **A Dittie upon the death of certain Judges . . .** 1590, rejoices in the death of these masters-at-law, who judge the poor and the rich according to different standards. John Tindall, master of the Chancery, is shot by one of the people he judged. [59]

Very few spokesmen in favor of law are to be found in the pamphlets. In **London's Cry ascended to God** Henry Goodcole relates the offences judged at the sessions of 1619, saddens at the number of executions following the trials, but concludes that it is a necessary evil. Order can be kept in London only at that price, and judges are Godsent.

Even the Crown does not trust judges. James I issues an act where he keeps the right to select only righteous men for the profession. This act was a pure formality but it indicates the dubiety of the reputation of the Bar. Yet this is the profession most represented in the House of Commons. Facing the title-page of **The House of Correction** by J. H., a judge is sitting surrounded by two magistrates and displays a Bible where "Take the oath" is inscribed. Another pamphlet shows the Court of the Palace of Justice in London, **Swetnam, the woman-hater, arraigned by women**, 1620. A woman seems to be judging when Swetnam appears at the bar.

The second most influential group in Parliament is the

class of merchants. Growing mercantilism in the age of Elizabeth slowly learns how to manipulate the intricate machinery of government, in London or in the provinces. The wholesalers in the provincial towns belong to any company, but often, one company only controls the trade for a town. [60] The Parliament of 1614 includes 42 merchants while that of 1640 has seventy. [61] Consequently, they control most of the prices and the conditions of marketing. Gradually England inclines toward greater centralization. **The laws of the Market**, 1595, proclaims that the prices of the goods to be sold and market-days are to be fixed by the Lord Mayor or the mayor of the town. It is forbidden to sell at the inn before reaching the market-place. The market is forbidden to any stranger to the town, not registered at the Chamber of Commerce. Any such stranger who may sell or buy anything in London, will have his goods confiscated. [62]

To enforce these laws and privileges, the merchants of London pay informers who thread the crowded streets, on the lookout for any fault. Corruptible Flood appears crushed under weights for having gone far beyond the call of duty, unfortunately, not to serve justice, but to serve his own ends. The pamphlet describes his activities and is illustrated by three woodcuts. They are typical of the misdoings of the informers of the time. (Plate 42).

Flood denounces the inn-keepers, the chamberlains and the stable-boys who have started working illegally in London, unless they pay him for his silence. The money paid, Flood will protect them from the inquisitive eye of other informers since the law stops one from being apprehended by two informers at cnce. From foreigners he requests monthly payments. Once his rabbits are caught, Flood forces them to leave the town, by exacting more and more from them. He meets his match in a shrew, who attracts him to her cellar and then accuses him of rape. Merchants would have delighted in the punishment of Flood, all the more so, since suicides sometimes ensued from his rounds.

Whether the pamphlet is strictly true or whether the facts have been exaggerated for the pleasure of the readers, one thing remains certain. London's trade was in a state of confusion and the mercantile middle-class endeavored to put some order into it.

Another consequence of the centralization of commercial power is the establishment of monopolies. There are two sorts of monopolies: those given by the Crown to rid itself of a debt, and those that are the consequence of letters patent given for a discovery or an invention. [63] For instance, the monopoly given to Raleigh for the pewter in Cornwall, [64] or to Sir Richard Conningsby on cards, since he can require five shillings for the making of twelve dozen games of cards, belongs to the first category. On the other hand, the monopoly granted William Humfrey for the lead of Derbyshire belongs to the second: indeed he had thought of using a sieve and a tank of water to separate the ore from the rest of the rock debris. [65] The companies of merchant adventurers also belong to the second class of monopolies.

Many speak against monopolies. Satirists like Gascoigne, in **The Steel Glas**, 1576, attack the merchants who enrich the clothes of the courtiers while impoverishing them. [66] Misselden, the economist, thinks that the trade should be regulated by law, that the coffers of the Crown should fill up thanks to letters patent. Yet, to his mind, it is bad for national economy to see trade within a few powerful hands who can fix prices according to their whim and their profit, and only remedy the immediate crisis. [67]

Both Misselden and satirists agree that serge looks better than it really is and that drapers do not care whether it will be long-lasting, provided it looks good and sells. Greene adds that shoe-makers and tailors often sew with too hot a needle and thus burn the fabric. [68] Corruption steals into every craft; to the salesman, every trick is fair play is the theme of the end of **The Steel Glas**. Gascoigne adds, when merchants are honest, [read, when pigs begin to fly], priests will have no need for prayer. Mompesson, one of the monopolists, censured by Parliament, is the subject of public ridicule. (Plate 69)

Although some of the provincial towns are ruled by the oligarchy of merchants, they are generally only satellites of the **Urbs**, London. The country complains that its head is so disproportionately large, compared to its limbs. **Penny-wise Pound foolish**, 1631, displays on its title-page a draper from Bristol traveling to London and Venice, which serve as conventional locations for the fable. In order to thrive, a merchant from Bristol goes to London at regular intervals. There he establishes some relationships with other drapers, more powerful and richer than he, who bring business to him. Should the merchant be weak and naive, he will let himself be lured into taverns and will be cheated by his wiser fellow-members. Thus in the sixteenth and the seventeenth centuries, provincial merchants both hate and depend on the London hegemony. [69]

The more adventurous are not content with the national markets, but push on to the East, to find new products and gain international markets for England. These are the heroes of our pamphlets, as the taste for exoticism, the desire for pathos and the feeling of national pride all converge in their stories. New markets open during the Elizabethan era; they spread through Russia to the East Indies to Africa and to the West Indies and America. [70]

The stories about merchants relate the dangers of foreign trade, the merits of which are extolled in Th. Mun's **A discourse of the Trade,** 1621. Spending for foreign trade is great, but the return in riches is greater still. Therefore one should not hesitate to spend. The hazards are also summed up. Sometimes the cargoes are seized by foreign ships and remain confiscated in their harbors; one could give as an example, the Great Carrack, thus confiscated by the English from the Spanish. Pirates are also numerous, another hazard at sea. **The lives of the two pirates Purser and Clinton,** leads us to believe that many more were running free on the ocean. [71] One can also assume that if England had its privateers, other privateers were running loose, catching boats for the sake of other countries.

Other illustrated pamphlets tell us about the difficulties of the trade in the East Indies. Their route generally starts from Alexandria, goes through Jerusalem, crosses over to Persia through Syria and from there to India. Attempts at reaching Persia through the North of Europe are still fairly rare, since the expense of freight on land is rather more expensive than shipping a cargo. One of the most interesting stories of the pamphlets can be found in **News from the East Indies,** 1638. It tells of the difficulties in establishing a new market with Bengal. The story is said to be true, but most of the like profess the same. This one seems precise in its details and devoid of the sensational, which gives it verisimilitude: John Norris sends over two merchants to establish a trading center in Bengal. He shows how from one town to the next, Ralph Cartwright sends money to the governors to assure them of his good intent. But he and his companions always divide to prevent both being taken as prisoners, should there be foul play. His trust in Muslims is very limited and, though he praises their hospitality, he never turns his back to them for fear of being robbed, or worse, murdered. After disembarking at Alexandria, he travels on rivers, with small boats laden with precious metal. On land he carts his load with the help of camels and donkeys and at each town where he stays, enlarges his freight. Once he has reached the court of the Nabab, he brings presents to the king in order to display his riches. After several days of delay and deliberation, the king grants him the trade he asked for, provided that English boats help Bengali boats in distress. During those few days, an unexpected incident with his rivals, the Portuguese, endangers the negotiations, but finally all goes well and England gets the desired market.

Francis Knight's narrative, **A relation of seaven yeares slaverie under the Turkes of Argeire,** 1640, is just as credible. It describes, among other things, the difficulty for the European mind to comply with the habits of the Moslem trade, with its deviations, its cups of teas, and its ever-deferred decisions. Monsieur de Sampson wants to buy back some French prisoners. The Turks give him hearing after hearing without ever concluding the bargain. Finally Monsieur de Sampson burst out into a fit of anger, to the great amusement of the Turks, who attack Sardinia. The pamphlet is devised to warn would-be merchants that trade with the East Indies and Africa, not only requires commercial knowledge and craft, but also a patience hitherto unknown to the Europeans. (Plate 70)

Any rising class arouses both admiration and envy. The second feeling is expressed in the epigrams and satires that rail at merchants for casting their fortune on the ocean. In J. H(eath)'s **House of correction**, 1619, Venter, whose name suggests his profession, loses his mind at the news that his ships are destroyed. Why should he lose both his goods and his mind, the author asks? [72] This work also contains epigrams on the voyages of Drake and of Sir Walter Raleigh.

As a necessary evil resulting from the growth of capitalism, usury, that is lending money for a profit, is the subject of general outrage and denunciation. Numerous sermons deal with it. But the most famous work, necessary for the understanding of the illustration of one pamphlet, is Wilson's **A Discourse uppon usurye**, 1572. [73] Wilson was a high official, the ambassador to the Netherlands, and the author of the well-known **Arte of Rhetorique** and **The rule of reason.** He voices the ethical standpoint of the majority of the moralists of the sixteenth century. Loans at interest are incompatible with charity and mere justice. The lender steals the usufruct of the money since he has not worked for it. This is why, in Blaxton's **The English Usurer**, 1634, the usurer is represented in a woodcut as the creature of the devil. He is sitting at his table and counts his ill-gotten gold. He holds a debenture-bond in his hand and two coffers are resting on the floor. On his table, bonds, purses, a pair of scales and a hook lie, pell-mell. A diabolical advisor sits on the back of his arm chair; the devil assures him that he will get both the capital and the interest. In a corner of the picture, on the right, two pigs represent him. The first, on top, digs the ground with his snout, for he is ready to look for gold even in the mire, just like the usurer, the unclean man. Right underneath, the swine, on the point of dying, prays that he should be spared and shared after his death. A poem compares man and beast, who spend their lives groaning. The usurer is dressed according to the old fashion and his hands are closed, tight-fisted, as a sign of stinginess. [74] Thus, he feeds on the labor of other people, but does not spend any money that might encourage industry. He is no good to anyone, until he dies. (Plate 67)

This is unfortunately the only visual representation we know of. Yet illustrated pamphlets often refer to the usurer and

his brother, the pawnbroker. Both are found among Greene's characters. [75] Caleb in Dekker's **Penny-wise, Pound foolish** bears
an extraordinary likeness to the Shylock of **The Merchant of Venice**,
[76] while Melton, in **The Astrologaster**, 1620 compares him to
the mole who feeds on the dark entrails of the earth. [77] The
usurer is a dark, gloomy character, a satanic figure.

Yet the texts of the illustrated pamphlets echo the
change that is taking place in the seventeenth century. Blaxton
defines usury in terms acceptable to the sixteenth century: a
loan which will bring back some profit, whether in kind, in labor,
or in cash. But he mainly criticizes those who lend money at
more than the eight per cent legal rate. [78] This is a step towards
the acceptance of the capitalist system.

This evolution can be perceived in linguistic evolution.
Breton, in **Pasquil's Nightcap**, says that the usurer now wants
to be called moneyman, or money-master, in order to make his
profession respectable. [79] Euphemism is a way towards the
acceptance of an old taboo. Usury, which was so vehemently condemned by Crowley, Sandys, Jewell, King, Williams, Sutton, and
other preachers, as an ignoble intruder, has come to stay. Gradually
the word becomes applicable only to those who lend at a higher
interest than the legal rate. We have travelled far from the statutes
of 1487 and 1495, which were applicable up to 1571. [80] So
much so, that **Cupid's Messenger**, 1622, a compilation of fictitious
letters, contains a letter from a pedlar to a merchant in London,
regretting that neither banks nor usurers can be found in the
part of England where he was travelling. This was a serious impedi-
ment to him and to his trade, since immediate payment was difficult
to obtain from the gentlemen he was dealing with. [81] As time
goes by, another sign of the evolution of the mind towards usury,
the profession of lender passes from the hands of the Jews in
the area of Houndsditch in London to the hands of Christians. [82]

The oligarchy of the merchants necessarily affects the
conditions of craftsmanship. We shall not endeavor to refer to
all the crafts described in the illustrated pamphlets as all of
them are represented. Instead we shall confine ourselves to the
iconography. [83] We are mainly concerned with what they reveal
of the lives of the apprentices, a cause of worry among the peace-
loving middle-class.

The unruliness of artificers and apprentices hardly con-
forms to the ideal of middle-class morality and social order. Apprentices, especially, most of them adolescents, like ribaldry and noise-
making in the streets of London. The feast of each guild, celebrated
the day of their patron saint, is particularly feared by the authorities for everyone enjoys food and drink to their hearts' and stom-
achs' content. With their liveries, they are easily recognizable

on the streets of the city and these joyous extroverts match in behavior the brightness and color of their dress. From 1583, apprentices are subject to national rules as well as craftsmen. Before they only obeyed the rules of their guilds. [84]

As they belong to the proletariat, they do not participate in the political life of the realm, no more than journeymen. The everyday life of apprentices and of artificers is vividly depicted in Dekker's **Shoemakers' Holiday.** Heywood sets them in action in his play, **The four Apprentices,** 1615, and card-like characters show them jousting on the title-page. The plot bears on the necessity for the count of Burgundy, dispossessed by the king of France, to send his four sons to become apprentices. This is not strange as the impoverished nobility were more and more compelled to send their children into business in order to survive. [85]

The choice of the father for his sons indicates the degree of consideration held by each craft in the Elizabethan mind. First and foremost comes the draper: to him international markets are open and voyages to the Near East. Guy, the second son, becomes a goldsmith: he works not only on jewelry but also for the growing clientele of those who want to eat on silver and gold dishes. [86]

The third son becomes a mercer; he also works for the refined as they come to choose garters to adorn the lower part of their breeches or lace for their rebato, or a handkerchief to offer the lady they sigh for. Eustace the youngest, finds that being a grocer is a harder profession than his brothers', as seven years of apprenticeship is a long time to wait before he can himself run a shop. He particularly suffers from all the restrictions imposed on apprentices, and he has a severe master. He hardly has time for breakfast, works six days a week and is only allowed to go and see a joust once a week. He is forbidden to attend any parade, even on Mayday. London was at the time under constant fear of a riot. Eustace therefore is forbidden to attend any sports events like football or dancing. Needless to say, he is severely reprimanded if he bends to pick up a staff in the street. [87]

If apprentices are feared in peace for the boisterousness of their young blood, they are appreciated in war, as their valor makes them the flower of England's recruits. Heywood represents all of them armed on the title-page. As Grivelet rightfully notes, they are the modern knights. [88] They serve on land and sea. **Our Ladie of the Sea,** illustrated by a ship, sings their praise. [89] A "small" English caravelle is facing four "huge" Portuguese caravelles. So the captain gives a drink to all his good apprentices and citizens of London, who, crying, "St George for England", put to flight the Portuguese. This tract, in praise of the valor of the Londoners, is worth any of the narratives of the **Song of Roland** or the **Gest** of William of Orange. [90] In the same way, the four apprentices of Heywood, on the way to Jerusalem, bear with pride the coats of arms of their guild. One recognizes on Godfrey, the crowned virgin, the badge of the drapers.

The praise of workers who according to their rank in society bring their stones to the national edifice can be considered one of the consequences of the growth of Calvinism in England and of the spirit of democracy. Not that the value of work was previously depreciated, but Protestantism tends to connect more closely work and achievement, whereas the Catholic spirit gives greater value to unseen work as in contemplation and prayer.

Before we deal with the idle, or caterpillars of the realm, we shall consider the other vocations illustrated in the pamphlets. Transportation is undergoing a partial change in the seventeenth century. Yet the horse remains the main mode of conveyance for the majority of people. **A post with a packet of madde letters,** a successful work of N. Breton, if one is to count its numerous editions and enlargements, shows a postman about to blow the horn that announced that the mail had arrived. Underneath him, his vigorous horse is galloping. (Plate 15)

In town, the refined used to take sedan chairs. The carriers get angry as this is replaced by the coach drawn by two, four or six horses which puts them out of work. The pamphlets are full of the quarrel illustrated by some fine woodcuts. In **Knave of Hearts,** S. Rowlands jeers at coaches. [91] **Coach and Sedan,** 1636, shows three modes of transportation: [92] the cart is the most common of the three, it would correspond to a bus today. It is sometimes used to convey prisoners, as in **A Caveat for Common Cursetors,** by Harman. Used for convenience between the country and the town, it is found in **The lives and deaths of the two English pyrats, Purser and Clinton,** 1639. The countryman and a pursuer happen to be travelling together, a happy encounter since their incompatibility gives great joy to all who happen to meet them. The pursuer reads a proclamation of the king against the two pirates and the dull rustic mispronounces all his words.

The sedan appears on the bottom right part of the woodcut in **Coach and Sedan.** The carrier has two bands around his waist in order to carry the chair with little effort. (Plate 71) The coach on the left lacks both horse and coachman. On the box may be discerned what is either the coachman's staff or possibly the pole of a cart. The driver appears right on top of the picture, praising the advantages of his work as opposed to that of the carrier. In Taylor's **The World runnes on wheeles,** 1623, the coach is a symbol of all the abuses of society. Satan and a whore are attached to it in the woodcut facing the title-page. Taylor mainly criticizes those who rent coaches without a patent and therefore, deprive saddle-makers, ferrymen and dealers in hackney-carriages of their livelihood. Taylor writes a petition to the king in 1633, because many men of high rank possess one or two coaches and some even possess five to seven and rent out a few of them. The ballad, **The coaches overthrow**, 1637, also shows how vehement various tradesmen were in opposing this new means of conveyance.

Taylor is hardly disinterested, as the coaches enable Londoners to go from London to Gravesend, without using his ferryman's services. He, himself is portrayed rowing on the title-page of **A Sculler**, 1612. **Westward for Smelts**, 1620, shows one of the same trade, bringing back some happy fishermen's wives who got merry at the Red Knight, one of the favorite taverns of the ferrymen. The too merry wives are all full of Bacchus. Each tells a story, each worthy of Chaucer's "Tale of the Wife of Bath", as they relate some cuckold's gossip. The ferryman, happy to be in such company, sings them some songs in order to encourage them. One can imagine the Thames at this late hour of the evening resounding with their vinous songs, despite the orders of the Lord Mayor who forbade disturbance of the peace at night. [**93**] (Plate 72)

Taylor is not the only writer who wants to be remembered by his readers. The two popular writers, Greene and Dekker, are also depicted in the title-pages of their works. Dekker prophesies from his bed like John of Gaunt in **Dekker his dreame**, 1620, whereas **Greene in Conceipt**, 1598, had shown himself clad in his shroud and giving news from hell. Donne, the preacher and metaphysical poet, will want his final sermon to be illustrated with his portrait exactly as he preached it, in his shroud. [**94**] Others will choose to be represented for what they are professionally, as teachers, like on the title-page of **Hornbyes hornbook**, or preachers . . . [**95**]

There follows a gallimaufry of professions, appearing on the title-page of pamphlets, bearing little connection to each other, or that contrived. The actors, Tarlton, Kemp, Armin and Greene open the ballet. [**96**] Capers are cut by the tailor's apprentice in Armin's **The Italian Taylor and his boy**, 1609, soon followed by the hairdresser, who cuts women's hair according to the masculine fashion, in **Hic Mulier**, 1620. The dance of the barber is followed by the pavane of the doctor. He nurses the gout of a rich glutton with a "pooh" of disgust, on the title-page of **The praise of the gout**, 1617. His dress is richly lined with fur and his long, pointed hat suggests all the science stored in his brains. Yet this hardly deceives the popular writers who hold him in the same esteem as Molière in France and numerous are the satires on his ignorance. [**97**] Then comes the physician of souls, the preacher with solemn tread. Sibbes, Sym and Donne left their portraits to posterity. Others want to be shown as they preach. Two pamphlets illustrate, one the sermons of St. Paul's Cross and the other the preacher in a church, with his audience half asleep. [98] Last of all comes the intellectual and the teacher Pedantius, tall, dubiously erudite, and boring as in the play of Th. Beard that bears its name. All these bow out to leave us those members of society, who by reputation, at least, feed on the English shrub.

Two main types of "caterpillars", or "cankers in the rose" can be discerned, those who are dressed in velvet and the dull, slimy ones. All have one thing in common: they do not seem to work for the betterment of society. The courtiers are avowed delinquents, while the poor are potential delinquents according to sixteenth century politics. Punishment comes to them according to their degree; the rich rogues are assassinated or executed, whereas imprisonment, the stocks and hanging are reserved for common-folk, and out their candles go, silently, unless they have achieved some notoriety by the extent or smartness of their crime.

Elizabethan work ethics was not tender to the weak. Any person, who on account of health, or unemployment, or any other reason, did not pull his weight, was considered a scavenger. He is compared to the cog in the wheel. Hence the extreme measures applied to those who happened to be out of work. And yet Christian minds are troubled by the problem of poverty. Who is going to be responsible for them after the dissolution of the monasteries? In fact, it has been proved that the poor were no worse off from the time of the Reformation, since the citizens, aware of the difficulty, are ready to take charge of them, since the duty can no longer be passed on to the ecclesiastical and feudal authorities. [99]

Two illustrated pamphlets appear in the first half of the century. **The hye way to the Spyttel hous,** by Copland is of uncertain date and shows Copland surrounded by a poor man and a mendicant leaning on a staff. The other was translated by one of the agents of Thomas Cromwell, W. Marshall, and is called **The forme and maner of subvētion for pore people practysed ī Hypres,** 1535. The preface indicates the aim of the work: to find in the regulations of the city of Ypres, a model for an English solution to the problem of the poor and the vagrant, who ceaselessly commit crimes. Marshall recognizes that the main cause of these crimes is poverty. The treatise divides the needy in two categories. Those who quit work without reason, like some fretful apprentices, should be sent back. [100] If they persevere in their delinquency, they should be delivered into the hands of the judicial authorities. But the orphans, the sick, the weak and the old, are entitled to social aid. Overseers of the poor should be appointed. Their task will be to visit the houses of the poor, shops and cottages, in order to answer their needs. Prefects, appointed among the laity and ecclesiastics will meet twice a week to provide for the poor's wants, whom they will hear without frowning. [101] They will love them as their own children. Each parish will be entitled to levy some funds by sending every week a tax collector for the alms of the poor. [102] Preachers are ordered to exhort their parishioners to generosity and, after the service, a box will be placed at the disposal of those whose hearts have been moved.

All these provisos make it possible for society to become less nomadic. In the middle ages, for instance, pilgrimages were loaded with poor people whose motive was more secular than sacred since their dignity as pilgrims entitled them to free room and board. As a legal system is conceived and enforced, providing the basics for the poor, however faulty it may prove, a punitive legal system is established, punishing vagrancy. A stable society is being created and each parish will be responsible for its poor. Should a poor man have to travel, he will be given food and drink for one night in each parish he will happen to cross; but no more. In no case should a parish accept a family loaded with children coming from another parish, as it would deprive its sister parish from being charitable. [103] One can easily imagine that uncharitable parishes might have gladly passed on their problems to others. But Marshall is a diplomat and would not express things so bluntly. The system had the advantage of providing some basic social rights for the needy and protection for the working citizens from depredation and rookery. [104]

But **London's cry ascended to God**, 1619, dedicated by the author, Goodcole, to Edward Sackville, proves that, despite the law and statutes, the provisions were faulty. Highwaymen still exist and robbery, murder and other crimes have not left the English soil. One cannot say with exactitude, which of those are represented on the title-page.

The Orphans Court or Orphans Cry written by M. S. in 1636, and poignantly illustrated also confirms that the measures in favor of the poor were insufficient. [105] He also divides the poor in two categories. The crooks and the prostitutes should go to prison, Bedlam being the most famous, or to a reformatory, or to the gallows. The blind and the impotent, would be better employed at spinning wool than at selling ballads. As for the poor old people, the orphans and the simple-minded of London, they are seen wandering in Cheapside or lying on the benches of St. Bartholomew's, whereas others are dying at Smithfield. M. S. proposes that the employers take a certain percentage of their staff from the ranks of the minorities or the disabled. He suggests that every boat weighing more than two hundred tons and every collier going from Newcastle to London should have two needy people among its crew.

The title-page is designed to awaken the public conscience: children in tatters on top are begging "for God's sake." A young girl is carrying a banner and the children cry that they are starving. Underneath, children are actually dying and the inscription condemns the sadism of the general judgment passed on the poor. To assert that only the lazy are poor is both unfair and cruel. [106] Two adolescents, male and female, appeal to everyone's pity. (Plate 73) Many of the authors of illustrated pamphlets are keenly aware of the problems of the indigent, and its consequence, crime. Copland, Awdeley plagiarized by Harman, Greene, Luke Hutton, Dekker, Rowlands and John Taylor, are among the best known.

The truth of the matter is that the streets of London are full of beggars. Some simulate poverty and dejection, others put all their gains in the window and dress superbly in the hope of baiting bigger fish. The courtier is assimilated to one of those. He is a Machiavellian adorning himself with peacock's feathers in the hope of getting a sufficient pension to fill up his ordinarily empty stomach. This is as popular a subject as the feminist and anti-feminist quarrel. Greene's **A quip for an upstart courtier,** 1606, and Breton's **The court and the country,** 1618, both present on the title-page cloth breeches and velvet breeches. Nicholas Breton, partial to the town as it seems, despite its defects, opposes its refinement of the Court to the rough life of the country. The countryman will not let the courtier have his way and eulogizes the beauty of country women and the liveliness of intellectual life in the country. Indeed, the sermon and the sessions offer as much wisdom and refinement as one needs. Also, he adds, at court you have your conies, but here we catch our conies and eat them, [107] thus alluding both to the immorality of the courtiers and to their hunger. The pamphlet finishes on the praise of the true courtier, who is involved in the res publica, and gives his life to it. He is a friend to the monarch, a supporter of nobility, and fights for honor and virtue. Breton's attitude to the court is totally different from that of Greene and, later, of Taylor.

Taylor, the farrier, in **The praise, antiquity and commodity of Beggary, Begger and Begging,** 1621, has no more time for the courtier than for the dissemblers, pretending that they fought and were wounded at war. His title-page shows various sorts of mendicants: the lame and wounded sit at the bottom of the tree, the wandering beggar carries a double bag on his shoulder--and cankers and lice decorate his garment. Thirdly, the courtier appears, with his refined sharp-pointed beard, his feathered hat and his elegant dress. **The beggar's ape** and **Machiavelli's dog,** 1617, both portray the courtier as an animal. The courtier apes the fashion coming from Italy and fawns upon his master like a hound expecting some food from the royal table. Though both pamphlets do not deal uniquely with him, he is the main actor and the subject of the two title-page woodcuts. Rowlands's **The Knave of Spades,** depicts him as turncoat. He changes his religion according to his economic interest. Certainly, the courtier is no more popular than the judge.

The prodigal is another potential beggar. This category includes the son who inherits and wastes his patrimony. He is found near the hospital in search of a scrap of bread as in Copland's **The hye way to the Spyttell hous,** n.d. **[108]** He may find his subsistence from the prison warden, like the young draper who is a wastrel in **Penny-wise, Pound-foolish,** of Dekker or like Spendall in **Greene's Tu quoque,** 1614, by Cooke.

Mendicancy is often associated with swindling. From Copland to Taylor, the water-poet, popular writers enjoy telling the feats of confidence men. One can hardly find any evolution from the sixteenth to the seventeenth century. The profession was well grounded in tradition. **[109]** The crutch-propped, seemingly lame mendicant is depicted by Copland and appears on the title-page of Taylor's **Praise of . . .Begging.** The false-seeming mariner or soldier, pretending to having been maimed at war is one of the two main roles played by Nicholas Jennings in a woodcut of Harman's **Caveat for Common Cursetors. [110]** When he plays the confidence man or the "upright man", he dresses tastefully as if he were in big business. He enters in St. Paul's where so many big deals are concluded and mixes with the merchants there. He takes one of them aside, gets him to lend him some money or some material, and then disappears for ever. In Dekker's **Lanthorne and Candlelight,** he finds a gull and passes the totality of his debt on to him. **[111]** Examples are numerous: Awdeley gives nineteen cases of swindling; Dekker, in **The Bellman of London,** cites eighteen or nineteen different callings for male rooks and seven or eight for the female.

To keep only to illustrated pamphlets, let us consider **The Groundworke of conny-catching** and Greene's pamphlets. The title-page of **The Groundworke** provides an amazing source of reference for other illustrations and variety of the tasks undertaken by the Elizabethan underworld. (Plate 38) The lock-picker is to be found on the title-page of Greene's **The second part of Conny-catching.** But sometimes diamond cuts diamond: Greene tells us of an ironmonger who took up lock-picking taken in by a gentleman who casually gives him a letter to carry to the warden of a prison. The coney-catcher becomes a coney in his turn, for the letter is actually a **mittimus** to send him to the gallows after the sessions of Lancaster.

Woman is not to be left behind in matters of trickery and stealing. This is the topic of Greene's **A disputation between a hee conny-catcher and a shee conny-catcher.** Its title-page is derived from **The Groundworke** and she holds a coney too. Women indeed are good at the work because they are least suspected. They generally know how to rook men out of their money by practicing the oldest trade in the world. At the time of the Renaissance, woman is reputed to be sexually voracious, and economically demanding. [112] This theme is continued in **Greene's Tu Quoque**, in which two prostitutes ignore their former lover when he falls into bankruptcy and the hands of the constable. Dekker describes the art of the prostitutes who pretend to be middle-class wives in **Lanthorne and Candlelight.** Some of them pretend to be the wives of merchants who went away on business, others of soldiers or of shopkeepers, according to the psychology of the customer. Some married women, indeed, sell their charms in order for their husband to catch them in the act; the husband threatens to expose his wife's lover and soil his name. To avoid this the gull often offers vast sums of money, as described in the second part of Greene's **A notable discovery of cosenage.**

No wonder most well-organized swindlers like having a female partner! The title-page of **A third part of conny-catching,** 1592, shows her in the company of a clown whom she embraces while behind her back she is hiding a coney she has caught by the hind legs. Cards are also to be seen, loose and in a pack, and a lock-picking tool. In fact, the text dwells more on male crimes than on female. Ballad-singers and pedlars are exposed and J. Gyfoon's **The song of a constable,** 1626, gives a picture of those. A merchant is deprived of a trunk full of dinnerware and linen, which was placed for safety at the bottom of his bed. About to be discovered as he is leaving the house, the robber asks him to help him carry his load, pretending he had come to rest on his door-step for a while. The merchant believes him as there was nothing distinctive about his own trunk, and helps him carry it away from his house, to the great secret joy of the rogue.

Some feats are indeed worthy of the most audacious stories. John Selman, for instance, used to attend worship at Whitehall and he was caught stealing the purse of a high-ranking courtier. The king at prayers required him to be detained until the end of the service; after Communion Selman had the rare honor of being addressed by his Majesty, though he is hardly to be envied since it led him to the gallows, between Charing Cross and Courtgate. **The arraignment of John Selman,** 1612, is adorned by a lively title-page woodcut; Selman, dressed like a gentleman, is fleeing, with the purse in his hand. The numerous stories of cutpurses are most entertaining. [113] There is that, borrowed from Greene by Dekker, of the man who has a knife made by a cutler. The knife has an odd shape and the cutler asks innocently what the knife was for. The cutpurse, instead of answering, severs the craftsman's purse. The special tool of the trade is seen lying at the feet of the she-coney-catcher on the title-page of **The third part of conny-catching,** but the story itself appears in **The second part . . .**

A female cutpurse, Moll, appears in the play of Middleton and Dekker that bears her name. On the title-page she is dressed like a man, smokes a pipe, and brandishes her sword that helps her earn her living. This theme of the golden-hearted prostitute develops with **A bawd** and **A whore** written by the water-poet, both illustrated; one must also name the unillustrated **The honest whore** of Dekker.

The Roaring girl is the story of an honest girl who defends her virtue with the edge of her sword. Act I tells us that Moll can be found in one of the taverns frequented by ferrymen. All the men who meet her want to date her for the body that accompanies her heroic spirit and her masculine femininity. [114] She offers to meet them in a duel and she beats them one after another. But she is really very kind-hearted. She helps Sebastian in deceiving his stern father who opposed his marriage to Mary Fitz-Allard, by making him believe that she is the one that Sebastian really wants to marry. Horrified, Sir Alexander quickly agrees to the other marriage for fear Sebastian might make a greater misalliance. It seems that the real Moll, Mary Frith, died a natural death instead of hanging at Tyburn, like most of her associates.

Taylor's defense of the bawd and of the prostitute are transposed into a different key. All are considered honest by the poet in comparison with the cheats of the court. At least, they do not hide their calling. In society, however, most people are hardly worth more, but they hide their game under the sign of respectability. Another of his pamphlets, **An arrant thief**, rings almost the same bell.

The description of the art of cheating at cards is related by Harman, then by Greene in **A notable discovery of cosenage** and by Dekker in **The bellman of London**, 1608. [115] The law of the Barnard requires four participants in order to catch a coney. The baiter or the hooker possess some superficial knowledge of all trades; he is friendly, outspoken and well-dressed. The second rook seems to be a rich farmer, a sign of respectability in a society still grounded in agriculture. The third fraud enters the inn, looking like an old farmer who came to the market in order to sell his products. As he was pleased with his gains, he had previously visited several other inns and is already tipsy. Number one then invites the coney for a game of cards or a throw of dice as well as number two and three. He plots with the coney to ruin the drunkard and the betting goes higher and higher. When a lot of money lies on the table, number four enters, who starts a quarrel with one of the players. While the whole crowd is assembled to view the fight and the attention is centered on the contenders, the barnard leaves with all the betting money. The law of the Barnard is the basis for all sorts of tricks described by Greene, Dekker and S. Rowlands. Cards serve to illustrate the latter's satires on society as we have already seen. [116] No wonder the law forbade the playing of cards and of dice since many were caught and rooked in the taverns.

In order to maintain some order in the streets of London and prevent crime, the bellman goes around at all hours, carrying a lantern and knocking at the door and the windows, giving the time and ensuring that all was well. Some dislike him, says Dekker, on whose pamphlets he regularly appears, because he wakes one up at night. But one should rather pity him, walking alone at night, whatever the weather. In **The Bellman of London,** he passes by a brick or stone house, followed by his faithful friend, his dog. Then he is seen again without his dog, agitating a bell with vigor on the title-page of **Lanthorne and Candlelight,** 1608, directly inspired from Rowlands's **Diogenes Lanthorne,** 1607. The latter shows Diogenes near his tub. All one needs to get Dekker's title-page is to add a bell in his hand and blacken his shoes.

The contents of the two pamphlets, however, are very different. To the realistic description of Dekker, Rowlands prefers watching a series of allegories in the manner of his master and model, Thomas Lodge. [117] The title-page of another edition of Greene's **A disputation,** under the name **Theeves falling out,** uses the same iconographic theme. The bellman has caught two rogues, one male, one female. The woodcut, obviously inspired by the previous ones, is nevertheless very different in style. It was engraved for the pamphlet, as by this time the printer was sure of success in the sale.

Most of the male robbers of London were at one time or another locked up in the prison of Newgate, which also served for the insolvent, whereas women usually went to Bridewell, until they were judged at the sessions. For a first and light offence either they were attached to the cart one sees on **A caveat for common cursetors,** and shamed around the streets of London, or they were condemned to the stocks. John and Alice West appear thus fettered, as they were condemned for having exacted money from the credulous; they pretended they were the king and queen of fairies and could grant any wish. [118] If the crime was serious or if it was their second offence, they would be hanged at Tyburn.

Mynshul's complaint on the conditions of imprisonment in **Essayes and characters of a prison and prisoners,** 1618, is only a weaker reiteration of Luke Hutton's fierce attack in **The black dog of Newgate,** 1596. Hutton dedicates his pamphlet to the supreme judge of England, Sir John Popham. There are as many rascals to be found, he says, among the prison staff as among its prisoners. In a vision, he sees the warden of the prison shaped like a black dog with a mane made of hissing serpents. His body is black like on the title-page woodcut, his breath is putrid, and smoke comes out of his nostrils. His heart is made of steel and locked in a cage of bronze. His enormous belly is a stove. One of his paws is a cloven foot, the other has a hound's claw. These are all satanic emblems and the warden is a bloodthirsty coward who feeds on the mishaps of others. [119] Furthermore, the warden is also accused of venality and sadism. Luke Hutton hates him so much that he rejoices at binding and fettering the cur, in his turn.

Unfortunately the evidence he gives on the terrible conditions of food and lodging given to the prisoners is confirmed by Cooke in his play, **Greene's Tu quoque,** 1617. All are not treated equally but those that can oil the warden's palm, get better quarters and nourishment. Spendall calls the warden the prison whore and describes the jail. Men fight for a piece of rotten meat, rejected by a child or a dog. [120] Dekker also despises jailers to whom he devotes ten chapters in **Lanthorne and Candle-light.** Some prison warders, nurses and cooks are not up to much, he says, and the preface of **Dekker his dreame,** 1610, is full of the bitterness that ensued from his incarceration.

London gangs are as jealous of their privileges and defend their territory with as much vigor as the ladies pacing up and down the pavements of Parisian Montparnasse, ready to abuse and injure any newcomer to the trade. The true Londoners greet a newcomer from the country, as they would a coney. It is healthier for him to stay away and keep stealing horses, like the character appearing on the title-page of Greene's **The second part of conny-catching,** 1591, or like the St. George woodcut deprived of his dragon on <u>sig</u>. C 2. The black man on the black horse suggests his evil intent. Greene tells us one pleasant story: one of the horse-stealers is audacious enough to sell a horse back to his original master, a few years after his crime. But the rogue is not yet content. He sends the proprietor a letter, a boast about the fact. But luck would have it that, as he was being tried for the stealing of another horse, the master turned up at the sessions and was able to prove that this was not his first crime. Instead of incurring the benevolence of the jury, the villain was sent to the gallows.

One language serves them all: slang. Awdeley gives a glossary of the argot of their various vocations. This is enlarged by Harman who also gives the list of the most famous swindlers at the end of the sixteenth century. Greene and Dekker take over and expand it to a small dictionary of in-words.

The pamphlets dedicated to the rogues of London are more numerous than those dealing with the sharks of the sea. Most of the writers indeed live in London, right on the spot. They only have contact with the pirates, when there is a proclamation read by a pursuer, or when they are caught, brought to trial, and hung. [121] These narratives appeal to the Elizabethan romantic spirit like the tribulations of merchants in the east. These old salts appear in ballads and are alluded to in the narratives of voyagers. Here, we shall mainly concentrate on three illustrated pamphlets.

Andrew Barker's pamphlet relates the lives of Ward and Danseker, the first English and the second Dutch, and, at the end, the narrative has a woodcut similar to Digges's **Prognostication.** [122] Both pirates are still loose but the English navy is actively searching for them, as their recent misdemeanor is a threat to the English sea-trade.

The second brochure, also of 1609, **Newes from sea, of two notorious Pyrats Ward and Danseker,** shows them hanging from the mast of their ship. Their flag is a crescent, like that of the Turks. At the verso of the title-page a rowing boat symbolizes the former condition of Ward, the fisherman, and underneath a merchant ship represents Mr. Neg's vessel, twice caught by the pirates. The text stresses the Elizabethan liking for social stability: Ward's main fault is that he aspired to a higher condition than the one he was raised in. Therefore he does not think of praying to God and goes drinking and gambling in Tunis among the unbelievers. Sir Anthony Shirley tries to reform him but his heart is hardened in sin and he does not listen to the wise advice of his patron. He allows drink among his crew, but will not tolerate any quarrel or any joust on board his ship. Finally he loses the esteem of his fellow seamen who raise a mutiny. Another effort is made to convert this obdurate sinner, but it bears no fruit. The narrative continues with a list of ships raided by the two pirates and letters of complaint sent by their legitimate owners.

The third pamphlet is half-serious, half-amusing in tone. [123] (Plate 74) It starts with a historical account of piracy. The same philosophy is expounded here as in the previous pamphlet. Ambition makes the pirate. Even though both Purser and Clinton are excellent sailors, nothing but evil can befall such upstarts. They will be ruthless in climbing the social ladder. The pirates first acquire one ship, then several, and soon they are in charge of a whole fleet. They operate around the straits of Gibraltar and around the Balearic Islands.

As before emphasis is laid on the attempts to save them. They are condemned to die on the beach of Wapping, for who lives by the depredation of the sea will perish by the sea. They are hung at low tide and the sea swallows those who have soiled its purity. The tide flows and ebbs and the bodies are then taken down. Since both of them were brave men, they are granted the privilege of being buried as Christians. The pamphlet also refers in passing to the execution of three other pirates in the Isle of

Wight and finishes on the relation of an earthquake in London. One hardly sees the connection. Pirates always die in the element of their crime, the sea. The pamphlet on Purser and Clinton includes many woodcuts. The sea-fight of the title-page, reprinted on sig. B 2 and C 3v is one of these old woodcuts that the printer took from his stock. But the images of sig. C and C 2 and C 4 are most amusing. A pursuer reading the proclamation stating that the pirates are wanted, travels in a cart with a countryman; [124] at the bottom of the picture people are laughing at this weird team. The same way of suggesting the crowd will be used in the intaglio engraved by Crispin Van Passe I for Th. Scott's **Vox Regis**. In C 4 the same crowd watches the hanging of the two pirates and the flowing sea has already reached their thighs. A rowing boat leaves them, while a larger ship passes by, implying that she will no longer have to fear them. [125]

* * * * * * *

The fascination for this kind of literature grows as public interest increasingly focuses on the feats of the merchant class in non-european civilizations. Cooke in **Greene's Tu quoque** notices that exoticism now intrigues English minds. European civilization was such old hat! Staines, in the play, is disguised as an Italian. He is introduced to Bubble, a goodman who wants to become a gentleman, in order to teach him the refinement of the Italian fashion. He boasts he is a traveller, has mastered several languages and is a writer in his own right. In his book he speaks of the wonders of the world and of his tribulations in many a country. After this introduction, he is well in with Bubble, who is a superficial snob.

It would be erroneous to think that the excitement caused by the reading of the news from the East, was due to sheer political or economic interest. There was genuine fascination for mores that were so far from the dull diurnal life. The Elizabethan fancy fed on other countries as we may escape into the civilizations of the past. They escaped from the restrictions imposed by their moral code by reading the narratives of the brilliant crooks whom they envied, pitied, and despised. Their thirst for power was partly quenched by the feast of fools. The narratives of the merchants were secular pilgrimages of the mind. Hence Coryate and Theodore de Bry were avidly read.

Illustrated pamphlets on this topic, open, as far as we know, on **Webbe his travailes**, 1590, a very chauvinistic pamphlet. Webbe was the son of a London gunner and himself a master gunner. The back of the title-page shows him firing the gun. He first goes to Russia with his father, the ambassador to Moscow.

The Russians, he says are akin to the Turks, except that they have warmer coats. They are very cruel by nature; the insolvent is beaten black and blue with a pole. Whoever offends the Czar is imprisoned with his family; as soon as the Moskva starts to freeze, a hole opens and the prisoners are pushed in. Soon it freezes over them and in the spring the bodies are far distant. Up to now there is nothing that makes us doubtful about the veracity of the narrative. English humanity is, of course, tacitly contrasted with the cruelty of the Russians. This is the only illustrated pamphlet giving information on Russia.

After the taking of Moscow by the Turks, Webbe is captured and enslaved by the Tartars. The babies' eyes only open at nine days, he adds, and at this point the wonder stories begin to titillate the imagination of his compatriots. In Syria, river trout and salmon only bite Christian or Turkish bait, but scorn Jewish lines. At the court of the Christian of Sentour and in Constantinople, a savage man is recorded to have eaten a quarter of a sheep per day. When a traitor is executed he is expected to eat a quarter of a man. His body is covered with hair, as we can see on sig. B 4v, facing animals. One of these is fictitious and the other real, like the narrative of Webbe. The first is a unicorn: its forelegs end as hands whereas the hind legs have hooves. Underneath there appears the Asian elephant, who unlike his African counterpart, has short ears. As the story proceeds, we meet with other monsters, a man with four heads, for instance. After he crossed the Red Sea and prayed at the tomb of Christ, Webbe is taken again by the Turks. Thanks to the Queen, he is released and he spends a few days at the Jesuit College in Rome, dressed like a fool, with blue and yellow back, and his head covered with a jingling cap. He has a discussion with Cardinal Allen. [126]

What is to be believed, what is to be rejected as fanciful in this story? Perhaps this is not the right question to ask at this point. What is noticeable is the Londoner's response, since within ten years at least four editions appeared. The English mind is turning from Europe to the East. [127]

The travels of the Shirley brothers are described by Anthony Nixon, in **The three English Brothers,** 1607. The eldest, Sir Thomas, is imprisoned by the Turks, as he is dispatched to the East. The year of publication of the pamphlet is the year of his incarceration in the Tower of London, for having unwisely crossed the interests of the East India Company. His younger brother, Anthony, conquered the Islands of Cape Verde. He is ordered to go to Persia by Essex in order to establish some markets. Emperor Rudolph II and Pope Clement VIII welcome him at their courts, but he is taken captive by the Venetians in 1607. Released, he is made an earl by the emperor for services rendered in Morocco. As for England, it disdains his talents. Last comes the youngest,

Robert, who left for Persia with his brother, fell in love with a Circassian lady and lived there till 1608.

Thomas Coryate's publications are as fabulous as they are long. His European travels appear in an enormous volume, **Coryats Crudities,** 1611. He also wrote two illustrated pamphlets on travels in the East. The first, **Thomas Coriate traveller for the English wit,** 1616, shows him riding an elephant with a book in his hand. The elephant's trunk is bent down towards the ground, angry at having to carry his weight. [128] At the back of the title-page he appears in travelling clothes. The text informs us that Coryate desired to walk from Jerusalem to Ashmere. To undertake this journey he has had to learn Italian, Arabic, Turkish and Persian. He meets Sir Robert and Lady Shirley who are returning from the court of the Great Moghul. This is not incredible, since most narratives show that the merchants followed approximately the same route. His eyes are mainly struck by elephants and antelopes. A visual representation of the latter appears on p. 16, as well as a woodcut of a unicorn, probably the Asian rhinoceros. But the elephant is most admired by Coryate. The king possesses so many of them, he says. Their golden head-dresses and coats laden with multicolored stones glitter and sparkle like so many Arabian nights.

On the title-page of **Mr. Coriat to his friends in England sendeth greeting** published by Purchas in 1618, Coryate is riding a camel. This posthumous work differs from the former pamphlet. Elephants are still honored but Coryate's linguistic performances are here emphasized: there is a supposed discourse of the Great Moghul in his own tongue, an answer in Italian to an insulting Muslim who called him an unbeliever, the supreme insult for an Arab.

This type of literature is so much in favor that Purchas keeps on and writes an enormous folio, **Purchas his pilgrimage. Good newes to christiendome sent to a Venitian in Ligorne from a merchant in Alexandria** is a pseudo-oriental prediction. An apparition in Arabia announces the fall of the Great Turk and the triumph of Christianity. This wonderful story describes desert convoys with lines of camels, a crocodile eating some aborigines . . . It criticizes the Catholic Church in satires which differ from the traditional ones thanks to touches of oriental spice. The pen, as Taylor says, often prostitutes itself according to the whim of the readers; [129] why not indeed unite two of the favorite subjects of the public, the hatred of Catholicism and the taste for exoticism? Why not indeed? The title-page shows the Turkish army in full flight, as a woman, with open book, threatens them with a sword. All of this happens over a European type of town, whereas a crowd in which one can discern normal English peasant head-dress and turbans, looks up, terrified.

Gradually the interest in oriental civilizations becomes less superficial and more scientific. One discerns growing interest in their ways of life and their religions. **A display of two forraigne sects in the East Indies,** 1630, is, as the title indicates, a comparative study of two forms of eastern religions. The engraved title-page reflects in a composite image the importance of the cow and of the couple among the Banians, and that of the fire and of funeral ceremonies among the Persians. The interest taken in the East, originally magical, has become anthropological.

The woodcut title-page of **A relation of the travels of two pilgrims** portrays the author, Timberlake, and a black native reaching Jerusalem upon a dromedary. The wall of the city can be discerned. (Plate 75) The pamphlet swarms with picturesque details. Peasants are told to bring their eggs to be hatched in containers that can travel on camels without breaking the contents. To keep the heat constant, a fire is made out of pigeon and camel excrement and covered by earth. The eggs are then placed on the fire and the chicks that come out develop monstrous claws within twelve days. One learns that merchants travelling from Alexandria to Damascus, seek lodging in Turkish cities in order to avoid the Arabs. Whenever they enter the city, they pay a fee per man and per beast. In Jerusalem the two travellers meet some problems. One of them, having pretended he was a Greek is invited by the patriarch. Upon discovering that he is an imposter, the holy man gets both pretenders imprisoned. They escape and go to a monastery. The brothers behave most courteously to them and wash their feet with water perfumed with rose petals. After having visited Calvary, the Holy Sepulchre and the Via Dolorosa, they return to Algiers through Arabia and Cairo. Contrary to the narratives of Coryate or of Webbe, this story is told simply, and almost credibly.

News from the East Indies, 1638, by William Bruton, attempts at historical and geographical truth. Along with a description of the town of Jaggernet is a woodcut map. [130] Though he considers that their religious ceremonies are idolatrous, nevertheless it seems that the engraved chariot facing the title-page corresponds to the precise and quantitative description given in the body of the pamphlet. Maybe the author does not keep to the bare truth, but at least he tries to keep anthropological verisimilitude.

A relation of seaven yeares slaverie under the Turkes of Argeire, 1640, endeavors to make the people aware of the number of Englishmen caught by the Turks and imprisoned. A woodcut shows a vivid image of a Turk beating a prisoner. The author, Francis Knight, who had a taste of their prisons, describes the tortures inflicted by the Turks. Some Englishmen are so afraid, he says that they become renegades. He describes the conspiracy of the Casbah, the negotiations attempted for the release of the prisoners, and the endless delays. Many Europeans like Monsieur de Sampson lose their tempers. Finally he manages to break out from jail. The second part of the pamphlet contains a description of Algiers, with a map. The latter, a woodcut, shows the two castles; the first was built by Emperor Charles V, the other by Targerine. A precise description of the manner of government, of the income, and of the naval and land forces of the city, ensues. He remarks upon the curious mixture of Turks and of Arabs that live together in Algiers and concludes on their apparent wealth. (Plate 70)

This pamphlet shows the broadening of the outlook of the seventeenth century mind. These narratives, unlike those of the West Indies, do not deal with colonial propaganda. The single example of anthropological interest in the pamphlets dealing with the West Indies, is undoubtedly the description of Captain Smith of the court of Powhattan, the Indian chief, whose daughter, Pocahontas, married John Rolfe.

The visit of the Indian princess to England in 1616, where she died a year later, may have awakened public interest in strange civilizations. And yet the West Indies and America did not attract the same purely intellectual curiosity or the same fascination as the coruscating universe of the East. This was probably due to the fact that the Indians became enemies for the majority of colonists who therefore viewed them with hostile rather than curious eyes.

To sum up, despite his domestic and social concerns, seventeenth century man awakens to the consciousness of a vast world. Certainly from the East came spices and silks, but henceforth Venice and Algiers bring in more than mere mercantile products: djinns escape from jars able at will to transport spirits towards the most exotic lands, where the daily reality of European conflicts will vanish. But without a basis in reality, fiction would become monotonous fancy. Eager for novelty, seventeenth century man found old perfumes merely stale smells. It is the perfume of natural flowers that he wishes from now on to discover in the distant gardens of the world, as he finds facts much more fascinating than fiction.

Chapter VIII

THE SUPERNATURAL

Auguste Comte, the father of modern sociology, divided the history of thought into three successive ages: religious, philosophic and scientific. The Renaissance, however, undergoing profound changes no longer knew how the silkworm should shed its chrysalis to reveal the precious thread, and thus distinguish the essential from the transient. From its standpoint the religious, the philosophical and the scientific were closely intertwined and frequently indistinguishable.

The readers of this period become disinterested in the purely fanciful. Such stories as **A Description of the King and Queene of Fayries** of R. S., 1635, were treated as fun, and **The severall Notorious and lewd Cousenages of John West and Alice West, falsely called the King and Queene of Fayries,** 1613, was hardly common currency. Fairies were effectively banished from life into escapist literature and a century hungering for magic and impregnated with credulity desired a more believable supernatural, like the evil spells of witches or the predictions of the astrologers.

The more rationalistic minds of the seventeenth century, including Richard Overton condemned as a propagator of egalitarianism in 1649, still believed in astrology. In 1648 Overton asked Lilly if he ought to join the party of the believers in the right of all to possess the earth. Lilly replied that Christianity and astrology were perfectly compatible, which was equally the view of the first historian of the Royal Society, Thomas Sprat, bishop of Rochester. [1] Bishop Wilkins, the first secretary of the Royal Society provides even more convincing evidence from the titles of three books he wrote in a decade, of the complete compatibility of religion and science. The titles are: **The Discovery of a world in the Moone,** 1638, **A discourse tending to prove that 'tis probable our earth is one of the Planets,** 1640, and, as a final surprise, **Mathematical Magick,** 1648.

Although Roman Catholic thought was slightly inimical to science, as the **De Contemptu Mundi** of Pope Innocent III showed, rational or natural theology was favorable to it. The Church in England took no action against science. If Luther was no enthusiast for the sciences, Calvin was clearly their supporter. Thomas Bacon in his **A New Catechism,** 1563, regarded science as the servant of religion and as an integral branch of the philosophical tree. Puritan education also gave it a significant role. Only the Brownists decried it and sent a petition to James I requesting him to forbid all studies in the universities other than the Scriptures. Fulke and Perkins, eminent Puritans, were both scientific men.

Science was not, of course, the sole aim of study; it was only a means or a servant, according to Thomas Bacon. Knowledge for its own sake was thought damnable and Doctor Faust sees the gates of Hell opening before him. Greene, whether sincere or not, swears off science at the end of his life. Euphues, Lilly's hero, after studying the natural sciences and philosophy for a decade, quits them for the study of theology. Science is therefore good, like philosophy, only so far as it enables us to know God's universe. In **A golden Chaine**, William Perkins points out that science proves the existence of God. [2]

Renaissance man is truly represented in emblematic form in **A feast for wormes** by Francis Quarles. He sees only the earth which he must study in contemplating death and the limits of his finitude. While angels protect him, yet the secrets of the heavens are hidden from him. He cannot proudly aim at knowing everything without damning himself through arrogance: this is only to rebuild the tower of Babel. The wise man's soul is fixed on heaven, where he looks for the crown kept for the servants of God, who have placed their hope and faith in Him.

It was previously seen that the Reformation forbade representations of divinity; yet in an age which is still more theocentric than anthropocentric, humanity will naturally expect a response to its prayers from a celestial sign. The supernatural which was natural in the life of those days reveals itself in very different ways. The dominant Manicheanism of the beginning of the English Renaissance continues to appear in the representation of God and Satan in their worldly manifestations. God sends prodigies and marvels to summon his people to repentance, while Satan sows the seeds of disorder in the world through his minions, sorcerers and witches. Astrology and divination are, however, blurred and ambiguous subjects. Do they express the power of God or of Satan? Are they a part of folklore like the dance of the fairies? Are they sheer charlatanism? Opinions are divided. What is certain is that the era still turns toward the supernatural as the only rational explanation of what is irrational and unpredictable in nature.

Representations of God were trinitarian or subordination-ist. Those of the first category appear to belong to the sixteenth century and to disappear entirely in the seventeenth. [3] One example of about 1535 is to be found on the back of the title-page of **The dialogue betweene the plaintiff and the defendaunt.** Its inspiration is gothic: the top of the illustration depicts the angels in threes, with a single angel in the central niche. The lower part is in a more modern style with pilasters bearing acanthus capitals; the Holy Trinity crowns the Virgin; at the left Christ, on the right God the Father wearing the tiara and bearing the orb, while from the level above in the center the Holy Spirit flies in the form of a dove. A trio of angels on each side are witnesses of the scene. (Plate 76)

The trinitarian conception of God also appeared on the back of the title-page of **A treatise of the immortality of the soul,** 1576, by Woolton. God the Father, accompanied by squadrons of angels, meets the Son of Man, followed by a crowd of the faithful. The heavenly Father is vested as a king, his right hand holding a sword, and his left hand resting on the globe of the world. Christ appears dressed in animal skins, the shepherd's crook in the hollow of his left hand. The encounter takes place in heaven since the Spirit flies above the clouds of glory.

Even though the Thirty-Nine Articles of the Church of England and the Westminster Confession of the Puritans both affirm the doctrine of the Holy Trinity, it will be found that the seventeenth century shows an increasing tendency towards subordinationism. God as Creator and as Providence tends to supplant in the imagery God the Redeemer and Sanctifier. God is inconceivable to the human understanding and so is almost always presented as surrounded by clouds of glory. The Jewish tetragrammaton appears on the title-page of Francis Mason's **The authoritie of the Church in making Canons and Constitutions concerning things indifferent,** 1607. A wise old man waters a tree, the leaves of which show that it is flourishing, while a simpleton regards it with envy and is holding a withered tree in his own hand. Above them both is the sign of God. The engraving is the mark of John Norton and warrants description because he is the printer royal. Furthermore, according to Psalm 1:3 the godly are like a flourishing tree, which was probably what the symbol was intended to indicate.

The lover by Robert Crofts, 1638, is interesting because parallel to God in the clouds of glory there are also visible the sun and the moon pierced by Cupid's arrow, and equally surrounded by clouds of glory. This is a curious mixture of Christian and pagan symbolism. [4]

The transcendence of God is shown in different ways. In John Dee's <u>Letter to His Majesty</u>, 1603, the clouds of glory emerge from the divine ear, the hand bearing the sword, and the eye. These metaphors represent the divine omniscience and God's desire to hear the prayers of men, as well as his omnipotence. The sword also shows that God chastises the impure. (Plate 77) With the exception of this unusual print, the presence of God is most frequently shown as the hand that guides or punishes. The printer's mark on the title-page of Chapman's **Andromeda Liberata**, 1614, depicts the hand of God holding a rod; the legend is <u>Mihi conscia recti</u>, God knows what is just and right, despite ocular illusions. This probably means that although the ways of God are mysterious, whatever the appearances may be, the hand that rules the world is just and righteous.

God, as the director of all human enterprises, appeared on the title-page of two pamphlets on Drake, **Sir Francis Drake Revived** by P. Nichols, 1628, and **The world encompassed by Drake** by F. Fletcher, 1635. In each case, the divine hand, <u>auxilio divino</u>, assists the vessel in its voyages around the world.

God as master of the universe wears the tiara and bears the globe surmounted with the cross reserved for Emperors, in the printer's sign on the title-page of **A short and pithye Discourse, concerning the engendering, tokens, and effects of all Earthquakes in Generall**, 1580. God, from the height of his glory, shoots forth rays that indicate His presence. The saint is the man who, with eyes fixed on Him, observes all His signs in a book which he rereads at will.

But the transcendence of God is occasionally manifested in divine anger. Black clouds emerge from the arm that brandishes the lash or the lightning. God in his anger sends his curses on the earth, such as the plague, in the title-page of Dekker's **A rod for runnaways**, or in Taylor's **The Fearefull Summer**, 1636. God's scourge is deserved; the effects of his indignation are paradoxically a mark of his goodwill, for He forestalls sinners and exhorts them to repent before the jaws of hell, blacker even than the leaden sky, come to enclose them for ever. (Plate 55)

The representations of Christ chiefly depict his maturity. Still, Taylor's **The Life and Death of the most blessed among women, the Virgin Mary**, 1620, shows the infant Jesus in the arms of his mother. The print is inspired by Catholicism since the Virgin's halo shines, while the Protestant tradition prefers a simple unradiating halo for Christ or the saints.

The smyth that forged hym a new dame presents an apocryphal Christ watching the smith moulding a woman. **A lyttle treatise** of Urbanus Regius, 1548, displays Christ as the Good Shepherd with his disciples reprimanding the fat monk who neglects his sheep, a typically Protestant topic. It is the renewal of a very ancient image of Christ, since in the Roman catacombs the Christians depicted Christ like Apollo bearing a lamb on his shoulder, a representation sufficiently ambiguous to be interpreted as a pagan or Christian divinity and therefore a source of security for those devotees of a forbidden faith. [5] Through such an image the Protestant expressed their disapproval of Catholic ceremonialism and their preference for a form of worship they thought simpler and more sincere.

There are also a number of woodcuts of the miracles of Christ. Rowlands in **A sacred Memorie of the miracles wrought by our Lord and Saviour Jesus Christ**, 1618, includes eight. The title-page displays the miracle of the wedding at Cana in Galilee. Jesus and his mother are surrounded by radiating aureoles and are eating at table with the host and hostess and two friends. The water-pots are near the Saviour. He stretches forth his hand to change the water into wine. The image is repeated three times in the course of the text.

The second print presents a problem. According to Rowlands's description, which alludes to Matthew 8, it is concerned with the healing of Peter's mother-in-law. The illustration is inappropriate because her cure took place in Peter's house and not out-of-doors. The same image can be found again with reference to the crippled woman who was bent double and whom Christ healed, (Luke 13), but the woman does not seem to be afflicted in the manner described by the biblical text and her cupped hands suggest begging rather than praying.

The third picture is clearly divided into two: on the left side, there is the healing of the paralytic who carries his mattress back into the house, while on the right there is a representation of a madman, a blind man, or a deaf-mute, one cannot tell which of the three he is.

All three illustrations are in the same style and present a mixture of Catholicism and Protestantism: in one part Christ has a radiating halo, a protocatholic sign, but in the other part the disciples lack aureoles, which is the Protestant way. Clearly, they were not cut for Rowlands's work, but for a larger work.

The Transfiguration on the mountain is also one of the most impressive images of the life of Christ, as in John Knox's **The first Blast of the trumpet against the monstrous regiment of women**, 1562. A traditional image faithful to Luke 9:30 shows the disciples awestruck when Christ appears between Moses and Elijah. Christ has shining rays and the disciples, aureoles, which implies that the print is of Catholic provenance.

Christ's Passion is the subject of a brochure by Rowlands,

The betraying of Christ. Each of the vignettes surrounding the title is an emblem for one of the events of Calvary. They are not chronologically arranged and there is some ambiguity about their provenance and religious affiliation. Besides the incidents related in the Gospels one finds additional traditional elements such as the pillar of flagellation and the conversion of Longinus. There are to be found the dice with which the soldiers played at the foot of the cross, the crown of thorns and the reed given mockingly to Christ as to a king, the cock that crowed thrice after the denial of Peter, the nails and the pincers of the crucifixion, the cross, the mounting ladder for attaching the condemned, the lance that pierced the side of Jesus and the sponge of vinegar, the paten and chalice of the Communion, the purse of Judas, the over-long leather thongs which suggest his hanging, the purple robe in which the Jews reclothed Christ in derision, the pillar and the instruments of the flagellation and, finally, the hand of the centurion Longinus (whose name the Bible omits), symbol of the future conversion of Rome to Christianity.

Harman's **A Caveat for common cursetors,** 1573, depicts a secularization of Christ. Below the image of the thieves in the pillory there is one of a man affixed to a horizontal pole, his limbs hanging vertically; one immediately associates it with the cross both because of the composition of the picture and the contraction of the flagellation and the crucifixion, for this does not appear to have been the usual punishment of criminals in the time of Elizabeth. [6]

Ascended into heaven, with God the Father, Christ sends his message to humanity. John Hilliard's **Fire from Heaven,** 1613, urges us to repent; but the title-page cut shows Christ blessing men from the starry vault, protected by the clouds of glory from which the light radiates. (Plate 68)

Finally, Samuel Ward the Ipswich Puritan in his diagram in **All in All,** 1627, displays Christ as the light of the world, Christus Consummator, under the different forms and figures which are attributed to him. [7] (Plate 30)

The most abstract of all these images of God are those of the tetragrammaton and that of Christ used by Samuel Ward. On the whole, the iconography of divinity remains more visual than conceptual, in spite of the sense that humans are incapable of making adequate representations of God. The majority of illustrations are symbols of the divine powers. But the Son of Man, being a historical personage, his human nature and his actions when incarnate are represented in graphic reproductions. Thus it is rare to see Christ at the right hand of God the Father as on the half-drums of so many Romanesque and Gothic cathedrals and abbeys. The impact of the Counter-Reformation can also be discerned in the iconography since interest grows in the human aspects of Christ.

Divine power is also exhibited in prodigies. Since the development of science was not yet powerful enough to explain all unusual and violent phenomena, they were viewed as an expression of the anger of God. To be sure, the Tudors and Stuarts did not believe like primitive men that every river and mountain, wind and tempest had its own god, yet the monotheist of the Renaissance read in the volume of nature what God had intended to inscribe there for the instruction of humanity. He believed that catastrophes came because man had broken the compact or covenant he had made with God. The common scourges he found in Deuteronomy: plague, famine and war. The devastation of a country caused by devouring animals was taken from Jeremiah 5:6 or 8:17, while the destruction of the royal coat of arms or royal sceptre derived from Jeremiah and Isaiah. The cursed nation eating the flesh of its children was taken from the sayings of II Kings 6:24-31 or Jeremiah 19:9. The pure water that quenches the people's thirst and is contaminated either by blood or by poison is found in Jeremiah 23:15, 9:14, and 8:14. The chastisement by flood appears in Genesis 6:5-17 and in Jeremiah 47:2 and 46:7-8. [8]

The curses of God were experienced in the daily life of the post-Reformation in the form of prodigies, earthquakes, bitterly cold winters, murders, and many other events in nature or human nature. Sometimes, as in **The warnings of Germany,** 1638, by Brinckmair, the scourges were so concentrated as to become hallucinations and the frequency of horrific images provoked nausea. In the apparition of the serpent in **True and Wonderful** by A. R. in 1614, the author informs us that monsters and prodigies are the portents of divine wrath; the serpents, so he says, have existed ever since the fall of Adam and Eve. [9] God sends them on the earth in new and different kinds and forms to punish us for the sins which we daily invent. [10] Having described snakes according to the authority of the Bible and of Macrobius, he gives a very warm description of their way of coupling. Next he considers winged serpents and dragons according to the descriptions of Plutarch. They have a deep moral sense; they punish the fault of men or prevent them from sinning. [11] The serpent of Sussex, a social satirist, exhorts men to repent for their excesses visible even in the exaggerations of their clothing. [12]

Punishment by flood is the theme of **Lamentable Newes out of Lincolne-shire,** 1614, where five small towns were drowned. This pamphlet is reminiscent of **The wonders of this windie winter,** 1613, which tells how air and water intervened to punish mankind. Gargoyle-faced angels simultaneously expel wind and water.

Air is the element employed most to demonstrate the

force of the divine power. **The wonderfull battle of starelings at Cork in 1621** wonders at the ways of God who, having made the world, is capable of changing the course of nature, if necessary, for the instruction of man. [13] The combat of animals in the air is one such means, which also reappears in **Prodigies of Germany,** 1638. Other apparitions and struggles in the sky such as **Looke up and see wonders,** 1628, which terrify observers, may also strengthen the soul against sin. This treatise explains that each of the four elements serves to edify man: the earth by its sterility and earthquakes, the sea by its monsters and pirates, the air by its thunder and lightning, while the comets and shooting stars are signs of fire. [14] Armies confront one another, drums roll, and the cannon roars, while two messengers from God cause the wind to blow that will purify mankind. A similar engraving of the battles of horsemen in the sky appears in **Prodigies of Germany,** [15] and in **Good Newes to Christendome,** 1620. The latter brochure is slightly different in content since it is concerned with a sign of the favor of God to Christendom whose champion He is against the Turks. The print is intended to reassure the elect against miscreants.

Finally, we have fire and comets. **Looke up and see wonders** links the two elements. **A True relation of a very dreadful earthquake** with a comet on the title-page also shows that the elements concur to instruct us.

The warnings of Germany, or **Prodigies of Germany,** 1638, add other scourges to those of nature. The text is a compilation of Dutch chronicles mixed with a sermon preached at Nuremberg. [16] Prodigies are the signs of God or His servants to indicate His good pleasure to men. The author has no credence in astrologers, but he does believe in the signs of God. He divides prodigies into natural, moral and divine. Moral prodigies are those which deal with human actions.

The best example of moral prodigies among illustrated pamphlets can be found in **The Lamentations of Germany** of Philip Vincent, 1638. The drift of the work is the same as that of the preceding one, but its eleven engravings illustrate the last point perfectly. There are to be seen side by side different atrocities, a pastor is burnt with his books; other tortures appear as well as rapes, thefts, assassinations; priests killed at the altar and children carved up by their famished mothers, crowded evictions from the countryside; inhabitants eating dogs and cats or even their like, living or dead. The dying, like General Holcke, leave this world without the consolation of the Church, and finally it is impossible to bury the dead because of their overwhelming numbers. Germany, as in the preceding brochure, characterized as an afflicted woman, cries: "Have pity on me." Other details of these prints can be omitted which, by their realism, are as effective as the most sinister films on the atrocities of war. (Plate 50)

Sometimes God gives a lesson to humanity by giving Satan free rein. One might have thought that the preceding work was such an example, but it is nothing of the kind. In **The Lamentations of Germany** God intervenes as vengeance and mercy at the same time. When He allows Satan to act, God retires from the world and shows men what the world is like without Him. This seems to be the point of **Strange Newes from Antwerpe,** 1612. God permits the devil to set fire to a priory, a center of idolatrous practices. In this case God has no need to remind monks of His presence but He shows His disapproval of their type of worship in removing His protection from them.

The miracle, of Miracles shows God at grips with Satan. T. I., the author, reminds us that Satan is there to seize us the minute we forget to act in accordance with the divine law. The woman seen on the bed is possessed. It is only by the constant prayer of her husband that the Satanic headless bear yields to the little child who bears the divine illumination. God thus comes to the aid of those who cry to Him relentlessly.

To recapitulate, it is the immanence of God which appears most commonly in our illustrated brochures. The tetragrammaton is the sign of his transcendence, but a growing pragmatism most frequently considers God in his relations with humanity. Since He is the guide of those who keep their eyes fixed on Him and the protector of the faithful, He chastises only to spare humanity from the greater punishment of everlasting damnation.

Milton's Christ appeared clothed in holiness and purity, but Satan, the fallen archangel, dominated the scene. One of the results of the Reformation was to suppress the exorcism of the medieval Church which, having defined the doctrines of possession and obsession theologically, had also found a remedy in exorcism. The rite of exorcism operated even at the moment of Baptism, since at the time of the signation of the cross, the insufflation of the Holy Spirit and the blessing of the water, the priest commanded Satan to leave the child. Then the manuals of exorcism helped those who in the course of their lives felt themselves to be in the hands of Satan. [17]

Protestantism denounced exorcism, whether, as Bishop Jewel because he thought it unnecessary at a time when the Faith was firmly established, or whether like Bishop Hall because deprived of the power to order Satan to depart, it found its only recourse in prayer. [18] Anglicanism's renunciation of exorcism and the problem it created is evident in reading Canon 72 of the new

Canons of 1604. It was handed on to the Puritans to find a substitute. Relying on Mark 9:29, the Puritans replaced exorcism by prayer and fasting, while the Recusants tried to retain it for their faithful members. The custom of the Recusants was to make the victim drink sherry mixed with holy oil and rue, while the victim's head was held above burning sulphur: the exorcist must have uttered Delphic oracles.

The person likeliest to be possessed probably had only nominal religion. In as troubled a period as the sixteenth century when European nations were required to profess the faith of their sovereigns, and particularly when Charles I was Protestant and his queen Henrietta Maria was Catholic, many found their faith shaken. The new religion, in lessening the power of guardian angels, and expelling the saints, left people without protection, while for others the satires against the papacy stressed the presence of Satan. Keith Thomas gives a striking example of this. In 1558, under the impact of Protestantism, in the annual procession of the guild of St. George at Norwich it was no longer possible to display the two saints: St. George and St. Margaret. So the dragon had to appear alone! [19] This incident admirably illustrates the situation when humanity faces the dragon without ecclesiastical protection.

The great decade for the representation of Evil in the pamphlets took place between 1610 and 1620, with the recrudescence of anti-catholic sentiment in England. In all periods, naturally, Satan appears as a distinct person as the adversary of the plans of God. God occasionally uses him without his knowledge when He wishes to punish men, as viewed in **Strange newes from Antwerpe.** The idea that a monster is the work of Satan and, by extension represents Satan in Catholic thought, is an inheritance from post-Babylonian Judaism. It is, however, under the influence of Zoroastrianism, that Satan becomes the king of the infernal universe and possesses a court of demons as his servants. [20] In our prints it is rare to see the Prince of Darkness himself appear, but it seems most common for his envoys to be delegated to inspire humans to commit the actions conceived by their sinister master.

However much one might wish to clarify and classify, it is very difficult to draw clear conclusions on the iconographic evolution of the devil in our period. All that can be said is that at first there is a preference for depicting him as a human monster. Then, in the seventeenth century, he is commonly represented as a dragon.

According to medieval iconography, the distinctive mark of the satanic personage is the head. Thus on the half-drums of the Romanesque churches, as for example, the west door of Conques, the demonic figures are distinguished by their horrific smile and their long ears and flamelike hair. [21] Most of these traits remain in our period, clearly in **The complaynt of the soule,** a little before our time in 1532. In **Of two wonderful popish monsters,** 1579, and **The beginning and endynge of all popery,** 1583, by Lynne, the monk in the form of a calf and the devil on sig. E are both of medieval inspiration, with the elongated ears and the tongue emerging from the mouth suggestively, lasciviousness being one of the attributes of the devil. The sexual power of the devil is even more clearly exhibited in the monster with the head of an ass discovered by Melanchthon in **Of two wonderful popish monsters,** previously described. An androgynous Satan mingles feminine characteristics in the upper part of his body with masculine characteristics in the lower part. The direct link between the projection of the tongue and the sex organ appears in the devil depicted in **The world runs on wheels** of J. Taylor, 1623. The prostitute allows herself to be led away by the devil with long ears, forked tongue and erect member. Furthermore, in the investigations of witchcraft, the allusions to the sexual potency of Satan recur frequently.

The elongated ears, the open mouth, and the often protruberant tongue, characteristic of the devil, are frequently depicted along with his very large eyes which shine with an infernal light. He appears so in **A pittilesse Mother,** 1616, and in Fennor's **Pluto his travailes,** 1618, where the eyes are round, while those in Taylor's **A world runs on wheels** are almond-shaped as in Sumerian statues. [22]

Finally, the noses of Satanic personages are sometimes elongated, sometimes flattened. The second engraving of evil in **The beginning and endynge of all popery** [23] belongs to the first category. The other noses depicted belong to the second category. The dilatation of the organs of the senses in Satanic creatures corresponds to the older Catholic iconography, itself inherited from the Byzantine tradition, and perpetrated in neo-platonic thought. A re-examination of this dichotomous vision of the universe pushed to its extreme dictated Pascal's celebrated phrase, "Qui veut faire l'ange fait la bête."

The devil is the BEAST. The tradition according to which he descends from a goat goes back to Leviticus 17:17 and to Deuteronomy 32:17. Doubtless the horns of the devil which can be seen in almost all the representations of pamphlets come from that origin. Satan in **Pluto his travailes** by Fennor is careful to hide them under his pilgrim's hat. The clogs which disguise his feet also come from the same source. [24] (Plate 79)

The devil is, however, the prince of this world, a bird of prey feeding on human carrion. His hands are rapacious like those of the usurer and his paws with claws exhibit his greed.

Most of our engravings show him with claws. In **Pluto his travailes** the index finger is uniquely elongated and the nail disproportionately long. Melanchthon's ass shows one foot clogged and the other predatory and grasping. [25] Lynne, Harrington and Taylor use this representation consistently, but in the first two authors the depiction of the hairy leg of Satan shows that the two traditions have amalgamated.

The engraving on the title-page of Samuel Ward's **Balme from Gilead,** 1618, is of dubious provenance. The Satanic head which unites with the Pope, the bishops and the monks to overturn England without success, has the same characteristics as the preceding ones; large ears, enlarged round eyes, sensual mouth showing the teeth, nose with flaring nostrils, but the horns and the general impression suggest a totemic devil.

The representation of Evil as a serpent goes back to Genesis 3. The Jewish tradition blends with the classical and oriental traditions of the serpent or the winged lizard--the dragon. Gessner's works assert that this fabulous monster really exists since Hercules fought against it as one of his famous labors in the garden of the Hesperides. The most recent accounts from Persia tell of the devil with seven heads who is enthroned in religious festivals. [26] It represents the forces of evil which are independent of the God of goodwill in the Persian and Iranian tradition; Ahriman or Anramainyu fights against the God of truth, Ormuz or Ahuramazda. Depicted in this fashion the devil is the source of all evil thoughts, the enemy of the Son of God. [27]

In ephemeral literature, the portrait of Satan, as God's tool and scourge, is confused with the image of the dragon, as Evil independent of God and opposed to Him. The confusion is evident vividly in the apparition of the serpent of Sussex, [28] where the good serpent who preaches repentance to men is obviously an emissary of God.

This theological confusion also creates an iconographical one. For example, Melanchthon's monster in **Of two wonderful popish monsters,** 1579, which belongs to the alternative tradition, nonetheless has a body covered with scales. There is an even clearer example in the depiction of the devil in **A pittilesse mother:** his body is covered with scales, but he also bears a dragon's wings. The devil of **Metamorphosis of Ajax** has clawed and winged paws, the legs of a satyr, and the claws of a bird of prey, but the face of a man.

An entirely snakelike serpent is found, so far as we know, only as the third satanic image in **The beginning and endynge of all popery,** 1583. The serpent is coiled through the key of the Pope and wears a crown. Here, as in Genesis, the serpent is the wicked adviser.

Serpents crown the head of the jailer of Newgate in **The Blacke Dogge of Newgate**, 1596, a mixture of biblical and classical traditions. The image of the hydra appears even more clearly in the engraving of **The Fierye Tryall of Gods Saints**, 1612, which is called "The Popes charge to his Bratts". Satan is the beast of the Apocalypse, 13:14 and 14:10-11. Toads, signs of evil possession, escape from the mouths of the Pope and his minions. The illustration uses an image common to exorcism although in reverse; the exorcised rather than the damned usually have mice or toads leaving their mouths. It is ironic to see a Protestant using an anti-papal illustration which presupposes the Catholic belief in exorcism. This is also the case in Williamson's **The sword of the Spirit**, 1613. On F 4 an imp with a pig's snout and a dragon's body emerges from the mouth of a Papist. [29]

Satan, the evil adviser, appears in the form of a completely black dragon in numerous brochures. It is he who urges the two servants of Edward Hall to assassinate their master in **A Horrible Creuel and bloudy Murther**, 1613, or who inspires the neighbor of a widow to kill her children in Cooper's **The Cry and Revenge of Blood.** (Plate 80) Behind the usurer's armchair the devil incites him to ask for more guarantees and money from his debtors. **The English Usurer** also shows him in the shape of a pig, one of the impure animals according to the Jews, which Christ commanded the demonic spirit to enter and caused the herd to rush into the sea. [30] Another engraving of the devil as a dragon, but without wings and the feet in the form of clogs, appears on the title-page of **A Courtly Masque** by Middleton and Rowley in 1620.

Satan the destroyer flies above the monastery of St. Michael in **Strange Newes from Antwerpe**, 1612. He carries the rock which will destroy the roof of the church, the cause of the burning of the monastery. [31] He causes the belfry of the church to fall in **The last terrible Tempestious windes and weather**, 1613. The dragon devil, whether tempter or destroyer, in the bending posture, leaning towards the man or the object which he desires to remove from divine influence, his fore paws extended in front of him, the favorite satanic illustration between 1610 and 1620.

The analysis of the iconography of the devil amply evidences the variety or the confusion that reigned at the time. Its inspiration is sometimes Judaic, sometimes Christian, sometimes Judeo-Zoroastrian, sometimes classical, and sometimes a combination of all traditions. In fact, the complexity of the images of Satan is equalled only by the variety of opinions on one of his misdeeds--witchcraft.

As defined by Keith Thomas, witchcraft is the employment of the occult for nefarious ends. The belief in it is based on attributing human misfortunes to an occult human power. [32] The evil, <u>maleficium,</u> is usually physical in character, the illness or death of a person or an animal. It can also be a relatively trivial mishap: cows refusing to give milk, or hens to lay, or the cream to become butter, or the beer to ferment. The witch works by "fascinating" her victim, or by pronouncing a curse, or more rarely, melting an image of wax, burning the name of the victim written on a piece of paper, or burning a piece of the victim's clothing. [33]

Witchcraft did not become a theological misdemeanor until the publication of **Malleus Maleficarum** in 1486, the work of two Dominican members of the Inquisition. Thereafter black magic became a Christian heresy: the accused renounced God in order to sign a pact with the devil, God's enemy. That is, the accused underwent the opposite process of Baptism in which Satan was renounced to enter into a covenant with God. In this respect the Protestants followed the example of the Catholics, and Perkins in **A Discourse of the Damned Art of Witchcraft** is the pioneer in writing treatises that proclaim the horror that witchcraft inspires in Christians. Three acts of Parliament reflect the evolution from <u>maleficium</u> to <u>malleus maleficarum</u>. The first two in 1542 and 1563 make no reference to a pact with the devil while the third in 1604 specifies that it is an act of felony to perform magic on a corpse. [34] It is worth remembering that in 1604 James I occupied the English throne. In 1597 he had written **Daemonologie** and since he became king of Scotland had followed with great interest the majority of the prosecutions of witchcraft. His treatise was a reply to Reginald Scot's **The discoverie of witchcraft** in 1584, which had taken the side of the witches. It is worth recapitulating briefly the arguments of the two adversaries upon which most of the contentions of the seventeenth century on this issue are based. [35]

Scot reduces the cases of witchcraft to four main categories. There are:

1. The innocents, those accused out of hate or jealousy;

2. Those who delude themselves because they wish to harm someone, and are half mad;

3. The witches who wish and perform ill to their neighbor by natural means;

4. The imposters who exploit the confidence of the ignorant populace and make them believe that they have magical powers which they do not possess.

The two latter categories include the true witches who should be punished by the law, but their sorcery owes nothing to the supernatural. [36]

King James VI of Scotland was opposed to this rationalistic view of the problem, because from his haunted castles he saw things differently. The ways of Satan are unfathomable since he can transform himself into an angel of light. [37] Satan works his will either by necromancy or through witchcraft. Among the sorcerers the king includes the astrologers and the fortune tellers who come in their train. The witches adore their master Satan, kissing his private parts as a sign of allegiance, in return for which he will grant them supernatural powers. These include: reducing the body to cinders and making statues of wax or clay by means of which they can weaken or kill the person against whom they cast a spell. One ought not to think that Satan works in this way independently of God, for he is sent by Him to punish or to test Christians. [38] The monarch gives an anti-papal color to the pamphlet in accusing Catholics of making pacts with the devil, and of achieving only the appearance of cures in exorcism. In any case, he adds with partiality if there is a genuine cure, God desired it and Catholic wisdom should receive no credit. This view was not shared by all; the Puritans, in certain desperate cases, sent the victims for exorcism to the priests. [39]

John Cotta in 1616 found that he had to discover a common measure between the two adversaries. Hence he divided the misdeeds of Satan into three categories: those accomplished without human consent, those effected by means of a pact with humans, and those which agreed with human reason.

Of these three treatises, the first and third are the most intellectual and both attempt a rational viewpoint. That of James VI of Scotland surprises by its pragmatism born of the experience he had of the legal process. He insists on the details of the life of the witches, on their misdeeds, on the way in which they can be recognized, and also on their punishment. For him, as for Perkins in 1608, witches deserve only death. Francis Bacon, for his part, analyzes the causes of superstition and attributes them to three factors: sensual rites and ceremonies, the Pharisaic pride of the Pelagian, and barbarism and emotional immaturity in the face of calamities. [40] In that respect he comes close to the categories of the monarch who attributes the fascination for witchcraft to the intellectual curiosity of ingenious spirits--one thinks of John Dee, to the desire for vengeance, or to covetousness born of poverty.

Each of these causes can be discovered again and again in the illustrated brochures that we have, accounts of witchcraft in England, or, like **The Damnable Life and Death of one Stubbe Peter, Newes from Scotland**, 1591, or **A Certaine Relation of the Hog-faced Gentlewoman called Mistris Tannakin Skinker**, 1640, from the European continent.

Lechery is most frequently represented by witches' nocturnal sabbaths or by the kiss with which witches have to show submission to the devil their master. In **Newes from Scotland,** 1591, Agnes Thompson declares that the devil goes to church in the shape of a man and punishes people for staying there too long. But, the witches affirm, the devil is too frigid in his relations with them which causes them great frustration. [41] This corresponds to the legend according to which diabolical sperm is dead sperm, one of the reasons why, when there is a conception, the devil can only engender monsters. Dr. Fian, the only man who was admitted in this coven of witches, obtained the love of a young wife by bewitching her husband. But the sorcerer more than met his match. When he wished to seduce a young girl, he asked her brother to bring him three of her pubic hairs. The mother, who was shrewder, cut three pubic hairs from a cow. The magic worked and the doctor saw himself being hotly pursued by the amorous cow. She appears on C iv near to the gallows with a pendulous and lubricious tongue. It is difficult to make out the meaning of the lower part of the illustration. There are two men on the back of a black horse which is carrying them to church; both have torches but the rider in front wears all black clothes. Is this preparation for a sabbath? One cannot say for sure. As in Dr. Fian's case, it was not rare to find witches young enough to offer themselves as sexual attractions to the devil, and probably some of them were perverts. [42]

The best example of Pharisaic intellectual curiosity--a defect and not a quality, for man's duty is to refrain from trying to learn what God has wished to conceal from him--is Dr. Faust, who signed a pact with the devil, to gain knowledge. By so doing he was turning from Christ to prelapsarian Adam. He could not be accused of committing the maleficium for he did no harm to anyone except himself by his obsession for excessive power and by his ambition. He is of the company of those astrologers that are jeered at and condemned throughout the period. [43]

The desire for vengeance and the covetousness of the poor is the most frequent motive given for black magic. Popular belief attributed the most effective powers for destruction to the poor and the disgraced. The description of the witch of Edmonton, Elizabeth Sawyer, is one of the most precise; her face is pale, her body is shapeless, and she lies and curses. [44] On the title-page she supports herself on a cane and she is hardly any different from the woodcut of the female beggar of Dekker's **O per se . . . O** by the general attitude of her bearing. Similarly, witches on the title-page of **The wonderful discoverie of the Witchcrafts of Margaret and Phillip Flower,** 1619, with angular faces are represented in begging posture, with their familiars.

The witch of Edmonton turned to magic voluntarily

because society took her for a witch and she decided she might as well be hung for a sheep as for a lamb. The play of Dekker, Ford and Rowley demonstrates this point very clearly. In Act II, Elizabeth Sawyer complains that she is condemned for her external appearance. [45] The same argument is taken up again in **The wandering Jew telling fortunes to Englishmen**, 1640. The author, Gad, recognizes that society is partly the reason for the misfortunes of witchcraft, but cannot find extenuating circumstances for agreeing to lose one's soul. [46]

Alan Macfarlane has shown that in Essex most of the cases of witchcraft involved neighbors. [47] It was also the case of the witch of Edmonton. Joan Vaughan in **The witches of Northamptonshire**, 1612, avenges herself for a slap given her by Miss Belcher whom she had previously insulted. [48] **The wonderful discoverie of the Witchcrafts of Margaret and Phillip Flower**, 1619, is the case of a domestic servant who had been sacked and took revenge on her masters by casting a spell over them. The two women, mother and daughter, were in the habit of helping themselves generously to the linen and the food of the master of the house. Lord Roos got tired of being robbed and discharged them. Certain domestic murders were attributed to witchcraft. Such was the case in **The Araignment and burning of Margaret Ferne-seede, for the Murther of her late Husband**, 1608. The woodcut of the title-page is divided in two parts: the left shows the witches preparing the brew while a man lies on the ground with his head supported by one hand; it is borrowed from **Newes from Scotland**, 1591, after having been cropped; the right part represents the guilty one, with a phial in her hand. She enters her house with a backward look for fear she might be caught red-handed.

The majority of these cases of witchcraft can be categorized as maleficia. In **Newes from Scotland** a witch conspires to kill King James VI. Agnes Sampson suspends a black toad by the hind legs for three days in order to obtain enough venom in an oyster shell. She keeps the venom until she can get a piece of the king's clothing, which she is unable to procure. At the time of the king's voyage to Denmark she took a cat, baptized it, attached to it the private parts of a corpse, went sailing with it, and left it at Leith, the port of Edinburgh. She thus caused a ship to be wrecked off the coast of Scotland which was laden with presents for the Queen. She also pretended to have been responsible for the winds that delayed the royal vessel. The reason why she was unable to kill the King of Scotland is explained by the devil in **The witch of Edmonton**: malefic power is limited if the victim loves the good and is charitable. Then it is possible to bring misfortune to his goods and his cattle but not to himself. [49] This belief makes the deaths of persons considered innocent, like the deaths of the two sons of Lord Roos killed by the magic of Margaret and Phillip Flower, extremely ambiguous. Where is the logic in the play where young Thorney is more friendly towards Elizabeth Sawyer than his father, yet the witch makes him pay for his father's rudeness to her? [50]

The narratives of witchcraft committed in England rarely report the changing of the witch or of her victim into an animal. However, two accounts, both translated from the Dutch, give credit to this peculiarity of continental Europe. The first, **A true discourse**, 1590?, deals with the life of a sorcerer Peeter Stubbe, who, in order to commit his crimes, changes himself into a wolf. An eight section woodcut on a broadsheet reveals his life, his arrest and his execution. From left to right and from above to below he can be seen killing a man in the shape of a wolf, driven by a horse and dogs in the plains of Germany near to Bedbur, then led under escort to the courtroom where he is indicted; the lower part shows the tortures applied to him: first the wheel and red-hot irons, then the wheel and the hatchet, the wheel a third time and his beheading by a sword, and, finally, he is burnt headless between two witches. **A certaine Relation of the Hog-faced Gentlewoman called Mistris Tannakin Skinker**, 1640, bears a title as promising as the woodcut. She is seen courted by a young man, while dressed in her best clothes, but she can only grunt "ouch" from her hog-faced head. The young girl bewitched in the bosom of her mother will not recover human form until she is married.

What is uniquely English, if one accepts the judgment of Keith Thomas, is the idea of the familiar. [51] The passion of the English for animals is well known and so this is hardly surprising. Elizabeth Sawyer speaks to her dog-shaped devil. All three witches of Northamptonshire travel on a pig. Generally, the familiar is nursed by the witch. In **Witches Apprehended . . .**, 1613, we learn that the Sutton women, one a widow, the other an unmarried mother, feed two spirits, Dick and Jude, with the diabolic breasts found between their legs as a mark of Satan. Were they androgynous? The devil assures Margaret and Phillip Flower, in a pamphlet of 1619, that he will appear in the shape of a dog, a cat, or a rat, as they wish. It was easy to accuse an old woman in the country of witchcraft. Indeed, most of them possessed a dog or a cat, at least in order to hunt the rats that infested the houses and barns. On the other hand, what woman had such a perfect body that no wart, scar, or mole marred her appearance?

In a period when witchcraft is feared like the plague, it is easy to prove that a single woman, or one on the margins of society in having an illegitimate child or an abortion, is a witch. In addition to the proof provided by marks on the body, the witch is put through other tests. The most eloquent pamphlet, as much for its text as for the image on its title-page, is **Witches Appre-**

hended, Examined and Executed, 1613. [52] The trial by water which is to be seen on the title-page is thought to be conclusive when an examination of marks on the body is not. The witch is brought to the millpond, tied up with ropes, and, after closing the dam, submitted to the water test. Her accusers are careful to attach the ropes round her body so that if she sinks, a proof of her innocence, she will not drown. If she floats, then her body is examined again for the marks of Satan. The second trial is to plunge her back in the river, attaching her right thumb to her left big toe, the position in which she can be seen. The third trial is that of the sieve which appears on the title-page but not in the narrative. (Plate 81) The witch is able to float on a sieve where all others would drown. This is the way in **Newes from Scotland** that Agnes Thompson brings the cat, which is destined to kill the king, to Leith. [53]

It was a daily concern to undo the evil caused by a witch. If one suspected anyone of being a witch, one of the surest ways to find out was to set fire to the thatch of her house; if she were a witch she would come out running. But who would not rush out to extinguish the fire? This is the prescription given by Goodcole in **The wonderfull discoverie of Elizabeth Sawyer.** Pinching and clawing the witch is another of the remedies which were used by the brother and sister of Miss Belcher who had been bewitched by Agnes Brown. [54]

The best remedy was the condemnation of the sorceress to death, generally to be burnt alive, as in the woodcut about Peeter Stubbe.

It is easy to imagine the panic into which the inhabitants of a village would be driven by witchcraft. Keith Thomas and many anthropologists see in this phenomenon the need to explain the inexplicable, such as the death of a person apparently in good health, misfortune, and an incredible series of mishaps in the same family. At a time when God was opposed by the devil, sorcery was a way of accounting for the immanence of the forces of evil.

* * * * * * *

Satan, however, with the agility of a serpent knew how to infiltrate everywhere. White magic was thought to be as much his province as black magic, for the magician has supernatural powers which derive from God's adversary, not from God himself, and could be converted into forces of evil. Hence there was a shadow of suspicion about John Dee, to take an example. Quite apart from medical charlatans who used herbs as well as charms,

England abounded in fortune-tellers and diviners. [55] James I was reluctant to continue exercising the powers of healing which were thought to belong to his predecessors, a power also believed to be inherited by the seventh son of a family. [56]

Divination awakened the most vehement quarrels and protestations, while becoming an obsession with both ignorant and cultured. Many Jacobean students at the universities were interested in magic, and conjuration was the craze of the age. Necromancy, or divination by means of the dead, was as old as Babylon from which it came. Doctor Faust and Friar Bacon practiced it and both renounced it at the end of their lives. [57]

Astrology proved attractive to the intellectuals. Begun by the Babylonians, continued by the Greeks first and then the Romans, and enlarged by the Arabs, astrology was the sister of astronomy. If the latter studies the movements of the planets, the former is concerned with their influence on humans. As long as astrologers were content with predicting the time and the almanac with giving the seasons for planting, cutting hay, harvesting the wheat, and gathering in the grapes, astrology was accepted. The psuedo-science was inoffensive. Astrologers were, however, often thought to be charlatans and their predictions false. The situation became worse when they pretended to foretell human destiny, predict the death and fall of kings, and the triumphs and defeats of kingdoms. Special legislation then became necessary for astrology had taken an inopportune hold on the credulity of the masses. Thus, what the English called "judicial astrology" was condemned.

Astrology, nonetheless, exercised an extraordinary fascination. It claimed to explain why two individuals differed in their behavior, why plagues ended the reigns of two sovereigns because the stars demanded that England should have a new start. [58] Many went to consult astrologers, like **The wandering Jew telling fortunes to Englishmen,** 1640, to recover property that had been stolen or lost, [59] or for other solutions to the problems of daily life. In Robert Greene's **Friar Bacon and Friar Bungay,** 1594, the son of King Edward and a young country girl, Margaret, have just consulted a fortune-teller about their difficulties in love. Edward sees in Friar Bacon's crystal ball that Friar Bungay is about to marry his best friend to the young girl he himself desired. By a magic trick Bungay is unable to move and the lovers must wait for the permission of Edward who, with a generous spirit, allows them to marry rather than killing them.

The aim of a horoscope is to discover in the solar system the influence of the moving bodies, the planets, against the fixed background which constitutes the signs of the zodiac. The four elements, earth, air, fire and water vary depending upon the influence of the celestial bodies. Experts, like Friar Bacon and his German protagonist, Vandermast, argued as to whether pyromancy or geomancy predominated in magic. [60] The almanacs nearly all reproduced a diagram of astrological man from which the reader could infer what medication he should use according to his astrological sign. Astrology remained influential until the beginning of the seventeenth century, tended to lose its prestige for a few years, then returned to greater favor during the revolution when men searched for certainties in scrutinizing the stars. The Copernican revolution and the discoveries of Galileo created a backwash of disbelief in astrology, but it was insufficient to dethrone the ancient belief which, despite all its efforts, never attained the status of a science. [61]

Satires on the almanac and its pretentions flourished from the moment that Erra Pater published his prediction which ran to at least twelve editions between 1536 and 1638. It was derived from the prediction of Esdras which circulated in the Middle Ages and was simply revived and rephrased in the taste of the day. Henry Peacham, Joseph Hall, and many others mocked popular credulity. The first of these satires is called **A mery prognosticacion**, 1544, and exhibits the astrologer in a fool's cap who is devising a horoscope with a companion, and showing him the sky in which appear the sun, the stars, and some birds. The woodcut is taken from the **Ship of Fools.** The satire emphasized two points, and served as a model for most of the satires that followed it: asserting facts in a pompous, doctoral tone, and pronouncing hypotheses with a maximum of ambiguity. [62]

Dawe's **Vox Graculi, or Jack Dewes prognostication,** 1623, is of the same type. The title-page represents a wise raven who writes while perched on a chair. A sundial and a compass are attached to the wall. The print recalls the title of Dekker's almanac, **The ravens almanach,** 1609, and **The Owles Almanacke,** 1618. Besides being a satire on gardening, it includes a counterpart to Erra Pater's prediction, the **Demogorgous,** supposedly borrowed from a wise man from the Antipodes. [63]

Political prediction awakened less the sarcasm than the indignation of both civil and religious authorities. Still one can find some amusing pamphlets. A prediction of Cypriano came from Italy; its title page and the exaggeration of the text showed that it was a joke. Two astrological experts are conferring with the devil in a room where the table is covered with a carpet; a book lies open between them--the proper setting if we are to believe John Melton, for the woodcut on the title-page of **Astrologaster,** 1620, depicts him at his table. [64] Cypriano's **A most strange and wonderful prophesie,** 1595, shows the astrologer in a turban, for exotic clothing makes the astrologer. He attaches the quadrant to his eye the better to observe the movement of the planets. Clouds of glory are present, but God is absent, as a sign of his disapproval. The moon seems to eclipse the sun, but it is only a partial eclipse because rays reappear and the moon is in the first quarter. Stars shine in the firmament. Then predictions follow in a cryptic language so that one cannot tell if they are serious. At the very least they are as fantastic as the conjurations in **Friar Bacon and Friar Bungay.** It is probable that the author is ridiculing such predictions, otherwise, the devil would not appear on the title-page. [65]

Without question the most serious treatise is **The Astrologaster** of John Melton, jurist and politician. (Plate 82) This best sums up the attitude of pamphleteers opposed to astrology. [66] The aim of the work is to confound the astrologer and fortune tellers, to refute the arguments of the philosophers, astronomers, geographers and cosmographers, to expose the frauds of Delphi, and to reveal the correspondence between the practices of the astrologers and the conjurations of Catholic imposters. He defines astrology as the school of falsehood. [67] The astrologer who consults the stars is a night bird and therefore a disciple of the devil. Melton transcribes the official opinion. Divine law forbids astrology; Hooper, Reginald Scot, and later James VI of Scotland, reiterate the argument that astrology goes contrary to the first commandment which ordains that God alone must be adored. This is also appropriated by John Chamber and William Perkins. Hence astrology, in the eyes of the religious authorities, is one of the satanic professions similar to witchcraft.

Civil authorities confirmed the voice of the Church; King James I could not deny what he had written in his Scottish kingdom. The legislation was not new, but it seems to have become more severe in the late sixteenth and early seventeenth centuries. The act of 1541 punishes only those who prophesy against the king; those of 1550 and 1563 impose a penalty of a year's imprisonment and a fine of ten pounds on all astrologers. At the time when Mary Stuart honored the jails of the kingdom with her presence and furnished the occasion for many insurrections in her favor, a law passed which condemned the astrologers to capital punishment like the witches. [68]

Being, as a good lawyer should, an expert in canon law, Melton proscribed astrology in the name of good sense. Pyromancy was above all the object of his sarcasms following the prediction of 1617 that fire would be the dominent element until the end of the world. The author jocularly concludes that one will certainly find heat in the brothels and that it continually reigns in tobacco shops! [69] Then he condemns the witches who think they can cure a malady with the help of superstitious ceremonies, [70] and the different branches of divination: necromancy, a study of the elements, the examination of entrails, palmistry, and spatalmancy. [71] Finally, Melton satirizes prophesy after dreams: dreams come, he argues, from worry or over-eating and all dreams do not come from God since even animals dream.

It is well known how important prophecies of this sort were thought to be at the end of the sixteenth century, so much so that Greene and Dekker were able to disguise their satires on society under the cover of dreams. The astrologer is therefore the raven for Dekker and Rowlands, the dispenser of the occult through rituals as elaborate as those of the Catholics who try to hide God from the eyes of the faithful. The author concludes that the only true remedy for the hardships of life is the Bible which Catholics refuse to believe in, and which England's official religion recommends. It may be recalled that the Authorized Version was published in 1611 under the aegis of King James I.

Astrologers were thought to imperil their souls. This conviction was strong enough to inspire at least two works. Friar Bacon abjured immediately after the bronze statue had uttered the magic words: "Time is, Time was, Time is past" while he was asleep; after having conjured up his lot once more he saw the evil effects of necromancy. He then smashed his crystal ball and renewed his trust in the providence of God. The title-page of the edition of 1630 shows the statue, the sleeping friar, and the fool beating the drum. The cropping shows that it must have illustrated a larger work. [72] (Plate 83a)

Marlowe's Faustus is as dominated by the will to power as Friar Bacon. Yet contrary to him, he does not know where to stop, and never repents. Before death he sees a vision of the jaws of hell. Whereas Bacon's servant Miles, hoping to become a tavern-keeper in hell, left the stage riding joyfully on a devil, Faustus's hell is a terrifying reality. He appears on the title-page amid the signs of the zodiac, while a horrific Satan waiting to claim him is shown at the bottom of the illustration, on the right. (Plate 83b)

In reading this type of ephemeral literature, what conclusions should be drawn other than that the representations of the sacred and the images of the satanic are only recognitions of the irrational in the world, and the inadequacy of science as a total explanation? Probably there was dissatisfaction with the liturgies of the times. It seems that magic finds a place each time that neither science nor religion can satisfy the needs of tormented people who find themselves caught in a bind between two equally unacceptable solutions: the fallibility of God or the blindness of fate.

CONCLUSION

Interpreting the images of illustrated pamphlets is like dealing with the remains of ancient civilizations. If one goes to Delos, then the setting, the arrangement of the town streets, the baths, and temples, as well as the Avenue of Lions, all mark the importance of the sanctuary. Nevertheless, the oak and the oracle are missing. It is the slow ascent of the sacred mount, the discovery of the islands below on which the sun sets, and the evening mist which create the sacred awe appropriate to mysterious places. In the same way, the illustration of texts allows us to recreate an historical approximation of reality, without which these remains cannot be interpreted.

In **Art and Illusion,** Gombrich asserts that an image performs many functions such as describing, illustrating, decorating, attracting or expressing emotions. It fulfills these functions successively or simultaneously. Most often these prints derive from the mixed motives characteristic of commercial life. They allure the buyer as much by their beauty as by their advertising power. The aesthete will be enticed by the technical perfection and the common herd by the suggestion of scandal in the contents. The bookseller has no desire to limit himself to a single type of illustration, since he would lose some of his clientele. For this reason, editors and booksellers who prefer to specialize find it necessary to diversify their wares. Although the Crown wished to increase its revenues by the granting of royal privileges for the publication of ballads, it had to give this up through the protest of the printers it had forced into unemployment. Illustrated pamphlets from Caxton and Bourne, therefore play an essential part in the economy of publishing.

From the artistic point of view, popular illustrations follow the vagaries of internal politics and economic necessities, as exemplified by royal proclamations. Royal policy, sometimes liberal, sometimes protectionist, invites or rejects the expertise of foreign printers. They skip into or bow out of England, according to the monarch's pleasure. Henry VIII encouraged Dutch talent; Elizabeth, preoccupied with religious issues after the reign of Bloody Mary and the danger created by the alliance of France and Spain, had neither money nor interest to devote to the arts. Only poetry and pageantry were kept up as necessary propaganda. It was sound politics for the queen to show herself to her subjects and her vassals with the pomp belonging to her rank.

In the seventeenth century, by contrast, thanks to their queens, the Stuarts' concern for royal pomp was backed up by a genuine interest in the arts. Once again foreigners were allowed to import their talents, while such Englishmen as Hilliard, Oliver and Inigo Jones were encouraged to go to Italy to study the new techniques. The nobles and courtiers, aping the Crown, gradually freed themselves from the prejudices against the graphic arts, encouraged by the Puritans who saw a practical value in them.

Technical progress in illustrations ensue as well as an evolution in their function. Some prints excel in the volutes, leather scrolls and foliage borrowed from the school of Fontainebleau, while others specialize in vignettes or lacy borders, and still others repeat the egg-and-dart motif in period furniture. This is purely ornamental or decorative material.

At the same time, under middle-class influence, informative illustration developed. Ramism insisted on the importance of logical demonstration at the expense of rhetorical ornamentation. Puritans and intellectuals applied its theories to the graphic arts. Images could both instruct and include a logical demonstration. Not that the Middle Ages had neglected the suggestive power of the visual: the fronts of cathedrals, their capitals, paintings, bas-reliefs, and stained-glass windows are vivid examples, to which should be added the carvings on the choir-stalls, which were well-developed in England. Generally, however, medieval images were static. That is to say, they recalled Biblical and hagiographical stories and described the archetypes of Christian ethics or of daily life. The transition was not abrupt, but images could henceforth be used for practical handbooks and husbandry. There is a change from the theocentric ideogram to anthropomorphic dynamism. It serves to instruct by reason or to awaken passions.

The authors of broadsheets had little concern for intellectual categories. However, the influence of rationalism is felt in the seventeenth century trend towards realism. One senses this evolution in the replacement of teratological images by realistic and individualized descriptions of murders. Even when the image is copied from one pamphlet to another or on a ballad, there is renewed effort to repeat reality in its concrete details. Criminal pamphlets display either the weapon and the murder, or its consequences, whether the hanging or the suicide of the guilty party. Sampson's **The vow-breaker** describes visually the entire psychological process of the human drama. Similarly, in **News from Perin**, the father kills himself on the body of the one he has assassinated in ignorance that this is his own prodigal son; while the mother takes her head in her hands, the daughter tears her hair in despair. The image therefore succeeds in depicting the violence of despair.

Finally, one of the functions of illustrated pamphlets is to serve as propaganda. Most of them, by showing the effects of passion exhort to virtue and reason. Other pamphlets are direct defenses of virtue by representing it in attractive forms. Humility for example serves to advance the Patient Griselda socially, while conjugal love is blessed by the spirit of God; and a mother and father exhort their child to follow the road of reason.

Political propaganda is also sometimes persuasive, sometimes dissuasive. Patriotism is encouraged in displaying the chief events in the lives of princes as well as in their deaths and effigies. In contrast, the national enemy appears with the blackest characteristics by means of an emblem or an emblematic image, or by illustrated accounts of naval warfare which boost the courage of the English in opposition to the supposed cowardice of their foes. Political propaganda passes from governmental into private hands in the seventeenth century. As external danger diminished, internal divisions were highlighted. Censorship was no longer effective, since prominent persons protected those who challenged the policies of the sovereign. In this way the tracts of Thomas Scott spread throughout England and Middleton's drama against the Spanish Marriage played for nine days before being stopped. The frontispieces of Scott constitute political sermons, while Middleton's make their point either by allegorical allusion or by realistic simplification. Gondomar will never be more than the man with the uncontrollable bladder. That _is_ caricature.

Religious propaganda remains chiefly directed against Catholicism in relation to Spain, the Pope and the Jesuits. It is the central topic of satirical illustration, which often uses emblems rather than realism. By 1641, after twenty years of Laudianism in the Anglican Church, woodcuts play an essential role in pamphleteering literature. Arminians accuse Puritans of sexual obsessions, while Puritans attack Laud's supporters for social ambition and stupidity. Evidently, Protestantism had become anchored in the hearts of the English.

The foreign policy of England up to James I was similarly motivated by a desire to help the Protestants. Allied with the Low Countries, England's relationship with France depended on the liberality with which the French sovereign treated the Protestants. Illustrations here were less truculent. Mostly, these were effigies in honor of sovereigns or generals, or representations of battle scenes: such were often informative. In this genre both emblems and caricatures are rare.

Internal economic propaganda is exemplified by encouraging the eating of fish and discouraging the importation of wheat. The rest was mainly colonial propaganda. The new world attracted the curiosity and cupidity of the learned, the rich and the poor. The Virginia Company and its promoters published tracts containing maps of Virginia to elicit donations and recruit colonists, voluntarily or by coercion, as was the case with poor children. Narrations about the East Indies depicted the daring merchants who ventured there as modern knights risking their lives to bring rich and colorful wares to the English market. These illustrations met the need for exoticism and the growing interest in distant lands.

Illustrated pamphlets also offered an almost complete picture of the life and beliefs of England from the Reformation up to 1640. Increasingly, they testify to the change from a theocentric to an anthropocentric universe. The earliest cuts are often taken from hagiographical books, illustrated Bibles and Books of Hours. As the seventeenth century proceeds, they increasingly depict humanity's daily life. There is no sudden transition, for God is still represented as helping or chastising men of goodwill. But pagan realism is often mixed with Christian faith.

The fear of death often obsesses these Christian souls, despite the neo-platonism inherent in their faith. Along with a genuine desire to prepare the soul for the after-life, there also appears a panic fear of death, as exemplified in illustrations of the plague. Death, which is an object both of revulsion and fascination dominates all concerns: sickness, murders and hangings. The bloodthirsty mob watched the body cut open while it was still alive. A strange relationship was that of the people of London with the Three Dark Sisters.

Worldly pleasures were not misprised. Comforts increased as England throve on its colonies. Homes became more habitable. Harington praised the water-closet; tableware became more luxurious. Nonetheless, we hardly ever visit the nobleman's mansion or the house of the rich upper-class. Feasts reflect the gargantuan enthusiasm of the period and the enormous appetite of a Falstaff, often accompanied by the delights of music, as in ancient banquets, where the minstrels sang while the company ate and imbibed. Tobacco which one "drank" according to the nomenclature of the time, caused as much ink to flow as today's controversy over marijuana.

The debates over social life dealt mainly with the role of woman. The subject was popular and Copland in the same year wrote two tracts, one for and one against marriage. Woman appeared wise or light-headed on numerous title-pages. The debate went on until the seventeenth century. The era of Patient Griselda had ended, and the wives and daughters of merchants prepared to assume a more responsible role. Women, armed with whalebones, threatened Swetnam, the male chauvinist.

No other social problem covered so much paper. Courtiers as judges, prison warders, physicians and pawnbrokers were generally despised as caterpillars of the commonwealth. Indeed any "character" in the social edifice was satirized at one time or another.

Graver social questions are concerned with the poor and the underworld of London. Greene, Dekker and many others, dealt with the subject fairly, and exposed the impostors and their enemy, the watchman of London. Copland and others, and in the seventeenth century, **The poore Orphan's Cry** speak of them with pathos. The government tried to impose some responsibility on the rich to be mindful of the poor, but their measures remained inadequate. Droughts, winter freezes, and the plague, weakened the labor force and impoverished agriculture. London, which depended on the country, was often near to starvation. The laws permitting the exportation of wheat were frequently revised, as well as the number of cattle allowed to be butchered. In such circumstances, the merchant vessel was surely a sign of hope.

The most marked change in the topics of the illustrated pamphlets during the reign of Elizabeth concerns the importance of the navy. In her reign there appeared a constellation of pamphlets on the achievements of the navy and on privateers. Many brochures and sermons are illustrated with ships. Both proclamations and ephemeral literature fluctuate according to the royal policy. Some allowed English privateers to take their revenge on the enemy, while others forbade this. But whoever dared attack the English navy was hanged at sea! Under James I and his successor, one still finds brochures on the bandits of the sea, but few deal with naval combats, because the Thirty Years War was a struggle on land.

The illustrated pamphlets that display progress in the military arts derive mainly from the seventeenth century, reaching their apogee as the Thirty Years War begins. Strategists published small tracts for the infantry. Butter and Bourne in **The Swedish Intelligencer** graphically represented the art of war and its fortifications. Similarly towards the end of Elizabeth's reign, there is a reduction in literature encouraging archery in favor of combat with the sword and rifle. These sports are recommended to be practiced each Sunday after worship in the heart of the parish.

The distractions of the Elizabethans and their successors are rigidly regimented according to the social category to which they belong. If chess is permitted for the nobility, it is forbidden to the common people as well as games of dice and theater-going. Each class is limited to its own distractions and wears clothes according to its rank. The society of this era seems therefore like a hierarchy whose stability depends on the vigilance of its directors. The three most dangerous personages who threaten the established order were: women, courtiers and merchants.

Although since the Reformation, the vicissitudes of royal policy in religion reveal a current of agnosticism or atheism, the majority of the population remains profoundly Christian. The evolution of the iconography of God is characterized by a revulsion at depicting Him as a Divine Father. As the sixteenth century draws to its close, printers use the tetragrammaton or the clouds of glory as signs of the divine transcendence, from which emerges the arm of God, a sign of his immanence and of his concern for human affairs.

Towards the end of our period, Rowlands and Taylor publish two versified pamphlets, one on the life of the Virgin, the other on the life of Christ. The existence of the former shows the renewed interest in Catholicism in the Church of England.

The need for the supernatural in an era when the foundations of faith were rudely shaken, is followed, as today, by a revival of belief in the occult. Popular credulity is exploited by astrologers and metaphysical insecurity is manifested in the progress of sorcery. Moreover news pamphlets appear where the behavioral or corporal deformities of human beings are attributed to their religious beliefs. Catholics and Separatists are thus considered responsible for numerous human misfortunes. The attitude of preachers often forms public opinion in these matters. Others express their skepticism about such interpretations of phenomena, which they believe are due to natural causes. This disagreement will continue for many centuries to come.

After this brief conclusion on the role of illustrations as testimony to historical and social life in England, one must ask what do they deliberately ignore? Two points seem significant to us. As essentially middle-class literature it leaves out of account the daily life of the nobility and the intrigues of the court. That is from our standpoint the essential difference between reading the journals compiled by G. B. Harrison and those of our pamphlets or royal proclamations. Information was carefully sifted. Only controversial decisions were publicly justified as in the case of the execution of the Earl of Essex. Court gossip might make the tongues wag, but this is not recorded in pamphlets. The sovereign, like God, was surrounded by clouds of glory, which also veiled most of the ruling class. This was an accepted fact in the sixteenth century which came to be challenged in the next.

At the other extremity of society there are the poor. Certainly the dregs of London are well described, as those of today are in detective novels, a literary genre one remove from reality. London's citizenry with its Calvinistic ethics, tended to believe that only the lazy were poor; and thus the poor were undeserving. Such is the impression to be derived from **The hye way to the Spyttel Hous** and the satires on the London gangs of thieves. From the iconographical standpoint, however, **The poore Orphan's Cry** is the most pathetic appeal for the awakening of consciences.

The literature of illustrated pamphlets is therefore guaranteed neither to lead to envying the ease of the aristocrats, nor to feeling remorse for the unfavored classes. In general it encourages personal initiative and industry with its capitalistic rewards: the acquisition of land and of the titles of the minor nobility.

The same veil is cast over the inner workings of political life. The English are instructed by proclamations of the essential decisions of the kingdom. But neither the debates between Parliament and the Crown, nor intrigues like that of Robert Cecil and Lord Cobham against Sir Walter Raleigh at the start of James I's reign ever reach the illustrated press. Censorship up to that point is effective. Under the Tudors the people are only informed of what they need to know, while subtle Elizabeth gives the people enough information for them to believe that they understand political life. James I does not even pretend to keep the people informed. Consequently the people of England resented being left in the dark, while at the same time being taxed heavily, and without representation during the lengthy abrogation of Parliament under Charles I. This resentment eventually resulted in the Revolution.

It is the final defeat of censorship and the explosion of this political turmoil as seen in the illustrated pamphlets which makes 1640 an important turning point. Since 1632 the foreign news of the Thirty Years War was avidly read in **The Swedish Intelligencer.** In 1641, the news of internal dissentions was spread by satirical illustrated pamphlets, which no censorship could stop. All England was conveyed to the arena where its political future was played out, in a struggle between Calvinist Parliamentarianism and the conservatism of Royalists and Laudians.

The political information thus diffused allowed all to take sides for one or other of the combatants, until in 1642 the spectators themselves descended into the arena to help their favorites, and ultimately in 1644 to dispatch the losers. The popular press and powers of governments passed from the Crown while illustrations became a political power to be reckoned with and finally turned against the government itself.

NOTES

Notes to pp. 1-2

Chapter One - A History of the Pamphlet and of Pamphlet Illustration

1. Sig. Aij v.

2. A pamphlet may be so successful as to reappear in a book or even be expanded into one.

3. Information furnished by H. G. Aldis in **The Cambridge History of English Literature**, eds. A. W. Ward and A. P. Waller (Cambridge: University Press, 1907-1932), I, 104, and reiterated prudently in R. B. McKerrow, **An Introduction to Bibliography for Literary Students** (Oxford: Clarendon Press, 1927; reimp. 1951), but of which I can find no trace in the copy of the documents of the period in W. W. Greg's **A Companion to Arber** (Oxford: Clarendon Press, 1967), nor in P. L. Hughes and J. F. Larkins, **Tudor Royal Proclamations** (New Haven, Conn.: Yale U. P., 1964-69). Perhaps it was less an ordinance than a custom whose value was repeatedly stressed.

4. This argument should not be overemphasized, as many books were also sold without binding.

5. H. G. Aldis, "The Book Trade, 1557-1625" in **The Cambridge History of English Literature**, IV, 407.

6. Except those who, like the Puritans, were uninterested in popular music and who occasionally read the pamphlets for the news they contained, or for their theological instruction; i.e. pamphlets on the Great Carrack.

7. This also includes the trade or importation of woodcuts as well as of translations. English pamphlets, unlike books, were almost never illustrated abroad unless they were completely printed abroad. Another market was the circulation of sensational news.

8. For the law of 1554, see Hughes and Larkin, **Tudor Royal Proclama-**

Notes to pp. 3-4

tions, 31-32, no. 404, and E. G. Duff, **A Century of the English Book-Trade, 1457–1557** (London: Bibliographical Society, 1948), xxvi. It also appears that certain foreigners had, despite all obstacles, succeeded in infiltrating into England. Such was Cawood, R. Jugge and G. Bishoppe who had immigrated from Duisburg with Mercator; cf. E. J. Worman, **Alien Members of the Book Trade during the Tudor Period** (London: Bibliographical Society, 1906), 41. Day, however, was one of the victims of the regime of Bloody Mary.

9. Aldis, op. cit., 378-415. However there appears to be no case where any printer or publisher was expressly forbidden to attend the book fair; at least Aldis does not mention any.

10. Greg, op. cit., 92, 290 and 304-94. The pamphlets edited by Prynne were **STC** 20454, 20459 and 20476. One of the bribed officers was Egerton.

11. Greg, op. cit., 59 and 177. Cf. the merchant mentioned by J. Gee in **The Foot in the Snare**, 1624, and cited by Helen C. White in **English Devotional Literature (Prose), 1600-1640** (Madison: University of Wisconsin Press, 1931), 178-182.

12. G. Duff, **The English Book Trade**, xxv–xxvi, mentions instructions to the Privy Council: "Thair is divers Prentaris in the Realme that daylie and continuallie prentis bukis concerning the faith, ballatis, songs, blasphematiounis, rymes, als weill of kirkmen as temporale . . . " The criticism could also apply to the theater.

13. The Company also desired the status of the liveried companies of London as well as the implementation of order within its members. A. W. Pollard's **Shakespeare's Fight with the Pirates** (Cambridge: University press, 2nd edition, 1920), 10, should be consulted for an interpretation which undermines the excessively political view on the granting of the royal privilege.

14. See Greg, op. cit., 12, and **STC** 10095: **Injunctions geven by the queenes Majestie. A. D. 1559.** R. B. McKerrow in **A dictionary of printers and booksellers in England, Scotland and Ireland and of foreign printers of English books, 1557-1640** (London: Bibliographical Society, 1910), xv, mentions many more laws. Despite these, aided by sympathizers, pamphlets succeeded in passing and printers were sometimes shielded by their colleagues. On the other hand, as in the case of witchcraft, personality differences were settled by reporting others to censorship. See Siebert, **Freedom of the Press in England, 1476-1776** (Urbana: University of Illinois Press, 1952), 63.

15. Henry Burton had his ears cropped later for having composed a tract against Cosin's **Devotions**, written at the instigation of Charles I for the Maids-of-Honor to the Queen, Henrietta-Maria.

16. G. F. Barwick, "The Laws regulating Printing and Publishing in France." **Bibliographical Society Transactions**, 1919, 69-107.

17. Pollard, op. cit., 15. See also Leland ˙Carlson, **Martin Marprelate, gentleman: Master Job Throkmorton laid open his colors.** (San Marino, CA: Huntington Library Publications, 1981).

18. Greg, op. cit., 40ff. and Siebert, op. cit., 145.

19. See H. R. Plomer, **New Documents on English Printers and Booksellers of the 16th Century** (London: Bibliographical Society, 1897), IV, and Greg, op. cit., 58 and 169.

20. Greg, ibid., 18.

21. Greg, ibid., 27, 33, 50, 120, 122, 124, 133, 153, 171, 233 and 108.

22. F. R. Johnson, "Printers, Copy Books and the Black Market in the Elizabethan Book Trade", in **The Library,** Vth series, I, 1946.

23. On the relationship between authors and printers see Pollard, op. cit., 24 and read Taylor, **The Penniless Pilgrimage** and **A Kicksey–Winsey;** also W. Ringler, **Stephen Gosson: A Biographical and Critical Study** (Princeton: U. P., 1942), 25-29. J. Stephens alludes to commanded poets in his epilogue to Fitzgeffrays' **Satyres and Satirical Epigramms,** 1617, sig. E4 v.

24. See for instance H. Parrot's **Lacquei ridiculosi** printed by J. Bushby without his consent.
     Proof–reading was often the subject matter of debates, contentions and railing. Chapman complains about the errata of **The Memorable Mask,** 1613, since he never received the galleys from the printer. Fletcher satirizes it in **The Nice Valour,** 1625. See on the subject Percy Simpson, **Proof–reading in the 16th, 17th and 18th Centuries** (Oxford: U. P., 1970). See also the epistle to the reader of **The Man in the Moone** (**STC** 17155).

25. On the relationship of the theater and the press, see Pollard, op. cit., 36-43.

26. S. Gibson, **Abstracts from the Wills and Testamentary Documents of binders, printers and stationers of Oxford** (London: Bibliographical Society, 1907).

27. Aldis, "The Book Trade", in **The Cambridge History of English Literature** (Cambridge: U. P., 1909), 388ff.

28. H. R. Plomer, **New Documents on English Printers and Booksellers of the 16th Century** (London: Bibliographical Society, 1897), IV, 158.

29. M. Plant, **The English Book Trade** (London: Allen and Unwin, 1939), 26 and 39.

Notes to pp. 6-8

30. Steinberg, **Five Hundred Years of Printing** (Harmondsworth: Penguin Books, 1955), 165.

31. Nash, in **Have with you to Saffron-walden or Gabriel Harveys Hunt is up,** 31, says "As newfangled and idle, and prostituting my pen like a curtizan, is the next item you tax me with: well it may or may not be so . . . There is no newfangleness in mee but povertie." Sir Thomas Overbury in **Characters,** 1638, sig. E7, says that the writer "Handles nothing that is not rare, and defends his wardrobe, diet . . . "

Dekker alludes to the browsers who do not buy in **Jests to make you Merrie,** 1607 and challenges them in **The Seven Deadlie Sinnes of London,** 1606: "You are able . . . to breade more infection on in **Pauls Church Yard** then all the bodies that were buried there in the Plaguetime, if they had been left still above ground. You stand sometimes at a Stationers stall looking scurvily . . . on the face of a new Booke, bee it never so worthy; and goe . . . mewing away."

32. Parrot, **The Mastive,** 1615.

> Printer or Stationer, or what ere thou proove
> Shalt me record to times prosperitie:
> Ile not enjoyne thee, but request in love,
> Thou so much deigne my Book to dignifie;
> As first it bee not with your Ballads mixt;
> Next, not at Play-houses, mongst Pippins sold:
> Then that on Posts, by th'Eares it stand not fixt,
> For every dull Mechanicke to behold . . . .

See also Earle's **Microcosmographie,** sig. H3, and Anton's satire in the epistle to the reader of **The Philosophers Satyrs,** 1616.

33. See Whetstone's **The Rocke of Regard,** 1576 and B. Rich's **A Souldiers Wishe to Britons Welfare,** 1604.

34. The classification used here, with some additions on my part, comes mainly from L. B. Wright, **Middle-class culture in Elizabethan England** (Chapel Hill: University of North Carolina Press, 1935), an outstanding piece of work.

35. **Winter's Tale,** IV, iv, 262f.

36. Overbury, **Characters,** 1638, sig, K2 v: "A Chamber-maid"-"She reade Greene's Works over and over, but is so carried away with the **Mirror of Knighthood,** she is many times resolv'd to runne out her selfe, and become a Lady Errand."

37. F. Madan, **The Oxford Press, 1468-1640** (Oxford: Clarendon Press, 2nd ed. 1895), 117.

38. See the tracts in reply to Swetnam the misogynist.

39. See Aldis and see Greg in **A Companion to Arber,** 264.

40. H. R. Plomer, "The Eliot Court Printing House, 1584-1674", **Library**, II, 1921-22, 176-184.

41. Greg, **A Companion to Arber** and P. McGrath, **Papists and Puritans under Elizabeth** (Oxford: Clarendon Press, 1967).

42. See the list drawn by D. Walker in his doctoral dissertation, **A Study of the Interaction of the Literary and Graphic Arts in England, 1535-1603** (Oxford University, 1972) 1038-1056.

43. H. Fitzgeffrey, **Satyres and Satyrical Epigrams**, 1617. See also **A Presse full of Pamphlets**, 1642.

44. Stubbes, **The Anatomie of Abuses**, sig. vi-viii.

45. B. Rich, **Allarm to England**, sig. iii-iii verso.

46. B. Rich, **A Soldiers Wishe to Britons Welfare**, sig. A3.

47. See **Greenes Vision:** "I crave pardon of you all, if I have offended any by lascivious pamphleting." Was this just a pose on the part of Greene? He also attacks pamphlets in **A disputation betweene a hee conny-catcher, and a shee conny-catcher**, 1592.

48. **STC** 4942. There equally can be found tricks of this kind: No. 213: "One seeing a printed book that was but one sheet of paper said it was not necessary for any man to libell it for it did penance in a sheet already." and No. 249: "One reading of a Curranto said he wondred that men did so affect to lye in paper and yet without sheets."

49. For the quarrel over images at the time of the Reformation see Calvin's **L'Institution de la religion chrétienne** (Geneva: Labor et Fides, 1958) I,xi,1, I,xi,5 and IV,ix,19. For Luther, see **The Oxford Dictionary of the Christian Church** (London: Oxford, U. P., 1957), 680a. See also **A necessary Doctrine and Erudition for any Chrysten Man, set furth by the Kynges Maiesty of Englande . . . ,** 1543. On the relationship between the Church and the visual see Horton Davies, **Worship and Theology in England** (Princeton: University Press, 1970), I, chapter X, "Religious architecture and art", 352-53 and **The Worship of the English Puritans** (Westminster: Dacre Press, 1948), appendix B, 268-69. **The Two Books of Homilies** were reedited by John Griffith (Oxford: Parker Society, 1859). On 189, we read: "Images be of more force to crooken an unhappy soul than to teach and instruct it."

50. **The Blindness of the Unhappy Jews** reads: "Thou shalt make the no graven image . . . There bee on this matter three opinions. Some do holde, that the is no manner of image to be made, not only in religion, but for no profane use neither. In that sorte they say, the Turks do use no images. Which appareth by their mony in whiche we see nothing but Arabike letters: and lyke wyse in their carpettes is found no ymagery of any beast or of man. This opinion is over

Notes to pp. 10-11

supersticiouse to be alowed. Neyther dyd Solomon understand it so . . . Others do not mislyke the use and arte of makyng images in profane matters: but mislyke to have them brought into Churches and into religion . . . Agayne there be some doe not disalowe that images by brought into Churches so that they be not honored and worshipped."

51. That sermons were first addressed to the listener and not to the reader may account for this lack of illustrations. It is also possible that the publisher, sure of the sale of this popular form of literature, did not want to add to their price by increasing their size.

For a Puritan defender of profane images even in religious books see William Perkins, **A Reformed Catholicke,** ed. 1604, p. 705: "The ninth point. Of image". Perkins even allowed the representation of cherubs in order to represent the majesty of God. His argument is very similar to that of St. Francis of Sales in **Introduction à la vie dévote,** edn. of 1614. He describes the angels, while decking them out in all the finery possible in order to prove that devoutness is the best of all possible virtues.

52. See Lawrence Stone, **The Crisis of the Aristocracy, 1558-1641,** (Oxford: Clarendon Press, 1965).

53. Henry Peacham, in **The Compleat Gentleman,** 1622, ch. XII, 102-05, attacks the twopenny-ha'penny works for their mediocre designs. Other attacks against bad drawing and the vulgarity of illustrations could be found in Peacham, **The Gentleman's Exercise,** 1612, 58-59 and in John Davies, **A Scourge for Paper Persecutors,** 1625, sig. A2 v.:

> So if upon the wall
> They see, an Antique in base postures fall:
> As, a Frier blowing wind into the taile
> Of a Babboone, or an Ape drinking Ale,
> They admire that, when to their view perhaps
> If ye should set one of Mercators Mapps
> Or a rare Piece of Albert Durer, they
> Would hardly sticke to throw the toy away,
> And curse the botching painter . . .

The author continues with a play upon Nathaniel Butter, the publisher of Corantos:

> But to behold the wals
> Butter'd with weekly News compos'd in Pauls . . .

54. Peacham, **The Gentlemans Exercise,** 23-25. He believes that the shape of a face translates a person's character. He also takes his examples from antiquity: Scylla's destiny as a great commander was written on his face.

55. **The Book of Homelies,** edn. 1859. See the homily "against excess of apparel". See also Hughes and Larkin **Tudor Royal Proclamations.**

56. S. Anglo, **Spectacle, pageantry and early Tudor policy** (Oxford: Clarendon Press, 1969). On 267 Anglo cites the words of Cromwell: "Into common

people thynges sooner enter by the eies, then by the eares: remembryng more better that they see then that they heere." M.-T. Jones-Davies in **Inigo Jones, Ben Jonson et le Masque** (Paris: Didier, 1967) insists that the masque is the best possible example of the union of the arts: painting, architecture, dancing and music. It is also an example of harmony between philosophy, painting and poetry. The masque is an emblem, a dynamic imprese.

For the love of tricks see L. B. Wright, "Juggling tricks and conjury on the English Stage before 1642", **Modern Philology**, 1927, 269-284.

Last, one might also remember the different roles of numerous disguises in the comedies of Shakespeare: for example in **Twelfth Night,** in **As You Like It** and in **Two Gentlemen of Verona.**

57. See Horton and Marie-Hélène Davies, **Holy Days and Holidays: the medieval pilgrimage to Compostela** (Lewisburg, PA and London: Bucknell University Press, 1980).

58. Horton Davies, **The Worship of the English Puritans,** 270. The author recalls also the principal Puritan poets: Spenser, Sidney, Milton and Marvell.

59. W. Perkins, **A Reformed Catholicke,** 1604, 705.

60. **Ten Books on Architecture** (repr. New York: Transatlantic Arts, 1966). The preface states: "Him I call an Architect, who by sure and wonderful Art and Method, both with Thought and Invention, to devise, and with Execution, to compleat all those Works, which by means of the movement of great Weights, and the Conjunction and Amassment of Bodies, can, with the greatest Beauty, be adapted to the use of Mankind . . . "

About the love-hatred between rhetoric and painting see F. Junius, **The Painting of the Ancients,** 1638, 48 and 54, Wille, **De Re Poetica,** 1573, reed. by the Luttrel Society, No. 17, 45, and Wye Saltonstall, **Picturae Loquentes,** 1631. Hakeville in **The Vanitie of the Eye,** 1608 consoles a blind girl by decrying the eye as a master of error and falseness, and John Calvin in **Institues,** I,xv,3, II,i,5, I,ii,17, II,vii,17,40, and 51, III,iii,9, and III,vi,1, had proclaimed the superiority of the rhetorical image. Henry Peacham in **The Gentlemans Exercise** says in the dedicatory epistle: "For my own part, I hope I shall not be imagined to speake as Dentrius did for his silver Images, as gaining ought hereby, since by profession I am a Scholler."

61. **STC** 18747, **A nunnes prophesie, or the fall of friers,** 1615.

62. William Camden, **Remains,** 1637, 164-171. P. 164 he says: "Whereas a poesie is a speaking picture and a picture a speechless poesie, they which lacked wit to express their conceit in speech, did use to depaint it out (as it were) in pictures, which they called Rebus, by a latin name well fitting their device." He enumerates all the devices of Islip. See also McKerrow, **Printers' and Publishers' Devices,** Nos. 169-171.

63. Whitney, **A choice of Emblems and other Devises,** 1586: "Such other figures, or workes, as are wrought in plate, or in stones in the pavementes,

Notes to pp. 14-15

or on the waules, or such like, for the adorning of the place: having some wittie devise expressed with cunning woorkemanship, something obscure to be perceived at the first, whereby, when with further consideration it is understood, it maie the greater delighte to behoulde . . . all do tend unto disciplin, and morall preceptes of living."

For example, there is an emblem representing the wall of virtue, a solid wall of stone, against which an arrow has struck and its tip has fallen to the ground; it bears this device: Calumniam contra calumniatorem virtus repellit. Another represents a king, with a sceptre in one hand and a sponge in the other which is being drained, while from afar a hanging scene can be made out. The device: Quod capit Christus, rapit fiscus is clarified by the poem: ill-acquired goods do not benefit a tyrant. The same type of emblem could be found in Wither; for instance sic transiit gloria mundi is illustrated by a rapier in the center of a brazier burning the symbols of worldly power: imperial, royal and papal crowns, mitres, scepters and orbs.

64. Quarles, **Emblems,** 1635, sig. A3.

65. See Jacques Maritain, "Signs and symbols", Journals of the Warburg Institute, 1937, I, 1-12, E. H. Gombrich, "Icones symbolicae. The visual image in neo-platonic thought", Journals of the Warburg Institute, XI-XII, 1948-49, 163-192, and Rosemary Freeman, **English Emblem Books** (London: Chatto and Windus, 1948; reed. 1967 and 1970).

66. McKerrow, **Printers' and Publishers' Devices,** where he enumerates a good twenty marks which can be called emblems and another twenty of emblem-atic origin. Some are occasionally borrowed from abroad, only requiring the initials to be changed; others are used for thirty or forty years. Booksellers also used heraldic devices and their ensigns as marks, which were passed on from hand to hand throughout Europe. Peter Short for example, adopted the serpent, which was the well-known mark of the Italian printer Vicentius. It was reused by Conrad Neobar, R. Wolfe, John Harrison, John Windet and Andrew Maunsell. See S. P. Thompson, "Peter Short, Printer and his marks," **Bibliographical Society Transactions** IV, 1897.

67. See **STC** 16698. Lomazzo, **A Tractate containing the Artes of curious painting, carving and building,** 1619. In the preface Haydock refers to the three chief painters of the time: N. Hilliard, I. Oliver and R. Lockey. How deeply the feeling of hierarchy is ingrained in the Elizabethans can be sensed from the fact that they even apply it to art: the portrait of a great man should raise him far above the technique used on a juggler.

68. See Alfred Shorter, **Papermills and paper-makers in England, 1495-1800,** published by Monumenta Chartae Papyracae Historiam illustrantia (Hilversum: Paper Publication Society, 1957). See also M. Plant, **The English Book Trade** (London: Allen and Unwin, 1939) and D. C. Coleman, **The British Paper Industry** (Oxford: Clarendon Press, 1958), which reiterates the theories of M. Plant.

69. M. W., **The Man in the Moone, telling strange fortunes, or the English fortune-teller,** 1609.

70. On the fabrication of paper, check the seventeenth century work of Moxon, **Mechanick exercises on the whole art of printing,** 1683-1684. Repr. (Oxford: University Press, 1962). His first treatise speaks of the art of printing in general and of the various techniques used. See particularly 82-84.

71. For an example of a line which is dark at the edge and pale in the middle, see **The pleasant and sweet history of patient Grissel,** ed. by Wright in 1630.

72. Jean Laran, **L'Estampe,** (Paris: P.U.F., 1959). For engraving and etching see 41 sq.

73. **STC** 23578 (Bod. 4° p. 35 Th).

74. (Bod. 4° p. 35 Th). For illustrations of this type, see also **STC** 25915, and the following: **STC** 13397, S. Hieron, **The dignitie of Preaching,** 1616, **STC** 18588, A. Nixon, **Londons dove,** 1612, **STC** 23772, J. Taylor, **A living sadness,** 1625.

75. Respectively **STC** 17155, **STC** 693, **STC** 10841a.

76. John Bate, **The mysteries of Nature and Art,** 1634, 136-140. On the techniques of printing and of the cutting of pictures see also the exhibit of the Bibliothèque Nationale, Paris: "Le Livre", 1972 which displayed the engravings of Louis Simmoneau on this particular subject, dating from 1694. More profitable reading can also be found in Félibien, **Les principes de l'Architecture,** Paris, 1675, or in the treatises of A. Bosse.

77. **STC** 17403 (Bod. 4° Th C 80).

78. **STC** 1609 (Bod. Godw. Pamph. 1114 (1).)

79. **STC** 20340. R. Pricket, **The Jesuites Miracles, or New Popish Wonders.**

80. **STC** 18545. Two other examples can be found: A. H., **A Scourge for paper-persecutors,** 1625 and R. S., **The counter-scuffle,** 1628.

81. **STC** 21125. (Bod. Douce B Subt 108).

82. **The Safeguard of sailers,** 1584 edition, **STC** 21545.

83. **STC** 13140 (B.M. 1195 c 3) **The sighes of Fraunce for the Death of their late King. The forme of the coronation of Prince Lewes,** 1610.

Notes to pp. 17-19

84. **STC** 17882 (<u>Bod.</u> Vet A 2 e 177) Middleton, **Game at Chaess,** 1625.

85. One can compare, for instance, the woodcut characters of two of Copland's interludes: **STC** 14113, **A new interlude of impacient Poverte,** 1525? and **STC** 14112, **Theterlude of Youth,** 1557.

86. Respectively **STC** 12012 and **Wing,** 1095.

87. Respectively **STC** 18588 and 13397.

88. This tremendous work could only be achieved by a team of special- ists in the field of Renaissance art. However, further complications would be added by the fact that libraries sometimes discarded pamphlets in order to make room for "fine books". It seems however that few of the English woodcuts of the sixteenth century were original.

89. (<u>Bod.</u> Arch G C 6) Compare with <u>B. N.</u> N 11 No D 133.

90. See the notes of a bibliographer to the edition of 1620. (<u>Bod.</u> Mal 186).

91. This information was provided by Jean Adhémar, chief curator of the Department of Prints and Drawings of the Bibliothèque Nationale, on October 19, 1972. This topic was the theme of his current research.

92. **STC** 639, **Christopher Angell, a grecian, who tasted of many stripes . . . ,** 1617.

93. See **The cry and revenge of blood,** 1620, 59 (<u>Bod.</u> 4° G 29 Art); **Pasquils Palinodia,** 1619 (<u>Bod.</u> Malone 211); **The baiting of the Popes Bull,** 1627 (<u>Bod.</u> 4° E 31 Th); **A post with a pack of mad letters,** 1633 (<u>Bod.</u> 4° F 2 Art BS); **The travels of Twelve pence,** 1635 (<u>Bod.</u> Mal 506).

94. **STC** 12027. N. Goodman, **Hollands Leaguer,** 1632; also **The Knight of Curtesy and the Lady of Faguell,** n.d. See R. B. McKerrow, **The decoration of Books,** iii.

95. **STC** 21388, 21389, 21390, 21392.

96. See, for instance, **STC** 6074, 13367, **Ben Jonson's execration against Vulcan,** 1640, etc.

97. Hind, **An introduction to the history of woodcut,** I, 90.

98. On the portraits of the Queen, see Hind, **Engraving in England** (Cambridge: U. P., 1952) and F. M. O'Donogue, **A descriptive and classified Cata- logue of portraits of Queen Elizabeth** (London: 1894).

99. See also the various editions of R. Greene's and Th. Dekker's pamphlets.

100. Compare this border to the Book of Hours for Englebert de Nassau executed around 1485-90, particularly folios 133r and 152v. (Bod. M.S. Douce 219).

101. STC 13759, **An homelye to be reade in the tyme of pestylence,** 1553.

102. For examples of transitional art, see STC 4370 (Bod. Facs e 3) and STC 6455 (B.M. C 12. 12).

103. Compare, for instance, the borders of **A fourme of common prayer,** 1572 (for the 27th of October) and E. Dering's sermon for February 25, 1569, or of **Riche his farewell,** 1581. The first is heavy, the others more delicate.

104. Heinrich Wölfflin, **Principles of Art History:** the problem of the development of style in later art (London: Bell and Sons, 1932). The whole first chapter dwells on the difference between what he calls the linear and the pictorial styles. According to him Dürer, Holbein and Hilliard are linear engravers, whereas Rembrandt and Bronzino work according to the new 'pictorial' theories.

105. See STC 731, J. Archbold, **The beauty of holiness,** 1621, and also STC 12650, J. Hall, Bp., **Contemplations upon the passages of the holie storie,** 1612.

106. One also finds an odd mixture of styles, architectural and pictorial, of Judeo-Christian inspiration in **The practice of pietie,** 1619, printed for J. Hodgetts.

107. See, for instance, **Here beginneth a litell treatise of the Knight of Curtesy and the Lady of Faguell** (Bod. S. Seld. d. 45) and **The frier and the boy** (Bod. 4° C. 39 Art. Seld.)

108. See STC 22915, **A true report of certaine overflowings of waters in Sommerset-shire,** 1607, and STC 25950, **The wonders of this windie winter,** 1613.

109. STC 1904, **Looke up and see wonders,** 1628.

110. In STC 5698, Th. Cooper, **The cry and revenge of blood,** 1620, the picture story can be read thus: up left, down left, up right, down right. In STC 24904, W. G., **Newes out of Cheshire** it is read top first and then bottom, whereas in STC 4768, T. Cash, **Two horrible murders,** it is read from left to right.

111. The same type of mistakes can be found in STC 6445.

Notes to pp. 22-25

112. The ambiguity of the picture should be noted. In the play which follows the historical record, the trial was judged by James I. But the woodcut clearly represents the judge as a woman. Are we then in the presence of an anti-feminist woodcut? After all Portia in **The Merchant of Venice** had won the praises of the Duke, for she was a wise young judge clad in man's apparel.

113. See, for instance, the title-pages of **STC** 11691, J. Gaule, **Practique theories,** 1628-29 or of the 1638 edition of **The Assizes of Bread.** Both could be categorized as books rather than pamphlets.

114. See respectively the printer's device on **STC** 25039; **STC** 6042 and 25844; and the etching of William Hole on the title-page of **The Sanctuarie of a troubled soul.** See also the evolution of astrological man in almanacs.

115. Pope-Hennesy, **The portrait in the Renaissance** (New York: Pantheon Books, 1966), 200ff.

116. **STC** 5257, Th. Churchyard, **A sparke of friendship,** 1588.

117. Bod. A. 13 8 Linc.

118. See, for instance, a pamphlet on the coronation of Henry IV of France. This is one of the few portraits of the king, if not the only one, to show both the line of his forehead and circles under his eyes. The king was usually painted with a serene forehead, expressing his kindness. (Talk with Mr. Adhémar, October 19, 1972, as previously in Fn. 23).

119. Hind, **Engraving in England,** II, plates 152 and 199.

120. **STC** 7031, J. Donne, **Deaths duell,** 1632.

121. **STC** 18165, **The arrival and intertainements of the ambassador from the Emperor of Morocco,** 1637.

122. **A funeral elegie,** 1625 (Bod. Vet A 2 e 146) shows James I recumbent on a couch.

123. Bod. 4º P 35 Th.

124. See, for instance, **STC** 25740, Williamson, **The sword and the spirit.**

125. J. J. Mayoux, **La peinture anglaise** (Paris: P.U.F., 1969), 18.

126. Erna Auerbach, **Nicholas Hilliard** (London: Routledge and Kegan Paul, 1961), 204ff.

Chapter Two - Images with an Essentially Decorative Function

1. **The true reporte of the forme and shape of a monstruous child,** 1562; the letter O contains a dragon.

2. **The description of a monstruous pig,** 1562. The letter T is entirely in the form of a scroll; from all appearances it is an embroidered letter intended for a table napkin or a tea-cloth.

3. The letter comes from E. Fenton, **Certaine Secrete wonders of nature,** 1569, 127. See, for a similar medieval example, "Le martyre de Saint-Victor", a manuscript from the end of the thirteenth century kept in the Library of Sainte-Geneviève in Paris.

4. (Bod. Arch. G C 6.)

5. For title-pages see R. B. McKerrow and F. S. Ferguson, **Title-page Borders used in England and Scotland, 1485-1640,** 1932.

6. See also that of the Duchess of Suffolk, an image of the great Protestant lady to whom Latimer dedicated **A Notable Sermon.** A widow in 1545, remarried in 1552, the Duchess had to become an exile in France during the reign of Mary Tudor who tried to decapitate Protestantism. Latimer himself succumbed.

7. **Proclamations of Parliament,** (Bod. Arch. G C 6).

8. **STC** 13159. See also Plate 27.

9. A proceeding often found in the seventeenth century, when the Company had the monopoly of the printing of almanacs; see for examples, those of Allestree in 1621 and 1637, or of Frende of 1621.

10. John Taylor, **The sculler, rowing from Tiber to Thames,** 1612.

11. (Bod. Fol. 659.)

12. **Cheap-side Crosse censured and condemned . . .** ANN. for I. R., 1641.

13. Charles Howard, Earl of Nottingham; an act written in Welsh, printed by Thomas Purfoot at London. The identification of this vessel is specially delicate. Is it a galleon or ship of the merchant navy? If the ship was a man-of-war, should it not have borne in honor of Howard, admiral-in-chief, the royal banner? Or is it rather a reminder of the role of the merchant navy in the time of Elizabeth, since all the great ships of war were in fact directed by merchant navy specialists?

238

14. Robert Hues, **The Seamans Kalendar**, 1602; this was an almanac and calendar intended for navigators and reflected the most modern theories. It ran to ten editions between 1602 and 1631. (Cf. David Waters, **The art of navigation in England in Elizabethan and early Stuart times,** 1958.)

15. **News from Perin in Cornwall: of a most Bloody and un-exampled Murther,** printed by E. A., 1618. (Bod. 4 G 29 Art.)

16. (Bod. Wood B 35.)

17. (Bod. Gough Essex 24.)

18. Thomas Heywood, **A true Discription of his Majesties royall ship built at Wooll-witch,** 1638. STC 13368.

19. **Proclamations,** (Bod. Arch. C 6).

20. For a description of the Elizabethan ships, see G. Mattingley, **The Armada,** (Boston: Houghton and Mifflin, 1959), xvi-xviii.

21. **Histoire mondiale de la Marine** (Paris: Hachette, 1965).

22. R. Mousnier, **Histoire générale des civilisations. Le XVIème siècle** (Paris: P.U.F. 1956), 142-145.

23. Bernard Capp, "Almanachs, 1500-1700."

24. Bosanquet, **English Printed Almanacks and Prognostications, A Bibliographical History to the year 1600** (London: Bibliographical Society, 1917).

25. See Bosanquet, ibid., passim as a work of reference.

26. See chapter I, 19-20.

27. Among others should be mentioned the almanacs of Cox in 1566 and of Securis in 1567. The signs of the zodiac reappear with White's prediction of 1615. It is the single survivor from a good hundred almanacs consulted after 1600.

28. See chapters I, 20-21 and chapter IV, 1.

29. Charles R. Morey, **Medieval Art** (New York: Norton, 1942), 195.

30. Butler's almanac of 1631. (Bod. Ashm. 68.)

31. See, for example, the illustration which decorates, or mars the almanac of Osborne or of John Vaux of St. Ellen in 1628: the statuette is hardly recognizable because it is so confused. Or, again, see the woodcut for the almanac

of Bretnor in 1615, which is split and found in numerous other almanacs; with the passage of the years the split gets larger.

32.   See an example in (Bod. Ashm. 62).

33.   See, for example, Woodehouse's almanac for 1628.

34.   See Rudstone's for 1613.

35.   There is a renewal of this ancient image in the seventeenth century: see White, Neve and Johnson in 1613, and Frende in 1621 . . .

36.   See the recto of page 2 of the almanac of Rivers, 1630, depicting a man in red.

37.   See chapter I, 19-20.

38.   See chapter III, 56.

39.   No systematic study of ballads is included here which would demand a colossal book; instead, there is an overview of those seen in our research in the Bodleian and British Libraries.

40.   See chapter I, 18-19.

41.   D. Carrick, **Here begynneth a dialogue betwene the comen Secretary and Jelowsy touchynge the unstablenes of harlottes.** (B.M. C. 21. c. 19).

42.   Lydgage, **Here foloweth the Churle and the byrde,** 1550.

43.   **The debate and stryfe betwene somer and wynter with the estate present of Man.** (B.M. C. 40 c. 5).

44.   **A new Enterlude for children to playe, named Jack Jugeler,** 1565.

45.   See also the illustration of **A Merry Jest of Robin Hood,** 1590, which has the same vignettes as the 1557 edition of **Adam Bell** (B.M. C. 21. c. 64). The trick is an easy one: to write beneath the person on the right "Adam Bell" in one case and "Little John" in the other. The same illustration can be used for the same poem by a simple modification of certain woodcuts. The same image decorates the 1605, 1628 and 1632 editions of **Adam Bell**; but the second part of the brochure in 1616 shows these differences: the cap and footwear of the three persons have been blackened; in addition the doublet and the handle of the halberd of the middle person have also been blackened.

46.   For additional references see **Theterlude of youth,** published in 1557 (Bod. Mal 231).

Notes to pp. 39-42

47. For the caparisoned knight, see Copland's **Here begynneth a propre tretyse of a marchauntes wyfe, that afterwarde went lyke a man and became a grete lorde, and was called Frederyke of Jennen.** (B.M.) It is hardly surprising that we have to do with a French image because of the fleur-de-lys that ornaments the shield of the knight. This type is often found in the middle of the seventeenth century. See, for example, **The famous delectable historie of Cleocreton and Cloryana** (1630?) by C.S. On the verso of the last page there is an inscription: "The renowned Cleocreton, Prince of Hungary." For the other kind of illustration, see, among others, **A merrie pleasant and delectable Historie, betwene King Edward the fourth, and a Tanner of Tamworth . . . ,** 1596. See also the same illustration reappearing in **STC** 25409, **The martyrdome of Saint George of Cappadocia.**

48. **The wyfe happed on Morel's Skypp.** (Bod. S. Seld. 45 (14)).

49. **The Maydens Crosse rewe,** 1540.

50. **The Notable Hystory of two faithfull Lovers named Alfagus and Archelaus,** 1574. **(STC 14498).**

51. It is difficult to decide: the proportions suggest either a tomb as one possibility, (but tombs were then often ornamented with recumbent figures), or a stone altar. Nor can the idea of a chest be excluded, since medieval art enlarged the object or person which was of great importance. It would therefore seem perfectly normal for the reliquary chest of a saint to attract the attention of the reader, whence our lack of certainty.

52. Another example of an illustration entirely independent of the text, is that of a centaur and a man brandishing a club at the top of **Dreme,** 1554, and of **Heir follouis the Tragedie of the Umquihyle maist Reverend father David . . . ,** 1547, the first printed at Edinburgh and the second by John Day. Both are satires on the great persons of the kingdom and, particularly in the second case, of Cardinal David Beaton, archbishop of St. Andrews and Papal Legate, who, through his cruelty and ambition was one of the plagues of Scotland. He was assassinated in 1546. The allusion to Hercules might be an indication of where the sympathies of Sir David Lindsay lay: the superman who overcomes the tyrant lives, in which case this is a subtle emblem. But, since the image can be found in other poems, it loses its force and seems to us to be merely decorative.

53. The exact date is unknown, but Copland is the printer.

54. Edition of 1560. (Bod. S. Seld. d 45).

55. The author of the work appears under this pseudonym. See the Bodleian Library edition, S. Seld. 45 (14), 1580.

56. Immediately under the cut is an allusion to St. Sim, whether Simon or Simeon. **The Oxford Dictionary of the Christian Church** mentions 7 saints

under these names, but none of them has a serpent for an emblem. There is therefore no direct connection between the story and the decorative woodcut.

57. According to the words of Christ: "Be as wise as serpents and
as harmless as doves."

(a) Examples of approximation are abundant. See also **The history
of Jacob and his twelve Sonnes**, 1570; the king is surrounded
by four princes recognizable from their ermine capes, but the
tongues of fire, symbols of Pentecost in the New Testament,
fall upon them.

Another example: in **A merrie pleasant . . . Historie, betwene
King Edward the fourth, and a Tanner of Tamworth**, 1596,
the title-page depicts two knights riding together. One of the
customary illustrations representing a knight depicts in fact
the king whom the tanner fails to recognize. The last illustration,
by contrast, shows the king and his court. One of the courtiers
is kneeling, which corresponds to the text, except that this
act of submission takes place outdoors and not in the palace.

(b) It is sometimes possible to trace the origins of certain images.
For example, **The Historie of graund Amoure de la Bel Pucell . . .
The pastime of pleasure** furnishes the image of **Wynter and
Somer** (STC 6445), that of the caparisoned knight in **A propre
treatyse of a merchauntes wyfe** (STC 11362), that of the lovers
in the garden in **The wyfe happed on Morel's Skypp**, 1580,
the monster of **Bevis of Hampton**, the title-page of . . . **Historie
betwene King Edward the fourth, and a Tanner of Tamworth**,
1596, and, finally, the title-page of **The Knight of Curtesy
and the Lady of Faguell**. It was an important book and in all
probability the images of our brochures were taken from it.
However, we cannot affirm positively that these illustrations
were all made for the book; to say that would require us to
know all the books which preceded it.

58. **STC** 23684, edition of 1638.

59. See chapter I, p. 23.

60. (<u>Bod</u>. Mal 296.)

61. **STC** 19333.

62. **STC** 23748.

63. **STC** 21642 (<u>Bod</u>. Mal 296).

64. See the same illustration in **I would and I would not**, without
date or author's name.

Notes to pp. 43-46

65. One does not want to be arbitrary, however. Works like **The seven sorowes that women have when theyr husbandes be dead,** of Copland, **A mery Jest of Dans Hew Munk of Leicestre,** 1560, and **Sir Bevis of Hampton** cannot be placed in this category because every image in the text or on the title-page recounts the story and has been prepared in all probability exclusively for the text itself.

66. See, for example, **A sermon of Spiritual Life and death,** 1626, by John Preston. The border of the title-page represents, among other things, four cardinal virtues: Justice, Fortitude, and Prudence, while the fourth, Temperance, is replaced by Mercy. It would be intersting to know whether Preston, a distinguished Puritan, chose Mercy because it implies the three theological virtues which are the superstructure of Catholic teaching (namely, Faith, Hope and Charity), without actually naming them, which might have been contrary to his Protestant convictions. (Commentary of Horton Davies on 6 July, 1974). This, however, may be no more than conjecture. Perhaps Preston had this intention, perhaps the editor changed the terminology of the virtues to satisfy theological exigencies, or possibly it was only an accident.

Chapter Three - The Image as a Source of Information

1. For education, see in particular the work of Cole, **A History of Educational Thought** (London: Oxford University Press, 1931) and W. Ong, **Rhetoric, Romance and Technology: studies in the interaction and expression of culture** (Ithaca, N.Y.: Cornell University Press, 1971).

2. **Palladis Tamia,** 1598.

3. See J. W. Blench, **Preaching in England** (Oxford: Blackwell, 1964) a study of the evolution of preaching in the sixteenth century.

4. On the insecurity of the Elizabethans and their contradictory views of the world, see H. B. Parkes, "Nature's Diverse Lawes - the double vision of the Elizabethans", Sewanee Review, LVIII, 1950.

5. Here we intentionally use Platonic terminology. It appears that the opinion of the ancients corresponds with the Platonic idea for this conception of knowledge. Sixteenth century felt its limitations since, as inheritors of the philosophy of the ancients, their knowledge was in fact twice removed. It was a debilitating and, in a sense, a contradictory situation, since it implied, as Bacon says, a great confidence in the spirit of man who could thus bind the rest of humanity by his discoveries: **Advancement of Learning,** I, v, 6: "Another error hath proceeded

from too great a reverence and a kind of adoration of the mind and understanding of man . . . " The word "adoration" suggests that Aristotle has become a god. As the Christianity of the Renaissance would not allow such blasphemy, we prefer to use neo-platonic categories.

The complexity of Renaissance thought on its position in the world is ably summarized in Herbert Weisinger's article, "Ideas of History during the Renaissance," Journal of the History of Ideas, VI, 1945, 415-433.

6. Although Peter Ramus best formulated the desires of modern education in Europe, they were already in the air. Sir Thomas Elyot in **The Governour** expressed certain ideas which announced the advent of Ramism in England. On the debate between the two schools, see the excellent study of W. S. Howell, **Logic and Rhetoric in England, 1500-1700** (Princeton, N.J.: University Press, 1956).

7. See J. W. Blench, op. cit., for the evolution of preaching in England. Otherwise one can find the influence of Ramism on the metaphysical poets, especially John Donne. See R. Tuve's article, "Imagery and Logic: Ramism and Metaphysical Poetics". The chief effect of Ramism was to intellectualize the images. Journal of the History of Ideas, III, 1942, #4, 365-400.

8. Perkins, **Works**, Cambridge, 1603.

9. Horton Davies, **The Worship of the English Puritans** (London: Dacre Press, 1948), 196.

10. Allen G. Debus, **Science and Education in the seventeenth century** (New York: American Elsevier, 1970), 9.

11. Sir Thomas Elyot, **The Governour**, 1531, fol. 26: "Experience we have thereof in lernynge of geometrie/ astronomie/ & cosmographie called in engliss be the discriptiō of the worlde. In which studies I dare affirme/ a mā shal more pfite in one wike by figures & chartis/ well and perfectly made/ than he shall by the only reding or hering the rule of that sciēce by the space of halfe a yere at the lest . . . "

12. This dispute corresponds to the time when the Puritan controversy reaches its height in Parliament when the Puritans hope to reform the English Church. Further, the Puritans always recommend the simplicity of expression and the clarity of the message of the preacher. It is no less interesting to note Puritanism's links with the middle classes, who were often Puritan in philosophy and even in religion, according to the Calvinist principle which encouraged the elect to work to occupy key positions in society and thus propagate their faith.

13. Walter J. Ong, **Rhetoric, romance and technology.**

14. See chapter I, 5-6.

15. See chapter II, 38-39.

244

Notes to pp. 49-51

16. Luther, **A ryght notable sermon uppon the twentieth chapter of Johan,** 1548.

17. On the title-page of the edition of 1620 beneath the emblem it reads:

This Naked Pourtraiture before thine Eye
Is Wretched, helplesse MAN, MAN borne to Die;
On either side, an ANGELL doth protect him
As well from EVILL, as to GOOD direct him:
Th'one poynts to DEATH, the t'other to a CROWNE:
Who THIS attaines, must tread the OTHER downe:
All which denotes the Briefe of MANS Estate,
That HEE's to goe from HENCE by THIS, to THAT.

18. Besides its iconographic interest, the work presents a tableau of the psychological and physiological conceptions of man in the time of Charles I. See above all 11–15. Another emblem intended for religious edification is that of R. Croft's **The terrestrial Paradise or Happiness on Earth,** 1639. The author praises the riches of the earth and the moderation which enables them to be enjoyed with prudence. The harmony of human life depends on the strength of the lion and the wisdom of the monkey. (**STC** 6044).

19. Taylor is here playing on the words "sun" and "son"; here is the citation:

My looking on the Sunne, doth heere expresse,
I care to see the Sonne of righteousness . . .

Earlier Taylor played also on the word "want" as desiring and "want" as a need.

20. The emblem serves also to praise a person or a family: as proof see the back of the title-page of **A most true relation of the affaires of Cleves and Gulick,** 1615, by Henry Peacham in honor of Sir John Ogle, colonel of a regiment of infantry.

21. Taylor also uses an emblematic image as a cover for a personal advertisement. The legend beneath the image representing him rowing on the Thames is: "Sum primus homo, Vis ire mecum Remis? Est mihi proxima Cimba." It should be observed that many of the devices of booksellers and printers were emblem-images. It would be interesting to consider McKerrow's **Printers' and Publishers' Devices in England and Scotland 1485-1640,** with a view to comparing those of the signs of booths and of taverns.

22. Sir Thomas Elyot, **The Governour,** fol. 25 verso and fol. 26 reads:

And when he happeneth to rede or here any fable
or historie/ forthwith the apprehendeth it more
desirously and retaineth it better thā any other/
that lacketh the sayd feate: by reason that he
hath foũde mater apte to this fantasie...
And he that is perfectly instructed in portrayture/

Note to p. 51

and hapneth to rede any noble and excellent historie/
Wherby his courage is inflamed to the imitation of
vertue/ he forthwith taketh his penne or pensill/ and
with a grave and substanciall studie/ gatherynge to
him all the partes of imagination/ endevoureth him
selfe to expresse lively/ and...actually in portray-
ture/ nat only the faict or affaire/ but also the
sondry affections of every personage in the historie
recited which mought in any wise appiere or be perceived in their visage, coutenance or gesture.

The image therefore has here an edifying function.

23. We are limiting ourselves to the comparison of two editions: that
of 1565 (B.M. C 21 c. 62) and that of 1582, which represent two types of illustration. That of 1565 contains a certain number of woodcuts of modern make which
are completed by those of 1639. The title-page of both editions is, of course,
different; that of 1565 represents a knight armed only with a sword, that of 1582
a knight followed by his escort. In each case the horse bears the white rose of
Southampton. For the correlation of the two editions we have prepared a comparative table. The images are identical (=) or different ($\neq$), deal with the same theme
or not (id./$\neq$), exist in one edition but not in the other ($\emptyset$).

1565		1582			
A iv, v	=	A iii		same theme	The father of Bevis, Guy, is killed by his enemies while he hunts the wild boar for his perfidious wife.
B ii	$\neq$	A iv		id.	Bevis looks after the sheep.
$\emptyset$		B			Bevis kills the door-keeper of his father's house and wounds his wife's mother.
$\emptyset$		B ii			Bevis is sold as a slave to the king of Armony.
C ii	=	B iii		id.	The combat of Bevis against the Saracens.
C v, v	=	B iv, v		id.	Bevis kills a wild boar in the forest.
E iv	$\neq$	C iv		$\neq$	1565: image representing a town. 1582: at Damascus, Bevis gives the king a message.
G i	$\neq$	D ii, v		id.	The king of mambrant marries Josiane who would have loved to marry Bevis.
K i, v	$\neq$	(E i			
		(E iv, v		id.	Bevis combats the giant.
K iii	=	F		id.	Bevis and Josiane subdue the giant.
$\emptyset$		F ii			Bevis fights the dragon.

Notes to pp. 51-53

N ii	≠	G	id.	Josiane is married against her will.
∅		G ii, v		A message is sent around to help Bevis reconquer his lands. (Same image as C iv).
P i	=	H i, v	id	Bevis at a tourney, who has rediscovered Josiane.
S iii	≠	I iv	id.	Marriage of the son of Josiane to the daughter of the king Bevis fought: solution of the conflict.

The different editions of **Bevis** include all the illustrations which are fairly close to the text. A second conclusion is that since it is impossible for the printer to reuse the first illustrations, he created other images for the same scenes in the same spirit.

24. See earlier, chapter II, note 57(B).

25. We have found it impossible to examine three numbers: 23757, 23758, 23808.

26. Here we are not including the decorative images.

27. See the bibliography for the correspondences between Taylor and **STC.** Most of the illustrations are on the title-page. However, they are found opposite the title-page in STC 23747, **Divers crabtree lectures,** 23748, **A dog of Warre,** 23766, **Juniper Lecture,** and 23781-82, **The olde old, very old man.**

28. On the title-page and the opposite page the two illustrations are found in **The Watercormorant his complaint,** STC 23813. Further, on the verso of the title-page we find the coat of arms of the merchant marine in **STC** 23726, **An Armado; Taylor his motto** which has a variation between its two editions (**STC** gives only one): a microfilm of **STC** 23726 shows this image on the title-page and the explanation of the emblem on the verso, while that of the Bodleian Library (8° 019 Art) shows it on A 2 with the explanation of the emblem opposite, on the back of the title-page. Both editions seem to be of 1621.
Finally, the illustration on the title-page of **A Kicksey Winsey** is repeated beneath the general plan of the little work where Taylor lists five catego-ries in which he can classify his debtors. Also, **An Englishman's love to Bohemia** includes an illustration on the back of the title-page.

29. If the gaps in the chronology of the iconography of Taylor up to 1660 are kept in mind, it is clear that they correspond to the vicissitudes and displacements of his life. In 1616 and 1617 he travelled in Europe. In 1626, having fled the plague that then ravaged London, he found himself in Oxford far from his printers. From this time on his life is relatively unknown. However, between 1628 and 1630 he prepared the edition of his complete works, but it is difficult to know why he apparently produced nothing new between 1630 and 1634. Nor

are there any illustrated works in 1637-1638, while five appeared in 1635. How is the irregularity of his productions to be explained? Did his clientele change? Or, did he only publish when economic difficulties put the knife to his throat?

30. It is interesting to note in this connection that Taylor prided himself on having weeded out anything that might displease Protestants without offending the Catholics.

31. How did this illustration pass from E. Allde to Purslowe, Taylor's printer? However, the relationship between the two printers must have been fairly close since both worked for Gosson and for Wright.

32. See Lavalleye's **Pieter Bruegel the Elder and Lucas van Leyden. The complete Engravings, Etchings and Woodcuts** (London: Thames and Hudson, 1967). In Bruegel's illustration the gourmand is found in the upper center and is thrown out of the kitchen. In Taylor's he is on the right.
Jack-a-Lent in the middle of Taylor's image is mounted on a fish, in Bruegel he is sitting and stirring the stew to the left. Hunger seizes the mussels on a plate in the middle of "The Poor Kitchen": in **Jack-a-Lent** he is found on the left brandishing some dry fishes. This person is inspired by Bruegel rather than a copy of his character.

33. See **An Englishman's love to Bohemia**, 1620.

34. Ibid.

35. **Divers crabtree lectures**, 1639.

36. **A Juniper lecture**, 1639.

37. See also for a similar genre the illustration to **Taylor's Goose** of which only a fragment is extant.

38. 159.

39. The emblematic illustration represents a winged shilling and corresponds to the text at sig. A4:

> A hundred strong men-midwives, digg'd their way
> Into her bowels, to find where I lay
> With Engine, Spade, Crowes, Mattocks, and such
> They ripp'd and tore her harmless womb to tatters,
> And but they did within the midway catch me
> They would have digg'd to hell it self to fetch me.

40. This matter will be reconsidered in Chapter VII.

41. It would be wrong to think that all the illustrated poems have been referred to, for only a selection has been presented of a representative char-

acter to avoid boredom and confusion. Other examples, like **Robin Goodfellow** will appear in other chapters, and yet others in the Bibliography.

42. Cf. Chapter I.

43. Cf. J. W. Blench, **Preaching in England** (Oxford: Blackwell, 1964). See also for the seventeenth century W. Fraser Mitchell, **English Pulpit Oratory** (London, New York: Macmillan, 1932), 102. He cites Mather referring to a Puritan, John Cotton: "But although he had been educated in the Peripatetic way, yet like the other Puritans of those times, he rather affected the Ramesian discipline; and chose to follow the Methods of the excellent Ramus...rather than the Empty, Trifling, Altercative Notions, to which the works of the Pagan Aristotle...have disposed his Disciples." It is not clear whether Mather does justice to Aristotle or confuses the master and the disciples. At least it shows the opposition between the Puritan and the Caroline divines.

44. Horton Davies in **Worship and Theology in England**, I, 305, summarizes the role of the imagination in the Puritan sermon in a formula as clear as it is poetical. He says: "If the form of the Puritan sermon was indeed so functional, was there a place for the imagination? The answer was that metaphors, similes, and exempla provided the illustrations that were the windows of the sermon, illuminating the doctrine while sustaining the interest of the auditors, and possibly even nerving their wills to action."

45. He says: "...things heard with the eare, oftentimes leave lesse impression behinde them then things seene with the eye. Therefore, I will now endevour in the more particular Application of that which hath beene spoken; to shew you, or to present before your eyes, such a very Woolfe as our Saviour speakes of in my Text.", 37.

46. See, on the possible interpretation of the iconographic framework, 145 note 66.

47. It should be noted that the 1615 edition of this work includes an error in that the Greek inscription has ὑμ ἦν instead of ὑμῖν . The fault is corrected in the 1627 edition of Ward's works.

48. The two most common monograms for Christ are the early Chi Rho, the labarum, which Constantine is supposed to have seen in the sky before the Battle of the Milvian Bridge, an abbreviation of "Christ Risen", and IHS, an abbreviation of Iesus hominum salvator, Jesus Savior of mankind.

49. The Biblical reference is to John 15:5.

50. A comparison can be made with the illustration from the sermon **All in All** and those of certain short moral treatises such as **Keepe within compasse,** which gives advice on moderation in love-making, liquor and the display of wealth.

This little work represents a compass. Beneath is the legend:

One God, one Baptism, and one Faith
One Truth there is, the Scripture saith.

See also **The mothers Counsel or live within Compasse,** 1623. The mother and her daughter are at the center of the compass; the mother holds the Bible in her hand, while the true North is marked by the cross of Christ. The chief virtue is modesty exhibited in the clothing of mother and daughter.

51. For another sermon illustrated by Ward, see B.M. Harl. M.S. 389, f. 13. This was part of the controversy against the Catholics for which he was imprisoned in 1621. Ward had to end his days in Holland after being twice incarcerated. As the middle of the century is reached the sermons become politicized. On this subject see G. Davies, "English Political Sermons, 1603–1640", in HLQ, III, 1–22, and John F. Wilson, **Pulpit in Parliament** (Princeton: Princeton University Press, 1969). As a cover for the author it happened that the publisher undertook the responsibility for the printing of the work: see Ward's attack against the Catholics, a controversial work: **Balme from Gilead to recover conscience** which uses one of the preferred themes of sermons of that time, "cases of conscience."

52. Printed in 1619 by E. Griffin, (Bod. Arts 4° B 32).

53. (Bod. Ashm, 133.)

54. **A Prognostication for 1613.**

55. **The discovery of a world in the moone,** 1638.

56. For the sixteenth century see above all the illustrations of the almanacs of Harvey, Dade and Westhouse with their images of equinoxes, solstices, or both.

57. The two diagrams will be found in White's prediction for 1613.

58. Harvey, in 1584, explained the partial eclipse of the sun, but the illustration gave no help at all. See also the design of Pond in 1630 which merely placed the moon on the sun. There it deals with a total eclipse: the sun is printed in red and the moon in black. The moon glides over the sun.

59. **The Cosmetographia** of Lawi, Baronia, 1578, we mention in passing without analysing it, since it is not directly concerned with the center of our study.

60. **STC** 6545.

61. W. Bourne's Almanac for 1572 contains a mariner's card, sig. Diii and a compass on sig. Civ.

62. Cf. Bosanquet, **English Printed Almanachs** (London: Bibliographical Society, 1917), 55.

63. Cf. Bosanquet, **The Flye** (London: Bibliographical Society, 1937). The illustration belongs to the almanac of Philip Moore (**STC** 484).

64. Unhappily we have no maps of Hollar because the celebrated cartographer did not come to work in England until 1635.

65. **STC** 21828; (<u>Bod</u>. 4 C 62 Art.)

66. See also the map of Algiers in **STC** 15048.

67. For military arts and fortifications, see G. Cataneo, **Most briefe tables** which shows the disposition of the army, the new theories on the fortification of a camp, the art of making good gunpowder and how to shoot fireballs from a pontoon-ship. For fuller information see H. J. Webbe, "Military newsbooks during the age of Elizabeth", <u>English Studies</u> 33, 241-251, or P. A. Jorgensen, "Theoretical Views of War in Elizabethan England", <u>Journal of the History of Ideas</u>, 1952, XIII, 469f.

68. See chapter II, 37.

69. W. Hamond, **The Method of curing wounds**, 1617.

70. On this subject see Chapter I.

71. Among the favorite animals of man, see also the books of the period on falconry, which are addressed to the leisure class. See in particular the illustrations of Latham, 1618.

72. There is also a book on growing poppies: **Opiologia** (STC 21594) where the author praises opium and derides the physicians who refuse to use it. See also, R. Scott's treatise on growing hops, **A perfite platforme of a Hoppe Garden**, 1574.

73. Considering its smallness, it is remarkably illustrated:
   Sig. B, a man mounts a ladder to cut a tree for grafting in a V-shape.
   P. 33, represents another technique of grafting: the tree is hollowed and the graft is introduced into the tree trunk and held together by ligatures.
   P. 34, the instruments for grafting.
   Pp. 35-54, trace different plans of gardens growing more and more complex.
   P. 54, one of these gardens has a central pond and fish in it. The origin of these images is undoubtedly French or Dutch because it is a compilation.

74. See, for instance, the evolution of the illustrations of **Bevis of Hampton**. The oldest examples include floral motifs which catch our attention by the purely esthetic pleasure they evoke.

75. This audacious work was published by the University of Toronto Press in 1962. See 18.

Chapter Four - **The Image as Emotion**

1. See <u>The New York Times,</u> 5 August 1974: 14, which states that the members of the Committee were deeply emotionally affected when a false alert sounded according to which a plane was about to destroy the Rayburn tower where they were gathered. Then the following occurred: "No plane appeared. Mr. Rodine sat, as if at the wake of a friend, speaking of inconsequential things with Mr. Doar. Suddenly he rose without a word and walked from the office. And cried."

2. Respectively, **The education of children in learning,** 1588 and **Ludus literarius or the Grammar Schoole,** 1612.

3. For the preceding information see B. L. Joseph, **Elizabethan acting** (Oxford: University Press, 1961) and W. J. Ong, **Rhetoric, Romance and Technology** (Ithaca: Cornell University Press, 1971).

4. Quintilian, **De Oratore,** I, xi and XII, x.

5. 172-173 reads: "the passion passeth not only thorow the eyes, but also pierceth the eare and thereby the heart; for a flexible and pliable voice, accommodated in manner correspondent to the matter whereof the person intreateth (...with gesture correspondent, and flexibilitie of voice proportionat)...is either a flash of fire to incense a passion, or a basson of water to quench the passion incensed."

6. See in this regard the critique of Robert South in his sermon of 1660, **The Scribe instructed to the Kingdom of Heaven,** cited by Horton Davies, **Worship and Theology in England,** II, 1975, 174. He criticizes the Puritans in these terms, after accusing them of indecency in their way of expounding the Word of Scripture: "But to pass from these Indecencies to others, as little to be allowed in this sort of men, can any tolerable Reason be given for those strange new Postures used by some on the Delivery of the Word? Such a shutting the Eyes, distorting the Face, and speaking through the Nose, which I think cannot so properly be called <u>Preaching,</u> as <u>Toning a Sermon.</u>"

7. See the illustration on the title-page - S. Rowlands's **The Melancholie Knight,** 1615.

8. One thinks immediately of the difference between the Pietàs of the Middle Ages and those of the end of the seventeenth or the eighteenth centuries. The former show a pale Virgin, swooning with grief and reflecting her motherly love for her Son, incapable of being even the witness of his agony, and yet faithful to the very end. It is also the fidelity of the Virgin who believed in her Son which the latter representations emphasize, but Mary wears a mask of indifference and opposes a wall of stoicism to the world, and no sign appears on her face with its perfect unchanging beauty, for her spirit is turned totally towards God and nothing human can change that.

9. See Stephen Denison's sermon, **The white wolfe...**, 1627.

10. Cf. Muriel Bradbrook, **The rise of the Common Player, a study of actor and society in Shakespeare's England** (London: Chatto and Windus, 1962), 101 recalls the satire of Gosson who describes the enthusiasm of those attending: "[they]...generally take up a wonderful laughter and shout all together with one voice when they see some notable cozenage practised, or some sly contrivance of bawdry brought out of Italy."

11. Stephen Gosson, **Playes confuted in five actions,** 1582, F5v-F6, speaks of comedy in this way: "...Comedies make our delight exceede, for at the many times we laugh so extreemely, striving to bridle ourselves, we cannot;... where such excesse of laughter bursteth out yet we cannot holde it, there is no temperance, for the time; where no teperace is, there is no wisdome nor use of reaso."

12. Ibid., C5v-C6: "The beholding of troubles and miserable slaughters, that are in Tragedies, drive us to immoderate sorrow, heaviness, womanish weeping and mourning, whereby we become lovers of dumpes and lamentatio both enemies to fortitude."

13. Ibid., sig. D1: "The rudest of the people are...sometimes so headie, that they runne together by heapes, they know not whither; and lay about with their clubbes, they see not why."

14. A. L. Rowse, **The Elizabethan Renaissance: the Cultural Achievement** (London: Macmillan, 1972), 20-21.

15. It can happen that an image will create a doubt in the mind of the reader. In the edition of 1573, a man walks in rags and tatters amid the mountains. In the distance one can make out trees and possibly a town. Automatically the Christian reference makes one think of the temptation of Christ in the wilderness. The second example is as follows: one of the malefactors is attached to a horizontal bar, a cruciform image, while two men, one of them bearing a bundle of sticks, and the other a lance or a hook, approach to molest him. How is this to be interpreted? Were the prints deliberately ambiguous? Do they come from an old stock of woodblocks?

16. The 1591 edition of **The Second part of Conny catching** differs from that of 1592; there are two images of horse-thieves in sig. A and C2, just as of a hare carrying a card, the five of hearts.

17. It appears that these illustrations come from the workshop of John Wolfe. The first to appear, so far as we know, is that which decorates the pamphlets of Greene in 1591.

18. See Plate 6.

19. Most illustrated joke books, "jest-books", were in verse. For the illustration of poems, see Chapter IV.

20. **STC** 14923, **Kemps nine daies wonder,** 1600.

21. For the jocular mood see also **The severall Notorious and Lewd Cousenages of John West and Alice West,** 1613, except that the title-page displays their punishment which darkens the story considerably.

22. Henry Goodcole, **Heavens speedie hue and cry sent after lust and murther,** 1635, 4. It speaks of a young woman in these terms: "But unfortunately it happened, that shee grew acquainted with a young man in London, who tempted her unto folly, and by that ungodly act her suddain ruin insued."

23. Another example of the exemplary tract intended to exhort the people to repentance is the unillustrated brochure of Reynolds, **The Triumphs of Gods Revenge,** 1621. The author after having complained about the escalation of crime and violence in his times continues by claiming that he has collected "thirty severall Tragical Histories, which for thy more ease, and perfecter memory, I have digested into six severall Bookes; that observing and seeing herein as in a Christall myrrour the variety of the divels temptations and the allurements of sinne...the consideration of these bloudy and mournfull Tragedies, may by their examples, strike astonishment to our thoughts, and amazement to our sences, that the horrour and terrour thereof may hereafter retaine and keep us within the lists of Charity towards men and the bonds of filiall and religious obedience towards God who tells us by his Royall Prophet, that whosoever makes a pit for others, shal fal into it himselfe; for his mischiefe will returne upon his owne head and his crueltie fall upon his own Pate."
    The citation illumines our interest: the author first puts us on our guard against Satan in scattering our ignorance and making us hate error, but he is equally concerned to urge us to be charitable, for however horrible are the crimes of criminals they still remain a part of humanity. Even the innocent, by his nature capable of falling, is not sheltered from sin.

24. **STC** 10930-31.

25. For the discussion of this pamphlet, see Chapter I.

Notes to pp. 71-75

26. The reference is to **A Horrible Creuel and bloudy Murther.**

27. We have no idea how to interpret the significance of this person who has no connection with the text. One might have thought that it concerned a preacher before the attack, an erroneous hypothesis since the garments of the victim are shorter than those of the person on the right.

28. Compare this illustration which decorates **Prince Henries Obsequies.** Apart from the horses and feathers, the effect is much the same.

29. For example, one could contrast the decorum of the woodcut with the desire to express the horror in the reports of the murder of President Kennedy at the time of his assassination. We should recall that a king by divine right does not share in the weaknesses of ordinary human beings and, as a result, his death as his life are imprinted with a superhuman dignity.

30. See G. B. Harrison, **The Elizabethan Journals,** 1955 (Ann Arbor: University of Michigan Press) for 26 December, 1594. Chastel, a Jesuit seminarian, had wounded the king in his face and broken several teeth. His torture consisted in having his arms and thighs burnt by white-hot irons, his right hand chopped off, his body dismembered by four horses. His body was burnt and the ashes were scattered to the four winds. The latter was to terrify the Jesuits for whom burial in holy ground was the only assurance of having one's body in after life. By burning the body of the Jesuit, judicial authorities seemed also to dispose of his destiny in the next life.

31. The information contained in this account is derived from a French book which the editor has summarized and interpreted. Ravaillac, says the English editor, is a man of envy. He was both a lawyer and a brother of the order at the same time. In the course of his trial, he confessed his guilt. The attempt at finding his accomplices through torture was in vain; Ravaillac would admit nothing. Before going to his torture, Place de Grève, Ravaillac crossed himself "as an obstinate papist". Then follow the details of the torture occupying 4-7. None of the juicy details of his final torture were lost; we are told that since the "poor" horses did not succeed in tearing the members apart, his flesh had to be cut at all the joints. The blood-thirsty mob watched the torture and relished it. The author concludes with this wish:

> God in his Justice I will hope in the like manner reward all such as repine at their countries safety, and desperately attempt to lift their hands against Gods annointed.

Here there is no mention of burning Ravaillac's corpse. Cremation was a fitting punishment for one who in killing a king by divine right, committed a sacrilege. Hence it was unthinkable that the guilty one should be born again in life eternal.

32. What happened to the nose that Hacket so jealously wished to retain? No one knows. Some suggested that Hacket ate it... Cf. G. B. Harrison in **Elizabethan Journals,** entry for 16 July 1591. Hacket and his prophesying caused

a great deal of harm to the Puritan party in the Church. The art of "prophesying", a Puritan means of Biblical exposition, without specific reference to the future, was misconstrued by their enemies who recalled the incident in fullest detail. They insisted mainly on its treasonable aspect.

33. See the epistle to the reader.

34. See Harman, **A Caveat for common cursetors; Londons cry,** 1620; **A true relation of a barberous and most cruell murther,** 1633.

35. See G. B. Harrison, op. cit.

36. Harman, op. cit.

37. The commiseration of the crowd at Southwell's execution in 1595 should be recalled. See G. B. Harrison, op. cit. entry of 22 February.

38. See also on this matter the punishments and tortures kept for witches and sorcerers. This will be dealt with in Chapter VIII.

39. Gombrich in **Art and Illusion,** New York, 1962, 117-118, recalls that this phenomenon is common to most civilizations:
> Emanuel Loewy at the turn of the century first developed his theories about the rendering of nature in Greek art that stressed the priority of the conceptual modes and their gradual adjustment to natural appearances.

40. Modern authors are also aware of the repelling force of being eye-witnesses to horror. This message is brought home in Anthony Burgess's novel, **Clockwork Orange;** the horror of crime is inculcated in the hero of the narrative, formerly a murderer, in forcing him to look at films that make him physically ill, as a result of a chemical treatment. The moral conclusions of the novel, however, are entirely different.

41. Cf. **An example of Gods judgement....of Cornelius Pet,** translated from the Dutch. The preface reads:
> Make peace, Make peace in all countries for the LORD will come and punish the earth with Swoord and Rod, as my hands do represent...

42. Sig. A3 reads:
> These contrary colours in the creation of man, sometimes fayre, sometimes deformed, expresse the skill, power, and omnipotency of the Great Master, in whose hand it lyes to make a beggar a King, a beautiful body, or a monstrous...

43. **STC** 12186.

Notes to pp. 80-81

44. **STC** 6769. Cicero's definition in the **De Divinatione**, i, should be quoted:

> Monstra ostenta, portenta, prodigia appellantur, quoniam monstrant ostendunt, portendunt et praedicant.

On the role of monsters and prodigies in primitive societies, L. Lévy-Bruhl, **L'expérience mystique et les symboles chez les primitifs,** Paris 1938, offers interesting examples. Chapter II: "L'insolite, expérience mystique" covers our concern at the end of this chapter.

45. For whales, see also **A true report and exact description of a mighty Sea-monster or Whale...,** 1617.

46. **STC** 20569.

47. **The miracle of miracles,** by T. I., 1613 or 1614. Sig. A2 provides the moral:

> Wee have to consider by this strange discourse, how ready Sathan is to take hold on us, if wee fall from GOD never so little. Hee continually runneth up and downe seeking whom he may devoure.

48. This is the testimony recorded:

> Then her husband looking up in his bed, espied a thing come to the bedde much like unto a Beare, but it had no head nor tayie, halfe a yard in length, and halfe a yard in height; her husband seeing it come to the bed, rose up, and took a joyned stoole and stroke at the said thing, the stroke sounded as though he had stroken upon a Fetherbed...

49. This is a recent practice. The press is accused of publishing so many lies that the author or publisher thinks it wise to claim the veracity of the story, as for example **True and wonderfull,** sig. A3:

> The just Reward of him that is accustomed to lie, is, not to be believ'd when he speaketh the truth; so just an occasion may sometime bee impos'd upon a pamphleting press; and therefore if we receive the same rewarde wee cannot much blame our accusers...

Occasionally witnesses are cited as here. See also **Miraculous Newes,** 1616.

50. Other examples could probably be found among the ballads. It should be noted that some of the broadsheets are partly narrative, partly ballad.

51. See, for instance, the author of the broadsheet of 1554 (to which a ballad of 1565 corresponds). He asserts that one ought not to believe that this is a natural way for infants to be born:

> Or els as our common custome is, by and by to judge god only offended wyth the Parentes of the same, for some notoryous vyce or offence reygning alone in them: But they are lessons and scholynges for us all (as the word monster shewith).

52. These were found in the **Roxburgh Ballads** of the British Library, a collection that does not only contain ballads, but news items and broadsheets, or mixed prose and verse sheets.

53. **STC** 20511.

54. One might, however, suppose that the practice existed as frequently as in our backward country districts like the Creuse or Picardy, in France.

55. Sig. A3 reads:
> I have been an old Brier, and stood many of Northerly storms: the winds have often blowne bitterly in my Face. Frostes have nipped my Blood, icicles (you see) hang at my Beard, and a hill of Snow covers my Head. I am the sonne of Winter.

The comparison is not in the least original. It can be found throughout the Renaissance. See, for instance, the seven ages of man in Shakespeare's **As You Like It.**

56. The parallel between an inundation and the Flood is constantly mentioned. The author of this particular pamphlet reminds the reader:
> Albeit that these swellings up, and overflowing of waters proceede from naturall causes, yet are they the very diseases and monstruous byrths of nature, sent into the world to terrifie it, and to put it in mind, that the great God...can as well now drown all mankind as hee did in the first...

57. See J. F. D. Shrewsbury, **A history of bubonic plague in the British Isles** (Cambridge: University Press, 1970). The author correlates the seasons with the plague, which was most lethal during the hottest month, namely August. To give an idea of the frequency of the plague, we take the following dates from Shrewsbury: 1538, 1540, 1542, 1547-8, <u>1563</u>, <u>1569</u>, 1575, 1577, 1578, <u>1582-3</u>, 1593. Then for the first part of the seventeenth century, the important dates are: 1603, <u>1604</u>, 1608, <u>1625</u>, 1630 and <u>1636</u>. The most murderous attacks of the plague are doubly underlined. In Ireland, however, 1574 appears to have been the worst year, and 1597 the worst for Scotland.

58. We will return to the social problems caused by the plague in Chapter VI.

59. It may be of interest to note that the use of the cross to indicate the kiss of death has been maintained in our own time. In 1946, in the port of Hamburg in Germany where there were many casualties inflicted by bombing raids, crosses on the lintels of ruined houses marked places where corpses were still believed to be buried.

60. **STC** 23259.

61. **Strange Newes from Antwerpe,** 1612.

Notes to pp. 84-86

62. The narrative does not explain how a stone falling on a roof could start a fire. If it was a ball of fire the narrative would have mentioned it. One could assume that in the interior of the monastery there were illuminated tapers and that a draught set fire to the "idols". This, however, is only a conjecture.

63. In the epistle to the reader, it says:
Nothing is here presented to thine eyes to fright thee, but to fill thee with Joy that this storme fell so farre off...

64. White Horse Hill is so named because of a chalk formation shaped like a horse which is cut into the side of this dry and desolate hill. Even today it attracts a crowd of tourists. The choice of this place for the apparition of the armies in the sky is most appropriate, since one of the horsemen of the Apocalypse rides on a white horse (Rev. 6:2). For the mystical battle see Rev. 12:7.

65. 24. See also **The wonderfull battell of Starelings**, 1622.

66. It seems useful to provide a certain number of references to the Book of Revelation in the King James version of the Bible.
Earthquakes are associated with the eclipse of the sun and the reddening of the moon; Rev. 6:12:
And I beheld when he had opened the sixth seal, and lo, there was a great earthquake; and the sun became black as sackcloth of hair, and the moon became as blood.
Thunder, tempests and earthquakes come together; Rev. 16:18:
And there were voices and thunders and lightnings; and there was a great earthquake, such as was not since men were upon the earth, so mighty an earthquake, and so great.
The wars in the skies come from Rev. 12:7:
And there was war in heaven; Michael and his angels fought against the dragon; and the dragon fought and his angels...
The dragon is Satan; Rev. 12:9:
And the dragon was cast out, that old serpent, called the Devil, and Satan, which deceiveth the whole world...
The flood, poisoning of the waters and the tempest are the scourges sent by God on the earth; Rev. 8:7-9:
The first angel sounded, and there followed hail and fire mingled with blood, and they were cast upon the earth: and the third part of trees was burnt up, and all green grass was burnt up. And the second angel sounded, and as it was a great mountain, burning with fire, was cast into the sea: and the third part of the sea became blood; and the third part of the creatures which were in the sea and had life died; and the third part of the ships were destroyed.
Then follows the blazing star; Rev. 8:10:
And the third angel sounded, and there fell a great star from heaven, burning as it were a lamp, and it fell upon the third part of the rivers, and upon the fountains of water...

67. Our scientific century sees the same phenomenon reappearing. The Reverend Sun Moon preaches to his followers that Christ will come to choose a new Eve and repeople the earth with his elect. In England, there is a resurgence of witchcraft. Finally, at scientific conferences, there are predictions of the end of the world coming soon, as a result of wasting the resources of the world. Similar causes produce similar effects.

Chapter Five - **Propaganda**

1. See Jacques Ellul, **Histoire de la propagande.** (Paris: Que sais-je? 1967).

2. G. R. Elton, **Policy and police. The enforcement of the Reformation in the Age of Thomas Cromwell** (Cambridge: U. P., 1972), 171 sq.

3. Ibid.

4. On the Catholic side, very few images appear. One can only count a few devices such as a heart pierced by three arrows and crowned by a cross in a medallion, as on the title-page of Alfield, **A true report of the martydom of Campion,** printed by Verstegan, 1582. Yet, a few illustrated works seep into England, from the presses of Rouen or of Douai.

5. J. Christopherson, **Take hede of rebellion,** 1554. It republishes the genealogical tree, probably issued by the orders of the Queen, Mary Tudor, in 1554: see **STC** 17560.

6. See one of the rare comments on Elizabethan propaganda: Gladys Jenkins, "Ways and Means in Elizabethan Propaganda", in **History,** 1941, 105-114. On 105 she quotes the words of Queen Elizabeth: "And though God hath raised me high, yet this I account the glory of my Crown, that I have reigned with your loves." Yet one should not take her words at their face value. Information was carefully sifted and, from 1535 to 1603, only ten illustrated political works can be numbered.

7. James I, for instance, objects to the interest the people take in the Thirty Years War. F. Bacon refers to a proclamation forbidding the discussion of matters of state, "which are no themes or subjects fit for vulgar persons or common meetings...And although in our nature and judgment we do well allow of convenient freedom of speech, esteeming any overcurious or restrained hand carried in that kind rather a weakness or else overmuch severity of judgment than otherwise;..." <u>Works</u>, XIV, 156-7. The king goes on to forbid anyone, even

his supporters, to discuss political matters, since they could only speak lightly, out of habit or prompted by excessive passion. See also L. Stone, **The causes of the English Revolution**, 1529-1642 (New York: Harper and Row, 1972).

8. One should note with interest that most of the portraits appearing on illustrated pamphlets do not figure in Roy Strong, **Portraits of Elizabeth I**, (Oxford: Clarendon Press, 1963). They probably were too rough to attract the author's interest. See also chapter I.

9. A. M. Hind, **Engraving in England** (Cambridge: U. P., 1955), 58.

10. See ibid. and Roy Strong, **Tudor and Jacobean Portraits** (London: H. M. S. O., 1969), 178.

11. See both works by Nichols: **The Progresses and Public Processions of Queen Elizabeth**, I-II, (London: Nichols, 1823), and **The Progresses, Processions, and Magnificent Festivities of King James I, his Consort, Family and Court**, I-IV (London: Nichols, 1828).

12. **STC** 13159.

13. See **Wing**.

14. **STC** 4538.

15. Edward Jeninges, **A briefe discovery of the damages that happen to this Realme by disordered and unlawful diet**, 1590, (**STC** 14486).

16. **A briefe note of the benefits that grow to this Realme, by the observation of Fish-daies**, 1593 (Bod. fol. θ 659 (2)).

17. **Orders established, condiscended, and agreed unto the Societie of Armes** (Bod. 8° 0 19 Art).

18. About Heywood's patriotism, see Grivelet, **Thomas Heywood et le drame domestique élisabéthain** (Paris: P.U.F., 1957), ch. IV. This excellent book does not, however, ask this specific question.

19. Th. Heywood, **A true description of his Majesties royall ship**. He stresses that the beauty of the ship "should bee a great spur and incouragement to all his faithful and loving subjects to bee liberal and willing."

20. See Chapter II.

21. **STC** 18920. **The just downfall of ambition, adultery and murder**, n.d. See also Chapter IV.

22. The pamphlets on Edward Coke are also anti-royalist, since he was in Parliament the opponent of the system of prerogatives.

23. Eccl. 9:10: Whatsoever thy hand findeth to doe, doe it with thy might.

    Prov. 27:1: Presume not of to-morrow for thou knowest not what a day may bring forth.

24. Eccl. 10:2: A wise mans heart is at his right hand.

25. Judg. 5:20: The starres in their courses fought against Sisera.

26. Sumus ergo pares. (Therefore we are Peeres).

27. Judg. 5:9: My heart is towards, the governors of Israel, who offered themselves willingly among the people.

    2 Sam. 3:36: And all the people tooke notice of it, and it pleased them: as whatsoever the King did please all the people.

28. 22097: **Vox Dei: injustice cast and condemned. A sermon preached at Bury S. Edmonds,** 1623.

29. On the Black Legend, see the books of W. Maltby, **The Black Legend in England. The development of anti-Spanish sentiment, 1558-1660** (Durham, N.C.: Duke University Press, 1971) and of P. W. Powell, **Tree of Hate. Propaganda and Prejudices Affecting United States Relations with the Hispanic World** (New York: Basic Books, 1971). One should also consult the pamphlets bound under the title of **The Spanish War, 1585-1587,** published by The Navy Records Society, XI, 1898.

30. Ralph Norris, **A warning to London by the fall of Antwerp.** The woodcut of the town is the representation of the concept rather than the reality. Another pamphlet, **An historical discourse or rather a tragicall Historie of the citie of Antwerp,** 1586, printed by Windet, deals with the same theme. Finally, Churchyard attacks the evil mind of the Spanish power in **A lamentable and pitiful description of the wofull warres in Flaunders...** STC 5239.

31. Norris, op. cit., stanza 4.

32. Black, **The reign of Elizabeth** (Oxford: Clarendon Press, 1936; reprint 1959), 317-18.

33. On the lack of competence of the Duke of Medina as Admiral in chief, see G. Mattingly, **The Armada** (Boston: Houghton and Mifflin, 1959). The book explains, moreover, how after having heard of the death of the two main continental Protestant statesmen, Coligny, in France and William of Orange in the Low Countries, Elizabeth feels obliged, against her own private feelings, to have Mary Stuart killed.

262

34. Respectively: STC 6565, **The queenes visiting of the campe at Tilsburie**, 1588.

STC 6557, **A joyful new ballad declaring the happie obtaining of the great galleazzo**, 1588.

STC 6558, **A new ballet of the straunge whippes which the Spanyards had prepared to whippe Englishmen**, 1588.

All three can be found in E. Arber, **An English Garner, Tudor Tracts, 1532-1588** (London: Bibliographical Society, 1903), 485-502.

35. **STC** 15106 (Bod. Linc. B. 4. 3.) On the activities of Cardinal Allen in Rome, see G. Mattingly, "William Allen and Catholic Propaganda in England", in **Aspects de la propagande religieuse, Travaux d'Humanisme et Renaissance**, XXVIII, Geneva, 1957.

36. G. Edmundson, **Anglo-Dutch Rivalry during the first half of the Seventeenth Century** (Oxford: Clarendon Press, 1911), 1-15. The author also states that Holland sends some help on the sea at the time of Essex's raid on Cadiz, in 1595.

37. STC 3057, W. Bigges, **A summarie and true discourse of Sir Frances Drakes West Indian voyage**, R. Ward, 1589. Commentaries about the various editions of this pamphlet can be found in Hans P. Krauss, **Sir Francis Drake, A pictorial biography** (Amsterdam: N. Israel, 1970).

38. STC 9196, **A declaration of the causes, which mooved the commanders of the navie to take certain shippes of corne**, 1589.

39. STC 22140. Another story by Francis Seall does not appear in STC, but in **The Naval Miscellany**, II, 94-114 (Publications of the Navy Records Society, 1910). **A Fig for a Spaniard**, criticizing the Spanish for their indiscipline and their lack of patriotism also belongs to the Black Legend.

40. Richard Hasleton, **Strange and wonderfull things happened to Richard Hasleton in his ten yeares travailes in many forraine countries**, 1595. This anti-Spanish tract contains twelve illustrations which are more or less connected to the text. These appear sig. A4, Bii, C, Ciii, D, Dii, Dii^v, Diii^v, E, Eii^v, Eiii^v. As one can see, this is one of the rare pamphlets whose contents are illustrated whereas its title-page is not.

41. **A true relation of a wonderfull sea-fight betweene two great and well appointed Spanish ships or men of warre**, 1621, with the woodcut of a ship and the legend: The **Margaret** and **John**, or the **Blacke Hodge**. (Bod. 4. L 78 Art.).

42. F. Nichols and Sir Francis Drake, baronet, **Sir Francis Drake revived**, 1628. This pamphlet is not mentioned in Krauss's book.

43. Francis Fletcher, **The world encompassed by Sir Francis Drake,** 1635. There is also extant an edition of 1628.

44. Another pamphlet of the sort is written on a Spanish naval defeat: **A true and incredible report of a great and very dangerous fight at sea,** 1600 (Bod. 4 L 70 Art.).

45. See **Three to one, being an Anglo-Spanish combat,** 1625. This time the Spaniards are being defeated on land and the illustration shows the fight. (Bod. C 16 Art BS.).

46. This is the usual propaganda technique used by official writers as well as by private initiative. After the raid on Cadiz, the Queen declares that she does not in the least intend to attack Spain. But she says, she bears a grudge against Philip II who sent the Armada against her. This tract is published in England and sent to France, to the Low Countries, to Italy and to Spain. See on this matter, Gladys Jenkins, op. cit., 109-110. The same procedure is also used by William of Orange, in an even more subtle way; he argues that his quarrel is not with the King of Spain, but with his vile counsellors (read, the Duke of Alba). All the Low Countries are asking for is to recover their ancient privileges.

47. John Lynch, **Spain under the Hapsburgs, I, Empire and absolutism, 1516-1598** (Oxford: Blackwell, 1964), 272-280.

48. Black, **The reign of Elizabeth,** 89-90.

49. See chapter V, 99; Elizabeth's share in the conflict is analyzed by Charles Wilson, in **Queen Elizabeth and the Revolt of the Netherlands** (Los Angeles: University of California Press, 1970).

50. **A true discourse of the overthrowe given to a common enemy at Turnhaut,** 1597 (Bod. 4º L 70 Art.).

51. **A true coppy of the admonitions sent by the subdued provinces to the States of Holland,** etc..., 1598 (STC 18465).

52. **A true report of three straunge and wonderful accidents...,** 1603.

53. See chapter V, 97-98, 2 sq.

54. These are not the only publications by Th. Scott, against the Spanish and the Catholics. William Maltby reckons that he must have had some powerful friend at court or in the Parliament, as the bishop of Norwich disregarded the orders he had received, according to which he should have prosecuted the pamphleteer. See Maltby, ibid., 102-108.

55. See on Th. Scott and on Middleton's play, Margot Heineman's "Middleton's Game at Chess: Parliamentary-Puritan and Opposition Drama", in

264

English Literary Renaissance, Spring 1975, V, No. 2, 232-250. This article also includes the reproduction of the etchings of **Vox Dei** and of **Vox Regis,** printed on brown paper.

56. Th. Robinson, **The anatomie of the English nunnery at Lisbon,** 1623 and 1630 editions. This pamphlet has extant four editions, of which two are illustrated. Middleton alludes to the convent in **A game at Chess,** IV, ii, 1, 116-121: "Promised also to Doctor Lopez for poisoning the maiden Queen of the White Kingdom, ducats twenty thousand; which said sum was afterwards given as meritorious alms to the nunnery at Lisbon, having at this present ten thousand pounds more in the townhouse of Antwerp."

57. **Copy of a letter sent into England by a gentleman from the towne of Saint-Denis in France** (Bod. 4° L 81 Art.).

58. **The orders of ceremonies observed in the annointing and Coronation of the most Christian King of France and Navarre, Henry the IIII,** 1594.

59. See the preceding chapter.

60. There are rather few pamphlets on France. **Antiduello,** 1609 is a broadsheet concerning a duel. It shows the duel between the English Warwick and the French de Guise. The device "Conquérir ou mourir" indicates that the etching is French. (Bod. Godw. Pamph. 1114(1)).
   Most of the extant pamphlets concern the life and death of Henry IV. The death of Henry IV both grieves and worries the English. We find various manifestations of this concern. One finds for instance an anti-Catholic tract under the form of the confession of a Catholic renegade, now become a Protestant: **The apologie of George Brisset, Lord of Gratence,** 1610. The title-page woodcut shows a man measuring the world. The satire on Catholicism is hardly any different from that of other pamphlets: they forbid the believers to read the Bible, they encourage murder, they believe in transubstantiation... But it is directed specifically against the France of the time of the Regency.

61. See chapter V, 100ff., 104ff.

62. See our analysis of this tract, chapter IV, 84-85.

63. **A true report and description of the taking of the Iland and Towne of S. Maries, by a shippe of Amsterdam, and foure English Pinasses, 1599-1600.**

64. On the crisis of 1618, see George Edmunson, **Anglo-Dutch Rivalry,** 43 sq. Despite this, England and Holland are capable of forgetting their differences to fight a common foe. See **A famous fight at sea,** 1627, where, in the Persian Gulf, four English and four Dutch ships joined together to dispel the Portuguese.

65. **STC** 7452-7455. **A true relation of the unjust proceedings against the English at Amboyna.** The fifth impression is in Dutch. The massacre had also inspired a ballad, inimical to Holland, **STC** 547, **News out of East India,** 1625?

66. Edward Pellham, **Gods Power and Providence: Shewed, in the miraculous preservation and deliverance of eight Englishmen, left by mischance in Green-Land, anno 1630, nine months and twelve days,** 1631.

67. "Thirty Years War", in **Encyclopedia Britannica,** XXII, imp. 1957, 136a-142b.

68. Opposite the title-page of the tract of Robert Burton, Gustavus Adolphus will be found, on foot, on the terrace of his palace, dominating the garden; above and to the right is his coat of arms.

69. Henry Hexham, **A Journall,** 1633 represents the Prince of Orange, opposite the title-page and a bird's eye view of the siege of Maestricht on the title-page.

70. Many works on this subject are illustrated: **The warres in Germany,** 1614, **The lamentations of Germany,** 1638, **The invasions of Germanie,** 1638, **The warnings of Germany,** 1638. Of these works, the most interesting from the point of view of iconography, is the second. It represents Germany as a victim of the plagues described in the books of Leviticus and Jeremiah: the rats eat the crops (Lev. 26:22), the water is polluted (Jer. 23:15; 9:14; 8:14), the dead are left unburied (Jer. 34:20; 7:33; 8:2, 9), etc. See, on the biblical curses, Delbert R. Hillers, "Treaty Curses and the Old Testament Prophets", Biblica et Orientalia, No. 16, Rome, 1964.

71. See chapter III.

72. See the preceding chapter.

73. See chapter V, 101ff.

74. An extract from this work, dealing with our immediate interest, is reproduced in Sydney Anglo, "An early Tudor Programme for plays and other demonstrations against the pope" in Annals of the Warburg Institute, XX, 1957.

75. This determination appeared in the work previously cited: Cotton MS Faustina, Cii, fol 15b.

76. S. Anglo, op. cit., 178 a-b. The author explains why the English, like the Hebrews, should rejoice: "In perpetuall memorye of the delyveraunce of the children of Israell out of thands of wicked pharao, under whom they lyved so wretchedly, forced to comytte idolatrie...who with his annates, peter pens, pardon monye, pilled, polled, robbed your subjectes and this your Realm yearly of innumerable treasure..."

Notes to pp. 113-116

77. Bod. Ashm. 995. The work cannot be found in **STC** under the name of Garter. According to the tradition, the monk is treacherous, crude, fat and libidinous. See on this matter, the tract of 1560, **Heere beginneth a mery Jest of Dans Hew Munk of Leicestre.** The woodcut on the title-page shows his just chastisement after having tried to seduce a middle-class woman who gets her own back on him.

78. For the interpretation of these symbols see G. Ferguson's book, **Signs and Symbols in Christian Art** (Oxford: U.P., New York, 1954). For the bear, see 5.

79. On sig. Ei the explanation of the relationship of the Pope and the devil is given: both are princes of this world.

80. It is also the theme of Cotton; S. Anglo, ibid., 178b. The English ought to rejoice that God has given them the victory against their enemy: "...that wicked dragon, the bisshop of Rome, who devoured us before as he now hath a great parte of all christendom...The priests yerely with procession make a perambulation rounde about the lymytes and extremes of their benifices, for the safeguard of their rightes and tythes."

81. Bod. Douce R. 261. Urbanus Regius, **A lytle treatise after the manner of an Epystle,** 1548. The device of Lynne, the fight between the ram and the goat, will be found at the end of the booklet.

82. Black, **The reign of Elizabeth,** 113 explains why the Ridolphi Plot never came off. For papist conspiracies see also the short anonymous tract, **A true report of the indictement, arraignment, conviction, condemnation, and execution of John Welden, William Hartley and Robert Sutton,** 1588, sig. A2. The three guilty men were executed in three different places of London: Mile-end, Hollywell and Clerkenwell, so that their deaths would serve as a warning to the largest number possible. Their portraits appear on the title-page.

83. **STC** 24269 and 24270. **The fierie tryall of Gods saints, as a counterpoyze to J. W. Priest, in his English Martyrologie.**

84. One cannot say where this work was printed. It attacks Bishop Gardiner, responsible for having burnt Cranmer, and accuses Bloody Mary of having reestablished Catholicism. It also attacks the ceremonial used by Bishop Gardiner.

85. Since the bull is hardly known for its intelligence, one can easily understand how the Pope was turned into a figure of ridicule. This woodcut toured Europe; it is found in Germany, its place of origin, and also in France. Two pamphlets appeared after the promulgation of the papal bull: unfortunately, they are not illustrated. The author of one is Bishop Jewel (**STC** 14614) but the other is anonymous, **A disclosing of a great Bull** (see Harl. Misc. I, 483-89).

86. **STC** 17797.

87. Anthony Nixon, the author, is one of the earliest journalists, like Butter and Bourne. His main themes are the triumphs of James I, foreign wars and the defeat of Catholicism.

88. G. Closse, **The parricide papist, or cut-throate Catholicke**, 1606.

89. This particular device and the usual device will be found in McKerrow, **Printers' and Publishers' Devices in England and Scotland, 1485-1640**, 1913, Plate 299.

90. See the title-page of **Trayterous Percyes and Catesbyes Prosopopeia,** 1606, by Edward Hawes, which represents him dreaming of Percy's ghost in hell. The woodcut, of which the left part is cut away, was not designed for the work.

See also William Fennor, **Pluto his travailes**, 1611, an attack against the Jesuits. The Jesuit father tells a brother Jesuit to go and kill the king; the devil, in monkish robe, promises his help; this tract alludes to the English College of Jesuits in Rome; its members entered England to evangelize it, under all kinds of disguises. Some of these missionaries were unafraid of preaching revolt against the sovereign. Parsons shocked English Catholic opinion in appealing for the aid of Philip II of Spain, on behalf of the Catholics. Campion, who had left Rome with him to evangelize England, suffered from the reputation of a traitor that the former had acquired. Under James I, John Gerard, E. Arrowsmith and H. More are numbered among this group. In 1632, there were 164 Jesuit priests in England (see ed. Henry Foley, **Records of the English Province of the Society of Jesus,** 1875, I, xxiii-lxv).

91. See Horton Davies, **Worship and Theology in England**, II, 57 sq.

92. On royal chapels, see Bryan Little, **Catholic Churches since 1623** (London: Hale, 1966), 22, and Margaret Whinney and Oliver Millar, **English Art, 1625-1714** (London: Oxford University Press, 1957), 287.

93. In the translation of the letter of Urban VIII to his English sons, one can read on sig. A3: "The Church well hoped indeed, that the mind of the most potent king who of a Catholique wife wished to beget heires, that might rule his Country Kingdomes, being mollified by the sighes of hise wives-piety, would permit the dowry of royall wedlocke to bee the liberty of faith; but now the vowes and counselles of your enemies are feared: and whereas the Orthodox religion is crowned with royall diademe in that most excellent Queene: yet there are not wanting those which dare threaten imprisonments and punishments to our sonnes." Burton takes up the letter point by point and recalls the Gunpowder Plot.

94. Stephen Denison, **The white wolfe**, 1627. Sig. F3 reads as follows: "...we have many Wolves in England, we have Popish Wolves which have fought by all possible meanes both by force and flatterie, to reduce all to blindnesse and superstition agine, as appeares by the hellish Gunpowder-plot never to be forgotten, in the yeare 1605, and other designees of theirs: wee have Arminian Wolves, which make a bridge betweene us and Popery, endevouring in some points to reconcile the Wolves and the Lambes..."

Notes to pp. 118-122

The Arminian tendency was condemned by the Synod of Dort in 1618-19. The initiative for the reunion came from the Low Countries, but it comprised the representatives from Switzerland, from the Palatinate and from Great Britain (**The Oxford Dictionary of the Christian Church**, 417b).

95. The application of the image of the wolf to the Roman Church appears to be a mixture of biblical and classical traditions. On the one hand the wolf is the symbol of the devil who seizes souls when the shepherd lacks vigilance (John 10:12) and on the other hand it is the classical symbol of the birth of Rome. John Dee, in his apologetical discourse, when accused of being a Catholic, employs the symbol of the wolf and the lamb on the title-page. The lamb is beside the pious man; the wolf is beside the devil who is called "legion" (**STC** 6461).

96. **STC** 4137, 4138, 4150.

97. **STC** 20461, 20469.

98. **An appeal to the Parliament**, Holland, 1628.

99. **STC** 21644. The reason for English indignation is explained in these terms: "The tumultuous Scotts, who under pretence of Religion, would overthrow the Hierarchy of the Church, pulling down the house of God, and building Babels of their own invention, and man'd with this furious zeale, they have of late raised great forces, and stand ready armed in the field to resist the head of the Church..."

100. See chapter V, 95-96.

101. See chapter V, 103.

102. See chapter V, 109ff. sq.

103. The work is known in two editions, one in 1631 and the other without date.

104. **A letter sent by I.B.**, 1572.

105. See also A. L. Rowse, **The expansion of Elizabethan England** (New York: Harper, 1972). See Massinger, **The maid of honour** (Act I, scene 1).

106. H. M. Jones, "The Colonial Impulse" in Proceedings of the American Philosophical Society, 90, May 1946, 132a.

107. See chapter V, 103ff.

108. Here England is in rivalry with Holland, see chapter V, 102-103, 109.

109. **A true relation of such occurrences and accidents of note as hath hapned in Virginia**, 1608. In this brochure, the first on Jamestown, Smith describes his difficult relations with the Indians, who sometimes are amicable and at other times provoke the members of his expedition to combat. He also depicts the difficulties that the colonists have in producing wheat and in beginning plantations.

110. Cf. ed. Arber, **Travels and Works of Captain John Smith**, 1910, II, 389-390. In fact, however, Watson does appear in the list of 1620, 559.

111. Ibid., 35.

112. **Newes of Sir Walter Raleigh**, 1618.

113. **The relation of a wonderfull voiage made by William Cornelison Schouten of Horne**, 1619.

114. This refers to **Sir Francis Drake revived**, of P. Nichols, which has two illustrated editions in 1626 and 1628 and **The world encompassed by Sir Francis Drake**, which has two editions in 1628 and 1635.

115. W. Goetzmann, **The Colonial Horizon: America in the sixteenth and seventeenth centuries** (Reading, Mass.: Addison Wesley, 1969), 97.

116. Robert C. Johnson, "The transportation of Vagrant Children from London to Virginia, 1618-1622" in **Early Stuart Studies** (Minneapolis, Minn., 1970).

117. See the ballad of 1639, **A zealous Puritain**.

Chapter Six - **Daily Life**

1. See chapter IV.

2. **Two most unnatural and bloodie murthers**, 1605. See also chapter IV. In **As You Like It**, Shakespeare alters the usual order of the planets which reign over the ages of men. The normal order as found in H. Cuffe's **The difference of the ages of man's life**, 1607, is the following: the Moon, Mercury, Venus, the Sun, Mars, Jupiter and Saturn.

3. **The deceytes of women**, sig. Hi and Kii.

4. See chapter VII

Notes to pp. 126-127

5. Edward Webbe's **The rare and most wonderful things which E. Webbe hath seen,** also known under the title **Webbe, his travailes.** Webbe is in fact loading the cannon, but it would serve as an admirable illustration to Shakespeare's verse in **As You Like It.**

6. This argumentation can be found in **Haec-Vir,** an answer to **Haec-Mulier,** both written in 1620.

7. Helen of Troy is often taken as the example of female fickleness. Swetnam in **The araignment...**also takes her as such. The reply of his adversary Ester Sowerman in **Ester hath hang'd Haman** should be noted: Helen, she says, was certainly not a model wife. But the Trojans were no better, since they were both stupid and lascivious enough to wage war because of her.

8. Another book echoes this one: **The mothers counsel or Live within compass,** 1623.

9. See **A bibliography of the Royal Proclamations of the Tudor and Stuart sovereigns** (Bibliotheca Lindesiana, Oxford, 1910), as well as Wilson's **The plague in Shakespeare's London** (Oxford: Clarendon Press, 1963). The best scientific survey, to our knowledge, is J. F. D. Shrewsbury's **A history of bubonic plague in the British Isles** (Cambridge: U. P., 1970), from which we abstracted the facts of the next page.

10. See **STC** 9342 bearing the arms of the Crown on the back of the title-page.

11. These can be found in F. P. Wilson, **The plague pamphlets of Thomas Dekker** (Oxford: Clarendon Press, 1925). Besides the quoted works, those of Moulton, Phaer, and of Bullein contain interesting medical advice. The influence of the plague on the behavior of pastors and congregations can best be studied from Godskall's **The Arcke of Noah,** 1603. Many broadsheets are devoted to the black sickness; many writers are haunted by the horrors they have witnessed. Such are Th. Nashe, J. Davies, Th. Brewer, Taylor and Wither, among others. Dekker stands apart as being particularly aware of poverty and misery in London.

12. **A looking-glass for city and country,** which was printed for Gosson and sold by Wright, <u>Bod.</u> Sutherland Collection. It can also be found in Maurice Ashley's **Life in Stuart England** (London: Batsford, 1964), 3.

13. In **The fearefull summer,** 1636, Taylor writes some interesting lines on the general psychosis which overtook countrymen as they saw Londoners flee the plague:

> Whilst Countrey people, where so'ere they went
> Would stop their noses to avoid their sent,
> When as the case did oft most paline appeare,
> 'Twas onely they themselves that stunke with feare.

14. B 2v reads:

> With good content I here was glad to stay,
> Where I beheld a number passing by
> That (as I heard) did in the high-wayes die:
> Some harbourlesse, and some through want of food,
> While faithless hearts did fear to do men good.

In **The fearefull summer**, Taylor confirms Dekker's testimony: the peasants would prefer to welcome infidels in their houses, he says, rather than a Londoner. His views are more radical than those of Dekker who understands the fear of the peasants. Taylor utterly condemns them.

15. See also in the same work, sig. B4.

16. Sig. B: "Our sinnes increasing with our yeeres, and like the Bells, never lying still."

17. None of the medical orders for the plague are illustrated, but they should be read for a medical understanding of the situation: **STC** 9342 and 18760. See also the remedies suggested by Bradwell: **STC** 3536. Taylor, like Dekker, thinks that all doctors are quacks; see **The fearefull summer** in **All the works of John Taylor the water poet**, 1630, in the re-issue of 1973, 60a: "Their Art is a meere Artlesse kind of Lying". Other trades which benefited from the plague numbered among them the grave-diggers and the dog-killers. In the country, cottages suddenly double or triple in price.

18. **STC** 93 42, I, Iv-v.

19. The same cut has been slightly modified for the title-page of Taylor's **The fearefull summer**, 1636.

20. It can be seen on a 1636 broadsheet (Bod. Wood. 416).

21. See Henry Raymond's **The worldes vanitie**.

22. Taylor, **A living sadness**, 1625.

23. S. Rowlands, **A terrible battle betweene time and death**, 1606.

24. **News from Hell.**

25. **A declaration of such greivous accidents as commonly follow the biting of mad dogges, together with the cure thereof**, 1613.

26. Book III, I, in the edition of 1877, 84-88. He quotes Holinshed's **The Chronicles of England, Scotlande and Irelande**, ed. W. Harrison, III, 94ff.

27. Sig. G 2v.

Notes to pp. 130-132

28. H. A. Monckton, **A history of the English public house** (London: Bodley Head, 1969), 40f.

29. Monckton, op. cit. Statistics should be revised, however. Children drank only "small beer". It was made by refilling the tun with water once the real beer had been drawn. Its alcoholic content was therefore much weaker. See also Harrison, ibid. II, 35, who describes the Englishman's passion for ale: "as pigs should lie in a row lugging at their dame's teats, till they lie again and be not able to wag. Neither did Romulus nor Remus suck their she-wolf or shepherd's wife Lupa with such sharp and eager devotion as these men hale at 'huffcap' till they be red as cocks and little wiser than their combs."

30. This cut is either borrowed from or inspired by **De Generibus**, Nuremberg, 1516.

31. Harrison's **Chronology** gives an interesting example, 269, in the Furnivall edition: "1573. In these daies, the taking-in of the smoke of the Indian herbe called "Tabaco", by an instrument formed like a little ladell, whereby it passeth from the mouth into the head and stomach, is gretlie taken-up and used in England, against Rewmes [Rheums] and some other diseases ingendered in the longes and inward partes, and not without effect." A note adds: "The use of tobacco spread very quickly in England to the disgust of Barnabe Rich, James I and many others. Rich 25-6 in **The Honestie of this Age** (1614) objects to the money wasted on it, says that 7000 houses live by the trade of tobacco selling, and contests the claim that it is good for the health."

32. Tobacco is one of the favorite topics of seventeenth century conversations. Gardiner prescribes it as a cure against tetanus. Popular writers take up the fight and Nashe, Harvey, Dekker, Philateres, Middleton, Parrot and Rowlands all satirize smoking.

33. 25 proclamations under Elizabeth are concerned with dress regulations. Writers make jokes about them. Everyone knows the picture of the naked man in Aiiii of **The fyrst boke of the introduction to knowledge of Andrew Borde and the verse accompanying it.** The commentary of Holinshed in **The chronicles of England,** edited by Harrison, 97a, is less familiar: "The picture of a naked man, unto whome he gave a paire of sheaves in one hande and a peece of cloth in the other, to the ende he should shape his apparrell after such fashion as himselfe liked, sith he could finde no kind of garment that coulde please him any whyle togyther, and this he called an Englishman." The author continues by referring to the varieties of changing fashions inspired from France, Spain, Germany or Turkey, with the gowns of Morocco and the sleeves of Barbary.

34. This type of disguise is rarely used in the English theater, but often appears in the French. One example can be found in Middleton and Rowley's **The changeling,** performed in 1623. Beatrice-Joanna, daughter of the governor of Alicante, seems to accept the marriage prescribed by her father. In fact she sends in her place her servant Diaphanta, on the night of her marriage. However, the device of disguise is constant in the theater and in court entertainments,

35. Gamaliel Bradford, **Elizabethan women** (Cambridge, Mass.: Houghton & Mifflin, 1936), 80-81. The art of starching seems to have been brought to England by the Dutch Vrouw Dinghen Van der Plaase. See A. C. Chapellow, **The old home in England** (London: Chapellow, 1953), 24 sq.

36. Here no claim is made to be exhaustive. It is enough to show that brochures are representative of the different fashions then current.

37. The apron was worn mostly by country women. That of Jyl is simple. Some of them were very ornate as Gosson indicates in **Pleasant quippes for upstart new-fangled gentlewomen,** 1596, sig. v.:

> These aprones white of finest thrid,
> So choicelie tide, so dearly bought;
> So finely fringed, so nicely spred;
> So quaintly cut, so richlie wrought;
> Were they in worke to save their cotes,
> They need not cost so many grotes.

38. C. W. and Phyllis Cunnington, **Handbook of English Costume in the Sixteenth Century** (London: Faber and Faber, 1970), 17 and 34.

39. Ibid., 43.

40. **Here beginneth a dialogue betwene the comen secretary and jelowsy,** 1560?

41. For the plain neckline, see **The Churle and the Byrde,** 1550, and **A new Enterlued...named Jack Jugeler,** 1565.

42. Cunnington, ibid., 93.

43. Ibid., 116.

44. See **A mournful dittie on the death of certaine judges...,** 1570.

45. The high collar and the ruff are satirized by Taylor in **The praise of cleane linnen,** 1624, in **All the works of John Taylor** (Menston: Scholar Press, 1973), 167b-168a.

> Now up aloft I mount unto the Ruffe,
> Which into foolish mortals pride doth puffe:
> Yet Ruffes' antiquity is here but small
> Within this eighty yeeres not one at all;

46. Bod. Arch. G. C. 6. 119b.

47. Jacques Rupert, **Le Costume,** II, (Paris: R. Ducher, 1930-31), 38.

Notes to pp. 137-138

48. See Heywood, **Englands Elizabeth,** and the portrait of Mary Stuart in the Proclamations (<u>Bod</u>. Arch. G. C. 6).

49. The fan, besides being decorative, was also functional. It protected the cheeks from being burnt as the ladies were sitting near the fire. See Gosson, **Pleasant quippes for upstart gentlewomen,** 1596, rep. 1847, iv. (the women)

> Were fannes and flappes of feathers fond,
> To flit away the flisking flies,
> As tailes of mare that hangs on ground,
> When heat of summer doth arrise;
> The wit of women we might praise
> For finding out so great an ease.

50. **The English usurer** (<u>Bod</u>. 40 E Jur.).

51. In **The first part of Churchyards chippes,** 1575, Thomas Churchyard describes the modern young peasant in para. 7:

> And at her gyrdle in a band
> A jolly bunch of keyes she wore
> Her petticoat fine laest before
> Her taile tucke up in trymmest gies
> A napkin hanging o'er her eies
> To kepe of dust and drosse of walles
> That often from the window falles.

52. The stiffness of the dress is criticized by many moralists, among whom is Stubbes; See G. Bradford, **Elizabethan women** (Cambridge, Mass.: Houghton and Mifflin, 1936), 81.

53. Examples of these collars will be found in R. Johnson, **A remembrance of the Honors due to the life and death of Robert Earle of Salisbury,** 1612, in **Three bloodie murders,** 1613, and in Rowlands, **The melancholie knight,** 1615.

54. The short beard, also called goatee, appears on the frontispiece of Dekker's **Lanthorne and candlelight,** and on the author's own face in **Dekker his dreame,** 1620. In **Superbiae Flagellum,** 1621, Taylor describes sixteen different styles; see **All the works of John Taylor,** 1973 ed., 34b:

> Some seeme as they were starched stiffe and fine,
> Like to the bristles of some angry swine;
> And some (to set their Loves desire on edge),
> Are cut and prun'd like to a quickset hedge.
> Some like a spade, some like a forke, some square,
> Some round, some mow'd like stubble, some starke bare,
> Some sharpe, Stiletto fashion, dagger-like,
> That may with whispering a mans eyes outpike;
> Some with the hammer cut, or Romane T,
> Their beards extravagant reform'd must be,
> Some with the quadrate, some triangle fashion,
> Some circular, some ovall in translation,

Some perpendicular in longitude,
Some like a thicket for their crassitude,
That heights, depths, bredths, triforme, square, ovall, round
And rules Geometricall in beards are found.

55. See Th. Brewer, **A knot of fooles,** 1624, and the title page hats of most of Taylor's illustrated pamphlets.

56. Cunnington, **A handbook of English costume in the seventeenth century** (London: Faber and Faber, 1955), 80.

57. See also, **A discourse against the painting and tincturing of women,** 1616.

58. <u>Bod.</u> 40 L 71 Art.

59. **STC** 13374.

60. **STC** 12386.

61. Ralph Dutton, **The English interior, 1500 to 1900** (London: Batsford, 1948), 20f.

62. E. Burton, **The Jacobeans at home** (London: Secker & Warburg, 1962), 58f.

63. Vicars, **Mischeefes mysteries: or treasons master-peece, The powder-plot,** 1617. The central hall still exists in the sixteenth century, but it gets smaller and rarer, as the sovereigns' progresses fall into disuse.

64. Harrison, ibid., 114. See also Dekker's **Lanthorne and candlelight.**

65. R. Dutton, **The English interior...,** 57-58.

66. In fact the distinction is not so simple: on the frontispiece of John Taylor's **A bawd,** the window is printed in black, from which one might suppose that the illustrator used it as a substitute for the red glass of taverns. In Dekker's **Bellman of London,** 1608, the new style door and the pavement can be observed.

67. H. Batsford and C. Fry, **Homes and gardens of England** (London: B. T. Batsford, 1933), 36-37; Harrison, ibid., II, XX. The most complete work on the Elizabethan garden is Th. Hill's **The gardeners labyrinth,** 1576, with varied illustrations.

68. Bacon, **Essays,** XLVI.

69. Batsford and Fry, op. cit. 37-38.

Notes to pp. 142-143

70. See also Bacon, **Essays**, XLVI: "... for the main garden, I do not deny that there should be some fair alleys ranged on both sides, with fruit trees, and some pretty tufts of fruit-trees, and arbours with seats, set in some decent order; but these to be by no means set too thick; but to leave the main garden so as it be not close, but the air open and free." The title-page of **The Spanish Tragedie**, 1615, also offers a striking example of an arbor.

71. He says in sig. Cv: "If within one large square the Gardner shall make one round labyrith or Maze with some kind of Berries, it will grace your forme, so there be sufficient roomth left for walkes, so will four or more knots doe."

72. **Architecture in Britain, 1530-1830** (Harmondsworth: Penguin Books, 1954), 62.

73. See **Jyl of Breyntfords testament**, 1560, and **The wonders of this windie winter**, 1613.

74. This custom, common at the beginning of the century, tended to disappear. See **Harrison's England,** ed. Furnivall, 1877, 237f.: "the mansion houses of our countrie townes and villages...are builded in such sort generallie, as that they have neither dairie, stable nor bruehouse annexed unto them under the same roofe, but all separate from the first, and one of them from another." Harrison, however, mentions that in some of the northern parts, men and beasts slept together.

> In 1610, bishop Hall gives the contrary testimony:
> Of one bayes breath, God wot! a silly cote,
> Whose thatched sparres are furr'd with sluttish soot
> A whole inch thick, shining like black-moor's brows,
> Through smok that down the head-les barrel blows;
> At his bed's feete feeden his stalked teme;
> His swine beneath, his pullen ore the beame...

75. Sidney O. Addy, **The evolution of the English house** (London: Swan, Sonnenschein, 1898), 66f.

76. <u>B.M.</u> C 40 a 13.

77. See Harrison, ibid., 239-240.

78. "Surveyor: We have in our dayes many and great buildings: a comly ornament it is to the face of the earth. And were it not that the smoake of so many chimneyes did raise so many duskie cloudes in the aire to hinder the heate and light of the Sunne from earthly creatures, it were the more tolerable..." <u>Bayly</u>: "Yea, Sir, that was a comfortable smoke; but <u>tempora mutantur</u>..." **The Surveyor's dialogue**, 1607, 178.

79. Harrison, ibid., II, xvii, 234-235.

80. The illustrations provide no example of the old type of sash window but the system existed as can be seen from the title-page of R. Record's **The groudes of artes**, 1543.

81. After the great fire of 1580, the reconstruction of London was undertaken with new vigor. Such is the description of a German traveller, cited by W. D. Robson-Scott, **German travellers in England, 1400-1800** (Oxford: Blackwell, 1953), 104: "All the houses newly built since the Fire are bright red with flat roofs and balcony over the entrance. There the occupier and his wife sit in summer, drinking to their neighbours opposite and smoking tobacco, while innumerable carriages drive past, making a frightful din (especially at night). The old houses which have survived the Fire all have pointed gables, and show that though London was formerly a very large city, it was very badly built." See also A. C. Chapellow, **The old home in England (A.D. 1100 to 1830), A running commentary on the life of the times, the home and its furniture** (London: Chapellow, 1953), 52.

82. See Stow, **Annales**, 1615, 892a.

83. The house is mentioned in the **Roxburghe Ballads**, I, 503 and I, 519. There is also a commentary on it in the appendix by W. Rendle to **Harrison's England**, ed. Furnivall, II, ix.

84. Ralph Dutton, ibid., 27. Rushes were also used as a carpet in the theater.

85. **A horrible creuel and bloudy murther**, (Bod. 40 G. 29 Art.).

86. R. Record's **The groudes of artes** shows a clearer image.

87. Ibid., 239. See also the bed with the baldaquin on the title-page of **Dekker his dreame**, 1620.

88. **A mournfull dittie on the death of certaine judges…**, 1590.

89. See **The famous game of chesse-play, A horrible creuel and bloudy murther, The praise of the gout, Hic Mulier, Vox graculi, A bawd**.

90. See E. Burton, **The Jacobeans at home** (London: Secker and Warburg, 1962), ch. 3.

91. **A horrible, creuel and bloudy murther**.

92. **A discovery by sea from London to Salisbury**, 1623.

93. Lilly C. Stone, **English sports and recreations** (Charlottesville, VA.: University of Virginia Press, 1960), 5.

94. **The book of sports**, version of Charles I, 1633, rpt. of 1862, sig. B4f.

95. See the editions of 1550?, 1605?, 1610, 1616, 1632 of **Adam Bell** and **Robin Hood.**

96. The entire history of Dover and the games he sponsored in the seventeenth century are contained in Chr. Whitfield, **Robert Dover and the Cotswold games** (London: Whitfield, 1962).

97. On sig. B2f. he reprimands the Puritans for not allowing the common folk to amuse themselves innocently. On sig. B4v, he forbids the Recusants to join in the parish sports since they do not attend the parish church.

98. Lilly C. Stone, ibid., 33f.

99. Sig. B. One wonders whether the Spaniards have similar biblical justification for the <u>corrida</u>.

100. Wilson, ibid., sig. D4.

101. **A history of cock-fighting** (London: Skibton, 1957), chs. I and IV.

102. See the title-page of **Tarltons Jests.**

103. See rev. ed. S. Taylor, **The history of playing-cards and their use in conjuring and card-sharping** (London: J. C. Hotten, 1865).

104. Sig. A 2. Chess fans could also read with profit H. J. R. Murray's **A history of chess** (Oxford: Clarendon Press, 1913), reprinted 1962. Chapters XI-XIII, explain the changes in the technique of the game during the Renaissance and add that the literature of the XVIth and XVIIth centuries gives no indication of the subtlety of the game.

105. For the iconographic description of this political allegory, see chapter V, the section on anti-Spanish propaganda.

106. **La grande encyclopédie,** vol. 33, 387a.

107. Fendry, ed., **Thomas Dekker** (London: Arnold, 1967); **The Gull's hornbook,** 101: "Before the play begins, fall to cards. You may win or lose as fencers do in a prize, and beat another by confederacy, yet share the money when you meet at supper."

108. See Greene, **A notable discovery of cosenage. Thart of conny-catching,** reprint of Bodley Head quartos, 27: "what will you play at, at Primero, Primovisto, Sant, one and thirty, new-cut, or what shall be the game?" Compare with **Taylor's Motto** in **Taylor's Works,** ed., 1630, 54b, where Taylor explains how the prodigal lost his fortune:

> The prodigalls estate, like to a flux,
> The Mercer, Draper, and the Silkman sucks:

The Taylor, Millainer, Dogs, Drabs and Dice,
Trey-trip, or Passage, or The most at thrice,
At Irish, Tick-tacke, Doublets, Draughts or Chesse,
He flings his money free with carelessenesse:
At Novum Mumchace, mischance, (chuse ye which)
At One and thirty, or at Poore and rich,
Ruffe, flam, Trump, noddy, whisk, hole, Sant, New-cut.
Unto the keeping of four Knaues he'l put
His whole estate at Loadum, or at Gleeke,
At Tickle-me quickly, he's a merry Greeke,
At Primesisto, Post and payre, Primero,
Maw, Whip-her-ginny, he's a lib'rall Hero;
At My-sow-pigg'd; and (Reader neuer doubt ye
He's skill'd in all games, except) Looke about ye.
Bowles, shone-groate, tennis, no game comes amiss,
His purse a nurse for anybody is:"

109. See chapter IV above for the four reporters of the underworld.

110. Others could be added to this list, such as **The Roaring Girle** by Middleton and Dekker, and N. Richard's **The tragedy of Messalina**.

111. See also the scene in the 1615 and subsequent editions of Kyd's **The first part of Ieronimo.**

112. Middleton's **A game at chesse** is omitted here because it was considered earlier in chapter V.

Chapter Seven - A Mirror of Society

1. Shakespeare, **Twelfth Night.** The same lesson can also be drawn from the reading of **King Lear.** One should also note that noble ladies enjoyed better status than commoners.

2. This biblical theme has inspired authors as different as Copland, who uses it in 1535, in **Here begynneth the Complaynte of them that ben to late maryed,** and Crofts in **The Lover,** 1638. The latter gives advice on how to seduce a woman.

3. See chapter II, 38-39.

4. **The first blast of the trumpet against the monstruous regiment of women,** 1558. In the Arber edition, one reads, 28: "For the same God that

hath denied the feet to see, hath denied to woman power to commande man, and hath taken away wisdom to consider, and providence to forsee the thinges, that be profitable to the commonwelth..." John Knox adds, at the end of the tract, an epistle to Queen Elizabeth, protesting, maybe too much, that this was not a personal attack against her, but that his conscience would not admit any compromise.

5. Cited by Roger Thompson, **Women in Stuart England and America, a comparative study** (London: Routledge, 1974).

6. Op. cit., 6. See also Smith, **De republica anglorum,** 1583, ed. L. Altson, 1906, 30. In the **De republica,** Smith excludes women and the minions from government: "In which consideration also we do reject women, as those whom nature hath made to keepe home and to nourish their familie and children, and not to medle with matters abroad, nor to beare office in a citie or common wealth no more than children and infantes: except it be in such cases as the authoritie is annexed to the bloud and progenie as the crowne, a dutchie or an erledome for there the blood is respected, not the age nor the sexe."

7. Ibid., 7. In fact among poorer classes, marriage was often delayed until the age of thirty.

8. Ibid., cited by R. Thompson, ibid., 162.

9. L. B. Wright, **Middle class culture in Elizabethan England,** 493.

10. Sig. D.

11. See Gen. 3:18 and also among the illustrated pamphlets, **The mothers counsell or live within compasse,** 16.

12. The 1945 edition of Stanley Pargellis, 10 sq.

13. Sig. E2. On the spendthrift middle-class, see also Henry Parrot, **The mous-trap,** 1606, epigram 31, sig. C2.

14. On the controversy, see Coryl Crandall, **Swetnam the woman-hater, the Controversy and the Play** (Purdue U. P., 1969).

15. She rails at Swetnam in these terms, sig. H.:
   The woman for an Helper, God made he doth say,
   But to helpe to consume and spend away,
   Thus, at Gods creation to flout and to jest,
   Who but an Atheist would so play the beast?

16. I, ii, 45 sq.

17. V, ii.

18. L. B. Wright, **Middle class culture in Elizabethan England** (Chapel Hill, N.C.: University of North Carolina Press, 1935), 495-97. Then comes a third work to back **Hic Mulier, Muld sacke: or the apologie of Hic Mulier**, 1620 (**STC** 21538).

19. See **Keepe within compasse**, and **The mothers counsell or live within compasse.**

20. William Harrison, a compiler and interpreter of Holinshed, **Chronicles of England, Scotland and Ireland**, 1577. The first part was edited separately and known under the title of **A description of England** (reprint, London: F. J. Furnivall, 1876).

21. Smith, **De republica anglorum**, 33 sq., Smith compares them to the roman <u>equites,</u> or knights.

22. **A royalist's notebook, The common place book of Sir John Oglander, Knight of Nunwell, 1622-1652**, ed. Francis Bamford, 1936, 45.

23. 12.

24. Thomas Wilson, **The state of England anno domini 1600**, ed. Fisher, 1936, 18.

25. John Norden confirms the presence of fruit trees in the hedges of Sussex, Dorset, Somerset, Norfolk and Suffolk. See M. St. Claire Byrne, **Elizabethan Life in Town and Country** (London: Methuen, 1961), 137.

26. See also chapter VI.

27. Grosart edition, XI, 231, which reads: "I am a severe censor to such as offend the law, provided there be a penalty annexed that may bring in some profyte..."

28. Among the characters disparaged, it is amusing to find the printer, which reflects more Greene's opinion than the viewpoint of the rustic.

29. Op. cit., 44.

30. Eric Kerridge, **Agrarian Problems in the Sixteenth Century and after** (New York: Allen and Unwin, 1969), 32 sq. The work contains a virulent criticism of Tawney.

31. This would be disputed by Kerridge who insists that the majority of leases were subject to legal control. However, he does admit that there were occasional abuses.

32. Sig. A4^V reads:

> That hath shepe in pastures goying
> Whiche grou̅de before this hath be put to tyllage
> Having thousa̅des his poore neybour lackynge
> He and his sheperds alone in a village
> Thus getteth his goodes by extortion and pillage
> If a man parte of his goodes withdrawe
> Shal he make answere therfore by goddes lawe.

33. **The pleasant and sweet history of patient Grisdelda,** 1630?

34. See John Selden, **The historie of Tithes,** 1618. He explains that it is a free gift agreed to by the peasants because their minister gives them the sacraments and preaches the Word to them, freely.

35. Brewer, op. cit.

36. Greene, op. cit., 251 sq.

37. See Wilson, op. cit., and Blaxton, **The English usurer,** 1634.

38. Greene, op. cit., 249.

39. W. Addison, **English Fairs and Markets** (London: B. T. Batsford, 1953), 46-52.

40. Harrison, op. cit., Book II, chapter 11, edition of 1557.

41. See William Lawson, **A new orchard and garden,** 1623, and **The expert gardener,** 1640, a compilation of French and Dutch authors.

42. Apricots were introduced in England by John Tradescant in 1620 on his return from Algiers. Sir Paul Harvey, **The Oxford Companion to English Literature,** 4th ed., 1967, 828b.

43. G. B. Harrison depicts them for us arriving in England in **A Second Jacobean Journal, 1607–1610** (Ann Arbor, MI: University of Michigan Press, 1958). The entry for May 1, 1609, 135 reads: "Last autumn and again this spring many hundred thousand of young mulberry trees have been brought out of France and planted in many shires of this land; and divers persons begin to breed worms and to make silk since by trial and experiment it hath been found that silk-worms will live and breed in England, and their silk is fit for taffeta, stockings and sewing-silk. Equal to the best that is made in Granada." See also the entry for 15 November 1609, 156.

44. A work of John Skelton, reedited in 1624.

45. Facing the illustration, 141 one reads on this duodecimo pamphlet:
Come Sirrah, you are a Drunkard and spend all your money
And when you come home you call me your honey
But all shall not serve thee, for have at thy pate,
My Ladle of the Crab-Tree, shall teach the to cogge and to prate.

46. The peasant in Brewer, **A dialogue...** says that he is so attached to his dog that he would not lose him for anything in the world. (Sig. A2^V) The dog is man's best friend, Taylor writes on a soldier's dog in **A dog of war.** This dog has also moral virtues; he barks whenever gallants and fops pass by.

47. **The praise of hempe-seed,** 1620. The greater part of the work tells of a voyage in a paper-ship on the Thames. In sig. E4 sq. the point is made that England would be in a sad case without hemp.

48. Fitzherbert, **A book of husbandry,** re-issued frequently between 1523 and 1598, ed. by Skeat, 1882, 94 sq.

49. **The wife happed on Morel's skypp,** 1580, sig. Eiv.

50. **STC** 12386.

51. Fitzherbert, op. cit., 65.

52. M. St. Claire Byrne, op. cit., 150.

53. About field agriculture, see the article by Robert A. Dodgson, "The landholding foundations of the openfield system" in Past and Present, No. 67, May 1975, 3-29.

54. **A horrible, creuel and bloudy murther,** 1614.

55. **STC** 16730.2, **The order of My Lord Mayor the Aldermen and the Sherifs for their meeting and wearing their apparel throughout the year.**

56. See A. H. Dodd, **Life in Elizabethan England** (London: Batsford, 1961), 36ff.

57. See, for instance, **The dialogue between the plaintiff and the defendaunt,** 1535, **A quipp for an upstart courtier,** by Greene, **The bellman of London,** by Th. Dekker, **A knot of Fooles,** 1624, by Th. Brewer, etc.

58. Johnson, **Nova Britannia,** 1609, sig. D. sq.

59. **A true relation of a most desperate murder,** 1617. One should notice that the title does not point out how heinous or horrible the murderer

is, but how desperate. This is confirmed by the narrative. The woodcut was commented on in chapter II.

60. See A. H. Dodd, **Life in Elizabethan England**, 1961, 42 sq.

61. Maurice Ashley, **Life in Stuart England** (London: Batsford, 1964), 50ff.

62. Sig. B2 shows that the word "foreigner" is applied to any person who does not reside in London. London, like Paris later on, is in fact, the overpowering metropolis of England, and the rest of England's inhabitants are small fry. The words of Maister Open in Middleton and Dekker, **The roaring girle**, II, i, warrant citation: "...she railes upon me for forraine wenching, that I being a freeman must needs keep a whore ith suburbs."

63. M. B. Donald, **Elizabethan Monopolies, The history of the Company of Mineral and Battery Works from 1565 to 1604** (London: Oliver and Boyd, 1961), viii. See also 198, the record of the lawsuit between L. Darcy and Th. Allen, about the renewal of the letter patent for the monopoly of playing cards.

64. A. H. Dodd, op. cit., 40.

65. M. B. Donald, op. cit., 3.

66. Sig. Fiii^v reads:
> And Master Merchant, he whose travail ought
> Commodiously, to doe his countrie good,
> And by his toyle, the same for to enriche,
> Can finde the meane, to make monopolyes
> Of every ware, this is accompted strange.
> Until the court, have courtiers cast at heele.

67. See Misselden, **Free trade or the meanes to make trade florish**, 1622, mainly 54-75.

68. **A quip for an upstart courtier**, 237-238. On life in the shops of London, see also Middleton and Dekker, **The roaring girle**, 1611 and J. Cooke, **Greenes Tu Quoque**, 1617.

69. See also A. H. Dodd, op. cit., 40.

70. On colonial propaganda, see chapter V.

71. See infra, 186f.

72. Sig. B8 sq. reads:
> Venter the Merchant is runne madde, they say,
> On the report his ships are cast away.

What, did he Venter with his goods his wits?
Then paradventure, it may well be found,
The sea his goods, and he his wits hath drown'd.

73. See the edition of Tawney and his excellent introduction, 169; see also the same author's **Religion and the rise of capitalism** (London: Murray, 1926).

74. It is interesting to see the Renaissance desire for the middle way in an apparent contradiction. On the one hand excess in apparel is severely satirized and punished by law. Poems, epigrams, satires and pamphlets scoff at it. On the other hand, satirists also come down heavily on the miser who never changes his garment out of stinginess. The <u>via media</u> is the right way.

75. **A quip for an upstart courtier,** 243 reads: The usurer is "the spoile of young Gentlemen, a bloud sucker of the poore,....a knave that hath intrest in the leases of forty baudy houses, a receiver for lifts and a dishonorable supporter of cut purses..."

76. A note in the edition consulted at the Folger Library in Washington, D.C., states that the work of Dekker is the only surviving piece of literature reiterating this old story which inspired Shakespeare's **Merchant of Venice.**

77. 73 reads: "The fourth and last Devill is your earthy Devill, and he is an Usurer, that like a Mole feedes in the bowels of the Earth, as Silver and Gold."

78. **The English usurer,** 60.

79. Here is the portrait of the usurer:
      The goutie Machiavilian murderer,
      Whose codpiece is neere 20 winters old,
      Now scornes the title of an usurer,
      And must be fashion'd in an other mold:
      The greybeard must a Monie-man be cleped,
      Because great store of monie he hath reaped:
      Of Mony-maister he to name must have;
      Though he unto his monie be a slave,...

80. Tawney, **A discourse upon Usury by Th. Wilson,** 130 sq.

81. See ibid.: in the Middle Ages and at the beginning of the Renaissance money was lent by the wealthy men of the town, by the merchants or the craftsmen. They are then not referred to by the name of usurer, but by the name of their trade. Tawney adds that money-lending, as a trade, only appears in England at the end of the XVth century or at the beginning of the XVIth, under the pressure of the rise of capitalism.

82. On the role played by the Jews, see A. M. Hyamson, **A History of the Jews in England** (London: The Jewish Society of England, 1908), 136.

83. In iconography one finds the following craftsmen: the tanner in **A Tanner of Tamworth**, 1596; the weaver in **A true discourse of the two infamous upstart prophets**, 1636; the shoemaker and the smith in T. H. **A discourse betweene Upright the Shoomaker and master Patent the Smith**, 1640, where each accuses the other of fleecing their customers. Of the three only the second woodcut shows the inside of a shop with the spinning wheel and the loom. We must also add the smith of **The Smith that forged him a new dame** and of **The English farrier**, 1636, a trade of the country as well as of the town.

84. A. H. Dodd, ibid., 133 sq.

85. The re-issue of Pearson, 1874, II, 169 reads:
> I prayse that Citty which made Princes Trades-men:
> Where that man, noble or ignoble borne,
> That would not practise some mechanicke skill,
> Whic might support his state in penury,
> Should die the death; not suffered like a drone,
> To sucke the honey from the publicke Hive.
> I hold it no disparage to my birth,
> Though I be borne an Earle, to have the skill
> And the full knowledge of the Mercers Trade.

The text is also quoted by Grivelet, **Thomas Heywood et le drame domestique élizabéthain** (Paris: Presses Universitaires, 1957), 138.

86. The passion for gold and silver dishes is attested by Misselden, ibid., 8 sq. See also Gascoigne, **The Steel Glas.** Everything will be fine, he says: "Whe goldsmithes get, no gains by sodred crownes..."

87. **The dramatic Works of Thomas Heywood**, II, 170.

88. Ibid., 138.

89. **STC** 20572.5.

90. The fame of the apprentices is said to reach the limits of the civilized world:
> The world reportes, what Londoners hath done,
> Freemen I meane, and prentices of worth:
> For countrie service, that are called forth.

91. Sig. A3^{v} sq. reads:
> Such Carting ne'er was seen before,
> A Coach must carry to Church doore
> An Asse that's with foure Horses drawne;
> Yea, Mistresse Easie, to the Pawne

> Must passe upon two paires of Wheeles,
> As though the Poxe were in her heeles...

92. Bod. Wood 614. On the quarrel, see also the ballad **The coaches overthrow**, 1636 (**STC** 5451)

93. One finds the same woodcut on a ballad in the Bagford Collection.

94. See **Deaths duell**, 1632.

95. See supra chapter II, 42.

96. They can be found respectively on the title-page of **Tarlton's Jest**, 1638; **Kemps nine daies wonder**, 1600; **The History of the two Maids of More-clacke**, 1609; and J. Cooke, **Greene's Tu Quoque**, 1614.

97. **STC** 19947. That the gout is the providential punishment of the rich is not a new idea. It is found in Chaucer's "Nun's Priest's Tale". See also Greene, **A looking glasse for London and England**, 1591, Sig. B2. On bad doctors, see Nicholas Breton, **The goode and the badde**, 1616, 16-17 and the ballad, **Dr. Do'good's directions...** (1635?). About the backwardness of the English medical publications as compared to those of the rest of Europe at the time, see C. D. O'Malley, "Tudor Medicine and Biology" in the Huntington Library Quarterly, XXXII, Nov. 1968. See also the issue of February 1969, S. K. Heninger, "Tudor Literature of the Physical Sciences", which shows the change that occurs in the approach to physical sciences in general and to medicine in particular at the end of the Elizabethan Age.

98. Both are to be found on the title-pages of **Saint Pauls Crosse her bill for the Parliament...** and of **The weeping lady** by Th. Brewer, 1625.

99. About this, see the two books of W. K. Jordan: **Philanthropy in England, 1480-1660. A Study of the changing Pattern of English Social Aspirations** (London: Allen and Unwin, 1959) and **The Charities of Rural England, 1480-1660. The Aspirations and the Achievements of the rural society** (London: Allen and Unwin, 1961).

100. Sig. B sq.

101. Sig. Civ^v: "without any sowre or grim countenaunce".

102. In 1572, after a famine, judges were given the right to levy every week money for the assistance of the poor from the rich freeholders in their jurisdiction. See A. H. Dodd, **Life in Elizabethan England**, 135-136.

103. Sig. Dvi sq.

Notes to pp. 179-181

104. The end of the work reads: "Fyrst, which is plesant to tell/ beggary, beggars and beggyne/ these thrē greues of the world rule nowe in the cyte as they did before. Parasytes por men smell festes/ which to the great hurte of the comen welth dyd abuse good mennes lyberal now dysapoynted of the wynnynge that they had by beggynge are brought to a quyet and sobre lyvynge. Such as used to bere about in the cytie countefeyte writynges of some fayned losse/ gettynge money so by crafte and disceyte/ now ferynge the eyes and handes of the prefectes and serchers disceyue nat the Cytizens so ofte as they were wonte to do."

105. However, the author states that there is no lack of statutes or laws for regulating the matter. He cites 22 Hen i. c. 12 and 27 H. 8. c. 25. Then I Edw. 6.c3.5., Edw. 6.c.2., 3 Phil. and Mar. c.5. Also 5 Eliz. c.3, 14 E. c.3, 18 El. c.3., 39 Eliz. c. 455 and finally 43 Eliz. c.2.3.4. But the surveyors and prefects were negligent and the magistrates did not bother to punish them.

106. This seems to be an attitude common to every nation living on a capitalistic economy.

107. Sig. B2.

108. It is worth quoting Copland's vivid description of beggars pressing against the door of the poorhouse to get some food:
> People as methought of very poor estate
> With bag and staff, both crooked, lame and blind,
> Scabby and scurvy, pock eaten flesh and rind,
> Lousy and scald, and peeled like as apes,
> With scantly a rag for to cover their shapes
> Breechless, barefooted, all stinking with dirt
> With thousand of tatters, drabbling to the skirt,
> Boys, girls, and luskish strong knaves,
> Diddering and daddering, leaning on their staves...

109. The fool of **A Maydenhead well lost** of Heywood, 1634, was not resigned, like his mistresses, to die of hunger, rather than condescend to the indignity of begging. On the contrary, he is master of the art of imitation, as can be seen in his speech in Act II: "I'le make all the high-waues ring of me with for the Lords sake. I have studied a Prayer for him that gives, and a Poxe take him that gives nothing! I have woe for the Horse-way, another for the Footeway, and a third for the turning-stile. No Madam, begging is growne a gentlemanlike calling here in our Countrey."

A beggar woman appears on the title-page of Dekker's **O per se—O**, 1612. Another edition of 1612 shows the bellman of London.

110. See **The hye way to the spyttell hous,** 7 and Harman, op. cit., chapter 10, and Dekker's **O per se—O**, 1612. In **The roaring girle** of Middleton and Dekker, Trapdore and Teare-cat are disguised as soldiers (v, i).

111. Ibid., chapter V.

112. See chapter VII, 160.

113. See also the image of the cutpurse among the characters of John Taylor's **The water-cormorant his complaint**, 1622.

114. Bowers, **The dramatic works of Thomas Dekker**, III, Act II, i, 320-32.

115. This is hardly an original work of Dekker since it is a compilation of Awdeley, Harman and Greene and only the banquet of the ruffians and his encounter with the bellman of London anticipate **Lanthorne and candlelight.**

116. In this type of literature, Rowlands lacks both the verve of Greene and the dramatic eloquence of Dekker. His satires are generally more abstract and the limitation of writing in verse causes him to lose much of the picturesque in his narrative.

117. See the Hunterian Club reprint of Rowlands's work, 1880, I, 15; the work to which Rowlands is indebted, according to the introduction to the new impression, is: **Catharos. Diogenes in his singularitie**, 1581. In his letter to the reader, in **A notable discovery of cosenage**, 1591, Greene also refers to Diogenes who, he says, although he was a forger, became a moralist.

118. **The severall notorious and lewd cousenages of John West and Alice West, falsely called the king and queene of fayries,** 1613. They were condemned at the Old Bailey sessions.

119. He describes the warder in these terms:
> A Cerberus, nay, worse, he thrice at wide did gape,
> His eares all snakes, curling, they will not part;
> Coal black his hue, like torches glow his eyes,
> His breath doth poison, smoke from his nostrils flies...
> Bribery his hand, spoil of the poor his trade...
> Methought his breast was all of burning brass
> Through which there grew a heart of hardest steel;
> His belly huge like scalding furnace was,
> His thighs both like unto a fiery wheel,
> His legs were long, one foot like a hind,
> The other foot a hound's of bloody kind.

120. See on sig. 12^V the comments of Spandall on the companions of his cell:
> Hunger will draw mee into their fellowship,
> To fight and scramble for unsaverie Scraps,
> That come from unknowne hands, perhaps unwash'd;
> And would that were the worst; for I have noted,

Notes to pp. 186-190

> That nought goes to the Prisoners, but such food
> As either by the weather has been tainted,
> Or Children, nay sometimes full paunched Dogges
> Have overlickt.

121. B.M. c 27 c 24: **The lives, apprehensions, arraignments, and executions of the 19 late pyrates,** 1609, shows that piracy was all too common. The title-page is only illustrated by a boat.

122. **A true and certaine report of the beginning, proceedings and now present estate of Captaine Ward a. Danseker, the two late famous pirates,** 1609. One can also read **The seamans song of Captain Ward...and the seamans song of Dansekar,** to the tune of **The Kings going to Bulloign.**

123. **STC** 20512. **A true relation of the lives and deaths of the two English pyrats, Purser and Clinton,** 1639.

124. For the narrative accompanying this woodcut, see above VII, 176.

125. Sig. 13^{v} reads:
> I have composed a Booke, wherein I have set downe
> All the wonders of the world that I have seene,
> And the whole scope of my Jornies, togeather with the
> Miseries and lowsie fortunes I have endured therein.

126. The narrative has a political interest. Webbe insists that in Italy, the false rumors spread by Mendoza on the victory of the Armada and the fall of England were believed.

127. An historical explanation of the origin of the marvels of the Far East can be found in Rudolf Wittkower, "Marvels of the East", in **Journal of the Warburg and Courtauld Institutes,** V, 1942, 159-197. A noteworthy citation is the view of St. Augustine in the **De Civitate Dei,** XVI, 8: "God has created fabulous races lest we should think that monstrous births among men are a defect of his wisdom."

128. The woodcut reappears opposite the dedicatory epistle with these lines:
> Loe here the wooden image of our wits;
> Borne, in first travaile, on the backs of Nits;
> But now on Elephants, &c:
> O'what will he ride, when his yeares expire?
> The world must ride him; or he all will tire.
The woodcut reappears for the third time on 97.

129. **A common whore,** 1635, sig. C3^{v} and C5.

130. See 29.

Chapter VIII - **The Supernatural**

1. Keith Thomas, **Religion and the Decline of Magic** (New York: Scribner's, 1971), 313. The author cites the Bodleian manuscript, Ashmole 420 attached to folio 267. For the sources of Overton's thought, he cites S. Hutin, **Les disciples anglais de Jacob Boehme aux XVIIème et XVIIIème siècles** (Paris, 1960), 62-215.

2. The source of the last two paragraphs will be found in Paul H. Kocher, **Science and Religion in Elizabethan England** (San Marino, California: Huntington Library, 1953), 1-45.

3. This fact can be explained by numerous philosophical and religious reasons. The Thirty Years War and the quarrels between Anglicans and Puritans that ended in the Civil War, made the mysteries of faith and undemonstrable dogmas, like that of predestination, difficult to accept. Further, the mystery of the Holy Trinity is one of the greatest since it insists on the triplicity of a being essentially One. On the other side, a world in which science was taking giant strides was readier to attach itself to God as the author of Nature than to God as Grace, and God's universal providence was easier to accept than the theory of the elect and the reprobate. Such considerations helped to nurture Deism which was born in the seventeenth century with Lord Herbert of Cherbury, whose **De Veritate** was published in Paris in 1624. On this subject, see Horton Davies, **Worship and Theology in England**, II, (Princeton: University Press, 1975), 178.

4. In passing, it is worth observing the Latin treatise, **Cometographia**, 1578, on the comet of 1577 which terrified all England, except its Queen, the virgin with the heart of a man whose superb alea jacta est filled the courtiers with that sacred fear felt before Caesar or divinity. The title-page includes the tetragrammaton in the star, while the message of God can be read in its tail.

5. On the sources and the significance of imagery at the beginning of Christianity, see the work of André Grabar, translated into English, and entitled, **Christian Iconography, A Study of its origins,** Bollingen Series, XXXV (Princeton, 1968). See also D. Talbot Rice, **The Beginnings of Christian Art** (London: Hodder and Stoughton, 1957), 41: "...iconographically that they are Christian is not always easy to distinguish. The evangelists thus resemble pagan philosophers, while our Lord takes on the character of a classical divinity. He was usually shown with long hair and youthful appearance like an Apollo." The image of the evil shepherd penetrates all the literature of the sixteenth century. It is found in **The Praise of Folly** of Erasmus, friend of Protestants, and also among Catholics, such as Ronsard.

6. Another example of the secularization of a religious theme is **A description of the King and Queene of Fayries**, 1635, by R. S., which makes use of the legends of the Saints and an image of Adam and Eve to illustrate imaginary and secular narratives.

Notes to pp. 198-203

7. See chapter III for the analysis of this image.

8. On the curses of God, see the excellent work of Delbert R. Hillers, "Treaty Curses and the Old Testament Prophets", _Biblica et Orientalia_, No. 16, Rome, 1964.

9. And the serpent of the garden of Eden? One is bound to ask.

10. Sig. A3v.

11. On the classifications of animals according to their physique, moral sense, astrological significance, their friendship for humans, and their pharmaceutical properties, see Madeleine Doran, "On Elizabethan credulity with some questions concerning the use of the marvellous in literature." _J.H.I._, 151-196.

12. Sig. Cv.

13. A3 reads: "Admirabilis Deus in omnibus operibus suis, God is wonderful in all his works. And with Saint Augustine, That as it was not impossible for Almighty God in his first creation to make what variety of creature He pleased, so it is not impossible for His divine Majesty to alter and change the ordinary course and disposition of the creatures which He hath made." The Londoners were haunted by visions of their beloved city consumed by flames.

14. 3f.

15. 30.

16. It is based on Luke 21:25. See also W. S. Reid, **Trumpeter of God: a biography of John Knox** (New York: Scribners, 1974), 48f.

17. Keith Thomas, **Religion and the Decline of Magic**, 1971, 478.

18. Ibid., 479.

19. Ibid., 494. Thomas cites D. Rock, **The Church of our Fathers**, ed. G. W. Hart and W. H. Frere, (London: Hodge, 1903-04), II, 343n.

20. For the development of the concept of Satan in Judaic thought, see the illuminating article in the **Encyclopedia Britannica** (New Werner edition, New York, 1903), VII, 136a-138a.

21. See, for example, the Romanesque church of Belin in the south of France, where on each side of the south doorway one finds the image of a holy man in opposition to that of a diabolical man. The latter has elongated ears, a sinister smile in which he displays decayed teeth and his eyes closed in an ecstasy of sensuality (visited on 29 June 1973 in the course of a research project). See

Horton and Marie-Hélène Davies, **Holy Days and Holidays: the medieval pilgrimage to Compostela** (Lewisburg, PA.: Bucknell University Press, 1982).

22. See also the devil in Harrington, **The metamorphosis of Ajax,** 1596.

23. It can be found between sig. E and F. since the pagination of the edition of 1548 appears to be incomplete.

24. The satyr, a man the bottom of whose body resembles a goat and whose sexual potency has changed a demi-god into a vulgar name, shows the same characteristics. It would be interesting, if it has not already been done, to trace the relations between Satan and the satyr and to discover to what degree the same oriental tradition was the cause of the representation of both.

25. **Of two wonderful popish monsters,** 1579.

26. See **Newes from the East Indies,** for the image opposite the title-page.

27. **Encyclopedia Britannica,** 1903, VII, 136b.

28. **True and wonderful,** 1614.

29. In these two illustrations the Papist is bewitched by the intervention of Evil. See later the role of Satan in witchcraft.

30. Matthew 8:28-32. This is the gospel most concerned with the possession of men by Satan and Christ's powers of exorcism.

31. See chapter VIII, 202.

32. **Religion and the Decline of Magic,** 1971, 436.

33. An outstanding glimpse of modern anthropological views on magic is provided in **Magic, Witchcraft and Curing,** edited by John Middleton, an anthology of extracts from the writings of the most renowned including Lévy-Strauss and Evans-Pritchard.

34. K. Thomas, op. cit., 176-182, 436-443.

35. See also Paul H. Kocher, op. cit., particularly the chapter entitled, "Satan exiled".

36. K. Thomas, op. cit., 573.

37. **Daemonologie,** 4.

Notes to pp. 207-209

38. Ibid., 47, which reads: "...there are three kinds of folkes whom God will permit so to be tempted or troubled; the wicked for their horrible sinnes, to punish them in like measure; the godlike that are sleeping in anie great sinnes or infirmities and weaknesse in faith, to waken them up the faster by such an uncouthe form; and even some of the best that their patience maybee tryed before the world, as IOBS was. For why may not God use anie kinde of extraordinarie punishment, when it pleases him; as well as the ordinarie roddes of sicknesse or other aduersities."

39. A number of treatises which took the part of James VI of Scotland against Scot can be found conveniently together in _Bod._ 4 B 71 Jur.

40. **Essays,** 1625, XVII.

41. In Bi verso an illustration depicts the witches, threatened by a rod, on their knees before two magistrates.

42. The myth according to which witches have immeasurable sexual voracity comes partly from the **Malleus Maleficarum,** and in part from the Elizabethan belief that woman is more avid than man.

43. See later VIII, 212. Faust became the complete opposite of the magician enamored of knowledge as expressed by Ficino. In selling his soul to the devil, Faust renounced the neo-platonic knowledge for an immediate power over which he had no control.

44. H. Goodcole, **The wonderful discoverie of Elizabeth Sawyer, a Witch, late of Edmonton, her conviction and condemnation and Death,** 1611, sig. A4 v.-B.

45. **The Witch of Edmonton,** II, i:
> Sawy: And why on me? why should the envious world
> Throw all their scandalous malice upon me?
> 'Cause I am poor, deform'd and ignorant,
> And like a bow buckl'd and bent together
> By some more strong in mischiefs than my self?

46. The argument is not new. Practically all Shakespeare's villains have a good reason for revenge, founded on injustice, but as soon as they take the evil path, the condemnation is theirs as much as the original offender: for instance, Iago, in **Othello.**

47. A. J. D. Macfarlane, **Witchcraft in Tudor and Stuart England; a regional study** (New York: Harper and Row, 1970), is a study on witchcraft in Essex. Most of the cases were outrages against persons or animals.

48. A similar case: **Witches Apprehended, Examined and Executed,** 1613. The widow Sutton avenged a quarrel of Master Sutton with Milton Mills,

49. The devil in the form of a dog reminds Elizabeth Sawyer of the limitations of her power: II, i, she cannot kill Old Thorney:

> Dog: Fool, because I cannot.
> Though we have power, know, it is circumscrib'd,
> Ans ti'd in limits: though he be curs'd to thee,
> Yet of himself he is loving to the world,
> And charitable to the poor. Now men
> That as he, love goodness, though in the smallest measure,
> Live without compass of our reach.

50. **Daemonologie**, 45-46.

51. Ibid., 445-446.

52. James, ibid., 79f. gives the criteria for recognizing a witch.

53. The ancient trial of bread and butter which Joan Flower requested to undergo in **The wonderful discoverie of the Witchcrafts of Margaret and Phillip Flower**, 1619, tends to disappear and give way to the trial by water.

54. **The witches of Northamptonshire**, 1612. On the cruelty of the trial, see the manuscript of the British Library, B. M. Sloane 972, f. 7, cited by B. Rosen in **Witchcraft**, 1969, 344.

55. For white magic, see C. G. Loomis, **White Magic** (Cambridge, Mass.: Medieval Academy of America, 1948).

56. Thomas, op. cit., 192-202.

57. Ibid., 324-328.

58. The narrator explains that he opened a shop because one day a tearful master came to him to ask him where his dog could be found. Having seen the dog pass in front of the house of this master, he replied that he would find it at home, whence his reputation as a diviner. This satire against fortune tellers continues. A crowd of credulous people comes to consult the diviner; the anxious walk by in a procession from the apprentice to the witch, receiving wise advice which has nothing supernatural in it.

59. In **The third and last part of conny catching**, Greene recounts the history of a gull who, having stolen silk from a merchant, and resold it to a mean pawnbroker, avenges himself by "divining" for the merchant, the street numbers where the silk could be retrieved.

60. Greene, ibid., sig. e3-e4.

61. For this purpose, see Kocher, ibid., ch. VII-VIII of Thomas, ibid., 284-285 and 349-351; and Francis Johnson, **Astronomical thought in Renaissance**

Notes to pp. 213-214

England (Baltimore: Johns Hopkins University Press, 1937), which explain the problems created by the discoveries of astronomy for astrology. Craig, in **The Enchanted Glass**, 1952, shows how, given the Renaissance propensity in England to make thought active, it would be natural to convert the stars into motile agents. Nor should the work of D. C. Allen, **The Star-Crossed Renaissance**, 1941, be ignored.

> 62. For example:
> The eygth day of Apryle it may chaunce to rayne...
> But I saye yf the nynth daye of Novembre
> Had fallen upon tenth of Decembre
> It had bene a mervaylous hote yere for bees
> For then had the Moone ben lyke a grene chese.
> Somer begyneth the fyrste daye of June
> And they shal go bare for that have no shewe
> Sometyme inclyned to be hot in the are
> Yf it be nat foule, then it shal be fayre.

63. In **Characters**, 1616, Overbury describes the maker of almanacs in these terms: "...is the worse part of an Astronomer: a creature compact of figures, characters and cyphers; out of which he scores the fortune of a yeare, not so profitably, as doubtfully. He is tenant by custome to the Planets, of whom he holds the 12. Houses by lease parol: to them he paies yearly rent, his study and time; yet lets them out again...for 40 s. per annum. His life is merely contemplative; for his practise, tis worth nothing...Ptolomy and Ticho Brahe are his Patrons, those volumes he understands not but admires." Nicholas Allen in **The Astronomical Game**, 1569, compares three almanacs for the same year. See F. P. Wilson, "Some English mock-prognostications" in The Library, 4th Series, XIX, 1939.

64. **Astrologaster or, the figure-caster**, 1620. We read: "A Square Table, covered with a greene Carpet, in which lay a huge book in FOLIO, wide open, full of strange characters, such as the Aegyptians and Chaldeans were never guilty of; not farre from that, a silver Wand, a Surplus, a Watering Pot, with all the superstitions or rather fayned instruments of his cosening Art. And to put a faire colour on his black and foule science, on his head he had a foure-cornered Cap, on his backe a faire Gowne, in his right hand he held an Astrolabe, in his left a Mathematical Glasse."

65. For political prediction, see also **The owles Almanacke**, 1618.

66. See also the excellent article of Warren D. Smith, "The Elizabethan Rejection of Judicial Astrology and Shakespeare's Practice", Shakespeare Quarterly, IX, 1958, 159-176.

67. 22-23.

68. There were, in fact, certain Catholic "astrologers" who thus hoped to influence the people in favor of Mary Stuart and of taking up again the reins

of the kingdom; see Warren D. Smith, op. cit., 162. See also, against the Jesuit exorcists, S. Harsnett, **A Declaration of egregious popish impostures**, 1603.

69. **The Astrologaster**, 32-33.

70. Ibid., 45-47.

71. Spatalmancy is divination with the aid of the shoulder blades of animals.

72. For the analysis of Greene's play see Kerstein Assarsson-Rizzi, **Friar Bacon and Friar Bungay. A structural and thematic analysis of Robert Greene's play** (Lund, 1972). See particularly the sources on 24-43. See also the book of the time, **The famous historie of Fryer Bacon, also the manner of his death**, 1627.

LIST OF ILLUSTRATIONS

1	Davies, Sir John	**A scourge for Paper-persecutors,** 1625. 4° T.P. (Folger 6340)
2	Sampson, W	**The vow-breaker. Or the faire maide of Clifton,** 1636. 4° Sig. A2. (Bodleian Douce S 1900)
3	Hooper, John	**An homelye to be read in the tyme of pestylence,** 1553. 4° T.P. (Bodleian Mason H 192)
4.	Benlowes, E.	**A buckler against the fear of death,** Cambridge 1640. 8° Frontispiece. (Bodleian 8° T 48 Th.)
5	Goodman, N.	**Hollands leaguer,** 1632. 4° Facing T.P. (Bodleian Douce G.G. 16)
6	Rowlands, S.	**The knave of clubbes,** 1611. 4° T.P. (Bodleian Facs. e. 30)
7	Gomersal, R.	**The tragedy of Ludovick Sforza,** 1628. 8° Frontispiece. (Folger 11995)
8	Musophilus, pseud.	**A new spring shadowed in sundry pithie poems,** 1619. 4° T.P. woodcut. (Bodleian 4° M 4 L. Art)
9	Swetnam, J.	**Swetnam, the woman hater arraigned by women,** 1620. 4° T.P. cut. (Bodleian Malone 197)
10	Tedder, W.	**The recantations...,** 1588. 4° T.P. verso (Bodleian A. 13.8 Linc.)
11a	Heywood, Th.	**If you know not mee, You know no body,** 1639. 4° T.P. (Bodleian Mal. 915)

11b		If you know not mee, You know nobody. – The Second part, 1633. 4° T.P. (Bodleian Mal. 915)
12	Morocco	The arrival and intertainements of the embassador from the Emperor of Morocco, 1637. 4° Frontispiece. (Folger 18165)
13		Newes out of Cheshire, 1600. 4° T.P. cut. (Bodleian 4° L. 78 Art.)
14	S., R.	The melancholie knight, 1615. 4° T.P. (Bodleian 4° L 71 Art.)
15	Breton, N.	A poste with a packet of madde letters, 1634. 4° T.P. (Folger 3693)
16	Churchyard, Th.	A light bondell of livly discourses called Churchyardes charge etc., 1580. 4° T.P. verso (Folger 5240)
17	Charles I, King	The entertainment of the high and mighty monarch Charles into his auncient city of Edinburgh, 1633. 4° (Folger 16680)
18	Wilkinson, R.	The merchant royall, 1607. 4° T.P. (Folger 25658)
19	Digges, L. and T.	A prognostication everlasting, 1556. 4° T.P. verso (Folger 6861)
20	Heywood, Th.	A true description of his Majesties royall ship built at Wool-witch, 1637. 4° Facing T.P. (Folger 13367)
21	Dauncy, G	His president for the starres...the almanacke, 1614. Sig. C v. and C2. (Folger 435)
22	Gray	An Almanack and prognostication for Dorchester, 1588. Sig. A v. (Bodleian [MS] Ashm. 62.[6])
23	Rudston, T.	A new almanacke and prognostication, 1607. 8° Sig. A2. (Bodleian Douce A 576)

24   Liturgie — **An order for publicke prayers on Wednesdayes and Frydayes,** 1586? 4° T.P. (Bodleian)

25   Jugeler, Jack — **A new enterlued for chyldren to playe, named Jacke Jugeler. Newly imprented.** (1565?) (Bodleian Facs. E 58)

26   Taylor, John — **Jack-A-Lent: his beginning and entertainment, with new additions,** 1620. 4° T.P. (Bodleian Douce JJ. 170)

27   Fletcher, J. — **The history of the perfect-cursed-blessed** man, 1629. 4° P. 7 and p. 34. (Folger 11079)

28   Taylor, John — **Divers crabtree Lectures,** 1639. 12° P. 140. (Bodleian Douce L 4)

29 — **A kicksey winsey: or a lerry come-twang: where-in John Taylor hath satyrically suited 800 of his bad debtors,** 1624. 8° T.P. (Bodleian B. 31 Med.)

30   Ward, S. of Ipswich — **All in all,** 1622. 8° T.P. (Folger 25033a)

31   Gedde, W. — **A booke of sundry draughtes principally for glasiers; whereunto is annexed how to anneil in glas,** 1615-16. 4° (Bodleian G 29. Art.)

32a   Harvey, J. — **An Almanach or annual Calender for 1584.** Sig. Dij verso (Bodleian Ashm. 62)

32b   Hopton, A. — **An Almanach and Prognostication,** 1607. Sig. Cvi verso (Bodleian Douce A. 576)

33   Burton, R. — **A brief treatise,** 1591. 8° P. 86. (Bodleian A. J. 17)

34   Pellham, Ed. — **Gods power a. providence: shewed in the miraculous preservation of eight Englishmen, left by mischance in Green-land...,** 1631. Folio map. (Folger 19566)

35 Swedish Intelligencer   **The Swedish Intelligencer. Second Part**, 1632. Map between 150 and 151. (Folger 23524)

36 Malbie, Sir N.   **A plaine and easie way to remedie a horse that is foundered in his feete, etc.**, 1594. 4° (British Library, C 31. g. 11)

37 Stallenge, W.   **Instructions for the increasing of mulberie trees a. breeding of silke-wormes**, 1609. 4° Sig. C 3v. (Folger 23138)

38 Harman, Th.   **The groundworke of conny-catching**, 1592. 4° T.P. (Huntington HEH 61333)

39 Fitz, Sir John   **The bloudy booke, or the tragical end of Sir J. Fitz**, 1605. 4° T.P. (British Library R. b. 41)

40 Goodcole, H.   **Natures cruell step-dames**, 1637. 4° T.P. (Folger 12012)

41 Ravaillac, F.   **The terrible and deserved death of F. Ravilliack, shewing the manner of his execution**, 1610. 4° (Folger 20755)

42 Flood, Griffin   **The life and death of G. Flood, informer**, 1623. 4° T.P., and verso. (Folger 11090)

43 Relation   **A true relation...**, 1609. 4° T.P. (Folger 20863.5)

44   **A true and wonderfull relation of a whale**, n.d. T.P. (Bodleian Wood B 35)

45 Year   **The cold yeare**, 1614: a deepe snow: etc., 1615. 4° T.P. (Bodleian L 68 Art.)

46 Scott, Th.   **Vox Dei**, 1623? 4° T.P. (Folger 22097a)

47 L., I   **The birth, purpose and mortall wound of the Romish holie league**, 1589. Folio map. (Bodleian B. 4. 3. Linc (4))

48	Drake, Sir Francis	**The world encompassed by Sir F. Drake...**, 1628. 4° T.P. (Folger 7161)
49	Netherlands	**A true copy of the admonitions sent by the subdued provinces to the States of Holland, etc.**, 1598. 4° T.P. (Folger 18465)
50	Vincent, P.	**The lamentations of Germany**, 1638. Folio map. (Folger 24761)
51	Lynne W.	**The beginning and endynge of all popery**, 1548? 4° (Bodleian Mal. 711)
52	Vicars, J.	**Mischeefes Mysterie**, 1617. 4° T.P. verso. (Bodleian H 21 Art.)
53	Johnson, R.	**The new life of Virginea: being the second part of Nova Britannia**, 1612. 4° T.P. (Folger 14700)
54	Crofts, R.	**The lover, or nuptiall love**, 1638. 8° Frontispiece. (Folger 6042)
55	Dekker, Th.	**A rod for run-awayes**, 1625. 4° T.P. (Bodleian Mal. 601)
56	Heywood, Th.	**Philocothonista, or the drunkard, opened, dissected and anatomized**, 1635. 4° T.P. (Bodleian Douce H H 227)
57	Copland, R.	**Gyl of Braintfords testament newly compiled**, 1560? 4° Sig. B3. (Bodleian S. Selden d. 45)
58	Rowley, S.	**When You see me, You know me**, 1613. 4° T.P. (Tudor Facsimile Texts, 1913)
59	Breton, N.	**The court and country, dialogue-wise between a courtier and a countryman**, n.d. 4° T.P. (Folger 3642)
60	Gosson, S.	**Quippes for upstart newfangled gentle women, etc.**, 1595. 4° T.P. verso. (Tudor Facsimile Text Reprint)
61	Ward, S. of Ipswich	Woe to drunkards, 1627. 8° T.P. cut. (Huntington Library)

62   Lawson, W.

A new Orchard and garden, etc. with the country housewifes garden, 1618. 4° P. 12. (Folger 15329)

63   Farley, H.

St. Paules-Church her Bill for the Parliament, 1621. 4° T.P. cut. (Bodleian H 21 Art.)

64   Walbancke, M.

Annalia Dubrensia: Dr. Dover's Olimpick games, 1636. 4° T.P. (Folger 24954)

65   Deceit

The deceyte of women, 1562? 4° T.P. (Huntington HEH 60965)

66   Haec Vir

Haec vir or the womanish-man, 1620. 4° T.P. (Folger 12599)

67   Blaxton, J.

The English usurer, 1634. 4° T.P. (Folger 3129)

68   Somerset, Co. of

A true report of certaine overflowings of waters in Summerset-shire, etc., 1607. 4° T.P. (Folger 22915)

69   Description

The description of Giles Mompesson late knight censured by Parliament, 1620. Folio sheet. (Folger 6769.5)

70   Knight, F.

A relation of seaven yeares slaverie under the Turkes of Argeire, 1640. 4° Facing the T.P. and facing p. 1. (Folger 15048a)

71   Peacham, H. Jr.

Coach and Sedan, pleasantly disputing, 1636. 4° T.P. (Folger 19501)

72   Westward

Westward for smelts, etc., 1620. 4° T.P. (Folger 25292)

73.   S., M.

The poore orphans court, 1636. 4° Frontispiece (Bodleian Gough. Lond. 7 (1))

74   Ward, Captain

Newes from sea of two notorious Pyrates, Ward and Danseker, 1609. 4° T.P. (Folger 25022)

75   Timberlake, H.

A relation of the travells of two English pilgrimes, 1631. 4° T.P. (Bodleian Arch. A e. 9)

76 Calverley, Wm.

A dyalogue betweene the **playntife and the defendaunt,** 1535? 4° T.P. verso. (Folger 4370)

77 Dee, John

A letter nine yeeres since, written and first published, 1603. 4° T.P. (Folger 6461)

78 Hilliard, J.

Fire from Heaven, 1613. 4° T.P. (Folger 13507)

79 Fennor, Wm

Pluto his travailes, 1611. 4° T.P. (British Library 4091, aa. 24)

80 Cooper, Th.

The cry and revenge of blood, expressing the haynousnesse of murther, 1620. 4° T.P. (Folger 5698)

81 Witches

Witches apprehended, examined and executed, etc., 1613. 4° T.P. (Bodleian E. 17 Art.)

82 Melton, J.

Astrologaster, or the figure-caster, 1620. 4° T.P. (Bodleian)

83a Greene, R.

The honorable historie of Frier Bacon and Frier Bongay, 1630. 4° T.P. (Folger 12268)

83b Marlowe, C.

The tragicall history of the life and death of Doctor Faustus, 1631. 4° T.P. (Folger 17436)

ILLUSTRATIONS

Illustrations have been taken from the Bodleian Library, Oxford; the Folger Library, Washington, D. C.; the Huntington Library, San Marino, California; and from Marie-Hélène Davies, **La gravure dans les brochures illustrees...**, 1979.

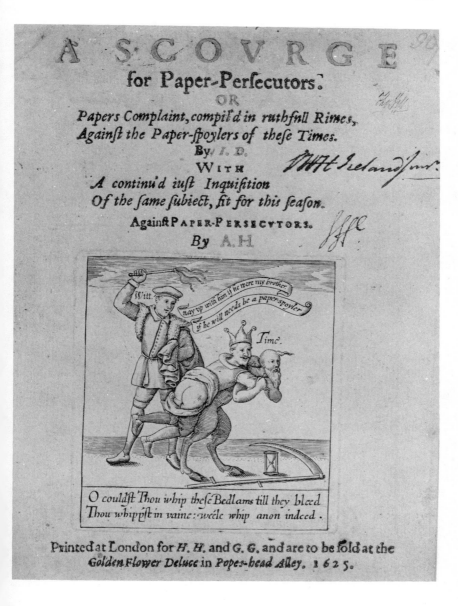

1. Davies, Sir John - **A scourge for paper-persecutors**, 1625.
4° T.P. (Folger 6340)

310

2. Sampson, W. - **The vow-breaker. Or the faire maide of Clifton**, 1636. 4°. Sig. A2. (Bodleian Douce S 1900)

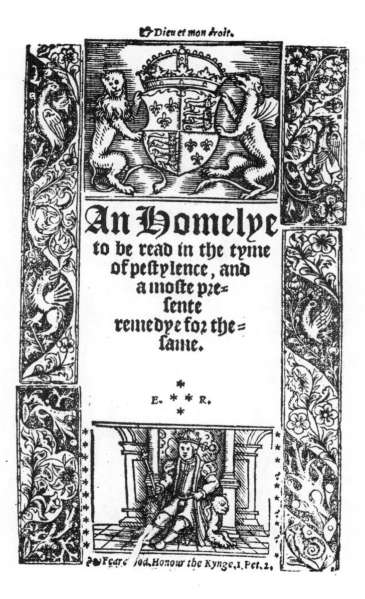

3. Hooper, John - **An homelye to be read in the tyme of pestylence**, 1553. 4° T.P. (Bodleian Mason H 192)

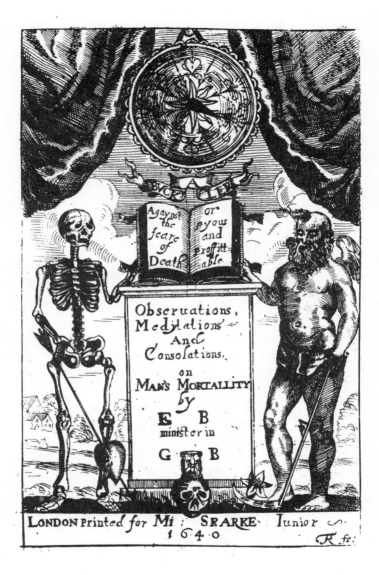

4. Benlowes, E. - **A buckler against the fear of death,** Cambridge 1640. 8° Frontispiece. (Bodleian 8° T 48 Th.)

5. Goodman, N. - **Hollands leaguer,** 1632. 4°
Facing T.P. (Bodleian Douce G.G. 16)

314

THE
KNAVE OF
Clubbs.

Printed at London by *E. A.* dwelling on Lambard hill
neere Olde Fish-street. 1 6 1 1.

6. Rowlands, S. - **The Knave
    of clubbes,** 1611. 4° T.P.
    (Bod. Facs. e. 30)

SFORZA
by
Rob: Gomersall

Printed for John. Marriott. 1 6 2 8. Tho:Cecill. Scul

7. Gomersall, R. - **The tragedy of Ludovick Sforza**, 1628. 8° Frontispiece. (Folger 11995)

316

MVSOPHILVS.
Quid nescis, si teipsum noscas?

LONDON,
Printed by *G. Eld*, for *Thomas Baylie*, and are to be sold at his Shop,
in the middle-row in Holborne, neere Staple-Inne.1619.

8. Musophilus, pseud. - **A new spring
shadowed in sundry pithie poems,**
1619. 4° T.P. woodcut. (Bod. 4°
M 4 L. Art.) [Repr. from M.-H.
Davies, **La gravure…**]

SVVETNAM,

THE
VVoman-hater,
ARRAIGNED BY
WOMEN.

A new Comedie,
Acted at the *Red Bull*, by the late
Queenes Seruants.

LONDON,
Printed for *Richard Meighen*, and are to be sold at his Shops
at Saint *Clements* Church, ouer-against *Essex* House, and
at *Westminster* Hall. 1 6 2 0.

9. Swetnam, J. - **Swetnam, the woman hater
arraigned by women**, 1620. 4° T.P. cut. (Bod.
Malone, 197) [Repr. from M.-H. Davies, **La
gravure ...**]

318

DIûa potens cuius decantant Sydera laudes,
 Quæ tibi dante Deo regia sceptra tenes.
Pro te pugnantem crûdelis sensit Hiberus,
 Quiq; domi volûit te spoliare, Deum.
Sceptra tibi sed firma manét,et firma manebût,
 Es quoniam fælix te protegente Deo.

If you know not mee,

You know no body.

O R

The troubles of Queene *Elizabeth.*
By Tho. Heywood.

LONDON:
Printed by *I. Raworth* for *N. Butter.* 1639.

11a. Heywood, Th. - **If you know not mee, You know no body**, 1639. 4° T.P. (Bod. Mal. 915) [Repr. from M.-H. Davies, **La gravure ...**]

If you know not me,

You know no body.

THE SECOND PART.

VVith the building of the Royall Exchange.
AND
The famous Victory of Queene Elizabeth, Anno 1588.

LONDON.
Printed for NATHANAELL BV... AT 16...

11b. Heywood, Th. - **If you know not mee, You know no body. The Second part,** 1633. 4° T.P. (Bod. Mal. 915) [Repr. from M.-H. Davies, **La gravure ...**]

The true Effigies of y^e Alkaid, (or Lord) Iaurar Ben Abdella, Embassador from y^e high and mighty Mully Mahamed Shegue, Emperour of Morocco, King of Fess and Suss. etc.

G. Glover fe.

12. Morocco - **The arrival and intertainements of the embassador from the Emperor of Morocco,** 1637, 4° Frontispiece. (Folger 18165)

NEWES OVT OF
Cheshire of the new found
Well.

Imprinted at London by F. Kingſton for T. Man, 1600.

13. **Newes out of Cheshire**, 1600. 4° T.P. cut. (Bod. 4° L. 78 Art.)
[Repr. from M.-H. Davies, **La gravure ...**]

THE
Melancholie Knight.

By S. R.

¶ Imprinted at *London* by R. B. and are to be sold by
George Loftus, in Bishops-gate streete, neere the
Angell. **1 6 1 5.**

14. S., R. - **The melancholie knight,** 1615.
4° T.P. (Bod. 4° L 71 Art.)

A POSTE
VVITH A PAC
KETOFMAD
LETTERS.

Newly imprinted.

For Love.
For Life.

LONDON,
Printed for *John Marriot.*
1637.

15. Breton, N. - **A poste with a packet of madde letters**, 1634. 4° T.P. (Folger 3693)

16. Churchyard, Th. - **A light bon-
    dell of livly discourses called
    Churchyardes charge, etc.,**
    1580. 4° T.P. verso. (Folger
    5240) [Repr. from M.-H.
    Davies, **La gravure ....**]

THE
ENTERTAINMENT
OF THE HIGH AND
MIGHTY MONARCH
CHARLES

KING of *Great Britaine*,
France, and *Ireland*,

Into his auncient and royall City of
EDINBVRGH, the fiftee ith
of *Iune*, 1 6 3 3.

Printed at EDINBVRGH by *Iohn Wreittoun*. 1633.

17. Charles I, King - The entertainment
of the high and mighty monarch
Charles into his auncient city of Edinburgh, 1633. 4° (Folger 16680) [Repr.
from M.-H. Davies, La gravure...]

146 **THE**

MERCHANT
ROYALL.

A SERMON PREACHED AT
White-Hall before the Kings Maieſtie,
at the Nuptials of the Right Honou-
rable the Lord H A Y and his Lady,
vpon the Twelfe day laſt
being *Ianuar.6.*
1607.

18. Wilkinson, R. - **The merchant royall**, 1607. 4° T.P. (Folger 25658) [Repr. from M.-H. Davies, **La gravure ...**]

19. Digges, L. and T. - **A prognostication ever-
     lasting**, 1556. 4° T.P. verso. (Folger 6861)
     [Repr. from Bosanquet]

20. Heywood, Th. - **A true description of his Majesties royall ship built at Wool-witch,** 1637. 4° Facing T.P. (Folger 13367)

March, October. 1614.

Mars paingit et virgile

MARS take in hand this fixt Age to dispose,
Thy thine, with bloody wordes obiectes confuse;
Sophisticate *Dreamme's*, woundes and smiles:
Let these commerce the doughtie, if Wit failes.
Thy time is past *felf* meane; how comes excesse
Of Manly minde, which doth so fiercenesse presse.
Thy trampling Steed doth champ his flaming Bitt;
Pride, Discord, Anger, ouerthrow thy wit:
With carefull Armes to secret tender Soules?
Thus lawlull b'owes dissembled Loue controules.
Ne, luckle *Vlcanus* on high Poles dost hang
Sterne *Magnanimitie*, with Fishes the hang:
Where Monarchies, subdue all places,
Doth heart courageous, not il-fauour'd faces,
Harpie Victorie doth not entreat'd come,
In hat e Labour, Violence, Care, and some
Exceeding Heat, rough Valiancie, and Skill,
Strength, Strategems, all these thy heart doe fill.
Why should Plebeian vulgar rumors hisse
At Martiall pompe? nay, they thy feete do kisse:
When braue Behauiour they behold in thee,
And Gestures sweete, to exalt thy Degree.
Thus auncient *Roman* Nobles did arise
By Warres and Eloquence, the Valiant Wise,
Now Giue tell me; Why in this our Time,

March. October. 1614.

Mars the fift Age afflicts.

No Noble Smiles to sudden Honours clime,
It is, because no new thing now is donne?
Armies beyond rewardes doe runne.
Mars, let thy solid ioyes i'th fickle world
Strike vp Ambition that pure Aire takes hold,
Addict the actions of Slaues vnto thy fame:
Oft with Barbarian Bandes thou captiue Kinges didst greete,
A foe of thy Flagge, ro th'top of windie Fame;
Thrust through with Pikes, a Flea-bite, and a Game:
Craue her such popular, hollow Honour pelt,
Among their flowers of Knights the foe that fought;
And looke then on those Clownes with haughtie brewes,
Which knowes not Warre, with Warlike minds on lowe,
To act absurd speech like *Selmes* charmes:
Great things pertaine t'haud strength to handle Armes.
Though Heauen and Earth should fall on thy iron backe,
To hurt all furious Eagles power lacke.
Obiect thy Battles; with Warres all Kingdomes shake;
Let Boldnesse adde thee Strength, and Courage take;
But suffer not in Furie; th'is that heede:
The lion he feeles, the more that Mars doth bleede.
Smite thy Helmet, and thy noble Crest
'Neath Olive branch; Sing out thy Cunty rest;
For thou art a worthy one; but that thy luft
Makes fearefull Death t'accompanie th'vniust.
And yet vnlesse so all things a time be free;
In minde and body, how can bodies be?
Where as both flesh and blood doe Warres atchieue;
In flesh and blood thou must both die and liue.
If madly he doe double strength to strive,
Reason can not dispersed powers yoke:
Then let Duke Mars fight lesse, giue counsell more,
Valesse when Vertue all lay when Armies roare:

C 2

21. Dauncy, G. - His president for the starres... the almanacke, 1614. Sig. C v and C2. (Folger 435) [Repr. from M.-H. Davies, La gravure ...]

22. Gray - **An Almanack and prognostication for Dorchester**, 1588, Sig. A^v. (Bod. [MS] Ashm. 62. (6))

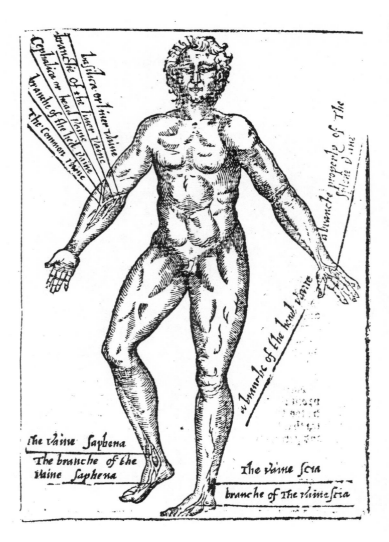

Basilica or Liver Vaine

branche of the Liver Vaine

Cephalica or head Vaine

branche of the hed Vaine

The Common Vaine

a branche properly of the Splene Vaine

a branche of the head vaine

the Vaine Saphena

The branche of the Vaine Saphena

The Vaine Scia

branche of The Vaine Scia

23. Rudston, T. - **A new almanacke and prognos-**
tication, 1607. 8° Sig. A2. (Bod. Douce
A 576)

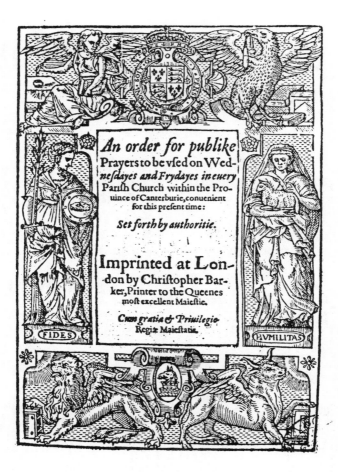

An order for publike Prayers to be vsed on Wednesdayes and Frydayes in euery Parish Church within the Prouince of Canterburie, conuenient for this present time:

Set forth by authoritie.

Imprinted at London by Christopher Barker, Printer to the Queenes most excellent Maiestie.

Cum gratia & Priuilegio Regiæ Maiestatis.

FIDES

HVMILITAS

24. Liturgies - An order for publicke prayers on Wednesdayes and Frydayes, 1586? 4° T.P. (Bodleian) [Repr. from M.-H. Davies, La gravure ...]

A new Enterlued for

Chyldren to playe, named Jacke Jugeler, both wytte, and very playſent. Newly Impꝛented.

The Players names.

Mayſter Boungrace	A galant
Dame coye	A Gentelwoman
Jacke Jugler	The vyce
Jenkin careaway	A Lackey.
Ales trype and go	A mayd.

Boūgrace.   Jacke Jugler.

25. Jugeler, Jack - A new enterlued for chyldren to playe, named Jacke Jugeler. Newly imprented, 1565? (Bod. Facs. E 58) [Repr. from M.-H. Davies, La gravure...]

26. Taylor, John - **Jack-A-Lent: his beginning and entertainment, with new additions,** 1620. 4° T.P. (Bod. Douce JJ.
170) [Repr. from M.-H. Davies, **La gravure ...**]

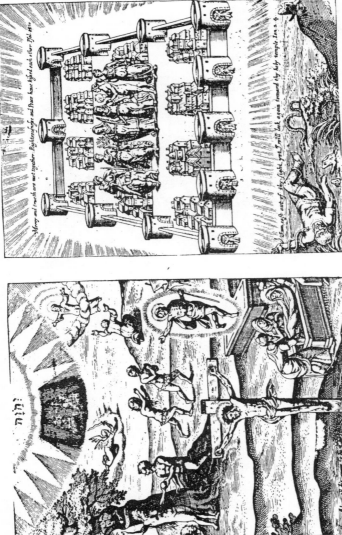

27. Fletcher, J. - **The history of the perfect-cursed-blessed man,**
1629. 4° P. 7 and p. 34. (Folger 11079) [Repr. from M.-H.
Davies, **La gravure...**]

140 *A Crab-tree*

28. Taylor, John - **Divers crabtree Lectures**, 1639. 12° P. 140. (Bod. Douce L 4)

A Kickſey Winſey:
OR
A Lerry Come-Twang:

Wherein *Iohn Taylor* hath ſatyrically
ſuited 800. of his bad debters, that
will not pay him for his returne
of his Iourney from Scotland.

*My debters like 7.eeles with ſlip'rie tailes,
One ſort I each, 6 ſlips away and failes.*

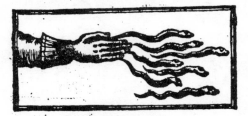

LONDON,
Printed by *Nicholas Okes,* for *Mathew
Walbancke,* dwelling at *Grayes Inne Gate,*
1619.

29. Taylor, John - A kicksey
winsey: or a lerry come-
twang: where-in John Tay-
lor hath satyrically suited
800 of his bad debters,
1624. 8° T.P. (Bod. B. 31
Med.) [Repr. from M.-H.
Davies, La gravure ···]

30. Ward, S. of Ipswich - **All in all**, 1622. 8° T.P. (Folger 25033a) [Repr. from M.-H. Davies, **La gravure ...**]

340

THE TRVE FORME, OF THE
Furnace, for the Anneiling in Glaſse, withall
the Inſtruments belonging therevnto .

31. Gedde, W. - A booke of sundry draughtes
principally for glasiers; whereunto is annexed
how to anneil in glas, 1615-16. 4° (Bod. G 29.
Art) [Repr. from M.-H. Davies, **La gravure...**]

32a. Harvey, J. - **An almanach
or annual Calender for
1584**. Sig. Dij verso (Bod.
Ashm. 62) [Repr. from
M.-H. Davies, **La gravure
...**]

32b. Hopton, A. - **An almanack
and prognostication**, 1607.
Sig. Cvi verso (Bod. Douce
A. 576) [Repr. from M.-H.
Davies, **La gravure...**]

5.

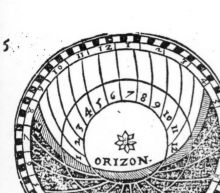

ORIZON

The vſe thereóf is thus.

❧ Know by the Table for that purpoſe, the riſing of the Sun for the day ye deſire, and vppon the ſame howres and neereſt quarter, in the vttermoſt margent lay the thredde, remoouing vp and downe the knot or Beade, till it lye vpon the Orizon lyne, there holde it ſtedfaſt at the center ende, and remoue your other hand to the howre of the clock, called the howre of the day, either before noone or after, the the knot among the Planets howers, ſhall ſhewe the iuſt howre of the Artificiall day expreſt by fygures of Arithmaticke, wherewith enter the Table of the Planets, with the day

The Inſtruction.

day at the head, and ſo the number of the howre ſhall ſhew you at the left ſide, the Planet that rules by day, and at the right ſide, the Planet that rules the ſame hower by night.

Example.

❧ The 20. of October being Tueſday, I would knowe what Planet raignes at three of the clock, 30. minutes after none. By the table of the ſunne ryſing I find that the 20. day of October, the ſun ryſeth at 7. of the clock 15. minutes, which found in the figure, I put the thred thereto, and ſet the knot on the Orizon, then remoue I the thred to 3, of the clocke, 30. minutes afternoone in the margent, and the knotte ſhewes the eleuenth houre of the artificiall day, wherwith I enter the table of Planets vnder Tueſday, and right againſt 11. at the leſe ſide is ♂ which rules that preſent howre.

❧ Againe at tenne of the clock at night I woulde do the like, I remoue the thred to ten in the margent, and the knot amongſt the howres of the night, ſhewes the 5. howre of the artificiall night. wherewith I enter the Table as before, and find right againſt 5. at the right ſide ♀ which rules that preſent howre, &c.

Thys doone, if ye deſire to know how long the Planet of that howre hath ruled, or how long hee ſhal rule, doe thus. Set the thredde to the time that ye deſire to know the Planets howre, and if the knot light vppon the time that deuides the artificiall houres, then and at that inſtant begins the planetarie houre, but if the knot fall within the ſpace, remoue your knot to the lyne proceding, then ſhall the thredde in the margent ſhew at what time the Planet began to raigne, after-ward remoue the knot to the lyne following, and the thred in the margent will ſhew you the inſtant of the clocke when the Planet ſhall ceaſe to rule, whereof take thys example. ❧ Sun-

33. Burton, R. - **A brief treatise,**
1591. 8° P. 86. (Bod. A J. 17)
[Repr. from M.-H. Davies,
La gravure...]

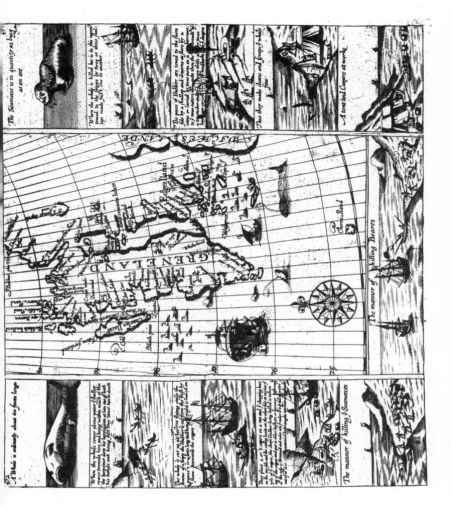

34. Pellham, Ed. - **Gods power a. providence: shewed in the miraculous preservation of eight Englishmen, left by mischance in
Green-land...**, 1631. Folio map. (Huntington Library)

344

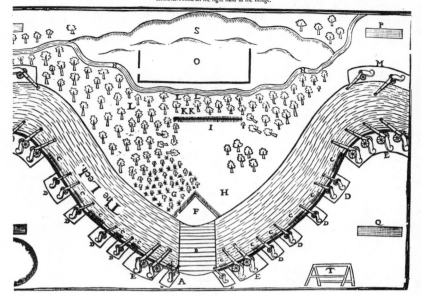

Place this betwixt pag. 150. & 151. Our Cutter hath made the Ordnance too long, and to lye too farre into the River. The Hole also marked with R, should have beene on the right hand of the Bridge.

35. Swedish Intelligencer - **The Swedish Intelligencer. Second Part,** 1632. Map between 150 and 151. (Folger 23524) [Repr. from M.-H. Davies, **La gravure...**]

36. Malbie, Sir N. - **A plaine and easie way to remedie a horse that is foundered in his feete, etc.**, 1594. 4° (British Library, C 31. g. 11) [Repr. from M.-H. Davies, **La gravure...**]

37. Stallenge, W. - **Instructions for the increasing of mulberie trees a. breeding of silke-wormes,** 1609. 4° Sig. C 3v. (Folger 23138) [Repr. from M.-H. Davies, **La gravure ...**]

38. Harman, Th. - **The groundworke of conny-catching**, 1592. T.P. 4° (Huntington HEH 61333) [Repr. from M.-H. Davies, **La gravure...**]

39. Fitz, Sir John - **The bloudy booke, or the tragical end of Sir J. Fitz**, 1605. 4° T.P. (British Library R. b. 41) [Repr. from M.-H. Davies, **La gravure ...**]

40. Goodcole, H. - **Natures cruell step-dames**, 1637. 4° T.P. (Folger 12012) [Repr. from M.-H. Davies, **La gravure...**]

41. Ravaillac, F. - **The terrible and deserved death of F. Ravilliack, shewing the manner of his execution**, 1610. 4° (Folger 20755) [Repr. from M.-H. Davies, **La gravure....**]

42. Flood, Griffin - **The life and death of G. Flood, informer**, 1623. 4° T.P. and verso. (Folger 11090) [Repr. from M.-H. Davies, **La gravure ...**]

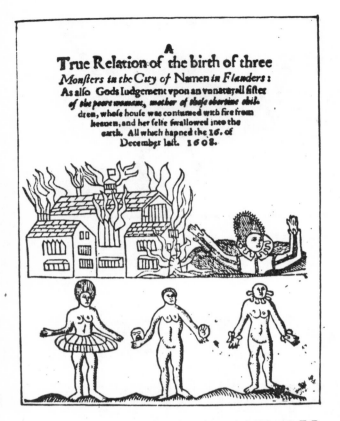

A

True Relation of the birth of three
Monsters in the City of Namen in Flanders :
As also Gods Iudgement vpon an vnnaturall sister
of the poore woman, mother of these obortine chil-
dren, whose house was contained with fire from
heauen, and her selfe swallowed into the
earth. All which hapned the 16. of
December last. 1608.

43. Relation - **A true relation...**, 1609. 4° T.P.
(Folger 20863.5) [Repr. from M.-H. Davies,
La gravure ...]

44.   **A true and wonderfull relation of
a whale**, n.d. T.P. (Bod. Wood B 35)
[Repr. from M.-H. Davies, **La gravure
...**]

THE COLD YEARE.
1614.

A deepe Snow : In which,

Men and Cattell haue perished,

To the generall losse of Farmers, Grasiers, Hus-
bandmen, and all sorts of people in the Countrie ; and no lesse hurtfull to Citizens.

Written Dialogue-wise, in a plaine familiar talke betweene a
London Shop-keeper, and a North-Country-man.
*In which, the Reader shall finde many
thinges for his profit.*

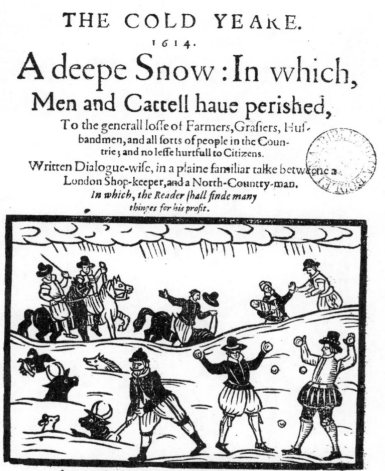

Imprinted at London by *W. W.* for *Thomas Langley*
in Iuie lane, where they are to be sold, 1615.

45. Year - **The cold yeare,** 1614: a deepe
snow: etc., 1615. 4° T.P. (Bod. L 68
Art.)

A time to love and a time to hate; a time of warre and a time of peace. Eccl. 3. 8.

46. Scott, Th. - **Vox Dei**, 1623? 4° T.P. (Folger 22097a)

The explanation of this Mappe appeareth in the 4. pages of profe next following, wherein you fhall finde from A. to M. *euery particular briefte handled.*

47. L., I. - **The birth, purpose and mortall wound of the Romish holie league**, 1589. Folio map. (Bod. B. 4. 3. Linc (4)

AVXILIO·DI·VINO

SIC PARVIS MAGNA

Drake penorati novit quem terminus orbis,
Et quem, bis mundi vidit vterq Polus:
Si taceant homines, facient te Sidera notum,
Sol nescit comitis non memor esse sui.

48. Drake, Sir Francis - **The world encompassed
by Sir F. Drake...**, 1628. 4° T.P. (Folger
7161) [Repr. from M.-H. Davies, **La gravure
...**]

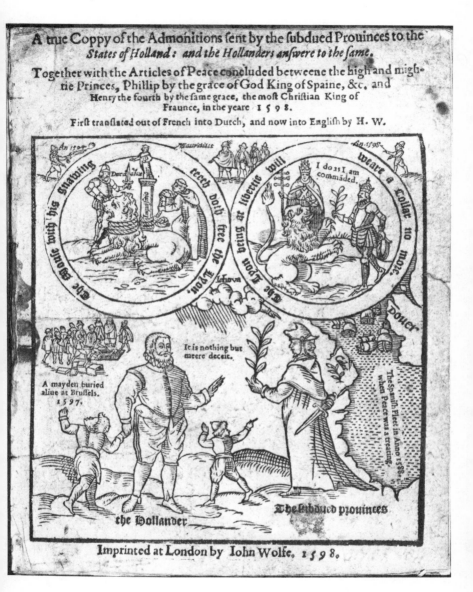

A true Coppy of the Admonitions sent by the subdued Prouinces to the *States of Holland:* and the Hollanders *answere to the same.*

Together with the Articles of Peace concluded betweene the high and mightie Princes, Phillip by the grace of God King of Spaine, &c. and Henry the fourth by the same grace, the most Christian King of Fraunce, in the yeare 1 5 9 8.

First translated out of French into Dutch, and now into English by H. W.

Imprinted at London by Iohn Wolfe. 1 5 9 8.

49. Netherlands - **A true copy of the admonitions sent by the sub-dued provinces to the States of Holland, etc.,** 1598. 4° T.P. (Folger 18465)

50. Vincent, P. - **The lamentations of Germany**, 1638. Folio map.
(Folger 24761)

51. Lynne, W. - **The beginning and endynge of all popery,** 1548? 4° (Bod. Mal. 711) [Repr. from M.-H. Davies, **La gravure ...**]

52. Vicars, J. - **Mischeefes Mysterie**, 1617 4°
T.P. & verso. (Bod. H 21 Art.) [Repr.
from M.-H. Davies, **La gravure** ...]

THE
NEW LIFE
of Virginea :
DECLARING THE
FORMER SVCCESSE AND PRE-
sent estate of that plantation, being the second
part of *Nova Britannia.*

Published by the authoritie of his Maiesties
Counsell of *Virginea.*

LONDON,
Imprinted by *Felix Kyngston* for *William Welby,* dwelling at the
signe of the Swan in Pauls Churchyard. **1612.**

53. Johnson, R. - The new life of
Virginea: being the second part
of Nova Britannia, 1612. 4° T.P.
(Folger 14700) [Repr. from M.-H.
Davies, La gravure...]

360

54. Crofts, R. - **The lover, or nuptiall love**, 1638. 8° Frontispiece. (Folger 6042) [Repr. from M.-H. Davies, **La gravure...**]

55. Dekker, Th. - **A rod for run-awayes**, 1625. 4° T.P. (Bod. Mal. 601) [Repr. from M.-H. Davies, **La gravure...**]

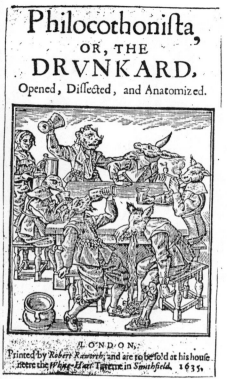

56. Heywood, Th. - **Philocotho-
    nista, or the drunkard,
    opened, dissected and anat-
    omized**, 1635. 4° T.P. (Bod.
    Douce H H 227) [Repr.
    from M.-H. Davies, **La gra-
    vure ...**]

57. Copland, R. - **Gyl of Braint-
    fords testament newly com-
    piled**, 1560? 4° Sig. B3.
    (Bod. S. Selden d. 45) [Repr.
    from M.-H. Davies, **La gra-
    vure ...**]

362

58. Rowley, S. - **When You see me, You know me**, 1613. 4° T.P. (Tudor Facsimile Texts, 1913) [Repr. from M.-H. Davies, **La gravure** ...]

The Country-man. The Courtier.

59. Breton, N. - **The court and country, dialogue-wise between a courtier and
a countryman**, n.d. 4° T.P. (Folger 3642)
[Repr. from M.-H. Davies, **La gravure ...**]

PLEASANT
Quippes for Vpſtart
Newfangled Gentle-
women.

Or, A Glaſſe

60. Gosson, S. - **Quippes for upstart newfangled
gentle women, etc.,** 1595. 4° T.P. verso (Tudor
Facsimile Text Reprint)

WOE TO
DRVNKARDS.

A Sermon by S A M V E L   W A R D
Preacher of *Ipſwich*.

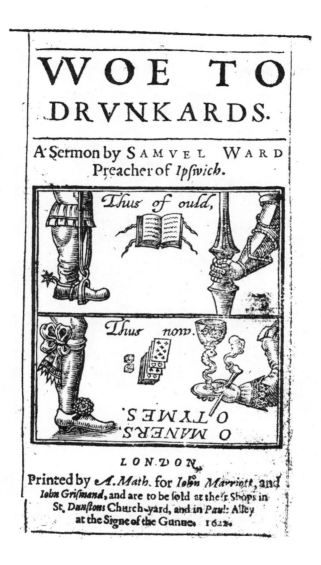

Thus of ould,

Thus now.

O MANERS O TYMES.

LONDON,
Printed by *A. Math.* for *Iohn Marriott*, and
Iohn Griſmand, and are to be ſold at their Shops in
St. *Dunſtons* Church-yard, and in *Pauls* Alley
at the Signe of the Gunne. 1622.

61. Ward, S. of Ipswich - **Woe to drunkards,**
1627. 8° T.P. cut. (Huntington Library)

366

A. All these square must bee set with trees, the gardens & orchards, and must stand in spaces be twixt the trees, and in the borders and fences.

B. Trees 20.yard asunder.

C. Garden knott.

D. Kitchin Garden.

E. Bridge.

F. Conduct.

G. Staires.

O. Walkes set with great wood thicke.

I. Walkes set with great wood round about your Orchard.

K. The out fence.

L. The out fence set with stone fruit.

M. Mount.

N. Still-house.

O. Good standing for Bees, if you haue an house.

R. If the Riuer run by your dore, and vnder your mouth it will be pleasant.

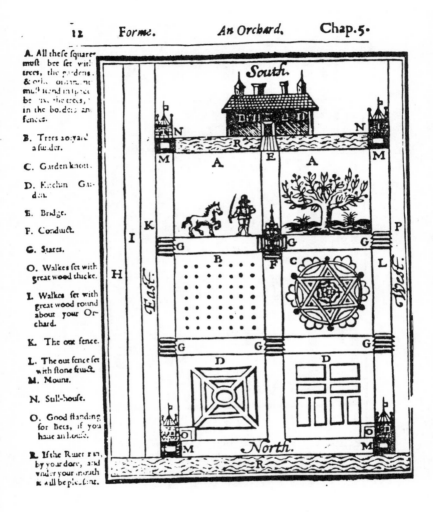

62.   Lawson, W. - **A new orchard and garden, etc. with the country housewifes garden,** 1618. 4° P. 12. (Folger 15329) [Repr. from M.-H. Davies, **La gravure** ...]

St.
PAVLES-CHVRCH.
HER BILL FOR THE
PARLIAMENT,

As it was prefented to the Kings Matie
on *Midlent-Sunday* laft , and intended for the
view of that moft high and Honorable Court,
and generally for all fuch as beare-good
will to the reflourifhing eftate of
the faid C H V R C H.

Partly in Verfe, partly in Profe.

Penned and publifhed for her good by H E N: F A R L E Y
Author of her Complaint.

For the Lord will comfort Zion
and repayre all her decayes: Hee
will make her Defert like Paradice,

and her Wildernesse like the Garden of the Lord. Mirth and joy
shall bee found there, Thankf-

giving and the voyce of melody.
Isaiah 11. 3.

Anno Dom. *M. D C. X X I.*

63. Farley, H. - **St. Paules-Church her Bill for
the Parliament,** 1621. 4° T.P. cut. (Bod. H 21
Art.)

COTSWOLD GAMES.

64. Walbancke, M. - **Annalia Dubrensia: Dr. Dovers Olimpick games**, 1636. 4° T.P. (Folger 24954) [Repr. from M.-H. Davies, **La gravure....**]

65. Deceit - **The deceyte of women**, 1562?
4° T.P. (Huntington HEH 60965) [Repr.
M.-H. Davies, **La gravure...**]

66. Haec Vir - **Haec vir or the womanish-
man**, 1620. 4° T.P. (Folger 12599) [Repr.
from M.-H. Davies, **La gravure ...**]

The English Vſurer.

67. Blaxton, J. - **The English usurer**, 1634. 4°
T.P. (Folger 3129) [Repr. from M.-H.
Davies, **La gravure...**]

68. Somerset, Co. of - **A true report of certaine overflowings of waters in Summerset-shire, etc.**, 1607. 4° T.P. (Folger
22915) [Repr. from M.-H. Davies, **La
gravure...**]

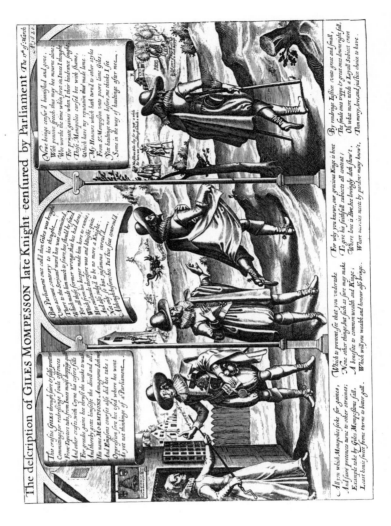

69.	Description - **The description of Giles Mompesson late knight censured by Parliament**, 1620. Folio sheet. (Folger 6769.5)

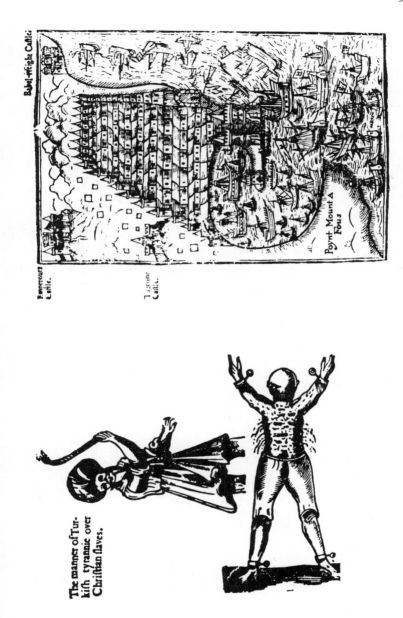

70. Knight, F. - **A relation of seaven yeares slaverie under the Turkes of Argeire**, 1640. 4° Facing the T.P. and facing p. 1. (Folger 15048a) [Repr. from M.-H. Davies, **La gravure ...**]

374

COACH and **SEDAN,**

Pleasantly Disputing for Place and Precedence;

The *Brewers-Cart* being Moderator.

Spectatum admiss, risum teneatis amici?

LONDON:

Printed by *Robert Raworth*, for *Iohn Crowch*; and are to be sold by *Edward Paxton*, dwelling at *Pauls* chayne, neere Doctors-Commons. 1636.

71. Peacham, H. Jr. - **Coach and Sedan pleasantly disputing,** 1636. 4° T.P. (Folger 19501) [Repr. from M.-H. Davies, **La gravure...**]

72. Westward - **Westward for smelts, etc.,**
1620. 4° T.P. (Folger 25292) [Repr. from
M.-H. Davies, **La gravure...**]

73. S., M. - **The poore orphans court**, 1636. 4°
Frontispiece (Bod. Gough. Lond. 7 (1))

74. Ward, Captain - **Newes from sea of two notorious Pyrates, Ward and Danseker,** 1609. 4° T.P. (Folger 25022) [Repr. M.-H. Davies, **La gravure ...**]

75. Timberlake, H. - **A relation of the travells of two English pilgrimes,** 1631. 4° T.P. (Bod. Arch. A e. 9) [Repr. from M.-H. Davies, **La gravure ...**]

76. Calverley, Wm. - **A dyalogue
betweene the playntife and
the defendaunt**, 1535? 4°
T.P. verso (Folger 4370)
[Repr. from M.-H. Davies,
La gravure...]

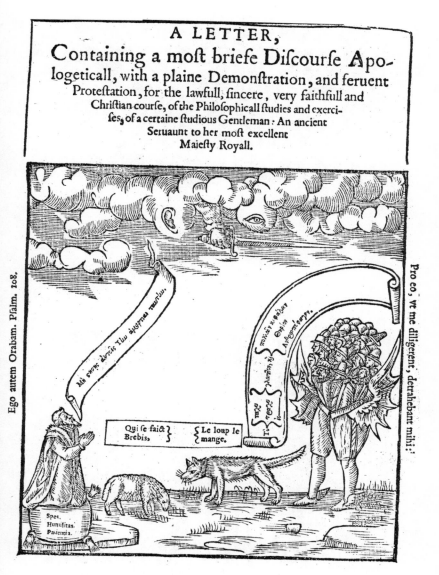

77. Dee, John - **A letter nine yeeres since, written and first published,** 1603. 4° T.P. (Folger 6461)

78. Hilliard, J. - **Fire from Heaven**, 1613.
4° T.P. (Folger 13507) [Repr. from
M.-H. Davies, **La gravure...**]

79. Fennor, Wm. - **Pluto his travailes**, 1611.
4° T.P. (British Library 4091. aa. 24)
[Repr. from M.-H. Davies, **La gravure...**]

80. Cooper, Th. - **The cry and revenge of blood, expressing the haynousnesse of murther**, 1620. 4° T.P. (Folger 5698) [Repr. from M.-H. Davies, **La gravure...**]

81. Witches - **Witches apprehended, examined and executed**, etc., 1613. 4° T.P. (Bod. E. 17 Art.) [Repr. from M.-H. Davies, **La gravure...**]

82. Melton, J. - **Astrologaster, or the figure-caster,**
1620. 4° T.P. (Bodleian) [Repr. from M.-H. Davies,
La gravure...]

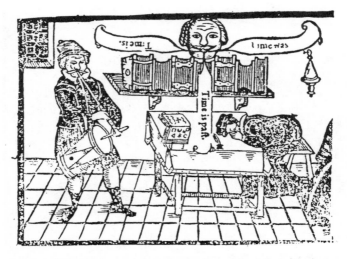

83a. Greene, R. - **The honorable historie of**
Frier Bacon and Frier Bongay, 1630. 4°
T.P. (Folger 12268) [Repr. from M.-H.
Davies, **La gravure...**]

83b. Marlowe, C. - **The tragicall history of the
life and death of Doctor Faustus**, 1631. 4°
T.P. (Folger 17436) [Repr. from M.-H.
Davies, **La gravure ...**]

SELECTIVE BIBLIOGRAPHY

Secondary sources appear fully described in the footnotes. Primary sources have been limited to a listing of illustrated pamphlets since the **Short-Title Catalogue** does not distinguish between illustrated and unillustrated pamphlets. Unless stated otherwise, the place of publication is assumed to be London.

I. PRIMARY SOURCES

A. ILLUSTRATED PAMPHLETS

Numbers refer to POLLARD and REDGRAVE, **Short-Title Catalogue,** from which most bibliographical descriptions are derived. Numbers followed by points refer to the **New STC.** Queries indicate that the works mentioned do not appear in **STC.**

3	A., G.	**Pallas armata, the Gentlemans armorie** wherein the use of the rapier and sword is displayed. 8° J. D. f. J. Williams, 1639.
5	A., J.	**A perfyte pronostycacion perpetuall.** 12° R. Wyer, (1555?).
16	A., R. Gent	**The valiant Welshman or Chronicle history of Caradoc the great.** 4° G. Purslowe f. R. Lownes, 1615.
23	ABBOT, Elizabeth	**The apprehension and execucion of E. Abbott.** 4° f. H. Gosson, 1608.
82	ABSTRACT	**An abstract of some speciall forreigne** occurences. 4° f. M. Butter a. N. Bourne, 1638.
109	ADAMS, Thomas	**Diseases of the soule; a discourse. 4° G. Purslowe f. J. Budge, 1616.**
197	AGE	**The phantastick age; or the anatomy of Englands vanity.** Ballad. f. T. Lambert (1634).
250	ALABASTER, William	**Roxana, tragaedia, a plagiarii unguibus vindicta, aucta & agnita.** 8° Gul. Jones, 1632.
339	ALEXANDER, William, Earl of Stirling	**An elegie on the death of Prince Henrie.** 4° Edinburgh, A. Hart, 1612.
341		**An encouragement to colonies.** 4° W. Stansby, 1624.
341a		(Variant dated 1625.)
342		(A. Imp.) **The mapp and description of New-England; together with a Discourse of plantation.** 4° f. N. Butter, 1630.

388

459		A new almanack for 1572 for the meridian of Oxenforde. fol. (R. Watkins a. J. Roberts).
461	HOPTON, A.	An almanack and prognostication serving Shrewsbury. 8° f. the co. of Stationers. 1606, etc.
462	HUBRIGH, J.	(An almanacke a. prognostication for 1553?) fol. N. Hyll f. J. Turke, s. d.
464	HURING, S.	An almanach a. pronostication for 1551. s. sh. fol. J. Turck, s. d.
474	LAET, Jaspar	An almanack a. pronostication of 1541. 16°.
477		1545, 46. 16° J. Herforde, s. d.
481	LOW, H.	An almanack a. prognosticacion for 1544, etc. 8° J. Kingston a. H. Sutton, 1554, etc.; T. Marshe, 1563, etc.
490.2	NEVE, John	A new almanacke a. prognostication for Norwich. 8° f. the co. of Stationers, 1636.
491	NORTON, Humfrey	An almanacke a. prognostication for 1581. 8° (Watkins a. Roberts, 1581).
492	NOSTRADAMUS	An almanacke for 1559. 8° H. Sutton f. L. Haryson, 20 fe. 1559.
492.2		An almanacke for the yere 1562. 8°
493		An alminacke and prodigious premonstration for 1566. 8° H. Denham, s. e.
493.8	OSBORNE, G.	Almanacke for...1622. 12° Co. of Stationers. 1622.
507	RUDSTON, T.	A new almanacke and prognostication. 8° f. the co. of Stationers, s. d. (1607, 1611, 12, 15, 19, 24, 27).
509	SECURIS, John	An almanacke a. prognostication. fol. J. Waley, (1562).
520	VAUGHAN, L.	A newe almanacke a. prognostication for 1559. T. Marshe, s. d.
526	WESTHAWE, R.	An almanacke a. prognostication for 1594, etc. 8° R. Watkins a. James Roberts, s. d. 1592.
527	WHITE, J.	A new almanacke a. prognostication. 8° f. the Co. of Stationers, 1613.
543	AMADIS, De Gaule	The ancient and honourable history of Amadis de Gaule. Tr. A. M. fol. N. Okes, 1618.
544		pts. 1 a. 2. fol. N. Okes, 1619.
546	AMANT	A certayn treatye most wyttely devysed, entytled, Lamant mal Traite de sa mye. 8° R. Wyer (1543).
547	AMBOYNA	Newes out of East India of the cruell usage of our English merchants at Amboyna. (Ballad) 2 pt. s. sh. fol. f. F. Coules (1625?).

564	ANABAPTISTS	A treuue nyeuu tydinges of the woderfull worckes of the Rebaptisers of Muster in Westuaell. 4º (s. n.).
598	ANDREWES, Lancelot, Bp.	The copie of the sermon preached on Good-Friday before the Kings Maiestie. 4º R. Barker (after 1610?).
639	ANGELOS, Christopher	Christopher Angell, a grecian, who tasted of many stripes inflicted by the Turkes. 4º Oxford, J. Lichfield a. W. Wrench, 1617.
693	ANTWERP	Strange newes from Antwarpe the 12 of August 1612. 4º R. Blower, 1612.
732	ARDEN, Alice	The complaint and the lamentation of Mistresse Arden, of Feversham in Kent. 2 pts. br. fol. f. C. W(right 1633?).
735	ARDEN, Thomas	The lamentable and true tragedie of M. Arden of Feversham. 4º Eliz. Allde, 1633.
773	ARMIN, Robert	The history of the two maids of More-clacke, with the life of John in the hospitall. 4º N. O(kes) f. T. Archer, 1609.
774		The Italian taylor, and his boy. 4º f. T. P(avier), 1609.
776	ARMS	The armes of the tobachonists. s. sh. fol. R. Shorleyker, 1630.
809	ARTHUR, John	Deeds against nature, or the murders committed by J. Arthur a. Martha Scambler. 4º 1614.
859	ASKHAM, Anthony	A prognostication for the yere mccccciiii. 8º W. Powell, (1553?).
903	ATTOWELL, George	Francis new jigge. Ballad f. J. W. (1595).
1026	B., G.	A fig for the Spaniard, or Spanish spirits. 4º J. Woolfe, sold by W. Wright, 1591.
1027		(A. Ed.) 4º J. Woolfe solde by W. Wright, 1592.
1048	B. J. Gentleman	A letter sent by I. B., gentleman unto mayster R. C. esquire. 8º H. Binneman f. A. Kitson (1572).
1049	B. J. (merchant)	The merchants aviso. 4º John Norton, 1607.
1208	BAINBRIDGE, John	An astronimicall description of the late comet from the 18. of Novemb. 1618 to the 16. of December following. 4º E. Griffin for J. Parker, 1619.
1243	BALDWIN, William	The funeralles of King Edward the Sixt. 4º T. Marshe, 1560.
1327	BALLAD	Come buy this new ballad, before you doe goe. 2 pts. Br. fol. Assignes of T. Symcocke (1625?).

1331		A new ballad, containing a communication between the carefull wife and the comfortable husband. Br. fol. f. H. Gosson (1630?).
1332		A pleasant new ballad you may behold, etc. 2 pts. Br. fol. f. H. Gosson (1630).
1376	BARBARY	A dolorous discourse, of a most terrible battel, fought in Barbarie. 8° J. Charlewood a. T. Man (1579).
1376.?		(A. Ed.)
1417	BARKER, Andrew	A true and certaine report of the beginning, proceedings and now present estate of Captaine Ward a. Danseker, the two late famous pirates. 4° W. Hall sold by J. Helme, 1609.
1421	BARKER, John	The plagues of Northomberland. s. sh. fol. T. Colwell (1570).
1422		The true description of a monsterous chylde. s. sh. fol. W. Gryffith (1564).
1445	BARLOW, W. (Archp.)	The navigators supply. 4° G. Bishop, R. Newberry and R. Barker, 1597.
1583	BATEMAN, Stephen	The golden booke of the leaden goddes. 4° T. Marshe, 1577.
1602–1605	BAYLY, Lewis Bp. of Bangor	The practise of pietie. 12° f. J. Hodgets, 1613, 1619, 1620, 1623.
1607–1611		ibid., f. R. Allot, 1625?, 1627, 1630 (in 8°), 1633.
1613–1614		ibid., f. R. Allot, 1635 (in 8°), 1735 (in 12°)
1670	BEAUMONT, F. a. FLETCHER, J.	A king and no king. 4° f. T. Walkley, 1619.
1676		The maides tragedy (Anon.). 4° f. F. Constable, 1619.
1677		(A Imp.) 4° f. R. Higgenbotham, 1619.
1678		Second impression, Newly perused, augmented and enlarged. (Anon.). 4° f. F. Constable, 1622.
1679		Third impression, revised and refined. 4° A. M(athews) f. R. Hawkins, 1630.
1680		Fourth impression. 4° E. G(riffin) f. H. Shepherd, 1638.
1681		Phylaster. Or love lyes a bleeding. 4° f. T. Walkley, 1620.
1791	BEDFORD, Thomas	A true and certaine relation of a strange birth borne at Stone-house. (Init. Th. B.) 4° A. Griffin f. A. Bowler, 1635.
1796	BEDWELL, William	Mesolabium architectonicum, that is a most rare instrument for measuring. 4° J. N(orton) f. W. Garet, 1631.

1797		(A. Ed.) 4° J. Norton, 1639.
1798		Trigonum architectonicum; or the carpenters rule, explained. s. sh. fol. (s. p. R. Field? 1614?).
1799	BEGGAR	The cunning northerne begger, who all the by-standers doth earnestly pray. Ballad. 2 pts. F. Coules (1634).
1807	BELL, Adam	Adambel, etc. 4° W. Copland, 1550?
1809		(A. Imp.) 4° (W. Jaggard f. J. Roberts, 1605?).
1810		(A. Ed.) 4° W. Jaggard, 1610.
1811		(A. Ed.) 4° T. Cotes a. R. Cotes sold by M. Trundle, 1628.
1812		(A. Ed.) 4° T. Cotes a. R. Cotes sold by F. Coules, 1632.
1813		Adam Bell. The second part. 4° f. J. Wright, 1616.
1817	BELL, Thomas	The downefall of poperie. 4° f. N. Butter, 1604.
1877	BENLOWES, Edward	A buckler against the fear of death. (Init. E. B.) 8° Cambridge, R. Daniel, sold by M. Sparkes, Junior.
1904	BERKSHIRE	Looke up and see wonders. A miraculous apparition in the ayre, seen in Barkeshire. 4° (M. Flesher) f. R. Michell, 1628.
1979	BETTE, T.	A newe ballad intituled. Agaynst rebellious and false rumours. s. sh. fol. W. Griffith, 1570.
1989	BEVIS, of Hampton	Syr Bevys of Hampton. 4° W. Copland (1565?).
1990		(A. Ed.) Sir Bevis of Hampton. 4° T. East (1582?).
1992		(A. Ed.) The historie of Bevis of Hampton. 4° (1620?) (wants t. p.).
1994		(A. Ed.) Syr Bevis of Hampton. 4° W. Stansby (1626?)
3056	BIGGES, Walter	A summarie a. true discourse of Sir Frances Drakes West Indian voyage. (Ed. T. Cates) 4° R. Field, 1589.
3056.1		(A. Ed.)
3057		(A. Ed.) 4° R. Ward, 1589.
3078	BIRCH, Wm.	A new balade of the worthy seruice done by maister Strangwige in Fraunce. s. sh. fol. A. Lacie f. W. Owen (1563).
3129	BLAXTON, John	The English Usurer. Or usury condemned by the most learned divines of the Ch. of Eng. Collected by J. Blaxton. 4° J. Norton, sold by F. Bowman, Oxford, 1634.
3129a		(A. Imp. called) Second impression.

3386	BORDE, A.	The pryncyples of astronamye in maner and prognosticacyon to worldes end. 8° R. Copland, c. 1542.
3435	BOWLE, John	A sermon preached at Flitton Bedford at the funeral of Henrie E. of Kent. (Init. I. B.). 4° W. Stansby f. R. Woodroffe, 1615.
3538	BRAHE, Tycho	Learned Tico Brahe his astronomicall conjectur of the new and much Admired (star) which appered in the year 1572. 4° B. A. and T. F. for Michael Sparke and Samuel Nealand, 1632.
3585	BRATHWAITE, Richard	A solemn joviall disputation briefly shadow-ing the law of drinking. (The smoaking age, with the life a. death of tobacco. 8° Oenozythopolis (London, Griffin) 1617.
3639	BRETON, Nicholas	Cornu–copiae. Pasquils nightcap. 4° f. T. Thorp, 1612.
3641		The court and country, dialogue–wise between a courtier and a countryman. 4° G. Eld. f. J. Wright, 1618.
3642		(A. Imp., with a new title and two wood-cuts at the bottom.)
3671		A murmurer. 8° R. Raworth, sold by J. Wright, 1607.
3685		A poste with a packett of madde letters. Newly enlarged. 4° f. J. Smethicke, 1603.
3685.2		(A. Ed.)
3685.8		(A. Ed.)
3686		The second part. 4° R. B. f. J. Browne a. J. Smethicke, 1606.
3687		(A. Ed.) The fourth time enlarged. 4° J. W(indet) f. J. Smethicke a. J. Browne, 1607.
3688		(A. Ed.) The fourth time enlarged. 4° J. W(indet) f. J. Smethicke a. J. Browne, 1609.
3689		(A. Ed.) 4° W. Stansby f. J. Marriot, 1620.
3692–3693		(A. Ed.) 4° F. J. Marriot, 1633, 1634, 1637.
3704		Strange news out of divers counties. (Init. B. N.) 4° W. Jones f. G. Fairbeard, 1622.
3717.5	BREWER, Thomas	A dialogue between a cittizen, and a poore country–man and his wife, in the countrey. 4° R. Oulton f. H. Gosson, 1636.
3718		A knot of fooles, etc. 4° f. F. Grove, 1624.

3719		The life and death of the merry devill of Edmonton, with the pleasant prancks of Smug the smith. 4° T. P(urfoot jr?) f. F. Faulkner, 1631.
3722		The weeping lady: or London like Ninivie in sackcloth. 4° B. A(lsop) a. T. F(awcet) f. M. Rhodes, 1625.
3759	BRINCKMAIR, L.	The warnings of Germany by wonderfull signes. 8° J. N(orton) f. J. Rothwell, 1638.
3791	BRISSET, Georges	The apologie of G. Brisset. Written upon consideration of the murther of the late French King. 4° f. W. Barley a. J. Baily, 1610.
3907	BROWNE, Agnes	The witches of Northamptonshire, A. Browne, J. Vaughan...who were all executed. 4° T. Purfoot f. A. Johnson, 1612.
3920	BROWNIST	A whip for the back of a backsliding Brownist. Ballad f. H. Chrouch, (1640?).
3946	BRUTON, William	Newes from the East Indies, or a voyage to Bengalla, with the state of the Court of Malcandy. 4° J. Okes, sold by h. Blunden, 1638.
4038	BULLEIN, William	A dialogue bothe pleasaunt and pietifull ag. the fever pestilence. 8° J. Kingston, 1578.
4104	BURDET, R.	The refuge of a sinner. s. sh. fol. R. Jones, 1565.
4137	BURTON, Henry	The baiting of the popes bull. (Init. H. B.) 4° W. J(ones) f. M. Sparke, 1627 (see also STC 4137.2, 4137 a. b. again poor cataloguing).
4163?	BURTON, Robertus	A brief treatise. 8° Charlwood 1591.
4241	BYLL, Thomas	A godly song, entituled, A farewell to the world. 2 pts. br. fol. f. H. Gosson (1630?).
4273	C. H.	Londons lord have mercy upon us. A true relation of five modern plagues. s. sh. fol. f. R. Harper (1637?).
4274	C. H.	Londons vacation, and the countries tearme. 8° f. R. Harper, 1637.
4279	C., I. or J.	A handkercher for parents' wet eyes. 12° E. A(llde) f. M. Sparke, 1630.
4370	CALVERLEY, William	A dyalogue bitwene the playntife and the defendaunt. 4° T. Godfray (1535?).
4537?	CAMPION, Edmund	A true report of the death and martyrdom of M. Campion Jesuite. 8° R. Verstegan, 1582.
4538	CAMPION, Thomas	The description of a maske, in honour of the Lord Hayes. 4° J. Windet f. J. Brown, 1607.

4658	CARLSTADT	Strange fearful a. true newes, which happened at Carlstadt in Croatia. Tr. 8º R. B(arker) f. G. Vincent a. W. Blackwell (1606).
4768	CASH, Thomas	Two horrible murders done in Lincolnshire, by two husbands, T. Cash, J. Dilworth. 4º f. J. Wright, 1607.
4790	CATANEO, Girolamo	Most brief tables to know howe manye rackes of footmen go to the making of a just battayle. Tr. H. G. 4º W. Williamson f. J. Wight, 1574.
4791		(A. Ed.) 4º T. East f. J. Wight, 1588.
4889	CAWWOOD, the Rooke	The pleasant history of Cawwood the rooke. 4º T. C(otes) f. F. Groves, 1640.
4981	CHAPMAN, George	The memorable mask of the Middle Temple, and Lyncolns Inne. 4º G. Eld. f. George Norton (1613?).
5023	CHARLES I, King	The entertainment of the high and mighty monarch Charles into his auncient city of Edinburgh. 4º Edinburgh, J. Wreittown, 1633.
5062	CHASSANION, Jean	The merchandises of popish priests. 4º J. Roberts, 1604.
5063		(A. Ed.) 4º f. H. Gosson, 1629.
5102	CHAUNCIE, William	The conversion of a gentleman long tym misled in poperie. 4º f. J. Perin, 1587.
5114	CHELMSFORD	The apprehension a. confession of three notorious witches at Chelmsford, 5 July 1589. 4º E. Allde (1589).
5115		A detection of damnable driftes practized by three witches arraigned at Chelmisforde. 8º (correction of STC) f. E. White, 1579.
5118	CHESTER, Town of	Chesters triumph in honour of her prince. As it was performed upon S. Georges Day, 1610. 4º J. Windet f. J. B(rowne), 1610.
5205	CHRISTMAS	Christmas carolles newely imprinted. 8º W. Copland (1550?).
5207	CHRISTOPHERSON, John, Bp.	An exhortation to all menne to take hede of rebellion. 8º J. Cawood, 1554.
5239	CHURCHYARD, Thomas	A lamentable and pitifull description of the wofull warres in Flaunders. 4º R. Newberie, 1578.
5240		A light bondell of livly discourses called Churchyardes charge, etc. 4º J. Kyngston, 1580.
5257		A sparke of friendship and warme goodwill. 4º (s. P.) 1588.
5262.5	CHUTE, A.	Tabaco. 8º f. William Barlow, 1595.

5324	CIPRIANO, Giovanni	A most strange and wonderfull prophesie upon this troublesome world. Tr. A. Hollaway. 4° 1595.
5376	CLAYTON, Giles	The approoved order of martiall discipline. 4° J. C(harlwood) f. A. Kitsonne, 1591.
5395	Cleland, James	Jacob's well and Abbot's conduit paralleled. 4° R. Allot, 1626.
5396		A monument of mortalitie upon the death of Lodovick, Duke of Richmond. 4° W. Stansby f. R. Rounthwaite, 1624.
5413	CLEVES, Duchy of	Newes out of Cleave-land. 4° T. H(aviland) f. J. Budge, 1610.
5430	CLIMSELL, R.	A warning for maides; or the false, dissembling young man. Ballad. 2 pts. f. J. Wright (1636).
5441	CLOSSE, G.	The parricide papist, or cut-throate Catholicke. 4° f. C. Hunt, 1606.
5451	COACHES	The coaches overthrow; or a joviall exaltation of divers tradesmen, etc. Ballad. 2 pts. London, (1636).
5457	COCKAINE, Sir Th.	A short treatise of hunting. 4° T. Orwin f. T. Woodcocke, 1600.
5530	COKE, John	The debate betwene the heraldes of Englande and Fraunce. 8° Rycharde Wyer, 1550.
5620	CONCINI, Concino	The ghost of the marquesse d'Ancre, with his spirits attending him. 4° f. N. Bourne, 1617.
5663	COOKE, Alexander	More worke for a masse-priest. 4° W. Jones, 1621.
5663.1		(A. Ed.) 4° W. Jones, 1621.
5664		Yet more worke for a masse-priest. 4° W. Jones sold by W. Sheffard, 1622.
5666		(A. Ed.) 4° W. Jones, 1630.
5673	COOKE, John	Greenes Tu quoque: or, the cittie gallant. 4° f. J. Trundle, 1614.
5674		(A. Ed.) 4°. f. T. Dewe, 1622.
5675		(A. Ed.) 4° M. Flesher (1628?).
5698	COOPER, Thomas	The cry and revenge of blood expressing the haynousnesse of murther. 4° N. Okes f. J. Wright, 1620.
5728	COPLAND, Robert	Here begynneth the Complaynte of them that ben to late maryed. (Anon.) 4° W. de Worde (1535?).
5729		A complaynt of them that be to soone maryed. (Anon.) 4° W. de Worde (date?).
5730		Gyl of Braintfords testament newly compiled. 4° W. Copland (1560?).
5731		(A. Ed.) Iyll of breyntfords testament. 4° W. Copland (1562).

5732		The hye way to the Spytell hous. 4° R. Coplande (1536?).
5732.5		The Knight and the swan. 4° Copeland, 1550.
5734		The seven sorrowes that women have when theyr husbandes be deade. 8° W. Copland, 1568?
5765	CORK, City of	The lamentable burning of the city of Corke. Ballad. 2 pts. E. A(llde) (1622).
5766		A relation of the most lamentable burning of the Citie of Corke. 4° J. D(awson) f. N. Bourne a. T. Archer, 1622.
5767		The wonderfull battell of starelings: fought at the Citie of Corke. 4° N. B(ourne), 1622.
5796	CORTANO, Ludovico	Good newes to christendome; sent to a Venetian in Ligorne. 4° f. N. Butter, 1620.
5796.2		(A. Ed.) 4°.
5809	CORYATE, Thomas	Mr. T. Coriat to his friends in England sendeth greeting: from Agra. October 1616. 4° J. B(eale?) 1618.
5811		T. Coriate traveller for the English wits: greetings from the Court of the Great Mogul. 4° W. Jaggard a. H. Fetherston, 1616.
5811.a		(A. Ed.) 1614.
5878	COURTNEY, Charles	The life and execution of C. Courtney. 4° f. E. Marchant, 1612.
5904	COWLEY, A.	Loves riddle, a pastorall comaedie. 8° J. Dawson, f. H. Seile, 1638.
6033	CRAWSHEY, John	The countrymans instructor; containing remedies for diseases to cattle. 4° T. Cotes sold by M. Allot, 1636.
6024	CROFTS, Robert	The lover, or nuptial love. 8° B. Alsop a. T. F(awcet) f. R. Meighen, 1638.
6044		The terrestriall paradise, or, happinesse on earth. 12° T. Harper, f. W. Aderton, 1639.
6073	CROUCH, H.	The industrious smith wherin is showne, How plain dealing is overthrown, etc. Ballad. 2 pts. f. R. Harper, (1635?).
6074		Loves Court of Conscience. 8° f. R. Harper, 1637.
6074a		The mad-mans morrice, wherein you shall finde his trouble and grief. Ballad. 2 pts. f. R. Harper (1637?).
6101	CUCKOLD	Cuckolds haven; or, The marry'd mans miserie. Ballad. 2 pts. M. P(arsons) f. F. Grove (1638).

6102		The merry cuckold. Ballad. 2 pts. Assignes of T. Simcock (1630).
6122	CUPID	Cupids messenger. 4º M. F(lesher) sold by F. Grove, 1629.
6122.2		(A. Ed.) 4º.
6123		Cupids schoole. 8º E. Purslow f. F. Grove, sold by S. Pemell, 1632.
6169	D., I. or J.	Doctor Do'good's directions, to cure many diseases. Ballad. 2 pts. f. R. Harper (1635?).
6191	DAINTY	A new northeren jigge, called, Daintie come thou to me. Ballad. Assignes of T. Symcock (1638).
6214.2	DAMIANO, da Oedemira	The pleasaunt a. wittie playe of the cheasts renewed. 8º R. Hall f. J. Rowbothum, 1562.
6215		(A. Ed.) (Anon.) 8º T. Marshe, 1569.
6216		(A. Ed.) Ludus Scacchiae: Chesse-play. 4º H. Jackson, 1597.
6222	DANCE	The daunce and song of Death. Ballad. (J. Awdeley, 1569).
6223		(Dance of Death) Begin. Marke well the effect purtreyed here in all, etc. s. sh. fol. (s. p.) (1580?).
6224		The doleful dance and song of death; intituled Dance after my pipe. Ballad. (London? 1625?).
6317	DAVID	The story of David and Berseba. Ballad. 2 pts. f. J. Wright (1624).
6340	DAVIES, John of Hereford	A scourge for paper-persecutors by J. D. with a continu'd inquisition by A. H(olland). 4º f. H. H(olland) a. G. G(ibbs), 1625.
6345		The writing schoole-master. Sixtene edition enlarged. obl. 8º f. M. Sparke, 1636.
6386	DAWE, Jack, pseud.	Vox graculi, or Iacke Dawes prognostication for the elevation of all vanity, etc. For this year 1623. 4º J. H(aviland) f. N. Butter, 1623.
6444	DEATH	Deaths dance. To be sung, to a pleasant new tune, called Oh no, no, no, not yet. Ballad. f. H. Gosson (1631).
6445	DEBATE	The debate and stryfe betwene somer and wynter. 4º L. Andrew (date?).
6451	DECEIT	The deceyte of women. 4º A. Vele (1560?).
6452		(A. Ed.) 4º W. Copland f. J. Wyght (1561?).
6461	DEE, John	A letter nine yeeres since, written and first published: containing a discourse apologetical. 4º E. Short, 1603.

6475.1 DEKKER	The **artillery garden**. A poem dedicated to the honour of all those Gentlemen who practize Millitary discipline.
6479	The **batchelars banquet**. (**A. Ed.**) 4° f. R. Bird, 1631.
6480	The **belman of London:** bringing to light the most notorious villanies. (Anon.) 4° f. N. Butter, 1608.
6481	Second impression (Anon.) 4° f. N. Butter, 1608.
6482	**Third impression, with new additions.** (Anon.) 4° f. N. Butter, 1608.
6483	**Fourth impression.** (Anon.) 4° f. N. Butter, 1616.
6484	**Fift impression.** (Anon.) 4° M. Flesher, 1640.
6485	**Lanthorne and candle–light, or the second part of the Belman.** 4° f. J. Busbie, 1608.
6486	Second ed. 4° F. J. Busby, 1609.
6487	O per se O, or a new cryer of lanthorne a. candlelight. (Anon.) 4° f. J. Busbie, 1612.
6487.2	(**A. Ed.**) 4°.
6488	**Villanies discovered by lanthorne and candlelight.** (Anon.) 4° f. J. Busby, 1616.
6489	(**A. Ed.**) **With canting songs; newly corrected and enlarged.** (Anon.) 4° A. Mathewes, 1620.
6491	**English villanies six severall times prest to death, now the seventh time discovered.** 4° A. Matthewes, sold by J. Grismond, 1632.
6492	**English villanies seven severall times prest to death, now the eighth time discovered.** 4° M. Parsons, sold by J. Becket, 1638.
6493	**Britannia's honor; brightly shining in several shewes or pageants.** 4° N. Okes a. J. Norton, 1628.
6497	**Dekker his dreame. In which the great volumes of heaven and hell were opened.** 4° N. Okes, 1620.
6515.2	The **owles almanacke.** (Anon.) 4° E. G. f. Laurence Lisle, 1618.
6516	**Penny–wise pound foolish.** (Anon.) 4° A. M(atthewes) f. E. Blackmore, 1631.
6517	The **pleasant comedie of Old Fortunatus.** 4° S. S(tafford) f. W. Aspley, 1600.
6518	The **pleasant comodie of Patient Grissil.** (Anon.) 4° f. H. Rocket, 1603.

6519		The ravens almanacke, foretelling of a plague, famine and civile warre. (Anon.) 4° E. A(llde) f. T. Archer, 1609.
6520		A rod for run-awayes. 4° f. J. Trundle, 1625.
6531		Warres, warres, warres. 8° f. J. G., 1628.
6557	DELONEY, Thomas	A joyful new ballad declaring the happie obtaining of the great galleazzo, (Init. T. D.) s. sh. fol. J. Wolfe f. E. White, 1588.
6558		A new ballet of the straunge whippes which the Spanyards had prepared to whippe English men. (Init. T. D.) s. sh. fol. T. Orwin a. T. Gubbin, 1588.
6564		A proper newe sonet declaring the lamentation of Beckles. (Init. T. D.) s. sh. fol. R. Robinson f. N. Colman of Norwich, 1586.
6565		The queenes visiting of the campe at Tilsburie. (Init. T. D.) s. sh. fol. J. Wolfe f. E. White, 1588.
6608	DENISON, Stephen	The white wolfe: or, a sermon preached at Pauls Crosse. 4° G. Miller, f. R. Milbourne, 1627.
6702	DERING, Edward	A sermon preached before the Quenes majestie. (A. Ed.) 8° J. Charllwood, 1578.
6767	DESCRIPTION	Ane breif descriptioun of the well of the woman-hill besyde Abirdene. 4° (Edinburgh, J. Ross) 1580.
6768		The description of a monstrous pig, etc. Ballad. A. Lacy f. G. Dewes (1562).
?		A description of a monstrous chylde borne at Chychester in Sussex, 1562. Ballad. Leonard Askel f. Fraunces Godlyf, 1562.
6769		The discription of a rare or rather most monstrous fishe, taken on the east cost of Holland, 17 Nov. 1566. Ballad. T. Purfoot (1566).
6769.5		The description of Giles of Mompesson, late knight censured by Parliament the 17th of March...1620. s. sh. fol.
?		The true description of a monsterous chylde borne in the Ile of Wight, 1564. s. sh. fol. Wylliam Gryffith (1564).
6774		The true discription of two monsterous chyldren borne at Herne in Kent. Ballad. T. Colwell f. O. Rogers, (1565).
?		The true description of a childe with ruffes borne in Surrey, 1566. s. sh. fol. John Allde and Richarde Johnes, 1566.

?		The true description of two monsterous children borne in the parish of Swanburne in Buckyngham shyre, 1566. Ballad. Alexander Lacy f. William Lewes (1566).
?		The true discription of this marveilous straunge fishe, whiche was taken 16 June 1569. s. sh. fol. Thomas Colwell.
6791	DEVEREUX, Robert	A lamentable dittie composed upon the death of Robert Lord Devereux late Earl of Essex. Ballad. f. M. Allde, 1603.
6807	DIALOGUE	Here begynneth a dialogue betwene the comen secretary a. jelowsy. 4º (J. Kynge, 1555). [Correction of the date given by STC]
6809		A merry dialogue betwixt a married man and his wife. Ballad. 2 pts. Assignes of T. Symcocke (1625?).
6840	DIGBY, Everard	A short introduction for to learne to swimme. Tr. C. Middleton. 4º J. Roberts, 1595.
6860	DIGGES, Leonard	A prognostication of right good effect. 4º T. Gemini, 1555.
6861		A prognostication everlasting. The seconde impression augmented. 4º T. Gemini (1556).
6863		(A. Ed.) 4º T. Marsh, 1567.
6864		(A. Ed.) Corrected a. augmented by T. Digges. 4º T. Marsh, 1576.
6865		(A. Ed.) 4º T. Marsh, 1578.
6866		(A. Ed.) 4º T. Marsh, 1583.
6867		(A. Ed.) 4º T. Marsh, 1585.
6868		(A. Ed.) T. Orwin, 1592.
6870		(A. Ed.) 4º F. Kyngstone, 1605.
6921	DITTY	A delicate new ditty composed upon the posie of a ring. Ballad. 2 pts. f. H. Gosson (1630?).
6922		An excellent new ditty: or-which proveth that women the best warriors be. Ballad. 2 pts. f. H. G(osson) (1630?).
6923		A pleasant countrey new ditty, merrily shewing how to drive the cold winter away. Ballad. 2 pts. f. H. G(osson) (1610?).
6924		A pleasant ditty of a maydens vow. Ballad. f. H. G(osson) (1633?).
6925		A pleasant new ditty intituled: Through rich golden booties, etc. Ballad. 2 pts. f. J. Wright (1635?).
6926		A pretty new ditty; or a young lasses resolution. Ballad. 2 pts. f. H. G(osson) (1633?).

6993	DOLPHIN, ship	A fight at sea famously fought by the Dolphin of London against five of the Turkes men of warre. 4° f. H. Gosson, 1617.
7031	DONNE, John	Deaths duell, or a consolation to the soule. 4° T. Harper f. R. Redmer a. B. Fisher, 1632.
7161	DRAKE, Sir Francis	The world encompassed by Sir F. Drake, being his next voyage to that to Nombre de Dios. (Anon.) 4° (G. Miller?) f. N. Bourne, 1628.
7162		(A. Ed.) 4° E(liz.) P(urslow) f. N. Bourne, 1635.
7292	DUGDALE, Gilbert	The time triumphant, declaringe the arival of King Iames into England, His coronation etc. 4° R. B(lore), 1604.
7357	DUNTON, John	A true journall of the Sally fleet, with the proceedings of the voyage. 4° John Dawson for Thomas Nicholes, 1637.
7448	EAST INDIA COMPANY	A letter written to the governours of the East Indian merchants, 4° f. T. Thorppe, 1603.
7451	EAST INDIA COMPANY OF THE NETHERLANDS	A true relation of the unjust proceedings against the English at Amboyna. 4° H. Lownes for N. Newbery, 1624.
7452	EAST INDIA COMPANY OF THE NETHERLANDS	A true relation of the unjust proceedings against the English at Amboyna. Second impression. 3 pts. H. Lownes f. N. Newbery, 1624.
7453		Third impression. 3 pts. 4° G. Purslowe f. N. Newberry, 1632.
7454		(A. Ed. of the first part). A true relation of the late cruell tortures at Amboyna. 4° 1624.
7481.5	EDEN, Richard	A treatyse of the new India...1536. 4° London, 1553.
7503	EDWARD IV, King	A merrie, pleasant and delectable historie between K. Edward the fourth and a tanner of Tamworth. 4° J. Danter, 1596.
7509	EDWARD VI, King	The prayer of K. Edward VI, whiche he made the vi july 1553. s. sh. fol. R. Jugge (s. d.).
7558	ELDERTON, William	A new merry newes, as merry as can be. 8° H. Jackson, 1606.
7565		The true fourme and shape of a monsterous chyld borne in Stony Stratforde. s. sh. fol. T. Colwell (1565).
7572	ELIAS, Chevalier au cygne	The Knight of the Swanne. 4° W. Copland (1550?) (STC 5734.5).

7573 ELIDAD, pseud.
A good and fruitful exhortation unto the Famelie of Love. 8º (1574?).

7588 ELIZABETH, Queen
Loe here the pearle
Whom God and man doth love, etc. s. sh. fol. G. Godhead (1563).

7593
The royall passage of her Maiesty from the Tower to White-hall. (A. Ed., s. d.) S. S(tafford) f. J. Busby.

7607 ELLIS, Thomas
A true report of the third voyage by Frobisher. 8º T. Dawson, 1578.

7678 MANUEL, Prince of Portugal
A declaration of the reasons, moveing Don Emanuel to forsake the Romish religion. Tr. I. R. M. D. 4º (London?) 1634.

7678.5 EMERY
Here followeth three practyses, nowe used at Mountpyllier by Monsyre Emery (London? date?).

10410 ENGLISH FARRIER
The English farrier, or countrymans treasure. (A. Ed.) 4º J. Beale, 1638.

10420 ENGLISH TRAVILLER
A direction for the English traviller. 8º Sold by M. Simons, 1635.

10521 ERRA PATER
The pronostycacion for ever. 8º T. Este (1607?).

10522
The pronostycacion for ever. 8º T. S(nod-ham), 1609.

10523
A pronostycacion for ever. 8º T. Snodham (1609?).

10524
A pronostycacion for ever. 8º T. Snodham (1610).

10525
A prognostication for ever. 8º F. Coules (1630?).

10526
The pronostycacion for ever. 8º R. Bishop (1639?).

10582 EVAN, Enoch ap.
A true relation of a barbarous murder committed by Enoch ap. Evan. 4º N. Okes, 1633.

10608.5 EXAMPLE
An example of Gods judgement shewn upon two children borne in high Dutch Land, in the Citie of Lutssolof, the first day of Julie. 8º f. William Bartlet HN.

10609
A most notable example of an ungracious son. Ballad. 2 pts. M. P(arsons), f. H. Gosson (1630?).

10612
A worthy example of a vertuous wife who fed her father with her own milk, etc. Ballad. 2 pts. f. W. W(right?) (1630?).

10627 EXHORTATION
A good exhortation to every man, etc. s. sh. fol. R. Ballard (1581?).

10646 F., I. or J.
A sermon preached at Ashby De-la-zouch, at the funerall of the Lady Elizabeth

10646	- cont'd	Stanley. (A. Imp.) T. P(laine), sold by J. Greenesmith, 1636.
10654	F., T.	A fooles bolt is soone shot. Ballad. 2 pts. f. J. G(rismond) (1625?).
?	F., T. W.	The shape of two monsters. 1564. s. sh. fol. John Allde (1564).
10690	FARLEY, Henry	St. Paules-Church her Bill for the Parliament. 4° (f. R. Milbourne), 1621.
10709	FAULCONBRIDGE, George, Lord	The famous history of George, Lord Faulconbridge. 4° J. B(eale), sold by J. Davies, 1616.
10710		(A. Ed.) 4° J. B(eale). sold by J. Wright, jun., 1635.
10712	FAUST, Johann, Dr.	The historie of the damnable life a. deserved death of Dr. J. Faustus. (A. Ed.) 4° J. Windet for E. White, 1608.
10714		(A. Ed.) The historie of the damnable life, etc. 4° f. J. Wright, 1636.
10826	FERNESEEDE, Margaret	The araignment a. burning of M. Ferneseede. 4° f. H. Gosson, 1608.
10841a	FIAN, Dr.	Newes....Declaring the damnable life a. death etc. 4° f. W. Wright, (1591?).
10877	FINCH, John, Baron	On winges of feare Finch flies away. s. sh. fol. (London? 1640?).
10930	FITZ, Sir John	The bloudy booke or the tragical end of Sir J. Fitz. 4° f. F. Burton, 1605.
10931		(2nd impression) 4° (1606?).
10936	FITZ-GEFFREY, Charles	The blessed birth-day, celebrated in some pious meditations. (2nd ed.) 8° Oxford. J. Lichfield sold by E. Forrest, 1636.
11029	FLANDERS	Newes from Flaunders: a new Ballad. s. sh. fol. (1600?).
11078	FLETCHER, Joseph	The history of the perfect-cursed-blessed man. 4° M. Flesher, 1628.
11079		(A. Imp.) f. N. Fosbrook, 1629.
11087	FLETCHER, Robert	The nine English worthies. 4° H. L(ownes) f. J. Harrison the Yonger, 1606.
11090	FLOOD, Griffin	The life and death of G. Flood, informer. 4° J. T., 1623.
11107	FLOWER, Margaret	The wonderful discoverie of the witch-crafts of M. a. P. Flower. 4° G. Eld f. J. Barnes, 1619.
11198	FORTUNE	Fortune's tennis-ball. 4° (London, 1640).
11281	FRANCE	Newes from France; or a relation of a fearfull accident, etc. 4° W. Jones f. N. Browne, 1618.
11358	FREDERICK I, King of Bohemia	The marriage of the two great princes. Frederick, Count Palatine and the Lady Elizabeth. 4° T. C(reed) f. W. Barley, sold by W. Wright, 1613.

11362	FREDERICK de Jennen	Here begynneth a propre treatyse of a marchauntes wyfe. (A. Ed.) 4º A. Veale (1560?).
11512	GAD, BEN–AROD, pseud.	The wandering Jew telling fortunes to English–men. 4º J. Raworth f. N. Butter, 1640.
11562	GARDENER	The expert gardener. 4º R. Hearne, 1640.
11629	GARTER, Bernard	A newyeares gifte, dedicated to the popes holinesse. By B. G(arter). 4º H. Bynneman, 1579.
11645	GASCOIGNE, George	The steele glas. A satyre, togither with the Complainte of Phylomene. 2 pts. 4º H. Bynneman f. R. Smith, 1576.
11695	GEDDE, Walter	A booke of sundry draughts principally for glasiers; whereunto is annexed how to anniel in glass. 2 pts. 4º W. Dight, 1615–16.
11727	GENEVA	The troubles of Geneva. Tr. W. P. 4º f. T. Nelson, 1591.
11747	GERALDSON, C.	An addition to the Sea Journal of the Hollanders unto Java. 4º John Wolfe, 1598.
11791	GERMANY	The invasions of Germanie. 8º J. Norton f. J. Rothwell, 1638.
11793		More newes containing the troubles in Germany. 4º f. N. Butter a. T. Archer, 1623.
11796		The wars in Germany. 4º f. N. Butter, 1614.
11875	GIL, Alexander	The new starr of the north, shining upon the King of Sweden. 4º A. Mathewes for R. Milbourne, 1632.
11876		The new starr of the north, shining upon the King of Sweden (A. Ed.) Anon. 4º A. Mathewes f. R. Milbourne, 1632.
11926	GOD	Gods handy–worke in wonder miraculously shewen upon two women. 4º G. Purslow f. J. W(right), 1615.
11992	GOMERSALL, Robert	The Levites revenge. 8º f. J. Marriott, 1628.
11995		The tragedie of Lodovick Sforza. 8º f. J. Marriott, 1628.
12009	GOODCOLE, Henry	The adultresses funerall day. 4º N. and J. Okes, 1635.
12010		Heavens speedie hue and cry sent after lust and murther. 4º N. a. J. Okes, 1635.
12011		Londons cry ascended to God. 4º B. Alsop, 1620.

12012		Natures cruell step–dames: or matchlesse monsters of the female sex. E. Barnes and A. Willis. (Anon.) 4º f. F. Coules, 1637.
12014		The wonderfull discoverie of E. Sawyer, a witch. 4º f. W. Butler, 1621.
12016	GOODFELLOW, Robin	Robin Goodfellow, his mad prankes and merry jestes. 4º f. F. Grove, 1628.
12017		Robin Good–Fellow. 2 pts. 4º London, 1639.
12018		The mad merry prankes of Robin Goodfel–low. (Ballad. 2 pts.) f. H. G(osson) (1631?).
12019		Good Fellows. A newe ballade intytuled, Good Fellowes must go learne to daunce. s. sh. fol. W. Gryffith, 1569.
12027	GOODMAN, Nicholas	Holland's leaguer: or an historical dis–course of Dona Britanica Hollandia. 4º A. M(athews) f. R. Barnes, 1632.
12027.?	GOODERIGE, Alice	The most wonderfull and true storie, of a certaine witch named Alse Gooderige of Stapenhill, who was arraigned and convicted at Darbie... 1597.
12096	GOSSON, Stephen	Quippes for upstart newfangled gentle–women, etc. (Anon.) 4º R. Johnes, 1595.
12102	GOSYNHILL, Edward	The prayse of all women, called Mulieru pean. 4º W. Myddylton (1542?).
12104		The vertuous scholehous of ungracious women. 8º (W. Lynne?, 1550?).
12136	GOULART, Simon	The wise vieillard or old man. Tr. T. W(illiamson?) 4º J. Dawson, 1621.
12169	GRAHAME, Simion	The passionate sparke of a relenting mind. 4º H. Lownes, 1604.
12186	GRANGER, Timothy	A most true and marveilous straunge wonder of 17 monstrous fisshes, taken in Suffolke. s. sh. fol. T. Colwell, 1568.
1222	GREENE, Robert	The historie of Arbasto. (A. Ed.) 4º f. F. Williams, 1626.
12234		A disputation betweene a hee conny–catcher, and a shee conny–catcher. 4º A. J(effes) f. T. G(ubbin), 1592.
12235		(A. Ed. with the title:) Theeves falling out, true men come by their goods. 4º f. T. G(ubbin), 1615.
12236		(A. Ed.) 4º H. Bell, 1617.
12237		(A. Ed.) 4º B. Alsop f. H. Bell, 1621.
12238		(A. Ed.) 4º f. H. a. M. Bell, 1637.
12264		Greenes cardie of fancie. (A. Ed.) 4º H. L(ownes) f. M. Lownes, 1608.

12267		The honorable historie of frier Bacon and frier Bongay. 4° f. E. White, 1594.
12268		(A. Ed.) 4° Eliz. Allde, 1630.
12279		A notable discovery of cousenage. (The art of conny-catching.) 4° J. Wolfe f. T. N(elson), 1591.
12280		(A. Ed.) 4° T. Scarlet, f. T. Nelson, 1592.
12281		The second part of conny-catching. (Init. R. G.) 4° J. Wolfe f. W. Wright, 1591.
12282		(A. Ed.) The second and last part of conny-catching. 4° J. Wolfe f. W. Wright, 1592.
12283		The third and last part of conny-catching. 4° T. Scarlet f. C. Burby, 1592.
12302		A quip for an upstart courtier. (A. Ed.) 4° E. A(llde) f. E. White, 1606.
12303		(A. Ed.) 4° G. P(urslow), 1620.
12304		(A. Ed.) 4° G. P(urslowe), sold by T. Dewe, 1622.
12305		(A. Ed.) 4° E. Purslow, 1635.
12386	GRISELDA	The pleasant and sweet history of patient Grissell. 8° E. P(urslow) f. J. Wright, (1630?).
12396.2		(A. Ed. with the new title page) The history of noble Marquess. s. d.
12522	GUNTER, Edmund	The description a. use of the sector, the crosse-staffe and other instruments. 2 pts. W. Jones sold by E. Weaver, 1624.
12523		The description a. use of the sector; (2 Ed.) 4 pts. 4° W. Jones f. J. Bowler, 1636.
12572	H., J., Gent.	The house of correction or certayne satyricall epigrams. By J. H(eath), gent. With a few characters called Par Pari. 2 pts. 8° B. Alsop f. R. Redmer, 1619.
12578	H., T.	The beautie of the remarkable yeare 1638. The yeare of the great covenant of Scotland (verse). 4° Edinburgh, J. Anderson, 1638.
12599	HAEC VIR	Haec vir or the womanish-man. 4° f. J. T(rundle), 1620.
12630	HALL, Edward	A horrible murder committed at Putney 21 Aprill last upon E. Hall. 4° f. J. Wright, 1614.
12724	HALLIARG, Arthur	The cruell shrow: or the patient mans woe. Ballad. 2 pts. M. P(arsons) f. H. Gosson (1610?).
12725	HAMDULTON, Valentine	A mery new jigge. Ballad. 2 pts. f. H. Gosson (1635?).

12771.5	HARRINGTON, Sir John	An anatomie of the metamorphosed Ajax. 8º R. Field, 1596.
12772		(A. Ed.) 8º R. Field, 1596.
12773		An apologie. I. Or rather a retraction. (Anon.) 8º (R. Field, 1596).
12774		(A. Ed.) An Apologie. I. or rather a retraction. (Anon.) (R. Field, 1596).
12774.3		An apologie. Or rather a retraction. (A. Ed.) J. Windet, 1596.
12779		A new discourse of a stale subject called a Metamorphosis of Ajax. Written by Misacros to his friend Philostilpnos. 8º R. Field, 1596.
12787	HARMAN, Thomas	A caveat or warening for commen cursetors. 4º W. Gryffith, 1567.
12788		(A. Ed.) 4º (H. Middleton, 1573).
12789		(A. Ed.) The Groundworke of conny-catching. (Anon.) 4º J. Danter f. W. Barley, 1592.
12790		The fraternity of vacabondes. (Anon.) 4º J. Awdeley, 1575.
12805	HARRIS, James	The lives, arraignements, etc. of the 19 late pyrates. 4º f. J. Busby (1609).
12863	HARRISON, Stephen	The arches triumph erected in honor of James the first at his entrance through London. fol. J. Windet, 1604.
12863a		[A. imp. with the addition:] to be sould by J. Sudbury a. G. Humble.
12887	HART, Henry	A godly newe short treatyse instructying every parson howe they shulde trade theyr lyves. 8º R. Stoughton, 1548.
12925	HASLETON, Richard	Strange and wonderfull things happened to Richard Hasleton in his ten yeares travailes in many forraine countries. 4º A. J(effes) f. W. Barley, 1595.
12931	HOUGHTON, William	English-men for my money; or a pleasant comedy called A woman will have her will. (Anon.) 4º W. White, 1616.
12940	HAWES, Edward	Trayterous Percyes Catesbyes prosopopeia. 4º S. Stafford, 1606.
12941	HAWES, John	The valiant a. most laudable fight by the Centurion of London against five Spanish gallies. 4º (London, 1591).
13128	HENRY IV, King of France	Brief declaration of the yielding of St. Dennis to the French king. 4º J. Wolfe f. W. Wright, 1590.
13135		An excellent ditty made upon the great victory which the French King obtayned against the Duke de Maine, 4 March 1590. s. sh. fol. (s. p., 1590).

13138		The order of ceremonies observed for the coronation of Henry the IIII. Tr. E. A(ggas) 4° ·J. Windet, sold by J. Flasket (1594).
13140		The sighs of Fraunce for the death of their late King. The forme of the coronation of Prince Lewis. 4° f. J. Budge, 1610.
13147		A true relation of the French Kinge his good successe. 4° J. Wolfe, 1592.
13157	HENRY, Prince of Wales	The funerals of the high and mighty prince Henry. 4° T. S(nodham) f. J. Budge, 1613.
13158		Great Brittans mourning garment. Given at the funerall of Prince Henry. 4° G. Eld f. A. Jonson, 1612.
13159		Londons love to the royal prince Henrie. 4° E. Allde f. N. Fosbrooke, 1610.
13162		Sundry funeral elegies on the untimely death of the Prince. Composed by severall authors. 4° H. Lownes, 1613.
13247	HERRING, Francis	Mischeefes mysterie; or treasons master-peece. The Powder-plot truly related. From the latine of doctour Herring trans-lated and dilated. (In verse) by J. Vicars. 4° E. Griffin, 1617.
13251	HESTER, Queen	A newe enterlude, drawen oute of the holy scripture of godly queene Hester. 4° W. Pickerynge a. T. Hacket, 1561.
13300	HEYWOOD, John	The playe the foure PP. 4° W. Myddylton (1545?).
13320	HEYWOOD, Thomas	The fair maid of the west. 2 pts. 4° f. R. Royston, 1631.
13321		The foure prentices of London. 4° f. J. W(right), 1615.
13322		(A. Ed.) Newly revised. 4° N. Okes, 1632.
13324		A funeral elegie upon the death of King James. 4° f. T. Harper, 1625.
13328		If You know not me You know no bodie. Or the troubles of Queene Elizabeth. (Anon.) 4° f. N. Butter, 1605.
13329		(A. Ed. anon.) 4° f. N. Butter, 1606.
13332		(A. Ed. anon.) 4° f. N. Butter, 1613.
13333		(A. Ed. anon.) 4° f. N. Butter, 1623.
13334		(A. Ed. anon.) 4° B. A(lsop) a. T. F(awcet) f. N. Butter, 1632.
13335		(A. Ed. anon.) 4° J. Raworth f. N. Butter, 1639.

13337		The Second part of Queene Elizabeths troubles. (A. Ed. anon.) 4° f. N. Butter, 1609.
13338		If you know not me, etc. The second part. (A. Ed. anon.) 4° f. N. Butter, 1623.
13339		(A. Ed. anon.) 4° f. N. Butter, 1633.
13340		The iron age. 4° 2 pts. N. Okes, 1632.
13356		Philocothonista, or the Drunkard. 4° R. Raworth, 1635.
13357		A pleasant comedy called A maydenhead well-lost. 4° N. Okes f. J. Jackson and f. Church, 1634.
13367		A true description of his Majesties royall ship built at Wool-witch. 4° J. Okes f. J. Aston, 1637.
13368		(A. imp.) Also a breefe addition to the first printed copy. 4° J. Okes, 1638.
13374	HIC MULIER	Hic Mulier, or, the man-woman. 4° (J. Purslowe) f. J. Trundle (1620).
13501	HILL, Thomas	A prognostication for the yeare 1572. 8° R. Watkins a. J. Roberts (1572).
13507	HILLIARD, John	Fire from heaven. 4° f. J. Trundle, 1613.
13525	HISTORIES	Two most remarquable a. true histories. (Tr. from the Dutch.) 4° J. E(ld) f. D. Speede, 1620.
13543	HOCUS-POCUS	Hocus Pocus Junior. The anatomie of legerdemain. 2nd Ed. 4° R. H(arper) f. R. M(abb), 1635.
13544		(A. Ed.) J. D(awson) a. R. M(abb) f. F. Grove, 1638.
13550	HODGSON, William	The plurisie of sorrow. 4° J. Legatt, 1625.
13567	HOLDT	Miraculous newes from the cittie of Holdt. Tr. (T. F.) 4° John Barnes, 1616.
13572	HOLLAND	The great victory which God hath given unto eight Holland shippes. Tr. out of the Dutch copie printed at Middle borough. 4° G. Eld f. T. Bushel, 1613.
13574		Newes from Holland, etc. 4° f. N. Butter, 1624.
13580	HOLLAND, Abraham	Naumachia, or Hollands sea-fight. 4° T. P(urfoot) f. T. Law a. W. Garrat, 1622.
13599	HOLLANDERS	An answere to the Hollanders declaration, concerning the occurrents of the East India. Pt. 1. 4° (N. Okes?), 1622.
13691	HOOD, Robin	A mery jeste of Robyn Hoode. (The playe of Robin Hoode) 4° W. Copland (1560?).

13695	HOOD, Thomas	The making and use of a sector. 4° J. Windet, solde by S. Shorte.
13697		The use of the celestial globe in plans. 4° J. Windet f. T. Cooke, 1590.
13699		The use of the two mathematicall instrumentes, the crosse staffe a. the Iacobs staffe. 2 pts. 4° f. T. Cooke a. R. Dexter, 1590.
13759	HOOPER, John, Bp.	An homelye to be read in the tyme of pestylence. 4° Warceter, J. Oswen, 1553.
13806	HORD, Richard	Black-Fryers. (Elegia, etc.) 8° Imp. J. Marriott & J. Grismand, 1625.
13814	HORNBY, William	Hornbyes hornbook. (In verse) 8° A. Math(ewes) f. T. Bayly.
13815		The scourge of drunkennes. 4° G. Eld f. T. Baylie, 1618.
13856	HOWARD, Charles Nottingham	(Brief authorizing collections in behalf of J. Salisbury.) s. sh. fol. T. Purfoote, 1591.
14029	HUTTON, Luke	The blacke dogge of Newgate, etc. (In verse) 4° f. G. Simpson a. W. White (1596?).
14030		The discovery of a London monster called the black dog of Newgate. 4° F. Eld f. R. Wilson, 1612.
14031		(A. Ed.) 4° M. P(arsons) f. R. Wilson, 1638.
14040	HYCKESCORNER	Hyckescorner (A. Ed.) 4° J. Walcy, (s. d.).
14050a	I., H.	An example for all those that make no conscience of swearing and forswearing. To the tune of Amy not too high. s. sh. fol. I. W. (C. 1600?).
?	I., P.	A mervaylous straunge deformed swyne. s. sh. fol. William How f. Richard Johnes s. d.
14066	I., T.	A discourse between Upright the shoomaker and master Pattent the smith. 4° B. Alsop a. T. F(awcett) f. F. Groves, 1640.
14112	INTERLUDE	Theterlude of Youth. (A. Ed.) 4° W. Copland (1562?).
14113		A new interlude of Impacient Poverte newly imprynted. 4° (W. Copland? 1561?)
14282	ISUMBRAS, Sir	Here begynneth the history of Syr Isenbras. 4° W. Copland, 1550?
14289	IVE, Paul	The practise of fortification, etc. 4° T. Orwin f. T. Man a. T. Cooke, 1589.

14378	JAMES I, King	His majesties gracious letter to the Earle of South-Hampton, and to the company of Virginia, etc. 4° F. Kyngston, 1622.
14419		God and the king; or a dialogue shewing that King James being immediate under God doth rightfully claime whatsoever is required by the oath of allegiance. 8° London, 1615.
14423		An excellent new ballad, showing the petigree of King James. s. sh. fol. f. E. W(hite, 1603?).
14486	JENINGES, Edward	A briefe discovery of the damages that happen to this realme by disordered and unlawfull diet. 4° R. Ward, 1590.
14521	JEST	Here begynneth a merry jeste of a shrewde and curste wyfe. 4° H. Jackson (1580?).
14523		A mery jest of the frier and the boy. (A. Ed.) 8° E. A(llde), 1617.
14524		(A. Ed.) A mery jest of the friar and the boy. 4° E. Alde, (s. d.).
14531	JESUITS	The Jesuites comedie, acted at Lyons. 4° E. Allde f. A. Johnson, 1607.
14543	JESUS CHRIST	Christs tears over Jerusalem, or a caveat for England. s. sh. fol. f. H. Gosson (1625).
14573		A sparke of Christs beauty. (A sermon on Isai. ix.6) 4° Oxford, J. Lichfield a. J. Short, 1622.
14577		Two pleasant ditties, one of the birth, the other of the passion of Christ (Ballade). assignes of T. Symcocke (1625).
14668	JOHNSON, John of Antwerp	A true relation of Gods wonderfull mercies in preserving one alive which hanged five days. (i.e. J. Johnson). 4° E. Allde (1606?).
14691	JOHNSON, Richard	A remembrance of the honors due to Robert Earle of Salisbury. 4° f. J. Wright, 1612.
14699	JOHNSON, Robert, gent.	Nova Britannia; offring fruits by planting in Virginia. (Init. R. I.) 4° (W. Stansby) f. S. Macham, 1609.
14700		The new life of Virginea: being the second part of Nova Britannia. (Init. R. I.) 4° F. Kyngston f. W. Welby, 1612.
14837	JUGELER, Jack	A new enterlued for chyldren to playe, named Jacke Jugeler. Never before imprented. 4° W. Copland, (1563).
14837a		(A. Ed.) Newly imprented. 4° W. Copland (1565?).
14899	KEMP	Keep within compasse: or the worthy legacy, etc. 8° f. J. Trundle, 1619.

14923 KEMP, William

Kempes nine daies wonder, performed in a daunce from London to Norwich. 4° E. A(llde) f. N. Ling, 1600.

14926 KEMPE, William

The education of children in learning (Init. W. R.) 4° T. Orwin f. J. Potter a. T. Gubbin, 1588.

14934? KENT

The forme and shape of a monstrous child borne at Maydstone in Kent, 1568. s. sh. fol. John Awdeley (1568).

14934

Strange newes out of Kent. 4° T. C(reed) f. W. Barley, 1609.

14935 KENT STREET

A wonder woorth the reading of a woman in Kent Street. 4° W. Jones, 1617.

14961 KIND

A mad kinde of wooing; or a dialogue betweene Will the simple and Nan the subtill. (Ballad, 2 pts.) assignes of T. Symcocke (1625?).

15048 KNIGHT, Francis

A relation of seaven yeares slaverie under the Turkes of Argeire. 4° T. Cotes for M. Sparke, jr., 1640.

15048a

(A. Ed.) T. Cotes f. M. S. jr., sold by T. Nicholes, 1640.

15091a KYD, Thomas

The Spanish tragedie. Newly corrected a. amended of suche grosse faults as passed in the first impression. (A. Imp.) W. White f. J. White a. T. Langley, 1615.

15092

(A. Ed.) 4° J. White f. T. Langley, 1618.

15093

(A. Ed. anon.) A. Mathewes, sold by J. Grismand, 1623.

15094

(A. Ed. anon.) 4° A. Mathewes f. F. Grove, 1633.

15106 L., I.

The birth purpose and mortall wound of the Romish Holie League. 4° (T. Orwin) F. T. Cadman, 1589.

15108 L., M.

A merry jest of John Tomas, and Jakaman his wife. (Ballad, 2 pts.) f. E. Wright (1635?).

15177 LAMBE, John

A briefe description of the notorious life of J. Lambe. 4° Amsterdam (London), 1628.

15186 LAMENTATION

The lamentation of a new married man. (Ballad, 2 pts.) assignes of T. Symcocke (1625?).

15193 LANGENES, Bernardt

The description of a voyage made by ships of Holland into the East Indies. Tr. W. P(hillip). 4° J. Wolfe, 1598.

15226 LANTERN

A lanthorne for landlords. (Ballad, 2 pts.) f. J. Wright (1640?).

15264 LASS

The lovely northerne lasse. (Ballad, 2 pts.) f. T. Coules (1632?).

15329	LAWSON, William	A new orchard and garden, etc. with the country houswifes garden. 4° B. Alsop f. R. Jackson, 1618.
15330		Now the second time corrected. 4° J. H(aviland) f. R. Jackson, 1623.
15331		Now the third time corrected. 4 pts. 4° J. H(aviland) f. F. Williams, 1629.
15341	LEAGUE	The necessarie league (against the house of Austria). Eng. a. Fr. 2 pts. 8° (London?) 1625.
15401	LEICESTERSHIRE LOVERS	The two Lestersheire lovers. (Ballad, 2 pts.) f. J. Trundle (1619?).
15428	LEIGH, William	Strange news of a monster borne at Adlington in Lancashire, 1613. 4° J. P(indley?) f. S. M(an), 1613.
15555	LEVETT, John	The ordering of bees. 4° T. Harper f. J. Harison, 1634.
15645	LINCOLN	A mournfull dittie on the death of certaine iudges and iustices, after the assizes, holden at Lincolne. s. sh. fol., J. Wolfe f. W. Wright, 1590.
15704	LISBON	Two most strange and notable examples, shewed at Lyshborne. 4° (A. Jeffes) f. W. Barley, 1591.
16513?	LITURGIES	An order for publike prayers on Wednesdayes and Frydayes. 4° C. Barker, 1586?.
16542		A short forme of Thankesgiving to God for staying the contagious sicknesse of the plague. 4° B. Norton & J. Bill, 1625.
16614	LLOYD, David	The legend of Captaine Jones. (In verse) 4° f. J. M(arriott), 1631.
16620	LLOYD Lodowick	An epitaph upon the death of Syr Edward Saunders. br. fol. H. S(ingleton) f. H. Disse (1576).
16622		Hilaria; or the triumphant feast for the fift of August. 4° S(tafford), 1607.
16730	LONDON, orders regulations	The order of my Lord Mayor the aldermen and the sheriffs for their meetings. 8° R. Young, 1629.
16761	LONDON, appendice	The manner of crying things in London. appendix. 4° (J. Wolfe? 1599?).
16766		A profitable and necessarie discourse for the meeting with the bad garbelling of spices; composed by divers grocers of London. 4° R. B. f. T. Man, 1591.
16767		(A. Ed.) 4° R. B. f. T. Man (1592).
16769	LONDON, College of Physicians	Certain necessary directions as well for the cure of the plague as for preventing the infection. 4° R. Barker a. assignes of J. Bill, 1636.

16801	LOOKES, John	The ragman; or a company that fell at odds one day. (Ballade, 2 pts.) f. F. Grove (1640?).
16825	LORD, Henry	A displaye of two forraigne sects in the East Indies, viz. The sect of the Banians, and the sect of the Persees. 4° T. a. R. Cotes f. F. Constable, 1630.
16836	LOUIS XIII, King of France	Articles concluded and agreed upon in the name of the King, etc. 4° G. E(ld) f. G. Fairebeard, 1619.
16855	LOVE	Fond love why dost thou dally: or the passionate lovers dittie. (Ballad, 2 pts.) F. Coules (1635?).
16862	LOVER	The discontented lover. (Ballad) f. F. Coules (1635?).
16863		The lovers complaint for the losse of his love. (Ballad) Assignes of T. Symcocke (1625?).
16864		The lovers delight; or a pleasant pastoral sonnet. (Ballad, 2 pts.) f. F. Coules (1640?).
16864a		The lover's dreame. (Ballad, 2 pts.) f. J. W(right) (1633?).
16865	LOVERS	The two kinde lovers. (Ballad, 2 pts.) Assignes of T. Symcocke (1635?).
16866		Two unfortunate lovers. (Ballad, 2 pts.) f. H. Gosson (1631).
16868	LOWBERRY, Peter	The constant lover, who his affection will not move. (Ballad, 2 pts. Init. P. L.) f. H. Gosson (1638?).
16869		A new dittie of a lover tost hither a. thither. (Ballad, 2 pts.) f. E. Wright (1630?).
16992	LUTHER, Martin	A ryght notable sermon uppon the twenteth chapter of Johan. (Tr. Argentine) 8° Ippeswich, A. Scoloker, 1548.
17013	LYDGATE, John	The churle and the byrde. (A. Ed.) 4° Canterbury, J. Mychel (1550?).
17014		(A. Ed.) 4° W. Copland (after 1561).
17036		A treatyse of the smyth whych that forged hym a new dame. 4° W. Copland (n. d.).
17115	LYNNE, Walter	The beginning and endynge of all popery (set forth out of hye almaine). 4° J. Herforde, at the costes of G. Lynne (1548?).
?	M., P.	News from the Tower Hill. (Ballad, 2 pts.) f. E. B. (n. d.).
17148	M., R.	Newes of Sr. Walter Rauleigh with the true description of Guiana. 4° f. H. G(osson), sold by J. Wright, 1618.

17155	M., W.	The man in the moone, or the English fortune–teller. 4° J. W(indet) f. N. Butter, 1609.
17156		A true discourse of the late battaill fought betweene our Englishmen and the Prince of Parma. 4° R. Ward, 1585.
17186	MAID	A constant and a kinde maid. (Ballad) fol. f. C. Coules (1635?).
17187		The maids comfort: or the kinde young man. (Ballad, 2 pts.) fol. assignes of T. Symcocke (1625?).
17188		The maydes metamorphosis. 4° T. Creede f. R. Clive, 1600.
17190	MAIDEN	The maidens complaint of her loves inconstancie. (Ballad, 2 pts.) f. H. G(osson) (1625?).
17191		(A. Ed.) f. E. W(right) (1630?).
17193		A maidens Nay; or I love not you. (Ballad, 2 pts.) f. F. Coules, T. Vere a. J. Wright (1640?).
17209	MALBIE, Sir Nicholas	A plaine and easie way to remedie a horse that is foundered in his feete, etc. 4° T. Purfoote, 1576.
17211		(A. Ed.) 4° T. Purfoot, 1594.
17232	MAN	The discontented married man; or a merry new song. Ballad, 2 pts. f. R. Harper (1640?).
17233		The marryed mans lesson, etc. Ballad (1635?).
17234		O Yes: If any man or woman, any thing desire. Ballad, 2 pts. f. F. Coules (1625?).
17235		The poore man payes for all. This is but a dreame. Ballad, 2 pts. f. H. G(osson) (1625?).
17259	MANSEL, Sir Robert	A true report of the service done upon certaine gallies. 4° F. Kyngston, sold by J. Newbery, 1602.
17403	MARKHAM, Robert	The description of that ever to be famed knight, Sir John Burgh. 4° 1628.
17432	MARLOWE, Christopher	The tragicall history of D. Faustus. Written by Ch. Mar. (A. Ed.) f. J. Wright, 1616.
17434		(A. Ed.) 4° f. J. Wright, 1620.
17435		(A. Ed.) 4° f. J. Wright, 1624.
17436		(A. Ed.) 4° f. J. Wright, 1631.
17437		The troublesome reigne a. lamentable death of Edward the second. As it was sundrie times publickly acted by the Earle of Pembrooke his servants. 8° f. W. Jones, 1594.

17444   MARMION, Shakerley   A morall poem, intituled the legend of Cupid a. Psyche. 4º N. a. J. Okes, sold by H. Sheppard, 1638.

17444a   (A. Imp. with a different engraved title-page) Cupid and Psiche, or an epick poem of Cupid and his mistress. 4º J. Okes f. H. Sheppard, 1638.

17466.5 MARRIOTT, Thomas   A briefe and true report of the new found land of Virginia, 1590.

17571   MARYLAND   A relation of Maryland 2 Pts. 4º N. 1635.

17572   MASCALL, Leonard   A booke of fishing with hooke & line (taken from the Treatise of fishing with an angle). (Init. L. M.) 4º J. Wolfe, solde by E. White, 1590.

17671a MAURICE, Prince of Orange   The battaile fought betweene Count Maurice and Albertus, Archduke. (A. Imp.) f. A. Wise.

17678b   A true discourse of the overthrow given to the common enemy at Turnhaut by count Moris of Nassaw. (A. Ed.)

17768   MEDE, Joseph   The name Altar anciently given to the holy table. 4º M. F(lesher) f. J. Clark, 1637.

17782   MEG, of Westminster   The life a. pranks of long Meg of Westminster. 8º f. A. Veale, 1582.

17797   MELANCHTHON, Philipp   Of two woonderful popish monsters, a popish asse wh. was found at Rome and a moonkish calfe calved at Friberge, witnessed, the one by P. Melanchthon, the other by M. Luther. Tr. out of French J. Brooke. 4º T. East, sould (by A. Maunsell), 1579.

17803   MELLYS, John   The true description of two monsterous children. s. sh. fol. A. Lacy f. W. Lewes (1566).

17804   MELTON, John   Astrologaster, or the figure-caster. 4º B. Alsop f. E. Blackmore, 1620.

17818   MENANTEL, François de   A congratulation to France, upon the happy alliance with Spaine. 4º (N. P.) 1612.

17878   MIDDLETON, Thomas   Civitatis amor. The cities love. An entertainement by water at Chelsey a. Whitehall. At the ioyfull receiving of the high a. mighty Charles, to bee created Prince of Wales. 4º N. Okes f. T. Archer, 1616.

17882   A game at chaess as it was acted nine days to-gether at the Globe on the banks side. (Anon.) 4º (London, 1625).

17883		(A. Ed.) 4° (London, 1625?).
17884		(A. Ed.) A game at chesse as it hath bine sundrey times acted at the Globe on the Banck side. 4° Lydden, J. Masse (1625?).
17908	MIDDLETON, Thomas, and DECKER, Thomas	The roaring girle. Or Moll Cut-purse. 4° f. T. Archer, 1611.
17910	MIDDLETON, Thomas, and ROWLEY, William	A courtly masque; the device called, The world tost at tennis. 4° G. Purslowe, 1620.
17911		A faire quarrell. As it was acted before the King, etc. 4° f. J. T(rundle), 1617.
17911a		(A. Imp.) With new additions.
17912		(A. Ed.) With new additions. 4° A. M(athews) f. T. Dewe, 1622.
17921	MILL, Humphrey	A nights search. Discovering the nature of all sorts of night-walkers. Digested into a poeme. 8° R. Bishop f. L. Blaicklock, 1640.
17994	MOFFETT, Thomas	The silkewormes and their flies. (Init. T. M.) 4° V. S(immes) f. N. Ling, 1599.
18009	MONEY	Money is my master: Yet once it was a servant unto mee. Ballad. 2 pts. f. F. Coules (1635?).
18021	MONMOUTHSHIRE	Lamentable newes out of Monmouthshire. 4° f. W. W(elby, 1607).
18075	MORE, Richard	The carpenters rule to measure ordinarie timber, etc. 4° F. Kyngston, 1602.
18165	MOROCCO	The arrivall and intertainements of the ambassador from the Emperor of Morocco. 4° J. Okes, 1637.
18211	MOTE, Humphrey	The Primrose of London, with her valiant adventure on the Spanish coast. 4° f. T. Nelson, 1585.
18272	MUNDAY, Anthony	The Englishe Romayne lyfe. 4° J. Charlewoode f. N. Ling, 1582.
18273		(A. Ed.) 4° J. Charlewoode f. N. Ling, 1590.
18286	MURAD IV, Sultan	A vaunting letter sent from Sultan Morat, etc. 4° J. Okes sold by J. Cowper, 1638.
18286.?	MURDER	The crying murther: contayning the cruell and most horrible butcher of Mr. Trat, Curate of olde Cleave. 4° Edw. Allde f. Nathaniell Butter, 1624.
18286.?		Murder upon murder, Committed by Thomas Sherwood, alias, Countrey Tom: and Elizabeth Evans, alias, Countrey Besse. Ballad (1635).

18287.?	MURDERS	**Sundrye strange and inhumaine murthers, lately committed.** 4⁰ Thomas Scarlet, 1591.
18287		**Three bloodie murders.** 4⁰ (London, 1613).
18288		**Two most unnaturall murthers.** 4⁰ V. S(immes) f. N. Butter, 1605.
18289		**Two notorious murders; one committed by a tanner** (J. Wright), etc. 4⁰ F. W. Blackwall a. G. Shaw, 1595.
18319	MYNSHUL, Geffray	**Essayes and characters of a prison a. prisoners. (A. Ed.)** 4⁰ (W. Jones) f. M. Walbancke, 1618.
18320		**(A. Ed.) . With some new additions.** 4⁰ J. O(kes) f. M. Walbancke, 1638.
18325	N., A.	**A true relation of the travels of M. Bush.** 4⁰ T. P(urfoot) f. N. Butter, 1608.
18417	NECK, Jacob Van	**The Journall, or daily register of the voyage of eight shippes of Amsterdam.** 4⁰ f. C. Burby and J. Flasket, 1601.
18447	NETHERLANDS	**A vision or dreame contayning the whole state of the Netherland warres. Eng. a. Dutch.** 4⁰ f. E. Marchant, 1615.
18452		**Answer made by the noble lords of the States to the ambassador of Polonia.** 4⁰ J. Windet, 1597.
18465		**A true coppy of the admonitions sent by the subdued provinces to the States of Holland, etc.** Tr. H. W. 4⁰ J. Wolfe, 1598.
18472a		**A proclamation touching the opening of the traffique of Spaine, with these countries.** (A. imp. with imp.:) W(hite) f. T. Archer, 1603.
18516	NICCOLS, Richard	**The beggers ape.** (Poem anon.) 4⁰ B. A(lsop) a. T. Fawcet f. L. Chapman, 1627.
18517		**The cuckow.** (Poem) 4⁰ F. K(ingston) sold by W. C(otton), 1607.
18532	NICHOLL, John	**An houre glasse of Indian newes. Shewing the miseries indured by 67 Englishmen sent to the planting in Guiana.** 4⁰ (E. Allde) f. N. Butter, 1607. .
18544	NICHOLS, Philip	**Sir Francis Drake revived.** 4⁰ E. A(llde) f. N. Bourne, 1626.
18545		**(A. Ed.)** 4⁰ (W. Stansby) f. N. Bourne, 1628.
18550	NICLAS, Hendrik	**Comoedia. A worke in ryme, contayning an enterlude of mynds witnessing the mans fall from God. Set forth by HN a. by him newly amended.** Tr. out of base-almayne. 8⁰ (1574?)

18588	NIXON, Anthony	Londons dove: or a memoriall of Maister R. Dove. 4° T. Creede f. J. Hunt, 1612.
18591		A straunge foot-post, with a packet full of strange petitions. 4° E. A(llde), 1613.
18591a		(A. Imp.) The foot-post of Dover. E. Allde solde by J. Deane, 1613.
18592		The three English brothers: Sir T. Shirley his travels, Sir A. Shirley his ambassage to the christian princes, Master R. Shirley his warres ag. the Turkes. 4° J. Hodgets, 1607.
18593		(A. Imp. with the title:) The travels of three English brothers.
18597	NOBODY	No-body, and some-body. 4° f. J. Trundle (1606).
18599		The wel-spoken nobody 'Nobody is my name' 'that beyreth evere bodys blame'. s. sh. fol. (n. p.) (1600?).
18656	NORRIS, Ralph	A warning to London by the fall of Antwerp. s. sh. fol. J. Allde (1585?).
18747	NUN	A nunnes prophesie or the fall of friers. 4° W. Wright, 1615.
18786	O'DOGHERTY, Sir Cahir	The overthrow of an Irish rebell. Or the death of Sir C. Odoughertie. 4° Dublin, J. Franckton, London, f. J. Wright, 1608.
18892.3	OSTENDE	The oppugnation and fierce siege of Ostende by the Archduke Albertus his forces, the fifth day of June. Tr. out of Dutch. 4° V. Simms, 1601.
18895		A true historie of the memorable siege of Ostend. Tr. E. Grimeston. 4° f. E. Blount, 1604.
18920	OVERBURY, Sir Thomas	The just downfall of ambition, adultery and murder, where-unto are added Weston, M. Turner and Franklin who all suffered death for the murder of Sir T. Overbury. 4° l. T. (1616?).
18921		The bloody downfall of adultery, murder, ambition. At the end are added Westons and Mistress Turners last teares for the murder of Sir T. Overbury in the Tower. f. R. H(igginbotham, 1635?).
19075	P., M.	Lord have mercy upon us; this is the humble petition of England, etc. s. sh. fol. f. T. Lambert (1636).
19120	PAINTER, Anthony	Anthony Painter, the blaspheming caryer. 4° f. J. Trundle, 1614.
19186	PARAGON	A peereless paragon. (Ballad. 2 pts.) f. T. Lambert (1633).

19190	PARÉ, Ambroise	An explanation of the fashion and use of instruments of chirurgery. 4° f. Michael Sparke, 1637.
19191		The method of curing wounds made by gunshot, done into English by W. Hamond. 4° J. Jaggard, 1617.
19230	PARKER, Martin	An exact description how his majestie went to the Parliament. 13 Aprill 1640. s. sh. fol. (n. p. 1640).
19238		Good newes from the north. Ballad. E. G(riffin), 1640.
19247		Keep a good tongue in your head. (Init. M. P.) Ballad. 2 pts. f. T. Lambert (1634).
19266		Robin Conscience or conscionable Robin. 8° f. F. Coles, 1635.
19274		A true subjects wish. s. sh. fol. E. G(riffin, 1640).
19275		A true tale of Robbin (Hood). 8° f. T. Cotes, sold by R. Grove (1632).
19276		Tyrall brings truth to light. (Init. M. P.) Ballad. 2 pts. f. T. Lambert (1634).
19277		The two inseparable brothers. Ballad. 2 pts. f. T. Lamb(ert), (1637).
19332	PARROT, Henry	Laquei ridiculosi; or springes for woodcocks. 16° f. J. Bushby, 1613.
19333		The mastive, or young-whelpe of the olde-dogge. (Init. H. P.) 4° T. Creede f. R. Meighen a. T. Jones, 1615.
19334		The mouse-trap. (Epigrams. Init. H. P.) 4° f. F. B(urton), 1606.
19454	PASQUIL	Pasquils Palinodia, and his progresse to the taverne. (By W. Fennor?) 4° T. Snodham, sold by F. Parke, 1619.
19455		(A. Ed.) 4° T. H(arper) f. L. Chapman, 1634.
19500	PEACHAM, Henry	The art of drawing with the pen, and limming in water colours. 4° R. Braddock f. W. Jones, 1606.
19501		Coach and Sedan, pleasantly disputing. (Mis-Amaxius, pseud.) 4° R. Raworth, f. J. Crowch, sold by E. Paxton, 1636.
19512		A most true relation of the affaires of Cleve and Gulick, with the articles of the peace propounded at Santen. 4° W. Stansby f. J? Helme, 1615.
19514		Prince Henrie revived; or a poem. 4° W. Stansby f. J? Helme, 1615.
19524	PEDANTIUS	Pedantius. Comoedia. 12° W. S(tansby) imp. R. Mylbourn, 1631.

19529   PEEKE, Richard

Three to one: being an English–Spanish combat performed by a westerne gentleman of Tavystoke. 4° f. J. T(rundle, 1626).

19566   PELLHAM, Edward

Gods power a. providence: shewed in the miraculous preservation of eight Englishmen, left by mischance in Greenland. With a description of that countrey. 4° R. Y(oung) f. J. Partridge, 1631.

19566.2

(A. Imp. The dedicatory epistle is different.).

19614   PERYN

Newes from Perin in Cornwall: of a murther. 4° E. A(llde), 1618.

19616   PERCY, Algernon
       Earl of Northumberland

A list of the colones, as also of ships, captaines and lieutenants, under A. Percey, etc. s. sh. fol. T. Paine f. T. Walkley (1640).

19625   PEREZ DE GUZMAN, Alonzo
       Duke of Medina Sidonia

Orders set downe by the duke of Medina to be observed in the voyage toward England. Tr. T. P., 4° T. Orwin f. T. Gilbert, 1588.

19628   PERICLES, Prince of Tyre

The painfull adventures of Pericles, prince of Tyre; being the true history of the play of Pericles as presented by J. Gower. 4° T. P(urfoot) f. N. Butter, 1608.

19766.3   PERNAU

A true report of 3 accidents lately happened in Pernau. Tr. from the Dutch. 4° R. B. f. Barley, 1603.

19792   PET, Edmund

Lamentable newes, showing the wonderfull deliverance of Maister E. Pet. 4° T. C(reed) f. W. Barley, 1613.

19803   PETOWE, Henry

The Countrie Ague. Or, London her welcome home to her retired children. With a true relation of the warlike funerall of Capt. R. Robyns. 4° f. R. Allot, 1626.

19845   PHILIP, John

The examination and confession of certaine wytches at Chelmsford 26 July 1566. 8° W; Powell f. W. Pickering, 1566.

19855   PHILIPS, Judith

The brideling, sadling and ryding, of a rich churle in Hampshire, by one Judeth Philips. 4° T. C(reed), solde by W. Barley, 1595.

19881   PHILO-BALLADUS

A womans birth, or a perfect relation, etc. Ballad. 2 pts. f. F. Grove (1638?).

19947   PIRCKHEIMER, Bilibaldus

The praise of the gout, or, the gouts apologie. Tr. W. Est. 4° G. P(urslow) f. J. Budge, 1617.

20126	PORTRAIT	Le vray purtraict d'un ver monstrueux qui a esté trouvé dans le coeur d'un cheval. s. sh. fol. J. Wolfe (1587).
20268	PRESTON, John	A sermon preached at the funeral of Mr. Arthur Upton, etc. 4° W. Jones, 1619
20290	PRICE, Daniel	The creation of the Prince. A sermon. 4° G. Eld f. R. Jackson, 1610.
20302		Sauls prohibition staide: a sermon. 4° (J. Windet) f. M. Law, 1609.
20317	PRICE, Lawrence	A monstrous shape, or a shapelesse monster. (Init. L. P.) Ballad. 2 pts. M. F(lesher) f. T. Lambert (1639?).
20340	PRICKET, Robert	The Jesuits miracles, or new popish wonders. (Init. R. P.) 4° f. C. P(urset) a. R. J(ackson), 1607.
20422	PROGNOSTICATION (anon.)	A mery pnosticacion for the yere a thousande fyve hundreth fortye & foure. 4° (n. p. 1544).
20449	PROTESTANTS	The protestants and jesuits in Gulicke–land. Tr. out of Dutch by T. Wood. 4° f. N. Bourne, 1611.
20511	PURMEREND	A strange and miraculous accident happened in the cittie of Purmerent. 4° J. Wolfe, 1599.
20512	PURSER, Pirate	A true relation of the lives and deaths of two English pyrats, Purser and Clinton. 8° J. Okes, 1639.
20569	R., A.	True and wonderfull. A Discourse relating a strange serpent in Sussex. 4° f. J. Trundle, 1613.
20570	R., C.	The true discription of this marveilous straunge fishe. s. sh. fol. T. Colwell, 1569.
20578	R., I. or J.	The taming of a shrew. s. sh. 8° f. F. Coles, (n. d.).
20754	RAVAILLAC, François	The copie of a letter written from Paris, declaring the manner of the execution of F. Ravaillart. 4° imprinted at Britaine Burse, 1610.
20755		The terrible and deserved death of F. Ravilliack, shewing the manner of his execution. 4° E. A(llde) f. W. Barley a. J. Baylie, 1610.
20778	RAYMOND, Henry	The maiden queene entituled the Britaine shepheardes teares for the death of Astrabomica, 1607. 4° I. W. f. J. Browne, (1607).
20778a		The worldes vanitie. (Init. H. R.).
20849	REGIUS, Urbanus	A lytle treatise after the maner of an epystle. 8° Gwalter Lynne, 1548.

20861	RELATION	A briefe relation of what is hapned since August 1598, by comming of the Spanish campe into the Dukedom of Cleve. 4° J. Wolfe, 1599.
20863		A true and strange relation of fire, etc. 4° f. N. Butter a. N. Bourne, 1639.
20863.5		A true relation of the birth of three monsters in the city of Namen in Flaunders, 1608. 4°
20891	REPORT	A true credible report of a great fight at sea. 25th May, 1600. 4° E. A(llde) f. W. Burre (1600).
20892		A true report of a mighty sea monster. 4° f. H. Holland, 1617.
		A true reporte of the forme and shape of a monstrous childe borne in the countye of Essex, 21 Apryll 1562. s. sh. fol. Thomas Marshe (1562).
20996	RICH, Barnabe	Riche his farewell to militarie profession. 4° R. Walley, 1581.
21005	RICH, Richard	Newes from Virginia, the lost flocke triumphant. 4° E. Allde, solde by J. Wright, 1610.
21011	RICHARDS, Nathaniel	The tragedy of Messallina. 8° T. Cotes f. D. Frere, 1640.
21083	ROBERTS, Henry	Lancaster his allarums, honorable assaultes, and supprising of block-houses in Brasill. (Init. H. R.) 4° A. J(effes) f. W. Barley (1595).
21124	ROBINSON, Thomas	The anatomie of the English nunnery at Lisbon. (A. Ed.) 4° sould by R. Milbourne a. P. Stephens, 1623.
21125		(A. Ed.) 4° f. P. Stephens a. C. Meredith, 1630.
21251	ROGERS, William	Youths warning-piece. In a true relation of the woefull death of Rogers. Ballad. 2 pts. f. A. K(emb), 1636.
21368	ROWLANDS, Samuel	Diogenes lanthorne. 8° (E. Allde) f. T. Archer, 1607.
21369		(A. Ed.) 4° f. R. P(avier, 1608).
21370		(A. Ed.) 4° J. H(aviland) f. R. Burre, 1628.
21371		(A. Ed.) 4° (J. Beale) f. R. Bird, 1631.
21378		The famous historie of Guy Earle of Warwick. 4° (E. Allde f. W. Ferbrand), 1609.
21379		(A. Ed.) 4° Eliz. All-de, 1632.
21381		A fooles bolt is soon shot. 4° f. G. Loftus, 1614.
21382		Good newes and bad newes. 4° f. H. Bell, 1622.

21387		The knave of clubbes. 4° f. W. Ferebrand, 1609.
21388		(A. Ed.) 4° E. A(llde), 1611.
21389		(A. Ed.) 4° E. A(llde, 1611).
21390		The knave of harts. Haile fellow well met. 4° P. S(nodham), solde by G. Loftus, 1612.
21392		More knaves yet? the knaves of spades and diamonds, 8° f. J. Tap, 1613.
21393		The letting of the humours blood in the head-vaine. (Init. S. R.) 8° W. White f. W. F(erbrand), 1600.
21401		The melancholie knight. 4° R. B(lore), sold by G. Loftus, 1615.
21402		The night-raven. 4° G. Eld f. J. Deane, 1620.
21405		The sacred memorie of the miracles wrought by Jesus Christ. 4° B. Alsop, 1618.
21406		Sir Thomas Overbury: or the poisoned knights complaint. s. sh. fol. f. J. White (1614).
21407		A terrible battell betweene time and death. 4° f. J. Deane (1606?).
21409a		Tis merrie when gossips meete. (A. Ed.)
21410.2		(A. Ed.) 4° f. J. Deane (1615?).
21411		(A. Ed.) Well met Gossip; or tis merrie when gossips meet. Newly enlarged. 4° J. W(right) f. J. Deane, 1619.
21418	ROWLEY, Samuel	When you see me, you know me. Or the famous chronicle historie of King Henrie the Eight. (A. Ed.) 4° f. N. Butter, 1613.
21419		(A. Ed.) 4° f. N. Butter, 1621.
21420		(A. Ed.) 4° B. A(lsop), a. T. F(awcet), f. N. Butter, 1632.
21451	RUSH, Friar	The historie of Frier Rush. 4° E. Allde, 1620.
21451a		(A. Ed.)
21452		(A. Ed.) 4° E. Allde, sold by F. Grove, 1626.
21457	RUSSELL, John	Corn-hoarder. A looking glasse for corne-hoarders, by the example of J. Russell. Ballad. 2 pts. f. H. Gosson (1632?).
21460	RUSSELL, John of Magd. Coll., Cambridge	The two famous pitcht battels of Lypsich and Lutzen. 4° printers to the Univ. of Cambridge, sold by P. Scarlet, 1634.
21503	S., I or J.	Match me this wedding. 2 pts. s. sh. fol. f. T. Lambert, (1640?).

21507	S., J. U.	The seafight in the road of Gibraltar. Tr. from the Dutch. 4° f. J. Hardie, sold by R. Jackson, 1607.
21509	S., M.	The poore orphans court. 4° A(nne) G(riffin) f. M. S(parke), jun. 1636.
21538	SACK	Muld sacke: or the apologie of Hic-Mulier. 4° f. R. Meighen, 1620.
21545	SAFEGUARD	The safeguard of sailers. Tr. R. Norman. 4° J. Windet a. T. Judson, 1584.
21548		(A. Ed.) 4° A. Islip, 1600.
21591	SAINT MARY'S ISLAND	A true report and description of the taking of the iland of St. Maries, 1599. Tr. out of Dutch. 4° J. Wolfe, 1600.
21642	SALTONSTALL, Wye	The country mouse, and the city mouse. Second edition. (Anon.) 8° T. Cotes f. M. Sparke, jun. 1637.
21688	SAMPSON, William	The vow-breaker. Or the faire maide of Clifton. 4° J. Norton, sold by R. Ball, 1636.
21772	SAUL, Arthur	The famous game of chesse-play. 8° R. Jackson, 1614.
21773		(A. Ed.) 8° (1620?).
21774		(A. Ed.) Now augmented by J. Barbier. (Init. A. S.) 8° f. J. Jackson, 1640.
21802	SAVOY	A true discourse of the occurrences in the warres of Savoy. Tr. E. A(ggas). 4° f. W. Burre, 1601.
21828	SCHOUTEN, Willem Cornelis	The relation of a wonderfull voiage. (Tr. W. P(hillip). 4° T. D(awson) f. N. Newbery, 1619.
21865	SCOT, Reginald	A perfite platforme of a hoppe garden. 4° H. Denham, 1574.
21866		(A. Ed.) Newly corrected a. augmented. 4° H. Denham, 1576.
21867		(A. Ed.) 4° H. Denham, 1578.
22097a	SCOTT, Thomas	Vox Dei: Injustice cast and condemned. A sermon preached at Bury S. Edmonds. (A. Ed.) 4° (s. p. 1623?).
22103		The second part of Vox Populi: or Gondomar appearing in the likenes of Matchiavell in a Span. parliament. 4° (s. p. 1620?). (A. Ed.) 4° Goricum. A. Janss, 1624.
22104a		(A. Ed.) 4°.
22105		Vox Regis. 4° (s. p. 1623).
22105.1		(A. Ed.) 4°.
22130	SEA FIGHT	A true relation of a wonderfull sea fight betweene two great and well appointed Spanish ships, and a small English ship. 4° f. N. B(utter), 1621.

22140	SEAMAN	The sea-mans triumph. Declaring the honorable actions of such gentlemen as were at the taking of the great carrick, lately brought to Dartmouth. 8° R. B(lore) f. W. Barley, 1592.
22183	SELMAN, John	The arraignment of J. Selman, who was executed neere Charing Crosse. 8° W. H(all) f. T. Archer, 1612.
22183a		(A. Ed.) 8°.
22183a.8		(A. Ed.) f. T. Archer, 1611.
22233	SERES	An almanacke and prognostication for M.D.LXXIIII, made in Salisbury. 8° (London) 1574.
22249	SERRES, Olivier de	The perfect use of silk-wormes. Tr. N. Geffe. 4° F. Kyngston, sold by R. Sergier a. C. Purset w. the assnmt. of W. Stallenge, 1607.
22404	SHELTON, Thomas	Shortwriting. second ed. 8° J. D(awson) f. S. C(artwright), 1630.
22431	SHERWOOD, Thomas	Murder upon murder committed by T. Sherwood, etc. Ballad. 2 pts. f. T. Langley, sold by T. Lambert, (1635).
22512a	SIBBES, Richard	The spirituall mans aime. A sermon. 12° E. G(riffin) f. J. Rothwell, 1637.
22528	SICILY	A famous victorie, atchieved by the christian gallies of Sicilia. 4° f. T. Thorp, 1613.
22554	SILVER, George	Paradoxes of defence, wherein is proved the true grounds of fight to be in the short auncient weapons. 4° (R. Field) f. E. Blount, 1599.
22614	SKELTON, John	Elynour Rummin, the famous ale-wife of England. 4° f. S. Rand, 1624.
22627	SKINKER, Tannakin	A certain relation of the hogfaced gentlewoman called Mistris T. Skinker. 4° J. O(kes), sold by F. Grove, 1640.
22645	SMELL-KNAVE, Simon, pseud.	Fearefull and lamentable effects of two comets which shall appeare in 1591. 4° J. C(harlwood) f. J. Busbie, (1590?).
22655	SMITH, Edward	The wofull lamentation of E. Smith, a prisoner in the jayle of Bedord. br. fol. Assignes of T. Symcock (1625?).
22787	SMITH, John, governor of Virginia	Advertisements for the unexperienced planters of New England. 4° J. Haviland, sold by R. Milbourne, 1631.
22791		A map of Virginia (the proceedings of the English colonie in Virginia). 2 pts. 4° Oxford, J. Barnes, 1612.

22795		A true relation of such occurrences as hath hapned in Virginia. 4º f. J. Tappe, solde by W. W(elby), 1608.
22872	SMITH, William	Chloris, or the complaint of the passionate despised shepheard. 4º E. Bollifant, 1596.
22872a	SMITH, William, inn-keeper	An elegie upon the death of that worthy house keeper, William Smith, of Crissing-Temple. 4º 1631 (B. M.11630. bb. 51).
22915	SOMERSET, County of	A true report of certaine overflowings of waters in Summersetshire, etc. 4º W. J(aggard) f. E. White, (1607).
22916		More strange newes of the late overflowings of waters, etc.
22977	SPACKMAN, Thomas	A declaration of such greivous accidents as follow the biting of mad dogges. 4º f. J. Bill, 1613.
23051	SPEED, Robert	The counter-scuffle. (Init. R. S.) 4º f. N. Butter, 1623.
23052		(A. Ed. Init. R. S.) 4º W. Stansby, sold by R. Meighen, 1628.
23053		(A. Ed. Init. R. S.) 4º W. Stansby, 1635.
23054		(A. Ed. Init. R. S.) 4º R. Bishop, 1637.
23138	STALLENGE, William	Instructions for the increasing of mulberie trees a. breeding of silke-wormes. (Init. W. S.) 4º E. A(llde) f. E. Edgar, 1609.
23201	STANDISH, Arthur	The Commons complaint; wherein is contained two special grievances. (A. Ed.) pp. 34. 4º W. Stansby, 1611.
23202		(A. Ed.) pp. 33. 4º W. Stansby, 1611.
23259	STEARLE, D.	A briefe sonet declaring the lamentation of Beckles, in Suffolke. s. sh. fol. R. Robinson f. N. Coleman of Norwich (1586).
23265	STEVIN, Simon	The haven finding art, by the latitude and variation. Tr. (E. Wright) 4º G. B(ishop), R. N(ewbery) a. R. B(arker), 1599.
23267	STILE, Elizabeth	A rehearsall both straung and true of hainous actes committed by E. Stile, etc. fower notorious witches. 8º f. E. White (1579).
23273	STOCK, Richard	The Churches lamentation for the losse of the godly. A sermon. 8º J. Beale, 1614.
23375	STUBBE, Peter	A true discourse: declaring the damnable life and death of one Stubbe Peeter, a sorcerer. Tr. out of the high Duch. 12º f. E. Venge (1590).
23421	SUDLOW, Edward	The arraignment and execution of E. Sudlow at West Chester. 4º (London, 1609).

23521	SWEDISH INTELLIGENCER	The Swedish Intelligencer. (By W. Watt). 4° (T. Cotes) f. N. Butter a. N. Bourne, 1632.
23522		(A. Ed.) Newly revised and corrected. 4° (T. Cotes) f. N. Butter a. N. Bourne, 1632.
23523		(A. Ed.) Now the third time revised, etc. 4° (T. Cotes) f. N. Butter a. N. Bourne, 1632.
23524		Second part. (By W. Watt). 4° f. N. Butter a. N. Bourne, 1632.
23533	SWETNAM, Joseph	The araignment of lewde, idle, froward and unconstant women. (Tho. Tel-troth, pseud.) 4° E. Allde f. T. Archer, 1615.
23534		(A. Ed.) 4° G. Purslowe f. T. Archer, 1615.
23535		(A. Ed.) 4° f. T. Archer, 1616.
23536		(A. Ed.) 4° f. T. Archer, 1617.
23537		(A. Ed.) 4° f. T. Archer, 1619.
23538		(A. Ed.) 4° B. Alsop f. T. Archer (1622).
23539		(A. Ed.) 4° A. M(athews) f. T. Archer, 1628.
23543		The schoole of the noble science of defence. 4° N. Okes, 1617.
23544		Swetnam, the woman-hater, arraigned by women. 4° f. R. Meighen, 1620.
23576	SYLVESTER, Joshua	Lachrimae lachrimarum. 4° H. Lownes, 1612.
23578		Third edition, with additions of his own a. other elegies. 4° H. Lownes, 1613.
23584	SYM, John	Lifes preservative against self-killing. 4° M. Flesher f. R. Dawlman a. L. Fawne, 1637.
23679	TAPP, John	The seamans kalender or an Ephemerides of the sun, moon and certaine stars. By J. T(app) 4° E. Allde f. J. Tapp, 1602.
23680		Fifth ed. Newly corrected and enlarged. 4° E. Allde f. J. Tappe, 1615.
23684	TARLTON, Richard	Tarltons jests drawne into these three parts. 4° J. H(aviland) f. A. Crook, 1638.
23730	TAYLOR, John	An arrant thiefe. With a comparison betweene a thiefe and a booke. (In verse) (A. Ed.) 8° (A. Mathewes) f. H. Gosson, 1635.
23731		A bawd. 8° (A. Mathewes?) f. H. Gosson, 1635.
23734		A brave and valiant sea fight. 4° f. N. Butter, 1640.

23735	A brave, memorable and dangerous sea-fight foughten neere the road of Tittawen in Barbary. 4° f. H. Gosson, 1636.
23744	A common whore, with all these graces grac'd, etc. (A. Ed.) 8° f. H. Gosson, 1635.
23747	Divers crabtree lectures. 12° J. Okes f. S. Sweeting, 1639.
23748	A dog of war. 8° (n. p. 1628?).
23751	An English–mans love to Bohemia. (In verse) 4° Dort (London), 1620.
23753	A famous fight at sea. 4° J. Haviland f. H. Gosson, 1627.
23754	The fearefull summer: or Londons calam-itie, the countryes discurtesie, etc. 8° Oxford, J. Lichfield a. W. Turner, 1625.
23756	(A. Ed.) Now reprinted. 4° E. P(urslow) f. H. Gosson, 1636.
23757	Fill gut and pinch belly, br. fol. E. Allde f. H. Gosson, 1620.
23760	Great Britaine all in blacke. For the incomparable losse of Henry, our late worthy prince. (In verse) 4° E. A(llde) f. J. Wright, 1612.
23762	The great O Toole. (In verse) 12° f. H. Gosson, 1622.
23763	Heavens blessing and earths joy. (On) the albeloved mariage of Fredericke & Elizabeth. 2 pts. 4° f. J. Hunt, 1613.
23765	Jack a Lent: his beginning and entertain-ment, with new additions. 4° f. J. T(run-dle), 1620.
23766	A juniper lecture: second impression. 12° J. O(kes) f. W. Ley, 1639.
23767	A kicsy winsey: or a lerry come–twang: where–in John Taylor hath satyrically suited 800 of his bad debters. 8° N. Okes f. M. Walbanck, 1619.
23768	(A. Ed., with the title:) The scourge of basenesse, or the old lerry with a new kicksey. 8° N. O(kes) f. M. Walbancke, 1624.
23770	The life and death of the virgin Mary. 8° G. E(ld), 1620.
23771	(A. Ed.) 8° G. E(ld) f. J. T(rundle), 1622.
23772	A living sadnes, in duty consecrated to the memory of our late soveraigne James. 4° (E. Allde f. H. Gosson, 1625).
23772 a	(A. Imp.) E. All–de f. H. Gosson.

23775	The Muses mourning, or funeral sonnets for the death of John Moray. 8° (1620?).
23776	The needles excellency. The 10th ed. inlarged. obl. 4° f. J. Boler, 1634.
23777	Twelfth edition inlarged, etc. obl. 4° f. J. Boler, 1640.
23781	The olde old very olde man: or the age and long life of T. Par. 4° f. H. Gosson, 1635.
23782	(A. Ed.) The old, old very old man. Whereunto is added a postscript. 4° f. H. Gosson, 1635.
23786	The praise, antiquity and commodity of beggery, beggers and begging, etc. 4° E. A(llde) f. H. Gosson, sold by E. Wright, 1621.
23788	The praise of hemp-seed: with the voyage of Mr. R. Bird and the writer hereof in a boat of brown paper, to Quinborough in Lent. 4° f. H. Gosson, 1620.
23789.5	(A. Ed.) 4° 1623.
23791	The sculler, rowing from Tiber to Thames. 4° E. A(llde), 1612.
23792	(A. Ed., with title:) Taylors waterworke or the scullers travels from Tyber to Thames. 4° f. N. Butter, 1614.
23793	A shilling, or the travels of twelve-pence. 8° (E. Allde, 1621).
23794	(A. Ed. with the title:) The travels of twelve-pence. 8° 1635.
23799	Taylors goose, describing the wilde goose, etc. 4° E. A(llde) f. H. Gosson, 1621.
23800	Taylor's motto: Et haveo, et careo et curo. 8° f. J. T(rundle) a. H. G(osson), 1621.
23801	Taylors pastorall: or the noble antiquitie of shepheards, 4° G. P(urslow) f. H. Gosson, sold at E. Wrights shop, etc., 1624.
23808a	The unnatural father: or a cruel murther committed by one J. Rowse. 4° J. T(rundle) and H. G(osson), 1621.
23809	A valorous and perillous sea-fight. 4° E. P(urslow) f. E. Wright, 1640.
23814	The water-cormorant his complaint. 4° F. Eld, 1622.
23816	The world runnes on wheeles. 8° E. All(de) f. H. Gosson, 1623.
23817	(A. Ed.) 4° f. H. Gosson, 1635.

23859	TEDDER, Will	The recantations by W. Tedder and A. Tyrrell at Paules Crosse. 4º J. Charlewood a. W. Brome, sold by T. Gubbin, 1588.
23923	TEXEDA, Fernando de	Texeda retexus; or, the Spanish monke his bill or divorce against Rome. 4º T. S(nodham) f. R. Mylbourne, 1623.
24047	THRACE	A pleasant history of a gentleman in Thraciae, which had four sonnes. Ballad. 2 pts. f. H. G(osson, 1633).
24066	TIDING	O marvelous tydynges both wonders old and new. s. sh. fol. C. Woltrop, (1570?).
24086	TIMBERLAKE, Henry	A true and strange discourse of the travailes of two English pilgrimes. (A. Ed. with the title:) A relation of the travells. (Init. H. T.) 4º J. N(orton) f. H. Perry, 1631.
24087	TIME	Take time, while time is. Ballad. 2 pts. M. P(arsons) f. H. Gosson, (1635?).
24098	TOKENS	Faire fall good tokens: or a pleasant new song, etc. Ballad. 2 pts. f. H. Gosson, (1630?).
24115	TOM THUMB	Tom Thumbe his life and death. 8º f. J. Wright, 1630.
24268.5	TRESWELL, Robert	A relation of such things as were observed in the journey of Charles, Earle of Nottingham, to Spaine, for the maintenance of peace betwene Great Brittaine and Spaine. (A. Ed.) to f. J. Seaton.
24269	TRIAL	The fierie tryall of Gods saints, as a counterpoyze to J. W. Priest, in his English Martyrologe. 4º T. P(urfoot) f. A. Johnson, 1611.
24270		(A. Ed.) 2 pts. 4º T. P(urfoot) f. A. Johnson, 1612.
24298	TRUSSELL, Thomas	The souldier pleading his own cause. (2. imp.) 8º N. Okes, sold by T. Walkley, 1619.
24299		Third impression. 8º N. Okes f. T. Walkley, 1626.
24301	TRUTH	Truths integrity: or a curious northerne dittie, called Love will find out the way. Ballad. 2 pts. f. F. Coules (1630?).
24316a	TUKE, Thomas	A treatise against painting (sic) and tincturing of men and women, whereunto is added the picture of Picture. (A Imp. with the title:) A discourse against painting and tincturing or women. 4º f. E. Marchant, 1616.

24370	TURTLES	The paire of northerne turtles. Ballad. 2 pts. f. F. Coules (1635?).
24413	TWYNE, Thomas	A shortie and pithie discourse concerning earthquakes. By T. T(wyne). 4° R. Johnes, 1580.
24435	TYNDAL, Sir John	A true relation of a murder committed upon Sir J. Tindall, etc. 4° E. All-de f. L. L(isle), 1617.
24518	UNDERHILL, John	Newes from America; or a new discoverie of New England. 4° J. D(awson) f. Peter Cole, 1638.
24585	VALESCO, Signior, pseud.	Newes from Rome of two mightie armies. Tr. out of Ital. by W. W. 4° J. R(oberts) f. H. Gosson, 1606.
24586		(A. Ed.) A Jewes prophesy, or newes from Rome. 4° W. J(aggard) f. H. Gosson, (1607?).
24713	VICARY, Thomas	A profitable treatise of the anatomie of mans body. Newly revyved. 8° H. Bamforde, 1577.
24740	VILLIERS, George, Duke of Buckingham	A journall of all the proceedings of the Duke of Buckingham in the Isle of Ree, etc. 4° f. T. Walkley, 1627.
24741		A continued journall. August 17. 4° f. T. Walkley, 1627.
24742		--August 30. 4° f. T. Walkley, 1637.
24744		--October 18. 4° A. M(athewes) f. T. Walkley, 1627.
24757	VINCENT, Margaret	A pittilesse mother, Being a gentlewoman named M. Vincent. 4° (London, 1616).
24761	VINCENT, Philip	The lamentations of Germany. 8° E. G(riffin) f. J. Rothwell, 1638.
24904	W., G.	Newes out of Cheshire, of the new found well. 4° F. Kingston f. T. Man, 1600.
24909	W., J., Gent	A speedie poste with certaine new letters. 4° M. F(lesher) f. W. Sheares, 1625.
24954	WALBANCKE, Matthew	Annalia Dubrensia; Mr. Dovers Olimpick games. 4° R. Raworth f. M. Walbancke, 1636.
25015	WANDERING JEW	The wandring Jew, or the shoomaker of Jerusalem. Ballad (n. p.) 1620.
25022	WARD, Captain	Newes from the sea, of two notorious Pyrats, Ward and Danseker. 4° f. N. Butter, (1609).
25022a		(A. Ed.) 4°.
25033a	WARD, Samuel of Ipswich	All in all. (A. Imp. with the date:) 1622.
25035		Balme from Gilead to recover conscience. (A. Ed.) 8° T. S(nodham) f. R. Jackson a. W. Bladen, 1617.

25036		(**A. Ed.**) 8° T. S(nodham) f. R. Jackson a. W. Bladen, 1618.
25037		(**A. Ed.**) 8° J. H(aviland) f. R. Jackson, 1622.
25039		**A coal from the altar. A sermon.** 8° H. L(ownes) f. S. Macham, 1615.
25055		**Woe to drunkards: a sermon.** 8° A. Math(ews) f. J. Marriott a. J. Grismand, 1622.
25056		(**A. Ed.**) 8° A. Math(ewes) f. J. Marriott a. J. Grismand, 1627.
25104	WATERHOUSE, E.	**A declaration of the state of the colony in Virginia.** 4° G. Eld f. R. Mylbourne, 1622.
25152	WEBBE, Edward	**The rare and most wonderfull things which E. Webbe hath seene.** Newly enlarged. 4° (J. Charlwood?) f. W. Wright, 1590.
25153		(**A. Ed.**) 4° A. J(effes) f. W. Barley, (before 1595).
25228	WELBY, Henry	**The phoenix of these latter times. Or the life of H. Welby.** (**A. Ed.**) Sig. A–F3. N. Okes, sold by R. Clotterbuck, 1637.
25229	WELDON, John	**A true report of the inditement and execution of J. Welden, W. Hartley and R. Sutton.** 4° R. Jones, 1588.
25230	WELL-WISHING	**A well wishing to a place.** A ballad. 2 pts. assignes of T. Symcocke, (1635?).
25265	WEST, Richard	**The school of vertue** (of F. Seager) **The second part; or the young schollers paradice.** 8° E. Griffin f. N. Butter, 1619.
25283	WESTERN KNIGHT	**The westerne Knight, and the young maid of Bristoll.** Ballad. 2 pts. F. Coules, (1629).
25611	WIFE	**A good wife, or none.** Ballad. 2 pts. f. F. Coules, (1635?).
25658	WILKINSON, Robert	**The merchant royall. A sermon.** 4° F. Kyngston f. J. Flasket, 1615.
25660		(**A. Ed.**) 4° G. Eld f. E. Blount, 1615.
25663		**The stripping of Joseph: or the crueltie of brethren. In a sermon.** 4° W. S(tansby) f. H. Holland a. G. Gibbes, 1625.
25723	WILLIAMS, John, Archbp.	**Great Britaines Salomon. A sermon.** 4° J. Bill, 1625.
25736	WILLIAMS, Wat	**Wat Williams Will.** Ballad. 2 pts. f. H. Gosson, (1640?).
25740	WILLIAMSON, Thomas	**The sword of the spirit to smite in pieces that antichristian Goliah who daily defieth the Lords people.** (**A. Ed.**) 8° E. Griffin, 1613.

25768	WILSON, George	The commendation of cockes, and cock-fighting. 4° f. H. Tones, 1607.
25783	WILSON, Robert	The pleasant a. stately morall of the three Lordes a. three Ladies of London. By R. W(ilson). 4° R. Jhones, 1590.
25840	WINDS	The last terrible tempestious windes and weather. 4° f. Jos. Hunt, sold by J. Wright, 1613.
25869	WIT	Wit's never good till 'tis bought. Ballad. 2 pts. f. T. Lambert (1634).
25872	WITCHES	Witches apprehended, examined and executed, etc. 4° f. E. Marchant, 1613.
25915	WITHER, George	Prince Henries obsequies. 4° E. Allde f. A. Johnson, 1612.
25937	WIVES	Halfe a dozen of good wives; all for a penny. Ballad. 2 pts. f. F. C(oules, 1634).
25950	WONDERS	The wonders of this windie winter. (A. Ed.) 4° J. Hunt, 1613.
25967	WOODHOUSE, Peter	The flea. 4° f. J. Smethwick, 1605.
25973	WOOER	The honest wooer. Ballad. 2 pts. f. F. Coules (1632).
25998	WORST	The worst is past, or A merry new song that lately was pend. Ballad. 2 pts. f. R. Harper (1640?).
26023	WRIGHT, Edward	A short treatise of dialling. 4° J. Beale f. W. Welby, 1614.
26091	YEAR	The cold yeare, 1614: a deepe snow: etc. 4° W. W(hite) f. T. Langley, 1615.
26104	YORKSHIRE LOVERS	A pleasant new northerne song called the two York-shire lovers. Ballad. 2 pts. f. J. Wright (1640?).
26118	YOUNG-MAN	A young-man's most earnest affection to his sweetheart. Ballad. 2 pts. (London, 1635?).
26119	YPRES	The forme and maner of subvētion for pore people practysed ī Hypres. Tr. (W. Marshall). 8° T. Godfray. 1535.

B. OTHER PRIMARY SOURCES

ALFIELD — A true report of the martyrdom of M. Campion, 1582.

ALLEN, Nicholas — The astronomical game, 1569.

ANTON, Robert — The philosophers satyrs, 1616.

ARBER, E., Ed. — An English garner, Tudor tracts, 1532–1588, 1903.

BACON, Francis — The essayes or counsels, civil and morall, 1625.

BACON, Friar — The famous historie of Fryer Bacon, also the manner of his death, 1627.

BARIONA, L. — Cometographia, quoedam Lampadis aeriae que 10 die Novemb. apparuit, Anno a Virgineo partu, 1577, 1578.

BEAUMONT, F. and FLETCHER, J. — The maids tragedy, 1630.

BECON, Th. — A new cathechism, 1563.

BERNARD, Richard — A guide to grand jury men, 1627.

BIBLE — The Bible and Holy Scriptures...with profitable annotations. At Geneva MDLX (1st ed. of the Geneva Bible).

The holy Bible..., 1568. (1st impr. of the Bishops' Bible).

The Holy Bible, Conteyning the Old Testament and the New; Newly translated out of the Originall tongues...by his Maiesties speciall Comandement (King Jame's Bible also known as the "authorized version").

BORDE, A. — ...A dyetary of health, (ed.), 1562.

BRIMSLEY, John — Ludus literarius, or the grammar schoole, 1612.

B(ULWER), J(ohn) — Chirologia, 1644.

CALVIN, J. — The institution of Christian religion wrytten in Latine by Maister Ihon Calvin and translated into Englysh...by Thomas Norton, 1582.

CHAMBER, John — A treatise against judicial astrologie..., 1601.

(CHARLES I, king) — The book of sports, 1633 (reprint, 1862).

CHURCHYARD, Thomas — The firste part of Churchyardes chippes, 1575.

CLELAND, James — Institution of a young nobleman, 1607.

COOPER, Thomas — The mystery of witchcraft; discovering the truth thereof, 1617.

COTTA, John — The triall of witch-craft, shewing the true methode of the discoverie, 1616.

CRAMER and SPRENGER — MALLEUS MALEFICARUM, 1487, (reed. by Montague Summers, Bungay, Suffolk, 1928).

DEKKER, Thomas — The Bellman of London, 1608.

The dead terme. Or, Westminsters complaint for long vacation, 1608.

The Gulls Horne-Booke, 1609.

Jests to make you merrie, 1609.

Satiro-mastix, or the untrussing of the humerous poet, 1602.

DEKKER – cont'd	The seven deadly sinnes of London, 1606.
	The wonderfull yeare, 1603.
--- ed. WILSON, F. P.	The plague pamphlets of Thomas Dekker, (Oxford, 1925).
DEKKER, Thomas, FORD, John and ROWLEY, William	The Witch of Edmonton, 1658.
E., T.	The lawes resolutions of womens rights, 1632.
FENTON, Edward	Certaine secrete wonders of nature gathered by E. Fenton, 1569.
GHISI, Andrea	Wits labyrinth, or the exercise of idlenesse, 1610.
GIFFORD, George	A dialogue concerning witches and witchcraftes, 1593.
GILBERT	Queen Elizabeth's Academy, 1572 (repr. Early English Text Society, 1869).
GOSSON, Stephen	Playes confuted in five actions, 1582.
	Quippes for upstart newfangled gentlewomen, etc., 1595 (repr. 1847).
	The schoole of abuse, conteining a pleasaunt invective against poets, pipers, _ plaiers, iesters, and such like caterpillers of a comonwelth, 1579.
HANMER, Thomas	The garden Book, 1659 (repr., edited I Elstob), 1935.
HARRISON, William	A Description of England (a separate edition of the first part of Chronicles of England de Holinshed, 1577), (repr. by F. J. Furnivall, 1876).
HEYWOOD, Thomas	Englands Elizabeth: her life and troubles, 1631.
	The four apprentices of London, 1613, 1632 (repr. of Pearson, The works, II, 1874).
HILL	The contemplation of mankinde, 1571.
JAMES VI, King of Ecosse	Daemonologie, Edinburgh, 1597.
JONSON, Benjamin	Bartholomew Fair, 1631.
KNOX, John	The first blast of the trumpet against the monstruous regimen of women, Genève, 1558 (repr. Arber, 1880).
MARKHAM, Gervase	The complete farriar; or the King's highway to horsemanship, 1639.
	The English Housewife, 1631.
	The English Husbandman, 1613.
MASSINGER, Philip	The Duke f Millaine, 1623.
	The Maid of Honour, 1632 (reed. in The dramatic works of Philip MMassinger, 1805.
MIDDLETON, Thomas	Works (Ed. A. H. Bullen, 1895-96).
MIDDLETON, Thomas and ROWLEY, William	The changeling, 1653.
MISSELDEN, Edward	The circle of commerce. Or the ballance of trade, in defence of free trade, 1623.
	Free Trade or the Meanes to make Trade flourish, 1622.
MOFFET, Thomas	Healths Improvement (ed. Christopher Bennet, 1655).

MULCASTER, Richard	Positions wherein those circumstances be examined necessarie for the training up of children, 1591.
NAVY RECORDS SOCIETY (collections of letters and tracts	Defeat of the Spanish Armada, 2 vols., 1894. The naval miscellany, vols. I–II, 1910. Naval tracts of Sir William Monson, Vols. I–III, 1902–1912. The Spanish War, 1585–1587, (1898).
NORDEN, John	The Surveyors dialogue, 1607.
OGLANDER, Sir John	A Royalist's notebook, The Commonplace book of Sir John Oglander, Knight of Nunwell, 1622–1652 (ed. Francis Bainford, 1936).
OVERBURY, Sir Thomas	New and Choice Characters of severall authors, together with the wife..., 1616.
PARKINSON, John	Theatrum Botanicum, 1640.
PEACHAM, Henry	The compleat gentleman, 1622. Graphice or the most auncient a. excellent art of drawing a. limming, etc., 1612.
PERKINS, William	A discourse of the damned art of witchcraft, Cambridge, 1608. A Golden Chaine...or, the description of theologie [including 12 other treatises] (Cambridge, 1600).
REYNOLDS, John, marchand	The triumphes of Gods revenge, 3 vols., 1621.
SCOT, Reginald	The discoverie of witchcraft, 1584.
SCOTT, Thomas	Vox populi. Vox Dei. Vox regis. Digitus Dei. The Begick pismire. The tongue–combat. Symmachia. The high–wayes of God and the King. The proiector. 1622–23.
SELDEN, John	The historie of tithes, 1618.
SHAKESPEARE, William	Shakespeare's works, 1623 (repr. Norton facs. ed. Charlton Hinman, New York, 1968). --King Lear --Macbeth --Richard II --Timon of Athens --Twelfth Night
SIDNEY, Sir Philip	Astrophel and Stella, 1591.
SMITH, Sir Thomas	De republica Anglorum, the maner of government of England, 1583 (repr., ed. by L. Alston, 1906).
SOWERNAM, Esther, pseud.	Ester heth hang'd Haman; or an answere to a lewde pamphlet, 1617.
STOW, John	The annales of England, from the first inhabitation untill 1592, 1592.
STUBBES, Philip	The anatomie of abuses, 1583.
TAYLOR, John	All the works of John Taylor the water poet, 1630. (reed., 1973).
WEBSTER, John	The White Divel, 1612.
WHITNEY, Geffrey	A choice of emblemes a. other devises. 2 pts. (Leyden: C. Plantyn, 1586).

WILKINS, John

WILKINSON, Robert

WILSON, Thomas

WRIGHT, Thomas

The discovery of a world in the moone, 1638.
A discourse concerning a new world...., 1640.
The merchant royall, A sermon, 1607 (reed. by Stanley Pargellis, 1945).
A discourse upon usury....1572 (edited with an introduction by R. H. Tawney, New York, 1925).
The state of England, anno domini, 1600, 1600. (reed. by Fisher, 1936).
The passions of the minde, 1601.

INDEX

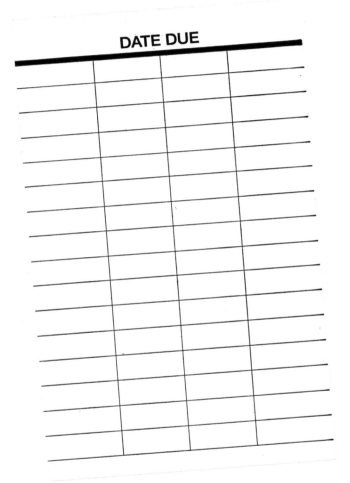

DATE DUE